Exchange Server 5.5

The Cram Sheet

This Cram Sheet contains the distilled, key facts about Exchange Server 5.5. Review this i͏͏͏
mation before you enter the test room, paying special attention to those areas where you͏
you need the most review. You can transfer any of these facts from your head onto a b͏
sheet of paper before beginning the exam.

Planning

1. Plan your Exchange Server locations to match the administrative and geographical layout of your organization.

2. An Exchange organization includes one or more sites under a single Directory (and possibly database) with connectors between sites. An Exchange site includes one or more servers that replicate and exchange data. An Exchange server provides access to mailboxes, applications, and Exchange folders.

3. An address space represents those remote addresses accessible through a connector. Each connector must have at least one entry for its address space. You must understand the address spaces related to each type of Exchange connector and be able to design and configure the necessary Exchange settings for connectors.

4. You can upgrade either Exchange 4 or Exchange 5 to Exchange 5.5 without losing any configuration data. But when up-

grading from Exchange 4 to 5.5, you m͏
assign the "log on locally" user right to th͏
Exchange Service account through the͏
User Manager For Domains for POP3 to͏
function properly.

5. The *Internet Message Access Protocol (IMAP)* is a newer email protocol that is becoming increasingly popular. Exchange 5.5 supports IMAP version 4 (IMAP4). IMAP4 permits users to read headers from messages stored on a server, so they can decide which messages they wish to download to their local systems. IMAP4 also permits users to store email messages on the client and the server simultaneously.

6. The *Lightweight Directory Access Protocol (LDAP)* is an IP-based standard protocol that may be used to share an Exchange Directory database across the Internet. The protocol even permits anonymous access. LDAP also permits administrators to configure which kinds of data (such as name, email address, or phone number) are made available to anonymous users.

33. A *server monitor* tracks Exchange services running on some remote Exchange servers. It can automatically generate alerts or perform specific tasks when certain events occur. Server monitors can even track non-Exchange services running on some remote Exchange servers.

34. Run the Exchange Optimization Wizard every time you change anything about an Exchange server. Such changes include adding more memory or hard-disk space, creating numerous new users, or altering a server's role (from a private message store to a public message store, for instance).

You may use the Simple Network Management Protocol (SNMP) to monitor an Exchange server.

Troubleshooting

36. Several Exchange utilities can handle connectivity, directory, and Information Store problems. These include the following:
   - EDBUTIL.EXE can defragment a database, run a consistency check on data, or recover a damaged database.
   - ISINTEG.EXE maintains the Information Store databases.
   - PATCH flag is used to patch an IS database after an off-line restore of Exchange.
   - FIX flag is used to repair a database that will not roll back to its last checkpoint.

37. The Exchange Key Management Server (KM Server) requires manual entry of a password, or a special-purpose installation diskette that includes a password, to start up properly.

Certification
Insider™ Press

Copyright © The Coriolis Group, 1998
Rights Reserved.

Exchange
Server 5.5
Exam # 70-081

MCSE Exchange Server 5.5 Exam Cram
© 1998 The Coriolis Group. All Rights Reserved.

Limits of Liability and Disclaimer of Warranty
The author and publisher of this book have used their best efforts in preparing the book and the programs contained in it. These efforts include the development, research, and testing of the theories and programs to determine their effectiveness. The author and publisher make no warranty of any kind, expressed or implied, with regard to these programs or the documentation contained in this book.

The author and publisher shall not be liable in the event of incidental or consequential damages in connection with, or arising out of, the furnishing, performance, or use of the programs, associated instructions, and/or claims of productivity gains.

Trademarks
Trademarked names appear throughout this book. Rather than list the names and entities that own the trademarks or insert a trademark symbol with each mention of the trademarked name, the publisher states that it is using the names for editorial purposes only and to the benefit of the trademark owner, with no intention of infringing upon that trademark.

The Coriolis Group, LLC
14455 N. Hayden Road, Suite 220
Scottsdale, Arizona 85260

480/483-0192
FAX 480/483-0193
http://www.coriolis.com

Library of Congress Cataloging-in-Publication Data
Tittel, Ed.
    MCSE Exchange Server 5.5 exam cram/by Ed Tittel, Barry Shilmover and Tim Catura-Houser
        p.   cm.
    Includes index.
    ISBN 1-57610-229-7
    1. Electronic data processing personnel—Certification.   2. Microsoft software—Examinations—Study guides.   3. Microsoft Exchange server.   I. Shilmover, Barry.   II. Catura-Houser, Tim.   III. Title
QA76.3.T5737   1998
005.7'13769--dc21   98-25782
                                                                CIP

Printed in the United States of America
10 9 8 7 6 5 4

President, CEO
Keith Weiskamp

Publisher
Steve Sayre

Acquisitions Editor
Shari Jo Hehr

Marketing Specialist
Cynthia Caldwell

Project Editor
Melissa D. Olson

Production Coordinator
Meg Turecek

Cover Design
Anthony Stock

Layout Design
April Nielsen

14455 North Hayden, Suite 220 • Scottsdale, Arizona 85260

The Smartest Way To Get Certified ™

Thank you for purchasing one of our innovative certification study guides, just one of the many members of the Coriolis family of certification products.

Certification Insider Press™ was created in late 1997 by The Coriolis Group to help professionals like you obtain certification and advance your career. Achieving certification involves a major commitment and a great deal of hard work. To help you reach your goals, we've listened to others like you, and we've designed our entire product line around you and the way you like to study, learn, and master challenging subjects. Our approach is *The Smartest Way To Get Certified.*

In less than a year, Coriolis has published over one million copies of our highly popular *Exam Cram, Exam Prep,* and *On Site* guides. Our *Exam Cram* books, specifically written to help you pass an exam, are the number one certification self-study guides in the industry. They are the perfect complement to any study plan you have, as well as to the rest of the Certification Insider Press series: *Exam Prep,* comprehensive study guides designed to help you thoroughly learn and master certification topics, and *On Site,* guides that really show you how to apply your skills and knowledge on the job.

Our commitment to you is to ensure that all of the certification study guides we develop help you save time and frustration. Each one provides unique study tips and techniques, memory joggers, custom quizzes, insight about test taking, practical problems to solve, real-world examples, and much more.

We'd like to hear from you. Help us continue to provide the very best certification study materials possible. Write us or email us at **craminfo@coriolis.com** and let us know how our books have helped you study, or tell us about new features that you'd like us to add. If you send us a story about how an *Exam Cram, Exam Prep,* or *On Site* book has helped you, and we use it in one of our books, we'll send you an official Coriolis shirt for your efforts.

Good luck with your certification exam and your career. Thank you for allowing us to help you achieve your goals.

Keith Weiskamp
Publisher, Certification Insider Press

About The Authors

Ed Tittel is a full-time freelance writer and the president of a small, Texas-based network consulting firm. Ed is the series editor for the Exam Cram books from The Coriolis Group. A contributing author to more than 60 books, he has written many hundreds of magazine articles. Ed is also a member of the program committee for NetWorld + Interop and a member of the faculty for that trade show. Ed has taught on a variety of subjects that range from Web technologies to Windows NT, and he enjoys encountering students inside and outside the classroom. In his spare time, Ed hangs out with his new Labrador pup named Blackie, shoots pool, and makes homemade chicken stock.

Barry Shilmover graduated from the University of Calgary with a mechanical engineering degree in 1992. Finding no work in his field, he sold shoes and decided to pursue a master's degree in biomedical engineering. After completing his first year at the Technion Institute of Technology in Israel, he decided that biomed was not his thing; he moved on to computer programming. From programming, he entered the networking field, where he ran a 325-node network at a local school. He also helped design and implement the school board's wide area network for 220-plus schools. After working for the school board, Barry helped start a small, local Internet Service Provider, where he was jack-of-all-trades. Shortly thereafter, he moved into consulting where he concentrated on the Internet, intranet, and security side of networks. Barry is an MCSE + I, and he owns a consulting company that concentrates on the Internet, intranet, and networking security. In his spare time, he teaches computer-related courses (Windows NT, Exchange, Web servers, and Novell) at a local technical school. Barry lives in Calgary, Alberta, with his wife, Shawna, and their new son, Jory.

Tim Catura-Houser of Seattle, Wash., began his digital journey with Control/Program Monitor computers for office solutions and point of sale systems. His certifications include Microsoft MCSE + I and MCT. With his first love being hardware, he carries certifications from Artisoft to Cisco and IBM. When Tim isn't writing, he is either teaching technical courses or leading classes as a Certified Technical Trainer/Microsoft Certified Trainer. For fun, he likes to beat up younger engineers at the Redmond campus. His single favorite toy is his battery powered Ricochet wireless modem. He has so much fun with computers, he has no time for anything else. Tim reads all his email, so you can question, pan, or praise him by email at **Tcat@usa.net**.

Acknowledgments

Every now and then a book comes along that proves to be a particular challenge. This book belongs in that category, but I'm pleased to say that the LANWrights staff, particularly Dawn Rader, David Johnson, and Mary Burmeister, were able to rise to this challenge and produce a book that is both jammed with information and readable to boot. Of course, we couldn't have done it without the wonderful team at The Coriolis Group, including Keith Weiskamp, our publisher; Shari Jo Hehr, our acquisitions editor; Sandra Lassiter, director of product development; Paula Kmetz, managing editor; Melissa Olson, project editor; and Meg Turecek, production coordinator; not to mention our bold and able copyeditor, Bart Reed. Thanks also to The Coriolis Group's outstanding sales staff, especially Jim Corbett, Tom Mayer, Cynthia Caldwell, Neil Gudovitz, and Anne Tull for their efforts to make this book sell. And finally, we're also grateful to the interior and cover design staff at Coriolis, who make these books look so sharp, including April Nielsen and Anthony Stock.

The real credit for this book goes to my co-authors—Barry Shilmover and Tim Catura-Houser—who contributed the bulk of the material. I would like to thank Chris Waters and Ramesh Chandak for their contributions as well. Thanks for being such a great team. I can hardly wait for Exchange 6 to come along!

—Ed Tittel

First, I would like to thank my wife, Shawna, for understanding the long hours I put into this book and for not serving me with divorce papers during the project. I would not have been able to complete this book without your help. You're the best! To my son, Jory, thanks for still knowing who I was even though you never saw me. I would like to thank the entire LANWrights team—Ed Tittel, for giving me a chance to work with your team; DJ, for putting up with my strange and wonderful questions; Dawn Rader and Mary Burmeister, for making the transition into the world of books relatively painless. Thanks to my family for understanding when I could not make it to get-togethers. To anyone I missed, thanks. And finally, to my ITP class, thanks for buying me a drink the day after I stayed up all night to meet a deadline—and for not enjoying my state of mind later that afternoon too much.

—Barry Shilmover

Acknowledgments

Without the fantastic assistance of several super people, I couldn't have gotten the concepts presented into print. Somehow, a mere mega-thanks doesn't seem to be enough for Marilyn, who let me stack servers like firewood in the living room, and for Compaq Computers, which helped me build the stack of servers. Most important of all, a very special thanks to Dawn, DJ, Mary, and Ed, all from LANWrights, for their patience in converting me (regardless of the pain and suffering it caused them) from a newsletter writer to a computer book author. Without the invaluable assistance of all of these grand folks, I never would have made it.

—*Tim Catura-Houser*

Contents At A Glance

Table Of Contents

Introduction

. . . .

Welcome to *MCSE Exchange Server 5.5 Exam Cram*! This book aims to help you get ready to take—and pass—the Microsoft certification Exam 70-081, titled "Implementing and Supporting Microsoft Exchange Server 5.5 Exam." This introduction explains Microsoft's certification programs in general and talks about how the *Exam Cram* series can help you prepare for Microsoft's certification exams.

Exam Cram books help you understand and appreciate the subjects and materials you need to pass Microsoft certification exams. *Exam Cram* books are aimed strictly at test preparation and review. They do not teach you everything you need to know about a topic (such as the ins and outs of managing an Exchange server). Instead, we (the authors) present and dissect the questions and problems we've found that you're likely to encounter on a test. We've worked from Microsoft's own training materials, preparation guides, and tests, and from a battery of third-party test preparation tools. Our aim is to bring together as much information as possible about Microsoft certification exams.

Nevertheless, to completely prepare yourself for any Microsoft test, we recommend that you begin your studies with some classroom training or some background reading. On the other hand, you might decide to pick up and read one of the many study guides available from Microsoft or third-party vendors on certain topics, including The Coriolis Group's *Exam Prep* series (for which a title on Exchange Server is also available).

We also strongly recommend that you install, configure, and fool around with the software that you'll be tested on, because nothing beats hands-on experience and familiarity when it comes to understanding the questions you're likely to encounter on a certification test. Book learning is essential, but hands-on experience is the best teacher of all!

The Microsoft Certified Professional (MCP) Program

The MCP Program currently includes eight separate tracks (five are discussed below), each of which boasts its own special acronym (as a would-be certificant, you need to have a high tolerance for alphabet soup of all kinds):

➤ **MCP (Microsoft Certified Professional)** This is the least prestigious of all the certification tracks from Microsoft. Passing any of the major Microsoft exams (except the Networking Essentials exam) qualifies an individual for MCP credentials. Individuals can demonstrate proficiency with additional Microsoft products by passing additional certification exams.

➤ **MCP+I (Microsoft Certified Professional + Internet)** This midlevel certification is attained by completing three core exams: "Implementing and Supporting Microsoft Windows NT Server 4.0," "Internetworking Microsoft TCP/IP on Microsoft Windows NT 4.0," and "Implementing and Supporting Internet Information Server 3.0 and Microsoft Index Server 1.1" or "Implementing and Supporting Microsoft Internet Information Server 4.0."

➤ **MCP+SB (Microsoft Certified Professional + Site Building)** This certification program is designed for individuals who are planning, building, managing, and maintaining Web sites. Individuals with the MCP+SB credential will have demonstrated the ability to develop Web sites that include multimedia and searchable content and Web sites that connect to and communicate with a back-end database. It requires one MCP exam, plus two of these three exams: "Designing and Implementing Commerce Solutions with Microsoft Site Server, 3.0, Commerce Edition," "Designing and Implementing Web Sites with Microsoft FrontPage 98," and "Designing and Implementing Web Solutions with Microsoft Visual InterDev 6.0."

➤ **MCSE (Microsoft Certified Systems Engineer)** Anyone who has a current MCSE is warranted to possess a high level of expertise with Windows NT (version 3.51 or 4.0) and other Microsoft operating systems and products. This credential is designed to prepare individuals to plan, implement, maintain, and support information systems and networks built around Microsoft Windows NT and its BackOffice family of products.

To obtain an MCSE, an individual must pass four core operating system exams, plus two elective exams. The operating system exams require individuals to demonstrate competence with desktop and server operating systems and with networking components.

You must pass at least two Windows NT-related exams to obtain an MCSE: "Implementing and Supporting Microsoft Windows NT Server" (version 3.51 or 4.0) and "Implementing and Supporting Microsoft Windows NT Server in the Enterprise" (version 3.51 or 4.0). These tests are intended to indicate an individual's knowledge of

Windows NT in smaller, simpler networks and in larger, more complex, and heterogeneous networks, respectively.

Note: The NT 3.51 version is scheduled to be retired by Microsoft sometime in 1999.

You must pass two additional tests as well. These tests are related to networking and desktop operating systems. At present, the networking requirement can be satisfied only by passing the Networking Essentials test. The desktop operating system test can be satisfied by passing a Windows 95, Windows NT Workstation (the version must match the NT version for the core tests), or Windows 98 test.

The two remaining exams are elective exams. An elective exam may fall in any number of subject or product areas, primarily BackOffice components. These include tests on Internet Explorer 4, SQL Server, IIS, Proxy Server, SNA Server, Exchange Server, Systems Management Server, and the like. However, it is also possible to test out on electives by taking advanced networking topics like "Internetworking with Microsoft TCP/IP on Microsoft Windows NT 4.0" (but here again, the version of Windows NT involved must match the version for the core requirements taken). If you are on your way to becoming an MCSE and have already taken some exams, visit **www.microsoft.com/mcp/certstep/mcse.htm** for information about how to proceed with your MCSE certification.

Whatever mix of tests is completed toward MCSE certification, individuals must pass six tests to meet the MCSE requirements. It's not uncommon for the entire process to take a year or so, and many individuals find that they must take a test more than once to pass. Our primary goal with the *Exam Cram* series is to make it possible, given proper study and preparation, to pass all Microsoft certification tests on the first try. Table 1 shows the required and elective exams for the MCSE certification.

➤ **MCSE+I (Microsoft Certified Systems Engineer + Internet)** This is a newer Microsoft certification and focuses not just on Microsoft operating systems, but also on Microsoft's Internet servers and TCP/IP.

To obtain this certification, an individual must pass seven core exams plus two elective exams. The core exams include not only the server operating systems (Windows NT Server and Server in the Enterprise) and a desktop OS (Windows 95, Windows 98, or Windows NT Workstation), but also include Networking Essentials, TCP/IP, Internet Information Server (IIS), and the Internet Explorer Administration Kit (IEAK).

Table 1   MCSE Requirements*

Core

All 3 of these are required	
Exam 70-067	Implementing and Supporting Microsoft Windows NT Server 4.0
Exam 70-068	Implementing and Supporting Microsoft Windows NT Server 4.0 in the Enterprise
Exam 70-058	Networking Essentials
Choose 1 from this group	
Exam 70-064	Implementing and Supporting Microsoft Windows 95
Exam 70-073	Implementing and Supporting Microsoft Windows NT Workstation 4.0
Exam 70-098	Implementing and Supporting Microsoft Windows 98

Elective

Choose 2 from this group	
Exam 70-088	Implementing and Supporting Microsoft Proxy Server 2.0
Exam 70-079	Implementing and Supporting Microsoft Internet Explorer 4.0 by Using the Internet Explorer Administration Kit
Exam 70-087	Implementing and Supporting Microsoft Internet Information Server 4.0
Exam 70-081	Implementing and Supporting Microsoft Exchange Server 5.5
Exam 70-059	Internetworking with Microsoft TCP/IP on Microsoft Windows NT 4.0
Exam 70-028	Administering Microsoft SQL Server 7.0
Exam 70-029	Designing and Implementing Databases on Microsoft SQL Server 7.0
Exam 70-056	Implementing and Supporting Web Sites Using Microsoft Site Server 3.0
Exam 70-086	Implementing and Supporting Microsoft Systems Management Server 2.0
Exam 70-085	Implementing and Supporting Microsoft SNA Server 4.0

* This is not a complete listing—you can still be tested on some earlier versions of these products. However, we have included mainly the most recent versions so that you may test on these versions and thus be certified longer. We have not included any tests that are scheduled to be retired.

The two remaining exams are elective exams. These elective exams can be in any of four product areas: SQL Server, SNA Server, Exchange Server, or Proxy Server. Table 2 shows the required and elective exams for the MCSE+I certification.

➤ **MCT (Microsoft Certified Trainer)** Microsoft Certified Trainers are individuals who are deemed able to deliver elements of the official Microsoft curriculum, based on technical knowledge and instructional ability. Thus, it is necessary for an individual seeking MCT credentials (which are granted on a course-by-course basis) to pass the related certification exam for a course and complete the official Microsoft training in the subject area, and to demonstrate an ability to teach.

This latter criterion may be satisfied by proving that one has already attained training certification from Novell, Banyan, Lotus, the Santa

Table 2   MCSE+Internet Requirements*

Core

All 6 of these are required	
Exam 70-067	Implementing and Supporting Microsoft Windows NT Server 4.0
Exam 70-068	Implementing and Supporting Microsoft Windows NT Server 4.0 in the Enterprise
Exam 70-058	Networking Essentials
Exam 70-059	Internetworking with Microsoft TCP/IP on Microsoft Windows NT 4.0
Exam 70-087	Implementing and Supporting Microsoft Internet Information Server 4.
Exam 70-079	Implementing and Supporting Microsoft Internet Explorer 4.0 by Using the Internet Explorer Administration Kit
Choose 1 from this group	
Exam 70-064	Implementing and Supporting Microsoft Windows 95
Exam 70-073	Implementing and Supporting Microsoft Windows NT Workstation 4.0
Exam 70-098	Implementing and Supporting Microsoft Windows 98

Elective

Choose 2 from this group	
Exam 70-088	Implementing and Supporting Microsoft Proxy Server 2.0
Exam 70-081	Implementing and Supporting Microsoft Exchange Server 5.5
Exam 70-028	Administering Microsoft SQL Server 7.0
Exam 70-029	Designing and Implementing Databases with Microsoft SQL Server 7.0
Exam 70-056	Implementing and Supporting Web Sites Using Microsoft Site Server 3.0
Exam 70-085	Implementing and Supporting Microsoft SNA Server 4.0

* This is not a complete listing—you can still be tested on some earlier versions of these products. However, we have included mainly the most recent versions so that you may test on these versions and thus be certified longer. We have not included any tests that are scheduled to be retired.

Cruz Operation, or Cisco, or by taking a Microsoft-sanctioned workshop on instruction. Microsoft makes it clear that MCTs are important cogs in the Microsoft training channels. Instructors must be MCTs before Microsoft will allow them to teach in any of its official training channels, including Microsoft's affiliated Authorized Technical Education Centers (ATECs), Authorized Academic Training Programs (AATPs), and the Microsoft Online Institute (MOLI).

Certification is an ongoing activity. Once a Microsoft product becomes obsolete, MCPs typically have 12 to 18 months in which they may recertify on current product versions. (If individuals do not recertify within the specified time period, their certifications become invalid.) Because technology keeps changing and new products continually supplant old ones, this should come as no surprise.

The best place to keep tabs on the MCP Program and its various certifications is on the Microsoft Web site. The current root URL for the MCP program is **www.microsoft.com/mcp/**. But Microsoft's Web site changes often, so if this

URL doesn't work, try using the Search tool on Microsoft's site with either "MCP" or the quoted phrase "Microsoft Certified Professional Program" as a search string. This will help you find the latest and most accurate information about Microsoft's certification programs.

Taking A Certification Exam

Alas, testing is not free. Each computer-based MCP exam costs $100, and if you don't pass, you may retest for an additional $100 for each additional try. In the United States and Canada, tests are administered by Sylvan Prometric and by Virtual University Enterprises (VUE). Here's how you can contact them:

➤ **Sylvan Prometric** You can sign up for a test through the company's Web site at **www.slspro.com**. Or, you can register by phone at 800-755-3926 (within the United States or Canada) or at 410-843-8000 (outside the United States and Canada).

➤ **Virtual University Enterprises** You can sign up for a test or get the phone numbers for local testing centers through the Web page at **www.microsoft.com/train_cert/mcp/vue_info.htm**.

To sign up for a test, you must possess a valid credit card, or contact either company for mailing instructions to send them a check (in the U.S.). Only when payment is verified, or a check has cleared, can you actually register for a test.

To schedule an exam, call the number or visit either of the Web pages at least one day in advance. To cancel or reschedule an exam, you must call before 7 P.M. Pacific Time the day before the scheduled test time (or you may be charged, even if you don't appear to take the test). When you want to schedule a test, have the following information ready:

➤ Your name, organization, and mailing address.

➤ Your Microsoft Test ID. (Inside the United States, this means your Social Security number; citizens of other nations should call ahead to find out what type of identification number is required to register for a test.)

➤ The name and number of the exam you wish to take.

➤ A method of payment. (As we've already mentioned, a credit card is the most convenient method, but alternate means can be arranged in advance, if necessary.)

Once you sign up for a test, you'll be informed as to when and where the test is scheduled. Try to arrive at least 15 minutes early. You must supply two forms of identification—one of which must be a photo ID—to be admitted into the testing room.

All exams are completely closed-book. In fact, you will not be permitted to take anything with you into the testing area, but you will be furnished with a blank sheet of paper and a pen or, in some cases, an erasable plastic sheet and an erasable pen. We suggest that you immediately write down on that sheet of paper all the information you've memorized for the test. In *Exam Cram* books, this information appears on a tear-out sheet inside the front cover of each book. You will have some time to compose yourself, to record this information, and even to take a sample orientation exam before you begin the real thing. We suggest you take the orientation test before taking your first exam, but because they're all more or less identical in layout, behavior, and controls, you probably won't need to do this more than once.

When you complete a Microsoft certification exam, the software will tell you whether you've passed or failed. Results are broken into several topic areas. Even if you fail, we suggest you ask for—and keep—the detailed report that the test administrator should print for you. You can use this report to help you prepare for another go-round, if needed.

If you need to retake an exam, you'll have to schedule a new test with Sylvan Prometric or VUE and pay another $100.

The first time you fail a test, you can retake the test the next day. However, if you fail a second time, you must wait 14 days before retaking that test. The 14-day waiting period remains in effect for all retakes after the first failure.

Tracking MCP Status

As soon as you pass any Microsoft exam other than Networking Essentials, you'll attain Microsoft Certified Professional (MCP) status. Microsoft also generates transcripts that indicate which exams you have passed and your corresponding test scores. You can order a transcript by email at any time by sending an email to **mcp@msprograms.com**. You can also obtain a copy of your transcript by downloading the latest version of the MCT Guide from the Web site and consulting the section titled "Key Contacts" for a list of telephone numbers and related contacts.

Once you pass the necessary set of exams (one for MCP, six for MCSE, or nine for MCSE+I), you'll be certified. Official certification normally takes anywhere from four to six weeks, so don't expect to get your credentials overnight. When the package for a qualified certification arrives, it includes a Welcome Kit that contains a number of elements:

➤ An MCP, MCSE, or MCSE+I certificate, suitable for framing, along with a Professional Program Membership card and lapel pin.

➤ A license to use the MCP logo, thereby allowing you to use the logo in advertisements, promotions, and documents, and on letterhead, business cards, and so on. Along with the license comes an MCP logo sheet, which includes camera-ready artwork. (Note: Before using any of the artwork, individuals must sign and return a licensing agreement that indicates they'll abide by its terms and conditions.)

➤ A subscription to *Microsoft Certified Professional Magazine*, which provides ongoing data about testing and certification activities, requirements, and changes to the program.

➤ A one-year subscription to the Microsoft Beta Evaluation program. This subscription will get you all beta products from Microsoft for the next year. (This does not include developer products. You must join the MSDN program or become an MCSD to qualify for developer beta products.)

Many people believe that the benefits of MCP certification go well beyond the perks that Microsoft provides to newly anointed members of this elite group. We're starting to see more job listings that request or require applicants to have an MCP, MCSE, MCSE+I, and so on, and many individuals who complete the program can qualify for increases in pay and/or responsibility. As an official recognition of hard work and broad knowledge, one of the MCP credentials is a badge of honor in many IT organizations.

How To Prepare For An Exam

Preparing for any Windows NT Server-related test (including Exchange Server) requires that you obtain and study materials designed to provide comprehensive information about the product and its capabilities that will appear on the specific exam for which you are preparing. The following list of materials will help you study and prepare:

➤ The Microsoft Windows NT Server 4 manuals (or online documentation and help files, which ship on the product's CD-ROM and also appear on the TechNet CD-ROMs).

➤ The Microsoft Windows NT Server 4 Resource Kit, published by Microsoft Press, Redmond, WA, 1996. ISBN: 1-57231-343-9. Even though it costs a whopping $149.95 (list price), it's worth every penny—not just for the documentation, but also for the utilities and other software included (which add considerably to the base functionality of Windows NT Server 4).

➤ The exam prep materials, practice tests, and self-assessment exams on the Microsoft Training And Certification Download page (www.microsoft.com/train_cert/download/downld.htm). Find the materials, download them, and use them!

In addition, you'll probably find any or all of the following materials useful in your quest for Windows NT Server expertise:

➤ **Microsoft Training Kits** Although no training kit is currently available from Microsoft Press for Exchange Server 5.5, many other topics have such kits. It's worthwhile to check to see if Microsoft has come out with anything by the time you need this information.

➤ **Microsoft TechNet CD** TechNet is a monthly CD-Rom subscription available from Microsoft. TechNet includes all the Windows NT BackOffice resource kits and their product documentation. In addition, TechNet provides the contents of the Microsoft Knowledge Base and many kinds of software, whitepapers, training materials, and other good stuff. TechNet also contains all service packs, interim release patches, and supplemental driver software released since the last major version for most Microsoft programs and all Microsoft operating systems. A subscription to TechNet costs $299 per year, but it is well worth the price. Visit **www.microsoft.com/technet/** and check out the information under the "TechNet Subscription" menu entry for more details.

➤ **Study Guides** Several publishers—including Certification Insider Press—offer Exchange Server titles. The Certification Insider Press series includes:

 ➤ **The *Exam Cram* Series** These books give you information about the material you need to know to pass the tests.

 ➤ **The *Exam Prep* Series** These books provide a greater level of detail than the *Exam Cram* books and are designed to teach you everything you need to know from an exam perspective. *MCSE Exchange Server 5.5 Exam Prep* is the perfect learning companion to prepare you for Exam 70-081, "Implementing and Supporting Microsoft Exchange Server 5.5." Look for this book in your favorite bookstores.

 Together, the two series make a perfect pair.

➤ **Classroom Training** CTECs, MOLI, and unlicensed third-party training companies (like Wave Technologies, American Research Group, Learning Tree, Data-Tech, and others) all offer classroom training on Exchange Server 5.5. These companies aim to help you prepare to pass the MCSE tests. Although such training runs upwards of $350 per day in class, most of the individuals lucky enough to partake (including your humble authors, who've even taught such courses) find them to be quite worthwhile.

➤ **Other Publications** You'll find direct references to other publications and resources in this book, but there's no shortage of materials available about Exchange Server. To help you sift through some of the publications out there, we end each chapter with a "Need To Know More?" section that provides pointers to more complete and exhaustive resources covering the chapter's information. This should give you an idea of where we think you should look for further discussion.

By far, this set of required and recommended materials represents a nonpareil collection of sources and resources for Exchange Server and related topics. We anticipate that you'll find that this book belongs in this company. In the section that follows, we explain how this book works, and we give you some good reasons why this book counts as a member of the required and recommended materials list.

About This Book

Each topical *Exam Cram* chapter follows a regular structure, along with graphical cues about important or useful information. Here's the structure of a typical chapter:

➤ **Opening Hotlists** Each chapter begins with a list of the terms, tools, and techniques that you must learn and understand before you can be fully conversant with that chapter's subject matter. We follow the hotlists with one or two introductory paragraphs to set the stage for the rest of the chapter.

➤ **Topical Coverage** After the opening hotlists, each chapter covers a series of topics related to the chapter's subject title. Throughout this section, we highlight topics or concepts likely to appear on a test using a special Study Alert layout, like this:

This is what a Study Alert looks like. Normally, a Study Alert stresses concepts, terms, software, or activities that are likely to relate to one or more certification test questions. For that reason, we think any information found offset in Study Alert format is worthy of unusual attentiveness on your part. Indeed, most of the information that appears on The Cram Sheet appears as Study Alerts within the text.

Pay close attention to material flagged as a Study Alert; although all the information in this book pertains to what you need to know to pass the exam, we flag certain items that are really important. You'll find what appears in the meat of each chapter to be worth knowing, too, when preparing for the test. Because this book's material is very condensed, we recommend that you use this book along with other resources to achieve the maximum benefit.

In addition to the Study Alerts, we have provided tips that will help you build a better foundation for Exchange knowledge. Although the information may not be on the exam, it is certainly related and will help you become a better test-taker.

This is how tips are formatted. Keep your eyes open for these, and you'll become an Exchange guru in no time!

➤ **Practice Questions** Although we talk about test questions and topics throughout each chapter, this section presents a series of mock test questions and explanations of both correct and incorrect answers. We also try to point out especially tricky questions by using a special icon, like this:

Ordinarily, this icon flags the presence of a particularly devious inquiry, if not an outright trick question. Trick questions are calculated to be answered incorrectly if not read more than once, and carefully, at that. Although they're not ubiquitous, such questions make regular appearances on the Microsoft exams. That's why we say exam questions are as much about reading comprehension as they are about knowing your material inside out and backwards.

➤ **Details And Resources** Every chapter ends with a section titled "Need To Know More?". This section provides direct pointers to Microsoft and third-party resources offering more details on the chapter's subject. In addition, this section tries to rank or at least rate the quality and thoroughness of the topic's coverage by each resource. If you find a resource you like in this collection, use it, but don't feel compelled to use all the resources. On the other hand, we recommend only resources we use on a regular basis, so none of our recommendations will be a waste of your time or money (but purchasing them all at once probably represents an expense that many network administrators and would-be MCPs, MCSEs, and MCSE+Is might find hard to justify).

The bulk of the book follows this chapter structure slavishly, but there are a few other elements we'd like to point out. Chapter 15 is a sample test that provides a good review of the material presented throughout the book to ensure you're ready for the exam. Chapter 16 is an answer key to the sample test that appears in Chapter 15. Additionally, you'll find the Glossary, which explains terms, and an index that you can use to track down terms as they appear in the text.

Finally, the tear-out Cram Sheet attached next to the inside front cover of this *Exam Cram* book represents a condensed and compiled collection of facts and tips that we think you should memorize before taking the test. Because you can dump this information out of your head onto a piece of paper before the exam, you can master this information by brute force—you need to remember it only long enough to write it down when you walk into the test room. You might even want to look at it in the car or in the lobby of the testing center just before you walk in to take the test.

How To Use This Book

If you're prepping for a first-time test, we've structured the topics in this book to build on one another. Therefore, some topics in later chapters make more sense after you've read earlier chapters. That's why we suggest you read this book from front to back for your initial test preparation. If you need to brush up on a topic or you have to bone up for a second try, use the index or table of contents to go straight to the topics and questions you need to study. Beyond helping you prepare for the test, we think you'll find this book useful as a tightly focused reference to some of the most important aspects of Exchange Server.

Given all the book's elements and its specialized focus, we've tried to create a tool that will help you prepare for—and pass—Microsoft Certification Exam 70-081, "Implementing And Supporting Microsoft Exchange Server 5.5." Please share your feedback on the book with us, especially if you have ideas about how we can improve it for future test-takers. We'll consider everything you say carefully, and we'll respond to all suggestions.

Send your questions or comments to us at **craminfo@coriolis.com**. Our series editor, Ed Tittel, coordinates our efforts and ensures that all questions get answered. Please remember to include the title of the book in your message; otherwise, we'll be forced to guess which book you're writing about. And we don't like to guess—we want to *know*! Also, be sure to check out the Web page at **www.certificationinsider.com,** and where you'll find information updates, commentary, and certification information.

Thanks, and enjoy the book!

Microsoft
Certification Exams

Terms you'll need to understand:

√ Radio button

√ Checkbox

√ Exhibit

√ Multiple-choice question format

√ Careful reading

√ Process of elimination

√ Fixed-length tests

√ Adaptive tests

√ Short-form tests

√ Combination tests

√ Simulations

Techniques you'll need to master:

√ Preparing to take a certification exam

√ Practicing (to make perfect)

√ Making the best use of the testing software

√ Budgeting your time

√ Guessing (as a last resort)

Exam taking is not something that most people anticipate eagerly, no matter how well prepared they may be. In most cases, familiarity helps offset test anxiety. In plain English, this means you probably won't be as nervous when you take your fourth or fifth Microsoft certification exam as you'll be when you take your first one.

Whether it's your first exam or your tenth, understanding the details of exam taking (how much time to spend on questions, the environment you'll be in, and so on) and the exam software will help you concentrate on the material rather than on the setting. Likewise, mastering a few basic exam-taking skills should help you recognize—and perhaps even outfox—some of the tricks and snares you're bound to find in some of the exam questions.

This chapter, besides explaining the exam environment and software, describes some proven exam-taking strategies that you should be able to use to your advantage.

The Exam Situation

When you arrive at the testing center where you scheduled your exam, you'll need to sign in with an exam coordinator. He or she will ask you to show two forms of identification, one of which must be a photo ID. After you've signed in and your time slot arrives, you'll be asked to deposit any books, bags, or other items you brought with you. Then, you'll be escorted into a closed room. Typically, the room will be furnished with anywhere from one to half a dozen computers, and each workstation will be separated from the others by dividers designed to keep you from seeing what's happening on someone else's computer.

You'll be furnished with a pen or pencil and a blank sheet of paper, or, in some cases, an erasable plastic sheet and an erasable pen. You're allowed to write down anything you want on both sides of this sheet. Before the exam, you should memorize as much of the material that appears on The Cram Sheet (in the front cover of this book) as you can, so you can write that information on the blank sheet as soon as you're seated in front of the computer. You can refer to your rendition of The Cram Sheet anytime you like during the test, but you'll have to surrender the sheet when you leave the room.

Most test rooms feature a wall with a large picture window. This permits the exam coordinator to monitor the room, to prevent exam takers from talking to one another, and to observe anything out of the ordinary that might go on. The exam coordinator will have preloaded the appropriate Microsoft certification exam—for this book, that's Exam 70-081—and you'll be permitted to start as soon as you're seated in front of the computer.

All Microsoft certification exams allow a certain maximum amount of time in which to complete your work (this time is indicated on the exam by an on-screen counter/clock, so you can check time remaining whenever you like). All Microsoft certification exams are computer generated and most use a multiple-choice format. Although this may sound quite simple, the questions are constructed not only to check your mastery of basic facts and figures about Exchange Server, but they also require you to evaluate one or more sets of circumstances or requirements. Often, you'll be asked to give more than one answer to a question. Likewise, you may be asked to select the best or most effective solution to a problem from a range of choices, all of which technically are correct. Taking the exam is quite an adventure, and it involves real thinking. This book shows you what to expect and how to deal with the potential problems, puzzles, and predicaments.

In the next section, you'll learn more about how Microsoft test questions look and how they must be answered.

Exam Layout And Design

Some exam questions require you to select a single answer, whereas others ask you to select one or more correct answers. The following multiple-choice question requires you to select a single correct answer. Following the question is a brief summary of each potential answer and why it is either right or wrong.

Question 1

Your company upgrades one of your Microsoft Exchange servers from version 4 to version 5.5. You enable POP3 support on the newly upgraded server. Your users complain that they cannot access their mailbox information using the POP3 protocol. What is the most probable cause of this problem?

○ a. The Exchange Service account is set up incorrectly.

○ b. POP3 is disabled for the server.

○ c. The clients are using the wrong POP3 client.

○ d. Windows NT Challenge/Response authentication is disabled.

Answer a is correct. The service account must be able to "act as the operating system"; this is not required in Exchange 4. If POP3 is disabled on the server, none of your users would be able to access the server. Therefore, answer b is incorrect. Basically, a POP3 client is a POP3 client is a POP3 client. POP3 clients may have extra bells and whistles, but they still use the same POP3 protocol to receive messages. Therefore, answer c must be incorrect. Windows NT Challenge/Response is not used with POP3. Therefore, answer d is incorrect.

This sample question format corresponds closely to the Microsoft certification exam format—the only difference on the exam is that questions are not followed by answer keys. To select an answer, you would position the cursor over the radio button next to the answer. Then, click the mouse button to select that answer.

Let's examine a question where one or more answers are possible. This type of question provides checkboxes rather than radio buttons for marking all appropriate selections.

Question 2

> If message transfers fail between Exchange servers, what tools can be used to help resolve this problem? [Check all correct answers]
>
> ❏ a. Link monitors
>
> ❏ b. Server monitors
>
> ❏ c. Disk Administrator
>
> ❏ d. Remote Access Admin
>
> ❏ e. None of the above

Answers a and b are correct. Link monitors are used to verify the efficient routing of test messages between Exchange servers. Server monitors are used to check the condition of one or more servers in a site. Disk Administrator is used to view (and optionally configure) storage devices, not message transfers. Because answers a and b are correct, answer e must be incorrect. Therefore, answers c, d, and e are all incorrect.

For this type of question, more than one answer is required. As far as the authors can tell (and Microsoft won't comment), such questions are scored as wrong unless all the required selections are chosen. In other words, a partially correct answer does not result in partial credit when the test is scored. For Question 2, you have to check the boxes next to items a and b to obtain credit for the answer. Notice that picking the right answers also means knowing why the other answers are wrong!

Although these two basic types of questions can appear in many forms, they constitute the foundation on which all Microsoft certification exam questions rest. More complex questions include *exhibits*, which are usually screen shots of the Exchange Server utilities. For some of these questions, you'll be asked to make a selection by clicking a checkbox or radio button on the screen shot itself. For others, you'll be expected to use the information displayed therein to guide your answer to the question. Familiarity with the underlying utility is your key to choosing the correct answer(s).

Other questions involving exhibits use charts or network diagrams to help document a workplace scenario that you'll be asked to troubleshoot or configure. Careful attention to such exhibits is the key to success. Be prepared to toggle frequently between the exhibit and the question as you work.

Microsoft's Testing Formats

Currently, Microsoft uses four different testing formats:

➤ Fixed-length

➤ Adaptive

➤ Short-form

➤ Combination

Some Microsoft exams employ more advanced testing capabilities than might immediately meet the eye. Although the questions that appear are still multiple choice, the logic that drives them is more complex than older Microsoft tests, which use a fixed sequence of questions, called a *fixed-length test*. Other exams employ a sophisticated user interface, which Microsoft calls a *simulation*, to test your knowledge of the software and systems under consideration in a more or less "live" environment that behaves just like the original.

For many upcoming exams, Microsoft is turning to a well-known technique, called *adaptive testing*, to establish a test-taker's level of knowledge and product competence. Adaptive exams look the same as fixed-length exams, but they discover the level of difficulty at which an individual test-taker can correctly answer questions. At the same time, Microsoft is in the process of converting some of its older fixed-length exams into adaptive exams as well. Test-takers with differing levels of knowledge or ability therefore see different sets of questions; individuals with high levels of knowledge or ability are presented with a smaller set of more difficult questions, whereas individuals with lower levels of knowledge are presented with a larger set of easier questions. Two individuals may answer the same percentage of questions correctly, but the test-taker with a higher knowledge or ability level will score higher because his or her questions are worth more.

Also, the lower-level test-taker will probably answer more questions than his or her more-knowledgeable colleague. This explains why adaptive tests use ranges of values to define the number of questions and the amount of time it takes to complete the test.

Adaptive tests work by evaluating the test-taker's most recent answer. A correct answer leads to a more difficult question (and the test software's estimate of the test-taker's knowledge and ability level is raised). An incorrect answer leads to a less difficult question (and the test software's estimate of the test-taker's knowledge and ability level is lowered). This process continues until the test targets the test-taker's true ability level. The exam ends when the test-taker's level of accuracy meets a statistically acceptable value (in other words, when his or her performance demonstrates an acceptable level of knowledge and ability) or when the maximum number of items has been presented (in which case, the test-taker is almost certain to fail).

Microsoft has recently introduced the short-form test for its most popular tests (as of this writing, only Networking Essentials [70-058] and TCP/IP [70-059] have appeared in this format). This test delivers exactly 30 questions to its takers, giving them exactly 60 minutes to complete the exam. This type of exam is similar to a fixed-length test, in that it allows readers to jump ahead or return to earlier questions, and to cycle through the questions until the test is done. Microsoft does not use adaptive logic in this test, but claims that statistical analysis of the question pool is such that the 30 questions delivered during a short-form exam will conclusively measure a test-taker's knowledge of the subject matter in much the same way as an adaptive test will. You can think of the short-form test as a kind of "greatest hits" (that is, most important questions) version of the adaptive exam on the same topic.

A fourth kind of test you could encounter is what we've dubbed the combination exam. Several test-takers have reported that some of the Microsoft exams, including Windows NT Server (70-067), Windows NT Server in the Enterprise (70-068), and Windows NT Workstation (70-073), can appear as combination exams. Such exams begin with a set of 15 to 25 adaptive questions, followed by 10 fixed-length questions. In fact, many test-takers have reported that although some combination tests claim that they will present both adaptive and fixed-length portions, when the test-taker has finished the adaptive portion (usually in exactly 15 questions), the test ends there. Because such users have all attained passing scores, it may be that a high enough passing score on the adaptive portion of a combination test obviates the fixed-length portion, but we're not completely sure about this, and Microsoft won't comment. Most combination exams allow a maximum of 60 minutes for the testing period.

Microsoft tests can come in any one of these forms. Whatever you encounter, you must take the test in whichever form it appears; you can't choose one form over another. Currently, the Exchange Server 5.5 exam may be adaptive, in which case you'll have 90 minutes to answer between 15 and 30 questions (on average), or short-form, in which case you'll get 60 minutes to answer exactly 30 questions. If anything, it pays off even more to prepare thoroughly for an adaptive or combination exam than for a fixed-length or a short-form exam: The penalties for answering incorrectly are built into the test itself on an adaptive exam or the first part of a combination exam, whereas the layout remains the same for a fixed-length or short-form test, no matter how many questions you answer incorrectly.

The biggest difference between an adaptive test and a fixed-length or short-form test is that on a fixed-length or short-form test, you can revisit questions after you've read them over one or more times. On an adaptive test, you must answer the question when it's presented and will have no opportunities to revisit that question thereafter.

Strategies For Different Testing Formats

Before you can choose a test-taking strategy, you need to know if your test is fixed-length, short-form, adaptive, or combination. When you begin your exam, the software will tell you the test is adaptive, if in fact the version you're taking is presented as an adaptive test. If your introductory materials fail to mention this, you're probably taking a fixed-length test. If the total number of questions involved is exactly 30, then you're taking a short-form test. Combination tests announce themselves by indicating that they will start with a set of adaptive questions, followed by fixed-length questions, but don't actually call themselves "combination tests" or "combination exams"—we've adopted this nomenclature for descriptive reasons.

You'll be able to tell for sure if you are taking an adaptive, fixed-length, short-form, or combination test by the first question. If it includes a checkbox that lets you mark the question for later review, you're taking a fixed-length or short-form test. If the total number of questions is 30, it's a short-form test; if more than 30, it's a fixed-length test. Adaptive test questions (and the first set of questions on a combination test) can be visited (and answered) only once, and they include no such checkbox.

The Fixed-Length And Short-Form Exam Strategy

A well-known principle when taking fixed-length or short-form exams is to first read over the entire exam from start to finish while answering only those questions you feel absolutely sure of. On subsequent passes, you can dive into more complex questions more deeply, knowing how many such questions you have left.

Fortunately, the Microsoft exam software for fixed-length and short-form tests makes the multiple-visit approach easy to implement. At the top-left corner of each question is a checkbox that permits you to mark that question for a later visit.

> *Note: Marking questions makes review easier, but you can return to any question by clicking the Forward or Back button repeatedly.*

As you read each question, if you answer only those you're sure of and mark for review those that you're not sure of, you can keep working through a decreasing list of questions as you answer the trickier ones in order.

 There's at least one potential benefit to reading the exam over completely before answering the trickier questions: Sometimes, information supplied in later questions will shed more light on earlier questions. Other times, information you read in later questions might jog your memory about Exchange Server facts, figures, or behavior that also will help with earlier questions. Either way, you'll come out ahead if you defer those questions about which you're not absolutely sure.

Here are some question-handling strategies that apply to fixed-length and short-form tests. Use them if you have the chance:

➤ When returning to a question after your initial read-through, read every word again—otherwise, your mind can fall quickly into a rut. Sometimes, revisiting a question after turning your attention elsewhere lets you see something you missed, but the strong tendency is to see what you've seen before. Try to avoid tendency at all costs.

➤ If you return to a question more than twice, try to articulate to yourself what you don't understand about the question, why the answers don't appear to make sense, or what appears to be missing. If you chew on the subject for awhile, your subconscious might provide the details that are lacking or you might notice a "trick" that will point to the right answer.

As you work your way through the exam, another counter that Microsoft provides will come in handy—the number of questions completed and questions outstanding. For fixed-length and short-form tests, it's wise to budget your time by making sure that you've completed one-quarter of the questions one-quarter of the way through the exam period. For a short-form test, as you may experience with the Exchange Server 5.5 exam, this means you must complete one-quarter of the questions one-quarter of the way through (the first 8 questions in the first 15 minutes) and three-quarters of the questions three-quarters of the way through (24 questions in 45 minutes).

If you're not finished when only 5 minutes remain, use that time to guess your way through remaining questions. Remember, guessing is potentially more valuable than not answering, because blank answers are always wrong, but a guess may turn out to be right. If you don't have a clue about any of the remaining questions, pick answers at random, or choose all a's, b's, and so on. The important thing is to submit an exam for scoring that has an answer for every question.

At the very end of your exam period, you're better off guessing than leaving questions unanswered.

The Adaptive Exam Strategy

If there's one principle that applies to taking an adaptive test, it could be summed up as "Get it right the first time." You cannot elect to skip a question and move on to the next one when taking an adaptive test, because the testing of software uses your answer to the current question to select whatever question it plans to present next. Nor can you return to a question once you've moved on, because the software gives you only one chance to answer the question. You can, however, take notes, because sometimes information supplied in earlier questions will shed more light on later questions.

Also, when you answer a question correctly, you are presented with a more difficult question next, to help the software guage your level of skill and ability. When you answer a question incorrectly, you are presented with a less difficult question, and the software lowers its current estimate of your skill and ability. This continues until the program settles into a reasonably accurate estimate of what you know and can do, and takes you on average through somewhere between 15 and 25 questions as you complete the test.

The good news is that if you know your stuff, you'll probably finish most adaptive tests in 30 minutes or so. The bad news is that you must really, really know your stuff to do your best on an adaptive test. That's because some questions are so convoluted, complex, or hard to follow that you're bound to miss one or two, at a mininum,, even if you know your stuff. So the more you know, the better you'll do on an adaptive test, even accounting for the occasionally weird or unfathomable questions that appear on these exams.

 Because you can't tell in advance if a test is fixed-length, short-form, adaptive, or combination you will be best served by preparing for the exam as if it were adaptive. That way, you should be prepared to pass no matter what kind of test you take. But if you do take a fixed-length test or short-form, remember our tips from the preceding section. They should help you improve on what you could do on an adaptive test.

If you encounter a question on an adaptive test that you can't answer, you must guess an answer immediately. Because of the way the software works, you may have to suffer for your guess on the next question if you guess right, because you'll get a more difficult question next!

The Combination Exam Strategy

When it comes to studying for a combination test, your best bet is to approach it as a slightly longer adaptive exam, and to study as if the exam were adaptive only. Because the adaptive approach doesn't rely on rereading questions, and suggests that you take notes while reading useful information on test questions, it's hard to go wrong with this strategy when taking any kind of Microsoft certification test.

Exam-Taking Basics

The most important advice about taking any exam is this: Read each question carefully. Some questions are deliberately ambiguous, some use double negatives, and others use terminology in incredibly precise ways. The authors have taken numerous exams—both practice and live—and in nearly every one have missed at least one question because they didn't read it closely or carefully enough.

Here are some suggestions on how to deal with the tendency to jump to an answer too quickly:

➤ Make sure you read every word in the question. If you find yourself jumping ahead impatiently, go back and start over.

➤ As you read, try to restate the question in your own terms. If you can do this, you should be able to pick the correct answer(s) much more easily.

Above all, try to deal with each question by thinking through what you know about the Exchange Server utilities, characteristics, behaviors, facts, and figures involved. By reviewing what you know (and what you've written down on your information sheet), you'll often recall or understand things sufficiently to determine the answer to the question.

Mastering The Inner Game

In the final analysis, knowledge breeds confidence, and confidence breeds success. If you study the materials in this book carefully and review all the practice questions at the end of each chapter, you should become aware of those areas where additional learning and study are required.

Next, follow up by reading some or all of the materials recommended in the "Need To Know More?" section at the end of each chapter. The idea is to become familiar enough with the concepts and situations you find in the sample questions that you can reason your way through similar situations on a real exam. If you know the material, you have every right to be confident that you can pass the exam.

After you've worked your way through the book, take the practice exam in Chapter 15. This will provide a reality check and help you identify areas to study further. Make sure you follow up and review materials related to the questions you miss on the practice exam before scheduling a real exam. Only when you've covered all the ground and feel comfortable with the whole scope of the practice exam should you take a real one.

If you take the practice exam and don't score at least 75 percent correct, you'll want to practice further. Though one is not available for Exchange Server 5.5 yet, Microsoft usually provides free Personal Exam Prep (PEP) exams and also offers self-assessment exams from the Microsoft Certified Professional Web site's download page (**www.microsoft.com/train_cert/download/ downld.htm**). If you're more ambitious or better funded, you might want to purchase a practice exam from a third-party vendor.

Armed with the information in this book and the determination to augment your knowledge, you should be able to pass the certification exam. However, you need to work at it, or you'll spend the exam fee more than once before you finally pass. If you prepare seriously, you should do well. Good luck!

Additional Resources

A good source of information about Microsoft certification exams comes from Microsoft itself. Because its products and technologies—and the exams that go with them—change frequently, the best place to go for exam-related information is online.

If you haven't already visited the Microsoft Certified Professional site, do so right now. The MCP home page resides at www.microsoft.com/mcp/.

Note: This page may not be there by the time you read this, or it may have been replaced by something new and different, because things change regularly on the Microsoft site.

The menu options in the left column of the home page point to the most important sources of information in the MCP pages. Here's what to check out:

➤ **Certifications** Use this menu entry to read about the various certification programs that Microsoft offers.

➤ **Exams** Use this menu entry to pull up a search tool that lets you list all Microsoft exams and locate all exams relevant to any Microsoft certification (MCP, MCSE, MCSD, and so on), or those exams that cover a particular product. This tool is quite useful not only to examine the options but also to obtain specific exam preparation information, because each exam has its own associated preparation guide. This is Exam 70-081.

➤ **Downloads** Use this menu entry to find a list of the files and practice exams that Microsoft makes available to the public. These include several items worth downloading, especially the Certification Update, the Personal Exam Prep (PEP) exams, various assessment exams, and a general exam study guide. Try to make time to peruse these materials before taking your first exam.

These are just the high points of what's available in the Microsoft Certified Professional pages. As you browse through them—and we strongly recommend that you do—you'll probably find other informational tidbits mentioned that are every bit as interesting and compelling.

Introduction To MS Exchange Server 5.5

2

Terms you'll need to understand:

√ Application Programming Interface (API)

√ CCITT X.400 originator/recipient addressing scheme

√ CCITT X.500 directory structure

√ Connectors

√ Distributed computer processing

√ Front-end and back-end programs

√ Interoperability

√ Messaging Application Programming Interface (MAPI)

√ Remote procedure call (RPC)

Techniques you'll need to master:

√ Understanding the concepts of Exchange Server

√ Examining client/server architecture

√ Reviewing industry standards that apply to Exchange Server

√ Understanding the key components of Exchange Server

√ Examining database objects associated with Exchange Server

In this chapter, we discuss the evolution of Microsoft messaging and how it has led to the development of Exchange Server. We then examine the inner-workings of Exchange Server by explaining several of the concepts involved in the messaging process. Next, we discuss how its design facilitates many of the features of the client/server architecture. We also examine and define many of the components and terms associated with Exchange Server. Additionally, we explain how the integrated features of Exchange Server enhance the messaging system.

Microsoft Messaging

The first email programs were designed to provide basic communication. There wasn't a need for very sophisticated messaging systems. Technology that would allow multiple systems to connect to each other was in the developmental stages. However, internetworking technologies quickly improved, allowing vast networks—consisting of various hardware platforms and network operating systems—to connect and interact with each other. As this technology improved, many corporations and organizations began implementing internal networks known as *intranets*. With the development of these intranets, the need grew for messaging systems that could communicate within intranets and pass information onto the Internet.

In 1991, Microsoft purchased an electronic messaging product called Network Courier. Shortly thereafter, Microsoft released its first email application, Microsoft Mail (MS Mail). MS Mail grew in popularity and shared a large portion of the market. Overall, MS Mail was a sufficient messaging system; however, it suffered from a number of problems, including security, platform dependency, and a shortage of administrative tools. These issues prompted Microsoft to develop a messaging system that would be more secure and robust. Microsoft also wanted to incorporate a suite of administrative tools that would provide a means for centralized administration and management.

Exchange Server was developed as a comprehensive communications solution. Currently, it's hard to find a single operating system capable of encompassing all the necessary functions of a corporation. Often, large corporations implement several operating systems, such as DOS, Windows 3.x, Windows 95, Windows NT Workstation, Macintosh, as well as some derivatives of Unix. Additionally, you may find several network operating systems, such as Banyan Vines, NetWare, and Windows NT. It is this multitude of hardware platforms and network operating systems that Exchange Server was designed to communicate with, thus providing a messaging system capable of servicing an entire enterprise.

Client/Server Architecture

Exchange Server is perhaps one of the most powerful messaging systems available today. It enables members of your organization to exchange information with users on the Internet, as well as with users on other systems. Exchange Server allows you to exchange information in the form of messages. Users can exchange items—such as documents, spreadsheets, and graphics—via email. Users can also access information within public folders, as well as post information or items in public folders for others to access.

Exchange Server is a client/server messaging system. Its design is based on the *client/server computing* model. Client/server computing is a process in which a network task is divided into client and server processes. Both computers process instructions to accomplish common tasks. These instructions occur on the network, which allows the two computers to maintain constant communication with each other. It is this communication between the computers that allows the tasks to be accomplished. The network is facilitated in such a manner as to relay requests and replies between the client computers and the server.

Client-side computing usually takes place on a user's workstation or desktop computer and includes the client software. As it pertains to the end user, the client software provides the interface for the messaging system. The interface also allows the user to manipulate data within the messaging system. Additionally, the interface allows the messaging processes to make requests and receive replies from the server. In the client/server model, the software that runs on the client's computer is usually called the front-end program. The front-end program (for example, Microsoft Outlook) provides an interface to messages and other data stored on the server. It also provides the users with access to their email, scheduling, and shared information stored on the server. When a user logs into a Windows NT Server running the Exchange Server software, the Exchange client, which resides on the user's system, logs into the Exchange Server software. This allows the user to access his or her email and other information. The processing power to carry out these tasks is provided by the user's computer.

The server-side processes take place on a server and include the server software. The server's software receives and processes the requests made by the client. The server software also provides the storage capabilities, implements security policies, and provides many of the administrative functions for the messaging system. The server software is referred to as the *back-end program* and consists of the main components of Microsoft Exchange Server. The Exchange Server software runs on a Windows NT Server. The back-end program provides the main administrative tasks, as well as the basic messaging services for the entire messaging system.

In the client/server model, both the client side and the server side are considered active participants. All the activities within the messaging system are divided between the two sides in such a manner that the messaging system takes advantage of both participants. The client software allows the user to engage in mail activities, such as creating, sending, receiving, reading, deleting, and forwarding mail. The server software allows the server to accomplish tasks, such as maintaining system security, placing messages in mailboxes, notifying clients of new messages, and all the tasks involved in routing messages. Client/server computing has many advantages, including the following:

➤ **Distributed computer processing** Network tasks use the computing power of both the server and the client. The client processor handles all the end user activities, whereas the server processor handles all of the messaging system activities. Here's an example of what occurs in distributed computer processing: A client sends a request to the server, the server processes the request and returns the result to the client. Depending on the client's request, the server could also send data back to the client for processing. This would occur if the client's request required a local process (for example, moving email files from the server to a local directory on the client's computer system).

➤ **Security** The server system is responsible for implementing security for the entire messaging system. The server software places messages into the user mailboxes. This means a user only needs access to his or her mailbox, thus restricting user access to other mailboxes, which makes the system more secure.

➤ **Reduced network traffic** Because the server software is responsible for notifying users of new messages, the client software does not have to poll the server to check for new messages. This means fewer broadcasts are sent on the network, which improves network performance.

Perhaps the only disadvantage to the client/server model (shown in Figure 2.1) is increased server hardware requirements, because the server is responsible for creating the storage capabilities as well as for processing all user requests. However, this should not be considered a large drawback in light of all the advantages of the client/server model.

Exchange In The Enterprise

Exchange Server was designed to be an enterprise messaging system. This means it's scalable enough to service an entire organization, regardless of its size or requirements. The term *scalability* refers to the ability to grow and adapt easily. To be considered scalable, Microsoft had to incorporate and facilitate

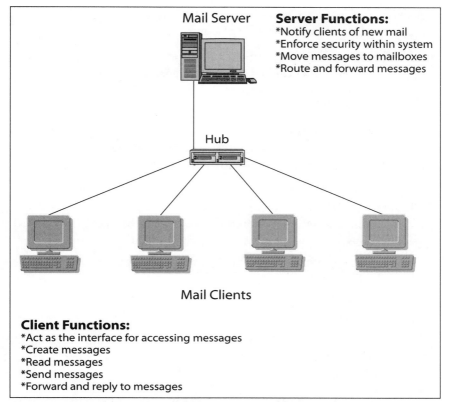

Figure 2.1   An example of the client/server mail system.

many of the technologies within Windows NT Server. This section briefly covers these technologies, which fall into six categories:

➤ Enterprise application platform

➤ Interoperability

➤ Administration

➤ Reliability

➤ Scalability

➤ Performance

Enterprise Application Platform

To be considered an enterprise solution, Exchange has to meet a series of requirements that allow it to service almost any organization, regardless of the organization's size. To accomplish this, several elements are incorporated into the Exchange platform. Here's a list of some of these elements:

➤ **Messaging services** Exchange must support the basic functionality of messaging services, including email, electronic forms, groupware, and the ability to support add-on products for faxing, paging, voice mail, video conferencing, and Internet access.

➤ **Platform independence** Exchange currently has client software that supports and runs on MS-DOS, Windows 3.x, Windows 95, Windows NT Workstation, Macintosh, Unix, and IBM OS/2.

➤ **Open architecture** Exchange uses an Application Programming Interface (API) for messaging services known as Messaging Application Programming Interface (MAPI). Through the use of MAPI, additional applications are created for use within the Exchange environment. This gives Exchange Server the ability to connect and communicate with many other existing messaging systems.

➤ **Industry standards** Here are some of the industry standards that Exchange currently supports:

   ➤ **Internet mail** The ability to send and receive mail through the use of mail standards, such as the Simple Mail Transfer Protocol (SMTP) and the Post Office Protocol 3 (POP3).

   ➤ **Internet directory access** The ability to provide access to directory listings on the Internet through the use of the Lightweight Directory Access Protocol (LDAP).

   ➤ **Internet news services** The ability to provide news services through the Network News Transfer Protocol (NNTP).

   ➤ **Internet Web protocols** The ability to support the Hypertext Transfer Protocol (HTTP), the Hypertext Markup Language (HTML), and the MIME Hypertext Markup Language (MHTML).

   ➤ **CCITT message transfer** The ability to support the CCITT X.400 messaging transfer protocol.

   ➤ **CCITT directory listing** The ability to support the CCITT X.500 directory structure.

Interoperability

Exchange Server can be deployed in enterprises with existing messaging systems already in place. The ability to coexist with other messaging systems is referred to as *interoperability*. A non-Exchange messaging system is referred to as a *foreign system*. If necessary, the data from the preexisting messaging system should be moved to the new messaging system. The process of moving the existing messaging system data over to a new messaging system is referred to as *migration*. For Exchange Server to be considered a true enterprise solution, it must address issues concerning both interoperability and migration. To communicate with foreign systems, Microsoft developed a series of programs known as *connectors*. Connectors act as translators between Exchange Server and other foreign systems. Also, third-party programs have been developed to accomplish this translation; they are referred to as *gateways*. Here are several of the systems with which Exchange can interoperate:

➤ Internet Mail

➤ Microsoft Mail

➤ Lotus cc:Mail

➤ Lotus Notes

➤ X.400 Mail systems

➤ IBM PROFS and SNADS

➤ Digital Equipment Corporation (DEC) All-in-1

Some of the mail systems that Exchange Server can migrate from include the following:

➤ Microsoft Mail

➤ Lotus cc:Mail

➤ Novell GroupWise

➤ Netscape Collabra

➤ IBM PROFS

➤ DEC All-in-1

Administration

Exchange provides several administration programs to effectively manage the messaging for an organization. The Exchange Administrator program provides a single point of administration for the entire organization. Within the enterprise, any Exchange server can be managed from the Exchange Administrator. Administration includes tasks such as creating mailboxes, managing connections with foreign systems, and changing or updating server configurations. In addition, Exchange Server incorporates the following administrative utilities:

➤ **Link Monitor** Examines the link between servers.

➤ **Server Monitor** Examines the status of a particular server.

Reliability

Exchange Server provides a status of high reliability, thus ensuring continuity of messaging services for the entire enterprise. It achieves this status through the following features:

➤ **Replicas** Exchange can be configured to maintain multiple copies (called *replicas*) of a single public folder on multiple servers. In terms of data access, this ensures user accessibility to these folders in the event of a server failure.

➤ **Transaction logs** These logs provide fault tolerance and recoverability by tracking and logging all transactions that take place within the system. In the event of a server failure, the transaction log continues to log activity, which the server resumes when it is brought back online.

➤ **Microsoft Cluster Server (MS Cluster Server)** MS Cluster Server provides fault tolerance for your hardware in the event of a system failure. A cluster consists of an *active node* and a *secondary node*. The active node acts as the primary mail server that processes and routes messages on your network. The active and secondary nodes monitor each other constantly. If the active node experiences a hardware failure, the secondary node assumes the role of the primary mail server without interrupting mail service or dropping client connections. MS Cluster Server is installed on the active node first and then on the secondary node. When the cluster is established, Setup detects that Exchange Server is installed on the active node and adds the Exchange Server resources, such as the System Attendant, directory, and Information Store, to the secondary node. Doing this enables the active node to failover to the secondary node. This failover protection ensures that another server is always available so that mail service is never interrupted in the event of a server failure.

Scalability

Exchange Server was developed to provide messaging services for an entire organization. The size of the organization does not hinder Exchange Server's functionality. This means Exchange Server is scalable. It can service both small and large organizations, regardless of their messaging requirements. Software scalability makes this possible.

When servicing an organization, Exchange Server can be implemented on a single server or literally dozens of servers, depending on the messaging requirements of the organization. Several Exchange servers may exist within an enterprise; however, only a single enterprise messaging system exists. This is due to the features of Exchange Server that allow the servers to communicate with each other. Several of these features include message routing, directory replication, and data replication. This functionality allows Exchange Server to be implemented on a single server or multiple servers.

Performance

A messaging system implemented at the enterprise scale must perform well enough to handle heavy loads. Exchange Server was designed to perform under these loads and to push the server's hardware to its fullest capacity. Exchange Server is a 32-bit, multithreaded application that runs on Windows NT Server's powerful operating system. In addition to capitalizing on the strengths of the operating system, Exchange Server integrates components that assist in maintaining performance. These components include the Exchange Performance Optimizer and the Load Simulator. The Performance Optimizer evaluates current system performance and adjusts the system automatically for peak performance. The Load Simulator is a component that simulates system loads and attempts to predict system performance during heavy loads. This information is then passed to the Performance Optimizer for evaluation.

Exchange Server And Industry Standards

Microsoft Exchange Server was developed to incorporate many of the industry standard technologies. Industry standard technologies ensure that programs comply with open architecture standards. By complying with open architecture standards, a program can easily be added to and is compatible with a multitude of hardware and software platforms. Here are a few of the most important standards Exchange utilizes:

➤ Messaging Application Programming Interface (MAPI)

➤ Remote procedure call (RPC) protocol

➤ CCITT X.400

➤ CCITT X.500

Messaging Application Programming Interface (MAPI) provides a standard API for client/server messaging interaction. To help you better understand MAPI, we'll define an API. All programs have certain built-in functions. Other programs, through the use of specific instructions, invoke these functions. Those specific instructions are referred to as *Application Programming Interfaces*. Every API has its own set of instructions called *function calls*. Function calls allow a program to access specific functions of another program. Several years ago, messaging products of the client/server model had their own APIs that enabled client/server interaction. Back then, client applications would only work with messaging systems whose APIs were compatible. This meant that if a user needed to connect to multiple messaging systems (Lotus Notes, Microsoft MS Mail, cc:Mail, and so on), the user would have to install multiple client applications (see Figure 2.2).

Microsoft created the Messaging Application Programming Interface to accomplish two goals. The first goal is to provide a standard API for client/server

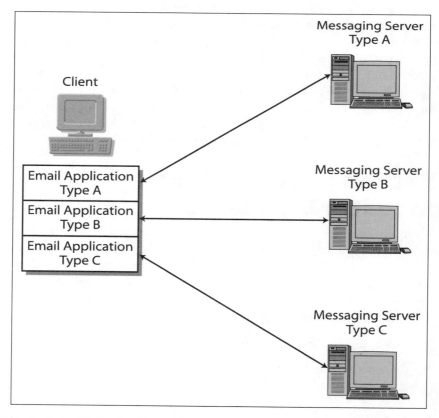

Figure 2.2 Multiple client programs interact with multiple APIs.

interaction. As implied by its name, this standard applies only to client/server messaging, hence the name Messaging Application Programming Interface. MAPI enables a single client application to interact with different messaging servers (see Figure 2.3).

The second goal of MAPI is to standardize services for client messaging applications. These services allow for the creation of universal address books and universal inboxes, as well as for a method of storing different types of data in the same folder. Through the use of standardized transport mechanisms, these services allow a single client application to connect to foreign messaging systems. MAPI deals with the actual instructions being passed between the client and server software. To pass these instructions between the client and the server, a series of protocols has been developed. Exchange Server uses the remote procedure call (RPC) protocol to pass the instructions between the server and

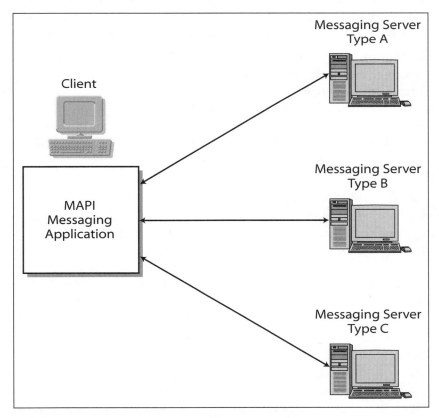

Figure 2.3 A single client interacting with different messaging servers through MAPI.

the client. However, before we get to the RPC protocol, let's review procedure calls. The following sections cover the two types of procedure calls: *remote* and *local*.

Remote Procedure Calls

The communication between the front-end (client-side) and back-end (server-side) processes are handled by RPCs. RPC is a protocol used for client/server communication specifically and is independent of any network protocols. This is important because it allows communication between servers and clients that may be running different network protocols. An RPC enables procedures (instructions) issued from one computer to be transmitted over the network to another computer, where the instructions are to be executed. The transfer of the instructions is completely transparent to both the program issuing the instructions and the user. In fact, to the program issuing the instructions, it appears as if the instructions are being executed locally. The RPC protocol is a key component of distributed processing within the client/server architecture.

For example, when a user reads a message, the client program issues a MAPI instruction. The client-side RPC protocol transfers this instruction to the server where the message to be read physically exists. The server-side RPC protocol receives the request, executes it, and sends the message to be read back to the client (which is viewed on the screen). RPC clients make requests, and RPC servers make replies; hence, RPC is also called the *request/reply protocol*. Figure 2.4 shows an example of an RPC protocol.

Local Procedure Calls

Programs issue commands to computer processors. When a program issues a command that's executed by the same computer on which the program resides (the local computer), this procedure is referred to as a *local procedure call*. Exchange Server implements a protocol known as the *local procedure call (LPC) protocol* to implement local procedure calls. To perform messaging activities, Exchange Server may issue several simultaneous commands on the same server. The LPC protocol allows the messaging system to issue multiple commands to the server's local CPUs.

CCITT X.400

Exchange Server uses a series of connectors, which allow it to communicate with other existing messaging systems. The Exchange Server X.400 Connector is based on the X.400 standard, which was developed by the International Telegraph and Telephone Consultative Committee (CCITT). X.400 is a set

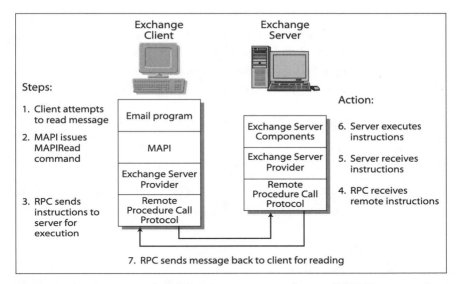

Figure 2.4 An example of the remote procedure call (RPC) protocol.

of standards related to the exchanging of electronic messages, such as voice mail, fax, telex, and email. This standard was developed to allow the creation of a global electronic messaging network. X.400 defines a series of protocols at the application level, and it's dependent on other protocols, such as the X.25 protocol, for the actual physical transportation of data. The X.400 standards are referred to by the year they were officially adopted and by a specified color. To date, here are the versions:

➤ 1984 "Red Book"

➤ 1988 "Blue Book"

➤ 1992 "White Book"

As this standard applies to Exchange Server, the X.400 Connector connects sites that have low bandwidths or preexisting X.400 backbones (such as public X.400 systems). Exchange Server supports X.400 with the following transports:

➤ Transport Protocol, Class 0 (TP0)/X.25

➤ Transport Protocol, Class 4 (TP4)/Connectionless Network Protocol (CLNP)

➤ Transmission Control Protocol/Internet Protocol (TCP/IP)

The Message Transfer Agent built into Exchange conforms to the 1984 "Red Book" and 1988 "Blue Book" X.400 publications.

To create a globally scaled messaging system, a standard numbering system was created. This numbering system had to be ambiguous enough to possibly scale the entire world's population. The address scheme that X.400 uses is called the *originator/recipient address (O/R address)*. This scheme uses a hierarchical format and consists of several categories. These categories include countries, communication providers, corporations or organizations, as well as several others. These categories are called *fields*, and they are represented in Table 2.1.

The X.400 O/R address specifies an unambiguous path to the location within the X.400 network, where the recipient is located. It does not specify the path the message will take, but only the path to where the recipient is located. An example of the X.400 O/R structure is illustrated in Figure 2.5.

CCITT X.500

X.500 defines the standard protocols for a global directory service. A directory service is a database that contains information about resources, such as user groups, mailboxes, printers, fax machines, and many other items. These resources are considered objects, and each object has its own set of properties. The properties associated with each object can include information such as the owner's name (owner of a mailbox), the owner's title, phone number, and so on. The purpose of the directory is to make this information available to other users and administrators. A good analogy of the purpose of X.500 would be the current global telephone system. Think about all the phone numbers that exist around the world. Imagine if you were trying to call a business without knowing the telephone number, and you didn't have a phonebook to look up

Table 2.1   X.400 O/R addressing field examples.

Field	Abbreviation/ Example	Description
Country code	c = US	Country
Admin. mgmt. domain (ADMD)	a = Sprint	Third-party network system (ATT, MCI, Sprint, and so on)
Priv. mgmt. domain (PRMD)	p = BestNet	Subscriber service to the ADMD (company name)
Organization	o = Best	Company name or organization
Surname	s = Morgan	Last name
Given name	g = Wesley	First name

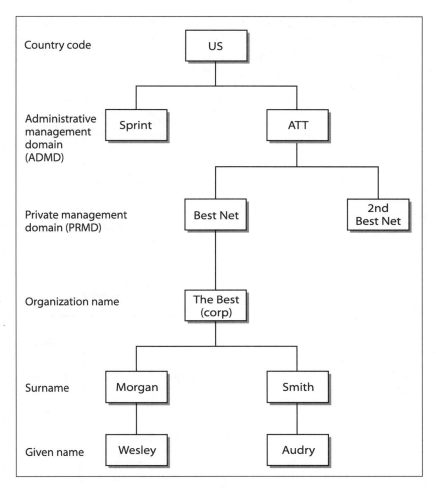

Figure 2.5   The X.400 O/R address scheme.

the number. The X.500 directory structure allows users to find other users' email addresses and so on. The X.400 standard allows users to communicate with other users on other systems so that everyone can communicate. This is the relationship between the X.400 and the X.500.

X.500 allows you to create a directory service, which is composed of two main areas:

➤ **Directory structure** All the objects on the Internet are organized within a certain directory structure, which is used to locate these objects.

➤ **Directory access** Users will need to be able to read, query, update, and modify the directory.

The X.500 directory structure is hierarchical and is composed of logical organizations of information. This permits users to find the information by making it more readily available. See Figure 2.6 for an illustrated X.500 directory structure. Table 2.2 further explains the structure.

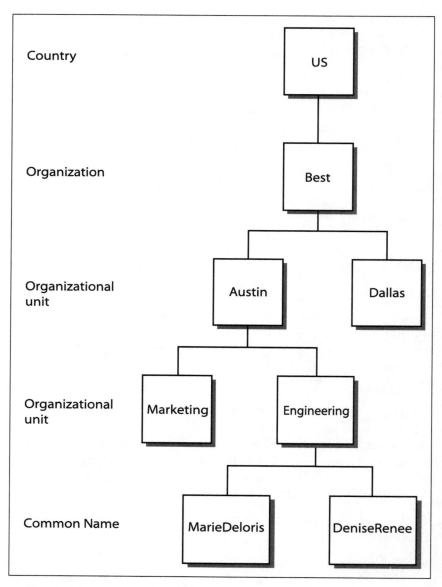

Figure 2.6 The X.500 directory structure.

Table 2.2 X.500 directory objects.		
Field	**Abbreviation/ Example**	**Description**
Country	c = US	Country of the organization
Organization	o = Best	Name of the organization
Organization unit	ou = Dallas	Subcategory of the organization, o = Best
Organization unit	ou = Marketing	Subcategories under ou = Austin, ou = Marketing
Common name	cn = MarieDeloris	Name of the resource (for example, username)

The structure of the X.500 directory is referred to as the *directory information tree (DIT)*. The information within the DIT is referred to as the *directory information base (DIB)*. The location of an object within the directory should be listed starting at the top, working your way down the tree. For example, the information in Figure 2.6 would be listed as this:

```
C=US; o=Best; ou=Austin; ou=Engineering; cn=MarieDeloris
```

The listing of the location of the object in Table 2.2 in this manner is referred to as the *distinguished name (DN)*. The purpose of the DN is to list the location of an object within a directory. The purpose of the X.400 address is to provide the location of an object within the messaging system. Now that we have discussed the X.500 directory listing, let's take a look at how users access this directory, and more importantly, what this directory provides.

With a directory structure in place, you now need access to this directory. However, to allow access to this directory, some other issues must be addressed: security (who can access this directory and at what level) and directory replication (a "global" directory, for obvious reasons, would have to exist on several computers). To address these issues, a series of directory access protocols were created. Within X.500, a standard access protocol known as the Directory Access Protocol (DAP) is recommended. However, DAP is extremely CPU intensive, especially on client computers. Because of this, a new directory access protocol has been designed. Although the new directory access protocol has not yet been standardized, software vendors have pledged their support for the newer protocol, and they are already implementing it. This protocol is known as the *Lightweight Directory Access Protocol (LDAP)*. LDAP is much less intensive on client computers, and it's considered an Internet protocol. It allows access to directories that comply with the X.500 directory structure.

Exchange Server

Exchange Server is a messaging system that's made up of several components. These components create and manage all the objects within the system. These objects are the resources within the messaging system, such as servers, mailboxes, public folders, address books, and so on. The way these objects are structured and organized is part of the Exchange architecture. Exchange is organized hierarchically, grouping objects and items by class, order, rank, and so on. Each of these objects is a member of the hierarchy tree. The highest ranked object (the parent) in the Exchange hierarchy sits at the top of the tree. Below the parent objects are other objects that represent the children, with their children located below them, and so on. The hierarchy tree shows the relationships among the objects. One of these relationships is called the parent-child relationship. In parent-child relationships, the children inherit traits from their parents. Additionally, child objects can also have other child objects below them, making them parent objects to the child objects below them. Here are three objects that constitute the main structure in the Exchange hierarchy (see Figure 2.7):

➤ Organizations

➤ Sites

➤ Servers

Organizations

The object that sits at the top of the Exchange hierarchy is called the *organization*. All the other objects within the messaging system are contained within the organization. The organization is the parent to all the sites within it. This allows administrators to configure the system at the organization level. The parameters with which the organization has been configured apply to all the sites within the organization. Because an organization encompasses the entire Exchange system, each corporation should create only one organization.

Sites

A *site* is a grouping of one or more Exchange servers. A single site can contain the resources from several different servers without reference to their locations. This grouping of resources makes use of the resources very easy through what is known as *location transparency*. For example, a user's mailbox may reside on site server A. This site server is referred to as the *home server* to that specific mailbox. All users sending mail to this mailbox do not need to know the physical location of the mailbox to send mail to it. To them, it simply appears within the site listing along with all the other mailboxes. This means that from the

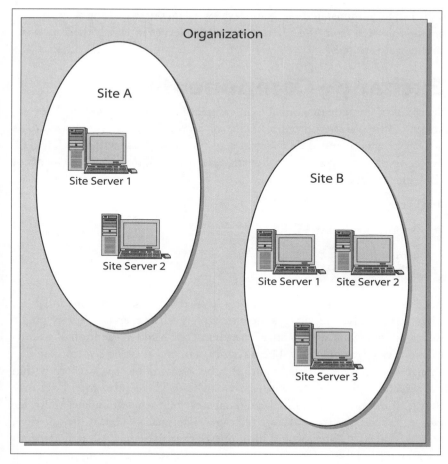

Figure 2.7   The three main objects within the Exchange hierarchy.

user's perspective, a site creates a transparent messaging environment. This also allows administrators to configure the site, and that site's servers will inherit those configurations. A permanent high speed connection must exist between all Exchange servers within a site; if multiple domains are involved, two-way trusts between each pair of domains will also be required.

Servers

Exchange servers are computers that run the Windows NT operating system as well as the Exchange Server software. On these servers are the mailboxes, public and private folders, data, and other information regarding the site. Each of the site's servers inherit configuration parameters from the site, while at the same time, they can be configured individually. For example, recipients within a site can be administered at the site level, while at the same time they can also be administered from their home server (the server in which their mail accounts were created).

Exchange Components

Several vital components provide functionality to Exchange Server. They are known as the *core components* of Exchange Server. They are also referred to as *services*, because many of them run as services on the Microsoft Windows NT Server operating system. The following are considered the core components of Exchange Server:

➤ Directory Service (DS)

➤ Information Store (IS)

➤ Message Transfer Agent (MTA)

➤ System Attendant (SA)

Exchange Server is designed to utilize a series of objects, containers, and databases. An *object* is a messaging system resource, such as a server, mailbox, public folder, address book, and so on. These objects are listed in the form of records within the system directory. The directory contains all objects within the Exchange Server system. This implies that because an object is a record within the directory, the directory must be a database. This is also true. Exchange Server stores information in several databases and then manipulates these databases to send, receive, and store messages. Examples of objects include sites, servers, folders, mailboxes, and files. The Exchange Server Administrator allows you to view the hierarchical relationship of these objects within your system.

A *container* is an object within Exchange Server that holds other objects. A good analogy is to think of storing a number of small containers within a larger container. For example, all the mailbox objects are stored within the recipient's container. This means the recipient's container is also an object, because it holds other objects. Containers and all the objects within them have the hierarchical parent-child relationships discussed earlier in this chapter. This structure controls the permissions for the objects. *Permissions* are rules that determine which users have access to which objects, and what rights those users have within the objects. Any permission granted to the parent object is automatically inherited by the child object.

As listed earlier, one of the main components of Exchange is the Directory Service. The function of the Directory Service is to create and manage the storage of all objects within the organization. The database that stores all the objects within the system is called the *directory*. The directory stores these objects in a hierarchical structure. The primary purpose of the directory is to provide a central location for all the objects within the system. This allows users and administrators to easily locate the system's resources to use and administer them. The objects stored by the Exchange Directory Service have *properties* (also called *attributes*) that are the characteristics of the objects. For example, an object can be a user (John Smith) or an entire Exchange organization (Best). Furthermore, objects have permissions, which determine the characteristics of the objects. The object John Smith can have properties, such as first name, last name, job title, email address, and many others, as shown in Figure 2.8.

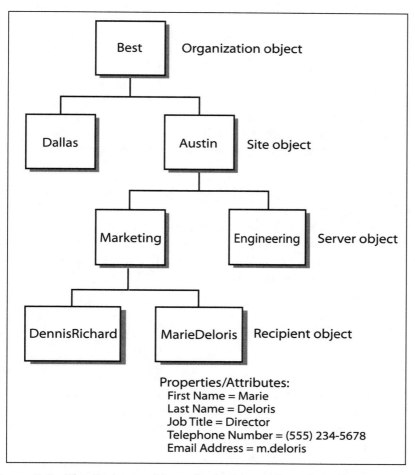

Figure 2.8   The Exchange hierarchy and some sample properties of an object.

The Information Store is responsible for creating and managing the message database on Exchange Server. This database stores information such as email messages, electronic forms, spreadsheets, word processing documents, graphics, audio files, and many other items from almost any application. Users can access the information within the Information Store through their mailboxes and folders in their client applications. The Information Store consists of two main databases:

➤ **Public Information Store** The Public Information Store database is contained in the file PUB.EDB. It contains all the public folders on the server. Public folders are containers that hold documents, messages, forms, and any other information your users want to share within the messaging system. Essentially, public folders act as public mailboxes.

➤ **Private Information Store** The Private Information Store contains the users' mailboxes and private folders. The Private Information Store database is contained in the file PRIV.EDB. Exchange utilizes the integrated security features within Microsoft Windows NT. This means that the user mailboxes and folders will only be accessible by their respective owners and to others who have been given access permission. These folders contain the users' private mailboxes. As such, users can keep any information they put into these folders private and inaccessible by other users.

The Message Transfer Agent (MTA) handles the routing of all messages, whether these messages are being routed within the same site, different sites, or to other foreign sites. Additionally, the MTA uses components known as *connectors*. Connectors manage the actual connection to other systems, as well as the transfer of data, whereas the MTA handles all the routing functions. The primary functions of the MTA include the following:

➤ Originator/recipient addressing

➤ Message format translation

➤ Message routing

The MTA is modeled after the X.400 standard (discussed earlier in this chapter) and, as such, uses the originator/recipient addressing scheme. If messages are being routed to an X.400 messaging system, the MTA will change the format of the message from the Exchange format, known as the Microsoft Database Exchange Format (MDBEF), to the X.400 format, known as the Interpersonal Message Format (IPM). The ability to translate messages to this format allows Exchange clients to exchange mail with X.400 mail users. When the MTA receives a message to be forwarded, it first determines a route for the message. It then examines the message recipient's distinguished name (DN). If this address does not resolve the next route, it then examines the originator/recipient address. The MTA will compare the address with the routing information contained within the gateway address routing table (GWART). Because there might be several available paths, the administrator can assign values to the different paths. These values are called *costs*. They allow priorities to be assigned to the different routes. When the MTA encounters multiple paths, it automatically chooses the path with the lowest cost. In the event that the MTA cannot resolve the address specified, it will send the message originator a report known as a *non-delivery report (NDR)*. This alerts the user or administrator that the message was undeliverable.

The System Attendant (SA) is a service that runs in the background. It monitors and logs almost all the Exchange Server processes, as well as builds and maintains the routing tables for the site. The SA logs data such as the tracking information that includes the route the message took and whether or not the message was received at its destination. The SA also compiles the routing tables for the entire site. This is the table the MTA uses when it's determining which route to take. In addition to these functions, the SA monitors the connection between servers, verifies the connection, and at the same time, checks the Exchange services running on other servers. It accomplishes this by sending test messages between itself and the other servers. Whenever new user accounts are created, the SA is responsible for generating their email addresses.

Exchanging Mail

When a client uses Exchange Server to send a message, the message is first delivered to the Information Store. The Information Store holds the messages being sent and received on an Exchange server. The Information Store is represented in the form of a database. It is considered the primary system database (SYSTEM.EDB), and it cannot be manipulated or directly accessed by users or administrators. The Information Store acts as a post office and has two main components—the Public Information Store and the Private Information Store.

After the Information Store receives a message, it processes the message by determining the destination of the message. It does this by searching the directory. As mentioned previously, the directory is a listing of all objects within the system, and it has two main functional units—the directory database and the Directory Service. The directory database (DIR.EDB) manages all objects in the organization and makes the information available to the appropriate users, administrators, and system processes. The Directory Service (DS) manipulates the information within the directory database. It also processes directory requests from users and other applications. The Directory Service also provides these other important functions:

➤ It maintains the objects stored within the directory database and displays them in a hierarchical tree structure.

➤ It sends replication notifications to directories on other servers, as well as receives directory replication notifications from other servers.

➤ It provides the interface between the Exchange clients and the directory database.

➤ It enforces rules that control the structure and contents of the directory.

After the directory has verified the destination information, the message is ready to be delivered. At this point, the message is relayed to the Message Transfer Agent (MTA), which is responsible for delivering the message. The MTA ensures that the message is successfully delivered to its destination. The MTA is an object that routes messages within your system, as well as to gateways that connect to outside email systems. It provides resolution for external addresses, and if necessary, it can convert message formats to ensure compatibility. The MTA uses four components to route data to other email systems and servers:

➤ **Exchange Site Connector** Connects two or more sites using RPCs. The sites must be linked via a permanent network connection. Site connectors use the RPC protocol and are fairly easy to configure. When you use RPC, you do not need to worry about configuring a network transport. The site connector will use whatever existing transport protocol is configured between the Exchange servers. The site connector is not protocol dependent.

➤ **Remote Access Service (RAS) Connector** Connects sites that do not have a permanent network connection. It provides a means to connect via asynchronous communications, such as a regular dial-up phone connection, ISDN, and X.25. The RAS Connector allows remote servers and users to communicate with Exchange Server.

➤ **X.400 Connector** As mentioned previously, the X.400 Connector can be used to connect to sites that have low bandwidths or existing X.400 backbones, such as X.400 public systems.

➤ **Internet Mail Connector** The Internet Mail Connector is used to communicate with other users on the Internet. This connector uses the Simple Mail Transfer Protocol (SMTP), which is integrated into Exchange Server. This integration makes the exchange of mail between users on the Internet transparent.

Exchange Clients

Exchange Server must run on a Windows NT Server computer. However, Exchange Server can coexist on a variety of network operating systems, including Novell NetWare and Banyan Vines.

The preferred client software to use with Exchange Server is Microsoft Outlook. Outlook is a desktop information manager that helps users organize and manage email, calendars, contacts, documents, and scheduling. Currently, you can install Outlook as the client for Microsoft Exchange Server on the following platforms:

➤ Microsoft Windows 3.x

➤ Microsoft Windows 95

➤ Microsoft Windows NT

➤ Apple Macintosh

➤ IBM OS/2

➤ Unix

Exam Prep Questions

Question 1

Which of the following is considered an email protocol?

- ○ a. POP3
- ○ b. LDAP
- ○ c. HTTP
- ○ d. TCP/IP

Answer a is correct. Of the protocols listed, only Post Office Protocol 3 is considered an email protocol. LDAP, HTTP, and TCP/IP are not considered email protocols. Therefore, answers b, c, and d are incorrect.

Question 2

Which of the following items allows you to transfer the actual data from a foreign system into the Exchange messaging system?

- ○ a. X.400 industry standard
- ○ b. Migration utility
- ○ c. X.500 directory
- ○ d. Message Transfer Agent

Answer b is correct. The migration utility, which is provided with Exchange Server, is used to migrate data from other messaging systems into Exchange Server. X.400 and X.500 are messaging standards, but they do not deal with data migration. Therefore, answers a and c are incorrect. The MTA is part of the Exchange Server architecture, but not part of the migration. Therefore, answer d is incorrect.

Question 3

The distinguished name (DN) is derived from which of the following?

- ○ a. Gateway address routing table (GWART)
- ○ b. Private Information Store
- ○ c. X.500 directory
- ○ d. X.400 originator/recipient addressing scheme

Answer c is correct. The distinguished name is derived from the X.500 directory scheme. The GWART is used by the MTA to determine through which connector the message should be sent. Therefore, answer a is incorrect. A Private Information Store contains a user's mailbox and private lists. Therefore, answer b is incorrect. X.400 O/R is a hierarchical addressing scheme, but it is not used to determine the DN. Therefore, answer d is incorrect.

Question 4

What is the X.400 message format?

○ a. X.400 Message Format (X4MF)

○ b. Interpersonal Message Format (IPM)

○ c. Microsoft Database Encoding Format (MDBEF)

○ d. Exchange X.400 Database Format (XDBF)

Answer b is correct. The X.400 message format is known as the Interpersonal Message Format (IPM). X4MF and XDBF are fictitious. Therefore, answers a and d are incorrect. MDBEF is the storage format used by an Information Store. Therefore answer c is incorrect.

Question 5

Which of the following protocols is designed for messaging specifically and is responsible for the client/server interaction of processes?

○ a. MAPI

○ b. Remote procedure call protocol

○ c. TCP/IP protocol

○ d. Directory Access Protocol (DAP)

Answer b is correct. The remote procedure call (RPC) protocol was designed specifically for client/server interaction. You may have thought it was the Messaging Application Programming Interface (MAPI). However, as implied by its name, it is an interface, not a protocol. Therefore, answer a is incorrect. TCP/IP is a suite of protocols, but it is not responsible for client/server process interaction. Therefore, answer c is incorrect. DAP was the predecessor to LDAP, but it was used for directory lookups, not client/server processing. Therefore, answer d is incorrect.

Question 6

Which of the following protocols replaced the Directory Access Protocol?

○ a. Local procedure call

○ b. TCP/IP

○ c. Lightweight Directory Access Protocol

○ d. Request/reply protocol

Answer c is correct. The Lightweight Directory Access Protocol (LDAP) was designed to replace the Directory Access Protocol (DAP). The DAP required too many resources and was too resource intensive on client computers. A local procedure call is used by applications within a system and is not a protocol. Therefore answer a is incorrect. Although TCP/IP is a protocol, it's been around a lot longer than DAP or LDAP, so answer b is incorrect. The request/reply protocol (RPC) is used to transfer instructions between clients and servers, but it has no relation to DAP or LDAP. Therefore, answer d is incorrect.

Question 7

Which of the following items are considered the three main components of the Exchange hierarchy structure? [Check all correct answers]

❏ a. Sites

❏ b. Organization

❏ c. Enterprise

❏ d. Servers

The correct answers are a, b, and d. The three main components of the Exchange hierarchy include the organization, sites, and servers. The term enterprise refers to a worldwide organization, but it is not part of the Exchange hierarchy. Therefore, answer c is incorrect.

Question 8

The Exchange Server software can issue multiple simultaneous commands to the client software.

○ a. True

○ b. False

The correct answer is b, False. Exchange Server can indeed issue multiple commands to the clients; however, these commands are not issued simultaneously.

Question 9

MAPI is responsible for the transfer of instructions between the client computer and the server system.

○ a. True

○ b. False

The correct answer is b, False. The remote procedure call protocol is responsible for the actual transfer of instructions between the client and server computers. MAPI allows client/server interaction or processing of instructions through the use of remote procedure calls.

Question 10

What is the remote procedure call (RPC) protocol?

○ a. A protocol designed for client/server communication specifically

○ b. The interface with which the user interacts

○ c. A protocol used specifically for Microsoft Networking

○ d. The protocol by which the System Attendant monitors the messaging system

Answer a is correct. The RPC protocol was designed specifically for client/server communication. Answers b, c, and d are incorrect.

Question 11

Which of the following items is considered the Exchange primary database?

○ a. SYSTEM.EDB

○ b. PRIV.EDB

○ c. The Information Store

○ d. PUB.EDB

Answer a is correct. SYSTEM.EDB comprises the Information Store and is considered the primary system database. PRIV.EDB and PUB.EDB make up the Private and Public Information Stores, respectively. Therefore, answers b and d are incorrect. The Information Store is the name for the combination of databases, but it is not the actual database. Therefore answer c is incorrect.

Question 12

On which network environments can a Microsoft Exchange Server reside? [Check all correct answers]

❑ a. Banyan Vines

❑ b. Novell NetWare

❑ c. Windows NT

❑ d. Unix

The correct answers are a, b, and c. Exchange Server can be installed on any Banyan Vines, Novell NetWare, or Windows NT networking environments. Exchange Server cannot reside on a Unix-only network. Therefore, answer d is incorrect.

Question 13

Which of the following is *not* a characteristic of client/server messaging?

○ a. Distributed computer processing

○ b. Reduced network traffic

○ c. Passive client application

○ d. Greater security

Answer c is correct. In the client/server messaging system, both the client and the server participate as active applications, both processing and receiving commands. Answers a, b, and d each represent a client/server characteristic and are therefore incorrect.

Question 14

> Which of the following items optimize the Exchange messaging system performance? [Check all correct answers]
>
> ❑ a. 32-bit architecture
>
> ❑ b. LDAP
>
> ❑ c. Load Simulator
>
> ❑ d. Exchange Optimizer

The correct answers are a, c, and d. Exchange Server implements the 32-bit architecture. The Load Simulator is a utility of Exchange Server that simulates loads on the system and adjusts the system automatically. The Exchange Optimizer is a component of Exchange Server that optimizes performance based on system resources. LDAP is a directory access protocol that is supported by Exchange Server, but it is not used to optimize performance. Therefore, answer b is incorrect.

Question 15

> Which of the following items are the main components of the Information Store? [Check all correct answers]
>
> ❑ a. Public Information Store
>
> ❑ b. Directory Service
>
> ❑ c. Private Information Store
>
> ❑ d. Directory replication

The correct answers are a and c. The Information Store is made up of the Public Information Store and the Private Information Store. They are subcomponents of the Information Store. The Directory Service and directory replication are functions of Exchange Server, but they do not comprise the Information Store. Therefore, answers b and d are incorrect.

Question 16

> When the Message Transfer Agent routes a message in the Exchange format, which format is used?
>
> ○ a. X.500
>
> ○ b. X.400
>
> ○ c. Microsoft Database Encoding Format (MDBEF)
>
> ○ d. Lightweight Directory Access Protocol (LDAP)

The correct answer is c. When the MTA is routing messages in the Exchange format, the data is formatted in the Microsoft Database Encoding Format (MDBEF). X.500 and X.400 are messaging standards, but not encoding formats. Therefore, answers a and b are incorrect. The LDAP protocol is used for directory lookups. Therefore, answer d is incorrect.

Question 17

> Which of the following are parts of the X.500 directory? [Check all correct answers]
>
> ❑ a. Directory information base
>
> ❑ b. Distinguished name
>
> ❑ c. Directory information tree
>
> ❑ d. Originator/recipient addressing scheme

The correct answers are a, b, and c. The DIB, DN, and DIT are all parts of the X.500 directory structure. The O/R addressing scheme is a part of the X.400 addressing scheme. Therefore, answer d is incorrect.

Question 18

> Of the following protocols, which ones does Exchange Server provide support for? [Check all correct answers]
>
> ❑ a. RPC
>
> ❑ b. LDAP
>
> ❑ c. DAP
>
> ❑ d. LPC

The correct answers are a, b, c, and d. The remote procedure call protocol, the Lightweight Directory Access Protocol, the Directory Access Protocol, and the local procedure call protocol are all supported by Exchange Server.

Question 19

> The RPC protocol is also known as the request/reply protocol.
>
> ○ a. True
>
> ○ b. False

The correct answer is a, True. The RPC protocol is responsible for transferring instructions between the server and the client. Therefore, it is also known as the *request/reply protocol.*

Question 20

> LDAP is a standardized protocol.
>
> ○ a. True
>
> ○ b. False

The correct answer is b, False. The Lightweight Directory Access Protocol has not yet been standardized. However, software vendors worldwide have endorsed it.

Need To Know More?

 On the Exchange Server 5.5 CD-ROM, Books Online is an optional component when you install Exchange Server. If you did not install Books Online during the installation process, you can always add it later.

 The Microsoft TechNet CD-ROM contains Knowledge Base articles and whitepapers related to Exchange.

 The official Web site for Exchange Server, www.microsoft.com/exchange/default.asp, offers information and assistance pertaining to Exchange Server. From the site, you may download an evaluation version of Exchange Server 5.5 to assist you in your studies.

Exchange
Server Installation

Terms you'll need to understand:

- ✓ Connectors
- ✓ Container
- ✓ Custom recipient
- ✓ Directory replication (DR)
- ✓ DirSync
- ✓ Domain controller (DC)
- ✓ Lightweight Directory Access Protocol (LDAP)
- ✓ Message Transfer Agent (MTA)
- ✓ Network News Transfer Protocol (NNTP)
- ✓ Organization
- ✓ Recipient
- ✓ Site
- ✓ X.400

Techniques you'll need to master:

- ✓ Understanding the options available for installing Exchange for an organization, site, or server
- ✓ Installing Exchange Server as the first server in an organization or as the first server on a site
- ✓ Configuring Exchange to communicate with other Exchange sites or other mail systems

In this chapter, we tell you what you need to know to install Exchange Server. We also take a look at foreign mail systems (foreign systems are non-Exchange mail servers, such as mail from the Internet). In addition, we examine the installation of a mail connector. Finally, we take you step by step through an actual Exchange Server installation.

Planning Your Installation

There's a famous adage that says, "The devil is in the details." It would not be surprising if the person who came up with this had been planning an Exchange rollout. Failure to stop and plan your installation will, at best, haunt you with a slow and expensive mail system. More likely, however, the mail system will not work at all. The following is a list of planning tips you should follow when preparing to install Microsoft Exchange Server:

➤ The security context within a site must be the same throughout.

➤ Provide your site with as much RAM and hard drive space as you can. It's easier to split one site than it is to merge two or more sites. Newcomers to Exchange are shocked to see how quickly drive space disappears.

➤ Replication is more network bandwidth intensive between servers within a site than it is between sites.

➤ For servers communicating within a site, the minimum net available bandwidth (NAB) between servers is 64Kbps. A more practical minimum is 128Kbps—unless your traffic is very light.

➤ Exchange can be installed on a Primary Domain Controller (PDC), a Backup Domain Controller (BDC), or a member server. A member server is the best choice because its hardware resources are not busy verifying login rights. To effectively install an Exchange organization, you must understand NT domains.

➤ When installed with the Complete option, Exchange will load on the drive, but connectors that aren't needed do not install. If you don't have Remote Access Service installed (with a modem), Exchange will not install the Internet Mail Service, for example.

When you're laying out your Exchange system, remember that you're working with a large and complex relational database. When planning your Exchange rollout, map as closely as possible to the way your firm is organized. For example, the organization name should match the company name; the California location should be named West; and there should be Exchange servers in the accounting, sales, and personnel departments. This will help you and your users in the actual use of Exchange.

You should be aware of what is new to a product version. The following is a list of new points that will enhance your effectiveness in a production environment. This list includes suggestions for designing and installing your Exchange system from field experts:

➤ Plan to add 100MB to the page file.

➤ NT 4 Service Pack 3 is required.

➤ IIS 3.0 or newer is required for Outlook Web Access.

➤ Exchange performs better when on a member server, instead of a domain controller.

➤ New service packs for Exchange 5.5 appear about every 90 days.

➤ Keep transaction logs on a FAT-based partition.

Some maintenance, such as moving a recipient's mailbox with the Exchange Resource Kit, is not a huge challenge. Other issues, such as splitting a site, involve a huge effort. Good planning on your part starts when you create your first Exchange server. All other servers within the site use the configuration information from the first server; therefore, you need to get it right the first time.

LOADSIM.EXE

LOADSIM.EXE for Exchange version 5.5 is now available. LOADSIM.EXE simulates the activity you expect to have. It assists your planning by simulating the load on your Exchange server with the number of users and the amount of mail that is expected to run on the server. Here are some helpful tips for running LOADSIM.EXE:

➤ Do not use LOADSIM.EXE on a production server.

➤ Run LOADSIM.EXE for at least eight hours to get an accurate picture. A couple days are preferable, if you have the time.

➤ Completely clean off the drive after testing (before putting it into a production environment). LOADSIM.EXE does not clean up well after itself.

Installing Exchange Server

Before you start SETUP.EXE on Exchange Server, you should preconfigure NT first. You must create a service account and install from it. If you install from an Administrator account, you'll end up with an Exchange installation that appears to work at first; however, when you log off, Exchange will have no way to validate and will fail. Therefore, the first step (creation of a service account) is critical.

Creating A Service Account

When creating a service account using User Manager For Domains, make sure it has been granted the Log On As A Service permission. Be sure to select a secure password, and store it in a safe place. Choose the Exchange server name carefully—you cannot rename the server without reinstalling Exchange. (You can, however, change the password later.) This account information is used if other Exchange servers are created within the site. This account must be in the same domain as the Exchange server.

To begin the installation, perform the following steps:

1. Click Start|Programs|Administrative Tools (Common)|User Manager For Domains.

2. Select New User from the User menu.

3. Enter a name and password from the service account.

4. Enable (check) the User Cannot Change Password & Password Never Expires option.

5. Remove (uncheck) the User Must Change Password at Next Logon & Account Disabled option.

6. Click Add.

7. Click Close.

From here, you'll create an Exchange Administrators group (shown in Figure 3.1). This global group has full control of Exchange.

To create the Exchange Administrators group, follow these steps:

1. Log on to the domain with administrative rights.

2. Click Start|Programs|Administrative Tools (Common)|User Manager For Domains|User|New Global Group.

3. Give a name and description to the new global group.

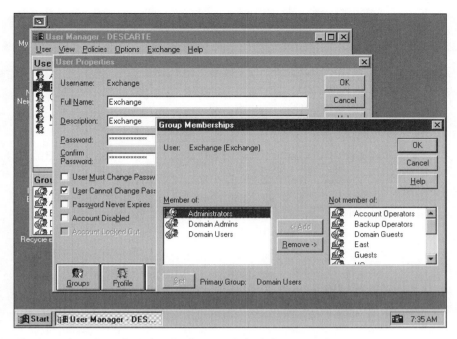

Figure 3.1   Creating the Exchange Administrators group.

4. Click Add.

5. Click Close.

Note: Refer back to your planning steps. Do you plan to use features such as Outlook Web Access (OWA)? If so, make sure you have Internet Information Server (IIS 3.0 or greater) installed. Also keep in mind that Exchange version 5.5 needs NT 4 with Service Pack 3 or greater.

Installing Exchange

To install Exchange Server, perform the following steps:

1. Using an account with administrative privileges, log on to the NT server.

2. With the program's CD in the CD-ROM drive, right-click Start|Explore or My Computer|CD.

3. Scroll down to the I386 or Alpha directory and click Setup, or you can enter Setup from the command prompt (Start|Run|Cmd.exe| *X*:\Setup\i386—where *X* is the drive where the CD-ROM is loaded).

4. Accept the licensing agreement and then choose the installation type.

5. Types of installation include Typical, Minimum, and Complete/Custom.

➤ **Typical** Installs the four Exchange components (Directory Service, System Attendant, Information Store, and Message Transfer Agent) and the Exchange Administrator.

➤ **Minimum** Installs the four Exchange components only.

➤ **Complete/Custom** Offers the following options (see Figure 3.2):

➤ It allows you to change the default installation directory and gives you the choice of MS Mail Connector, cc:Mail Connector, X.400 Connector, and Exchange Event Service (connectors are discussed in detail in Chapter 8).

➤ The Exchange Administrator can be installed on any NT machine for the administration of Exchange. It will not operate with Windows 95 or Windows 98.

➤ Books Online includes online Exchange documentation. It can be very useful; however, it consumes about 135MB of disk space.

➤ Internet Mail will not migrate some routing information.

➤ Outlook Web Access is a lightweight method for gaining access via an Exchange client in HTML. It requires IIS 3.0 or newer.

 If you don't see all the options described in the preceding list, it's because you don't have enough disk space. A complete installation (without data) uses about 143,700K of disk space.

6. Choose Licensing (the actual setting for the machine). Click OK.

7. Enter organization and site information. If this is an initial site, you'll be asked "Are you sure you want to create a new site?" Choose Yes if this is a new site. Otherwise, choose Join An Existing Site.

 To install additional Exchange servers into an existing site, choose "Join An Existing Site" when prompted during the installation process.

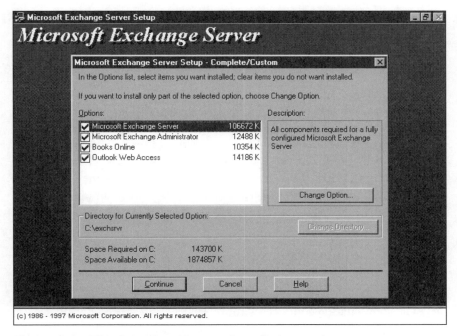

Figure 3.2   The Complete/Custom installation options.

8. Enter the information for the service account and password. Without a separate service account, Exchange cannot validate users and will not run.

9. Confirm that rights have been granted and then click OK.

10. Click OK to begin installation.

11. At this point, you can choose to run the Optimizer, or you can run it later after mailbox creation. (Do not use the Optimizer with Back Office SBS.)

The Exchange Administrator

The Exchange Administrator program is where you'll spend most of your time configuring Exchange. Be careful when making changes to your Exchange system. The default is to work at the site level. Exchange uses a container concept, similar to boxes within boxes. Exchange starts at the top level, called the *organization*, and below that is the site level. Modifications done at the site level affect all servers within the site. The site is the default permission level that you'll work with when launching the Exchange Administrator. This means that if you have 40 Exchange servers within a site and you effect a change on the site, you created a change on 40 servers. By design, you should plan to put as many Exchange servers as possible within a single site. It's much less effort to split sites than to combine them. The next level down is the single server level. You can drill down from the site level and then effect a change at the server level that will impact that server only.

Put another way, Exchange inherits configurations from top-level containers, unless you specify otherwise. Experienced Exchange administrators suggest that you create an NT group called Exchange Administrators and assign it the role Permissions Admin. Then you can add the administrative staff for the servers to this group. This is especially effective if you have changes in Exchange Administrators, because you'll only need to modify the users in the group, as opposed to affecting updates in all places in the Admin program.

The Admin program contains three main sections where you set the permission roles:

➤ The organization container (top level in the tree)

➤ The site container

➤ The configuration container within the site

The organization container is the topmost level. The next layer down is the site container. A site contains configuration data and servers, and it has a second container that contains the recipients (users). For reducing administration efforts, you may create multiple recipient containers.

Mailboxes

Mailboxes are assigned to recipients. The template for mailbox creation is set by selecting Options from the Tools menu. The first tab, Auto Naming (shown in Figure 3.3), allows you to designate how a name will be displayed. For example, John Smith or Smith, John. There is no right or wrong way, as far as Exchange goes. The issue is usually political. In the Auto Naming tab, you can also choose how to generate an alias name. In the Permissions tab, you choose your default NT domain as well as other useful options (for example, Try To Find Matching Windows NT Account When Creating Mailbox). If you have more mailboxes (recipients) than you can comfortably manage, you should organize by recipient containers.

Recipient Containers

Going back to your thoughtful planning of an Exchange organization, refer to the list you produced to guide you in the creation of recipient containers. You'll save yourself a lot of grief if you organize your containers in a logical order (for example, by geography and/or job function). Remember that you can nest containers (that is, a recipient container can contain another container).

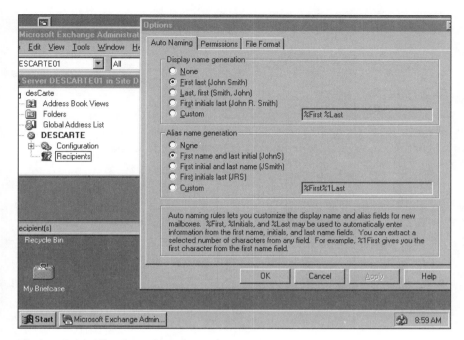

Figure 3.3   The Auto Naming tab.

To create a new container, follow these steps:

1. Select the site or recipient container.

2. Click File|New Other|Recipient Container.

3. Name your new container with a logical name.

Recipient Types

Recipients come in three different types: custom, distribution lists, and mailboxes. We'll explore each of these in the following sections.

Custom

A custom recipient is an email address added to your Exchange site with a pointer to a mailbox that exists on a foreign email system. Custom recipients provide an easy way for Exchange users to send mail to outside email users simply by selecting the user name from the global address list.

Here's how to create a custom address that can appear in a DS:

1. Pick a container.

2. Choose File|New Custom Recipient.

3. Select the type of mail address (Internet Address, X.400, and so on).

4. Enter the address.

Distribution Lists

This type of recipient borrows heavily from the format of user groups in NT. However, in Exchange they're called distribution lists. These are used to create a logical grouping of recipients (for example, sales and marketing).

Here's how to create a distribution list:

1. Pick a recipient container.

2. Choose File|New Distribution (you'll see six tabs on the list, beginning with the General tab).

3. Enter a display name (choose logically) and an alias. Then assign an owner. Ideally, the owner is not you (the administrator). This way, someone else can manage some of the workload with Outlook (as opposed to requiring rights to the Exchange Administrator account).

A required step in this process is to go to Properties and select your expansion server. An expansion server takes one copy of an email (and an attachment if it has one) and makes copies to all the mailboxes listed for distribution. You want a server capable of supporting this function. However, you should note that this does burden the RAM and CPU with quite a load.

Mailboxes

This is the area most users think of as a traditional mailbox. Although a mailbox usually has only one owner, it can assigned to an NT group. For instance, you could create a mailbox for the human resources group, and anyone in human resources may respond. Of course, in most cases you would also create a personal mailbox for each person in that department.

You have several mailbox creation choices available through Exchange Administrator, Extract and Import, or User Manager For Domains. If you're adding a new user to NT and Exchange is already installed, the fastest choice is to add the user by selecting Exchange while in User Manager For Domains. Extract and Import is most useful when you need to set up a large number of users, such as when you're migrating between systems.

Here's how to create a mailbox via Exchange Administrator:

1. Pick a container listed in the Exchange Administrator.

2. At the toolbar, select File|New Mailbox.

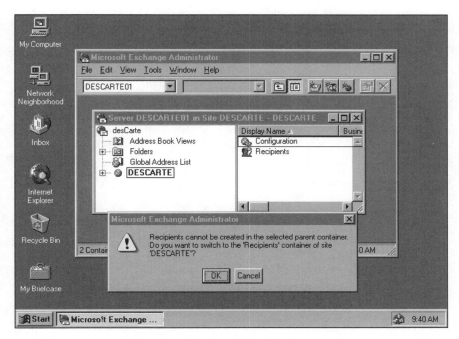

Figure 3.4   Incorrectly selected configuration container error message.

Notice that if you incorrectly select the configuration container, Exchange comes up with the error message shown in Figure 3.4.

To create a new user from User Manager For Domains, follow these steps:

1. From the User menu in User Manager For Domains, select New User.

2. Type the account information and then click Add.

3. In the Connect To Server dialog box, type the name of the Exchange server in which you want to create the mailbox.

To extract and import in Exchange Administrator, follow these steps:

1. From the Tools menu, choose to extract from either an NT domain or a NetWare 3.x or 4.x server (as shown in Figure 3.5).

2. Import your domain of choice into Exchange.

3. While importing, choose the recipient container to which you want to import, declare an existing mailbox as a template to set permissions, and optionally, declare an error log to monitor your success (or lack thereof).

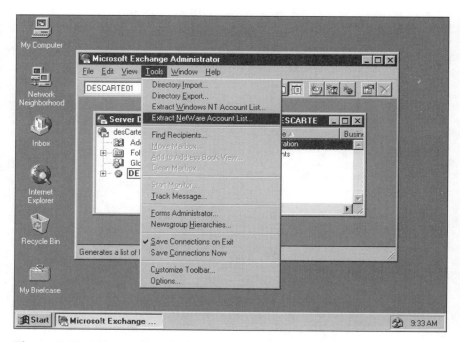

Figure 3.5 Microsoft Exchange Administrator Tools menu.

 As of Exchange version 5.5, mailbox storage no longer has the limitation of 16MB per server. This limitation existed in Exchange through version 5.

Sites

Moving up from the user level, let's look at sites and their properties. If you're not clear on the concept of sites, refer back to Chapter 2. Remember that Exchange uses the idea of a box within a box. When setting properties, double-check your container selection. Properties that you configure at the site level affect all servers within that site. By expanding the view of a site, you can adjust the properties of a particular sever, overriding the configuration at the site level.

Site Addressing

The Site Addressing tab (shown in Figure 3.6.) is where you configure the address properties of a default name. You can select a mail format (for example, SMTP) by clicking the Edit button. Be sure to recalculate the routing table in the Routing tab. If you fail to do this, mail delivery will fail. Remember that you can create more choices for routing mail in the event of a connection failure on the Routing tab. Exchange 5.5 will attempt to use the least costly route first.

MTA Configuration

Within your configuration container, you'll find the Message Transfer Agent (MTA). The MTA allows you to configure items such as Retry and Timeout values. The types of connections can include the following:

➤ **Internet Mail Service** Renamed from Exchange version 4, where it was known as the Internet Mail Connector. Microsoft did this to reflect the additional functionality (for example, LDAP and IMAP4).

➤ **Lotus cc:Mail** The "father" of Notes. This is a popular email system that competed with MS Mail.

➤ **Lotus Notes** The IBM/Lotus competitor to Exchange.

➤ **Microsoft Mail** The "father" to Exchange. MS Mail was Microsoft's first mail program. (Note: It's not year 2000 compatible!)

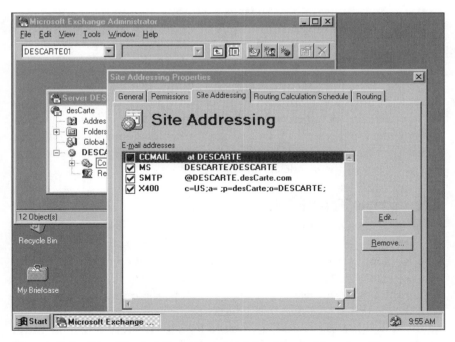

Figure 3.6   The Site Addressing tab of the Site Addressing Properties dialog box.

➤ **RAS (Remote Access Service)** A secure method for dial-up network-ing. Think of RAS as a way to extend the network, using a very long and very slow network connection from the server to the client.

➤ **Site Connector** A tool that connects sites within a local area network (LAN) or a wide area network (WAN).

➤ **X.400** This can be integrated with the MTA and can be configured to connect sites within Microsoft Exchange Server or to route messages to foreign X.400 systems. When handling communication between Microsoft Exchange Server and foreign X.400 systems, it maps ad-dresses and converts Microsoft Exchange Server messages to native X.400 messages, and vice versa.

Information Store

This is where actual data is stored for both individual mailboxes and public folders. Configuration options include specifying who can create new public folders (the default is Everyone, so be sure to control this or you'll have a plethora of public folders), configuring storage warnings, and replicating pub-lic folders.

 Remember that Exchange 5.5 includes a new feature that gives you the ability to refuse mail in a mailbox after the threshold you set has been reached. Previously, you could only block the sending of mail as a control method.

Storage warnings and limits, age limits for public folders, and DS listings are all adjusted here. Another tab on the Information Store is the Diagnostics Logging tab (see Figure 3.7). This is a great troubleshooting aid if you have a troubleshooting challenge. Keep in mind that if you turn logging on, it must be turned off before you can delete any messages.

Message Tracking

Tracking is a great way to keep messages flowing, as well as to find out why they aren't. You configure message tracking with the Exchange Administrator. Configuration is performed in two areas: the Information Store (IS) and the Message Transfer Agent (MTA). First, let's look at the IS. Messages bound within the site do not leave Exchange; therefore, these messages are tracked with the IS. When a message has a destination outside of the site, it's tracked by the MTA. Message tracking creates a log file. You'll find this file in the subdirectory \Tracking, under Exchsrvr. This log is created with the System Attendant (SA). The format is YYMMDD.LOG. (This log can be imported into Excel for detailed analysis, or even for graphing.)

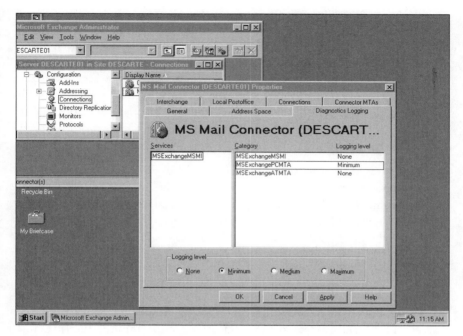

Figure 3.7   Detailed logging is enabled on the Diagnostics Logging tab.

Outside Mail Systems

Systems that are not part of your Exchange mail are called *foreign systems*. To update messages and attachments, you need a network link and a method for converting the data to something the foreign system can understand.

 Microsoft created a wizard for Internet Mail Service (IMS) with Exchange 5.5.

For the IMS wizard, you must have TCP/IP installed and configured; otherwise, the IMS cannot communicate with the Internet. Furthermore, you must have a DNS server available. Both the A record (host) and the MX (Mail Exchanger) must be configured. You or your ISP may do this. Small Business Server (officially titled *Microsoft Back Office Small Business Server*) will almost always use the ISP, and it will use ETRN. ETRN is a replacement to TURN. The details for ETRN are available by searching for RFC (Request For Comment) 1985. ETRN is normally used for dial-up connections, which are common for the low-traffic volume that an SBS-based server would experience.

Protocols

HTTP with Active Server Pages (ASPs) requires Internet Information Server (IIS) to be installed so that it can make an RPC request (it does not have to be on the same server as Exchange). This allows Exchange to be accessed with a browser, such as Outlook Web Access (the Outlook Web Access is covered in Chapter 7). Furthermore, by default, the Challenge Handshake And Response Protocol (CHAP) is required for security verification. Other protocols available in Exchange include the following:

➤ **Lightweight Directory Access Protocol (LDAP)** Used to query a DS and find an email address. Users may choose an internal LDAP server to find someone within their company, or they can use a public server (for example, Four11 or BigFoot). At first glance, it can be a confusing issue as to whether to use the Exchange GAL (Global Address List) or LDAP. The GAL is an Exchange phone book. LDAP is a subset of the international X.400 standard. You can use LDAP to query public phone books such as the two public servers just mentioned.

➤ **Network News Transfer Protocol (NNTP)** New in Exchange 5.5, NNTP provides access to any public newsgroups from the Internet. You also can select the newsgroups to be sent to your Exchange Server and place them in public folders. The preferable method is to subscribe to newsgroups from a public folder.

➤ **Post Office Protocol (POP3)** Currently, this is the most common way of bringing in mail from the Internet.

IMAP4 support is new to Exchange 5.5. Internet Message Access Protocol version 4 allows users to create and manage mail folders remotely and to scan message headers to retrieve only selected messages. For more information about IMAP4, consult RFC 1730.

Lotus cc:Mail Connector

The Lotus cc:Mail Connector's purpose is to connect to cc:Mail versions 5.15 or 6.0. This is useful if you need to connect to any cc:Mail servers that you have to transfer mail to or from.

Microsoft Mail Connector

Microsoft Mail Connector can be used for the migration to or coexistence of the older MS Mail program. In the real world, most Exchange administrators consider the MS Mail application to be a dinosaur. To connect to MS Mail, follow these steps:

1. Click the Connections container.

2. Select MS Mail Connector|File|Properties.

3. In the Interchange tab, select an account for the administrator. (The Maximize MS Mail Compatibility option will store OLE objects in the older format and the current format.)

4. In the Local Post Office tab, define the post office.

5. Select your connection type.

6. In the Connector MTA tab, define the MTA for each post office.

7. In the General tab, define the size limits.

8. In the Address tab, define which addresses will be used by the MS Mail Connector. You can balance the load by selecting different connectors for different mail sites.

 Remember that MS Mail can talk to both PC and Macintosh.

Site Connector

Site Connector is the fastest connector, and it doesn't require any conversion. It uses RPC, so a full-time connection is required. To configure a Site Connector, follow these steps:

1. Click File|New Other|Site Connector.

2. Enter the name of the other site (it may be the bridgehead server).

X.400 Connector

Lotus Notes relies on the X.400 format. Microsoft usually expects that you know how to connect to other systems. Notes has a large installed base.

A configuration of X.400 could look like this:

```
c=US;A=MCI;p=EXORG1;o=EXSITE2;s=Tim;g=Catura-Houser
```

Here's the breakdown:

```
Country = c
MCI=a The central message carrier
```

```
Private Management Domain = p Your Exchange Organization
Exchange Site for that mailbox = o
Surname or last name = s
Given name or first name = g
```

X.400 supports the MTA, RAS, TP4, TCP/IP, and X.25 protocols. The X.400 Connector is the most generic of the connectors. It's also slower than the Exchange Site Connector.

 You can override a configuration from the default level of a site at the server level, but not at the mailbox level.

Replication

Replication can be thought of as a cloning process for information. Let's assume you have an address list in your Global Address List (GAL) that's made up of everyone in your multinational company. Without replication, any time a user in Redmond wants to find the address of a coworker based in New York, that user has to go across the network link to find the address. This could be repeated many times a day, thus increasing network traffic and costs. If you replicate address lists and other data (such as public folders), the network traffic would only occur once, thus reducing costs and increasing performance. Use the Directory Replication Connector's General tab to establish local and remote bridgehead servers. You can also add an administrative note, which is visible only to administrators.

Replication is the process that updates the directories of all Microsoft Exchange Server computers within a site and between sites with the same information. Within a site, directory replication is automatic. You can reduce network traffic between sites by configuring directory replication so that only the desired information is replicated to other sites.

For directory replication between sites, create and configure a Directory Replication Connector, which is a bidirectional replication connection between two sites. You must designate and schedule one server in each site to request updated directory information from the other site. At the scheduled times, the local server requests directory updates from the remote server.

 To configure replication, follow these steps:

1. Select the configuration container.

2. Select File|New Other|Directory Replication Connector (see Figure 3.8).

3. Install the Directory Replication Connector.

4. Schedule a time when replication should occur (either when required or when network traffic is low).

Synchronization

Exchange would be pretty useless if you couldn't get information between Exchange and other systems such as MS Mail. Synchronization is an efficient process because only changed data is handled. Exchange will support this optional step with any system that supports MS Mail For PC Networks, version 3, Directory Synchronization (DirSync) protocol. The DirSync process has three steps. First, DirSync requestors send changes to the DirSync server. Second, DirSync creates a master copy. Finally, the master copy is sent back to the DirSync requestors. Exchange can be the requestor or the server. In the case of MS Mail, it already should have a DirSync server running, so Exchange will be a requestor. Keep in mind that MS Mail has an AppleTalk option.

To configure synchronization, perform the following steps:

1. Select File|New Other|DirSync Server.

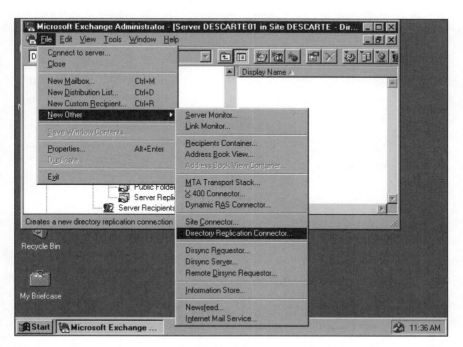

Figure 3.8   Configuring directory replication and other options.

2. Configure times for the DirSync master copy and the DirSync requestors. Click OK.

3. Select Start|Setting|Control Panel|Services|Start DirSync Service.

4. At the MS Mail server(s), select File|New Other|DirSync Remote Requestor.

5. While at the MS Mail post office, run ADMIN.EXE to send DirSync messages to the shadow post office of the Exchange server.

Here are the steps for Exchange Server:

1. Click File|New Other|DirSync Requestor.

2. Set the time for DirSync requestors to send changes to the DirSync server.

3. Select Start|Setting|Control Panel|Services|Start DirSync Service.

Importing Data

You can save a great deal of time if you import data rather than re-creating it (and thus increasing the chances of error). Some effort is required to create an import process. You must create connections so that you're running two systems while you test your migration. The alternative is to manually enter the users and to experience an interruption in mail service. Given these two options, importing is the better choice. A Migration wizard is available from Exchange (see Figure 3.9). Your other option is to import and kill the old system. Choosing this route is not advised.

 The wizard can import from Collabra Share, Lotus cc:Mail, MS Mail, and Novell GroupWise.

Importing can be a one- or two-step process. The wise administrator would choose a two-step process. This involves an export and import process. Some administrators use Excel to reconfigure the data in the process. This is very common with the Internet Alias list. Think of *alias* as another term for a.k.a. (also known as). For example, the mail name Tcat@descarte.com only works in the descarte organization (because the DNS entries were not configured). Tcat@usa.net is what is broadcast to the outside world. Keep in mind that Exchange also uses an alias to communicate to people who are not on your Exchange system.

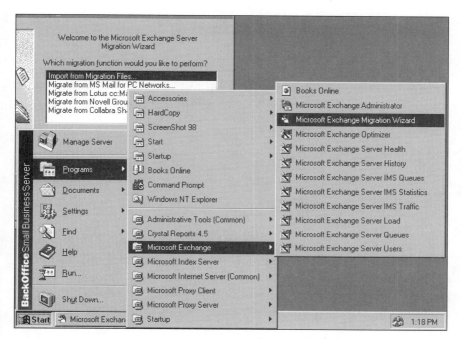

Figure 3.9   The steps to starting the Migration wizard.

Folder Replication

Public folders are created on the client side (see Chapter 7 for details). The critical concept is to remember how data is replicated. Exchange only creates one copy of data per server. You can configure replication between servers or between sites. This is set up in the Properties page of the public folder.

Exam Prep Questions

Question 1

> What is the service that routes information between servers in a
> single site?
>
> ○ a. Directory Service
>
> ○ b. System Attendant
>
> ○ c. Information Store
>
> ○ d. Windows NT security

The correct answer is a, Directory Service. The System Attendant (SA) verifies directory information, configures data, and generates routing tables;
therefore, answer b is incorrect. The Information Store holds public and private mail; therefore, answer c is incorrect. Windows NT security is used by
Exchange for preserving and observing sufficient rights; therefore, answer d is
incorrect.

Question 2

> What version of Windows can be used with Exchange 5.5?
>
> ○ a. Windows 95
>
> ○ b. Windows NT 3.5x
>
> ○ c. Windows NT 4
>
> ○ d. All of the above

The correct answer is c. Windows NT 4 is the required platform for Exchange
5.5. All other answers are incorrect.

Question 3

> Which of the following would you stop if you wanted to stop all
> Exchange services?
>
> ○ a. Server service
>
> ○ b. NT
>
> ○ c. Information Store
>
> ○ d. System Attendant

The correct answer is d. The System Attendant is responsible for overseeing all of Exchange. If you stopped the Server service, no one could log in to NT; therefore, answer a is incorrect. If you stopped NT, you have no server; therefore, answer b is incorrect. If you stopped the Information Store, there would be no place to send or get messages; therefore, answer c is incorrect.

Question 4

Where is the SMTP address set for a site?

○ a. The Site Addressing tab in Configuration

○ b. The Address page of a mailbox

○ c. User Manager For Domains

○ d. The Address properties of IMS

The correct answer is a. The Addressing tab in Configuration is where the SMTP address for a site is set. The Address page of a mailbox contains the alias name for Exchange; therefore, answer b is incorrect. User Manager For Domains contains the shortcut to adding a mailbox; therefore, answer c is incorrect. IMS is an MTA; therefore, answer d is incorrect.

Question 5

You would like to have addresses for outside consultants available to you in your Directory Service. Can you do this?

○ a. Yes

○ b. No

The correct answer to this questions is a, Yes. Create a custom recipient for each consultant.

Question 6

You are currently running MS Mail and you would like to upgrade to Exchange. How many steps are required to complete this process?

○ a. One step

○ b. Two steps

○ c. Not possible

The correct answer is b. The upgrade from MS Mail to Exchange is a two-step process. It's risky to create a single-phase migration; therefore, answer a is incorrect. If the migration blows up for any reason, you must restore from backups. If it were not possible to migrate, few users would buy Exchange; therefore answer c is incorrect.

Question 7

> You provided your administrator account and password when asked for the service account during an Exchange installation. What effect will this have on the installation?
>
> ○ a. None. Everything will work fine.
>
> ○ b. It won't work. You must reinstall.
>
> ○ c. It will appear to work just fine for a while.

The correct answer is c. It will appear to work just fine for a while. Exchange depends on NT security to function. When the password for the Administrator is changed, Exchange will not be able to validate and will fail. This is why you create a service account with a very cryptic password that is marked for no expiration. Answers a and b are incorrect.

Question 8

> You have just completed an Exchange installation. When is it desirable to run the Optimizer? [Check all correct answers]
>
> ❑ a. After installation of Exchange
>
> ❑ b. After a hardware change
>
> ❑ c. After a major software configuration change
>
> ❑ d. After the addition of many new users

Answers, a, b, c, and d are all correct. The Optimizer reviews the Information Store, database files, the Message Transfer Agent queues, the transaction log files, and the Directory database files. Changing storage, adding users, or changing the Exchange configuration would impact these files.

Question 9

> Which of the following statements is true about the X.400 Connector?
>
> ○ a. It will allow Exchange to send and receive mail from another site supporting X.400.
>
> ○ b. It removes the dirty words filter (which the FCC suggests to prevent children from reading adult messages).
>
> ○ c. It lets you send and receive mail from another Exchange site within your company.
>
> ○ d. All of the above

The correct answer is a. X.400 allows Exchange to send and receive mail from another site supporting X.400. Answer c is a possibility, technically; however, it would place an undue burden on the Exchange server, because your mail is already in an Exchange format. Answers b and d are untrue statements about the X.400 Connector and are therefore incorrect.

Question 10

> Your next project is to create users in your freshly installed Exchange server. How can you accomplish this?
>
> ○ a. Using User Manager For Domains
>
> ○ b. Entering them via Exchange Administrator
>
> ○ c. Exporting them from another system and importing them into Exchange
>
> ○ d. All of the above

Answer d is correct. All of the preceding actions should be performed.

Question 11

> All servers within a single site share a single service account.
>
> ○ a. True
>
> ○ b. False

This statement is true; therefore, answer a is correct. Because all servers within a site are granted security through the same domain, they use a single account.

Question 12

> The Exchange Administrator can be installed without a full copy
> of Exchange on which type of computers? [Check all correct
> answers]
>
> ❑ a. NT servers
>
> ❑ b. NT workstations
>
> ❑ c. Windows 9.x
>
> ❑ d. Windows 3.x

The correct answers are a and b. By choosing Complete/Custom, you can install just the Administrator program to any NT-based computer for the purposes
of administrating any Exchange servers within your security permissions. Because answers c and d are not NT based, these answers are both incorrect.

Question 13

> Exchange can talk directly to other Exchange servers within its
> site using which of the following?
>
> ○ a. Challenge Handshake And Response Protocol (CHAP)
>
> ○ b. Interprocess Communications (IPC)
>
> ○ c. Remote Access Service (RAS)
>
> ○ d. Remote procedure call (RPC)

Answer d is correct. RPC is required by Exchange. CHAP is a security method;
therefore answer a is incorrect. Interprocess Communications is used for NT-
to-NT communications; therefore answer b is incorrect. RAS is for dial-up
networking; therefore, answer c is incorrect.

Question 14

> Exchange version 5.5 is limited to how much storage space for
> the Information Store?
>
> ○ a. Depends on the version of NT
>
> ○ b. 16GB plus transaction logs
>
> ○ c. 16GB with transaction logs
>
> ○ d. No effective limit

The correct answer is d. No effective limit exists for how much storage space
there is for the Information Store. Therefore, answers a, b, and c are all incorrect.

Question 15

> Exchange can use third-party connectors because it was designed
> around Microsoft's Messaging Application Programming Interface
> (MAPI).
>
> ○ a. True
>
> ○ b. False

This statement is true; therefore, answer a is correct. It's possible to find third-
party add-ins that will even allow Exchange to be part of telephone voice mail
systems because of the Messaging Application Programming Interface (MAPI).

Need To Know More?

Gerber, Barry: *Mastering Microsoft Exchange Server 5.5 for Windows NT, 3rd Edition.* Alameda, CA: Sybex Press, 1998. ISBN: 0-7821-2237-X. With more than 1,000 pages, this offering is excellent for those new to Exchange. The author creates a fictional company that makes the Enter key for keyboards and then displays a masterful use of Exchange, based on real-life experience. He also manages to keep the deep subject of Exchange on the fun side.

Visit www.msexchange.org. This is a great site to get information about Exchange from the experts. Posting by "newbies" is not recommended.

Visit www.microsoft.com/exchange/default.asp. The official site for Exchange. At the time of this writing, it was possible to download an evaluation version of Exchange 5.5 for your study.

Exchange 5.5 CD. Books Online. This is an option when you install Exchange. If you did not install Books Online, it can be added later.

The Microsoft TechNet CD. Contains Knowledge Base articles and whitepapers related to Exchange.

Exchange Server Communications

Terms you'll need to understand:

✓ Connector

✓ Distinguished name (DN)

✓ Directory Service (DS)

✓ Information Store (IS)

✓ Knowledge Base (KB)

✓ Knowledge Consistency Checker (KCC)

✓ Message Transfer Agent (MTA)

✓ Remote procedure call (RPC)

✓ System Attendant (SA)

✓ Update sequence number (USN)

✓ X.400

✓ X.500

Techniques you'll need to master:

✓ Understanding how Exchange Server communicates

✓ Exploring the roles of MTAs in an Exchange Server environment

The usefulness of Exchange Server would be rather limited if you could only communicate with users on your own server. Therefore, the first question you need to ask yourself is what other mail systems do you need to connect with? When working with Exchange to connect to other mail sources, you use a Message Transfer Agent (MTA). If you need to refresh your memory about where the MTA fits in the Exchange scheme, refer to Chapter 2.

In this chapter, we look at Exchange's Message Transfer Agents. Remember that because Exchange was created with the Messaging Application Programming Interface (MAPI), you're not limited to only the MTAs provided by Microsoft. Third-party developers have created enhancements to Exchange, with options as diverse as telephone voice mail systems and faxes. We explore all of these factors throughout this chapter.

Planning Your MTAs

Before you do anything with MTAs, you need to plan how communications within your site will take place. To do so, you should be familiar with the following points:

➤ Within a site, all servers communicate by remote procedure call (RPC).

➤ Servers belonging to a single site are called *intrasite servers*.

➤ Replication of messages is more network bandwidth intensive between servers within a site than between sites.

➤ The minimum net available bandwidth (NAB) between servers within a site is 64Kbps, with 128Kbps being a more practical minimum.

➤ The connection must be permanent or, as current slang has it, *nailed up*.

If mail cannot be delivered, it stays at the server where the mail originated and waits until that server becomes available. If the wait exceeds the configured timeout, the message is returned to the user.

Information Transfer

Two components are required by Exchange to carry out the mail transport—the MTA and the Directory Service (DS). All types of information can be transferred. Table 4.1 shows the types of information and which Exchange service has the task of transferring the data.

Table 4.1	Exchange information types and the services that perform each task.	
Information Type	**Service**
Directory Replication	Directory Service (DS)
Directory Synchronization messages	Directory Synchronization
Link Monitor messages	System Attendant (SA) by using the Information Store (IS)
Mail messages	Private Information Store
Public folder hierarchy changes	Public Information Store
Public folder replication changes	Public Information Store

Remote Procedure Calls (RPCs)

RPCs run a program on a different server than the one that originally created the request. As a result, network traffic can reach the point where it floods the network. In most cases, a 64Kbps connection is the bare minimum, but a 128Kbps connection is more realistic.

Message Transfer Agent At Work

Any information moved among MTAs is always in the form of a message (see Figure 4.1). If it's not in a message form, it's placed within a message and then sent. The MTA performs the following functions:

1. The MTA looks up the recipient's server destination in the Directory Service (DS).

2. The MTA determines if the routing requires leaving the site.

3. The destination MTA opens an RPC session by using NT's system service user account, which is set up during the installation. Microsoft refers to this as an *association*.

4. The message is sent.

5. After successful delivery of the message, the MTA on the receiving end uses the local DS to determine if the message needs to be passed on to another server. In a single site, the receiving MTA is the final destination.

6. The MTA queues up the message and informs the IS of the new message.

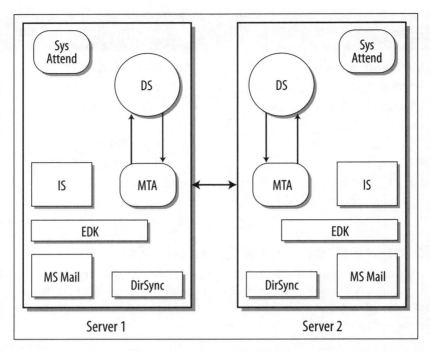

Figure 4.1   When information is transferred among MTAs, it must always be in a message format.

If your delivery attempt fails, several things can happen to the Exchange site that is loaded with data. If the glitch is a minor one, the update will occur in the next cycle. A more serious event may require the use of the Knowledge Consistency Checker (KCC). This may need to be run several times to get all Exchange servers back on track. On a very bad day, you may have to resort to using the EBDUTIL program. If you're reaching for EBDUTIL, don't plan to sleep in the near future. Troubleshooting programs such as this are examined in Chapter 14.

MTA Associations

Exchange is designed to use a single instance. That is, if a message is meant for more than one recipient on multiple servers, the MTA creates a single message for each server and sends the message to each remote MTA. This reduces network traffic. The bridgehead server does the expansion. Expansion servers consume resources. Review Chapter 2 if you're not clear as to why expansion servers take more resources.

The usual design for the MTA is a single connection to a server. You can increase the in-message traffic load by creating multiple associations to the destination server. This reduces the backlog that would be created if only a single connection existed. The Exchange Optimizer determines the correct number of connections to create, supporting 20 to 240 MTAs. (The default is 40.)

After an association has been created, all messages are delivered and received at the same time. This is called *two-way association*. After all mail has been transferred, the RPC session will remain open for five minutes. This increases the efficiency of the local MTA because it can reuse the RPC session if additional messages need to be sent.

 The Association setting can be configured in the MTA Site Configuration dialog box or by selecting the Advanced tab to a specific connector.

Distinguished Names

X.400 is an international standard that allows for a common method of electronic mail addressing among the digital citizens of the world. Exchange uses a subset of the X.400 standard to identify recipients. Because X.400 is part of Exchange, it can be used between other Exchange servers, Lotus Notes, as well as many IBM mainframes. For Exchange to be able to communicate with other mail servers, it uses a naming convention in the format of either the X.500 distinguished name (DN) or the X.400 originator/recipient (O/R) address. The MTA must be configured before it can be used by Exchange. Information on each transport stack is found in the Exchange Server Administrator's Guide.

To configure the MTA, follow these steps:

1. Choose File|New Other.

2. Select a transport stack (RAS, TCP/IP MTA, X.25, or TP4).

With a transport stack selected, configure the X.400 Connector by following these steps:

1. Select File|New Other.

2. Add the connector and enter your information on the Properties page.

3. Upon completing this task, you'll be shown a warning that this connector will not work unless the other system you're communicating with is configured with the information about your site.

An X.500 DN contains the information that identifies a recipient within an organization. It may help you to think of a DN as the digital equivalent of your formal name, address, city, state, and postal code or ZIP code. The DN has a specific path throughout the Exchange system, because a structure must be followed. Within the DN, there's also a relative distinguished name (RDN), typically found as the last attribute in the DN. For example, Tom Smith would have an RDN of Toms. In X.400, the X.400 O/R name and address represent both the recipient and the originator.

Advantages Of The X.400 Connector

The following points are advantages to using the X.400 Connector:

➤ It's supported by many different types of connectors on other systems.

➤ Restrictions can be placed on items such as message size and/or who can access the link.

➤ You have control over when data transfer takes place.

Disadvantages Of The X.400 Connector

The following points are disadvantages to using the X.400 Connector:

➤ It's complex and more difficult to set up.

➤ It's less efficient than an Exchange site connector (about 20 percent slower).

➤ It may cause a bottleneck because all mail must route through the bridgehead server.

Note: Distinguished names are based on X.500 relative distinguished names (RDNs), which are typically the last part of the DN. O/R names based on X.400 O/R are similar, but not identical, to DN. Exchange uses either DN and O/R for routing via the MTA.

Routing With The MTA

The MTA looks at the recipient address to determine where a message is to be delivered. The journey starts when an MTA, a connector, or a user sends a message to the MTA. The following logical steps are then followed:

➤ The site name is compared to the local site name by the MTA. If this is not a match, routing follows the multisite procedures.

➤ If the address has an O/R address and it does not match, the MTA confirms the validity of the O/R address. If it's not a valid address, it is returned to the sender, informing him or her that this message cannot be delivered.

If the DN or O/R address matches the local site, the next step the MTA has to take is to determine how to deliver the message. For DN and O/R addresses that are part of a distribution list (DL), the DL is expanded and the routing process is begun again; however, this time, the message goes out to each member of the distribution list as follows:

➤ For custom recipients, the MTA gets the recipient's DN address from the DS, and the process starts over again, this time with the new addresses.

➤ If the recipient is on the local server, the MTA passes the message to the local Information Store for delivery to the user's mailbox.

➤ For recipients on other computers in the same site, the MTA forwards the mail to the recipients on their home MTA for delivery.

If the MTA cannot transfer a message, it continues its efforts until it's successful or the timeout is exceeded, whichever comes first (see Figure 4.2). The default setting is one day. If this timeout is reached without delivery, the mail is bounced back to the sender as undeliverable.

Intrasite Service Communications

With the exception of DS, all Exchange services move data though email messages. It's a function of the IS to do this if the service itself cannot. Hidden mailboxes perform the needed task. IS, SA, Connector, and MS Mail DirSync are services that require this assistance. Don't worry about creating hidden mailboxes. Exchange will do this for you.

The multimaster model replicates data from each DS to other servers, as opposed to centralized storage. This provides fault tolerance as well as reduces network traffic. If you're unclear about the multimaster model (multiple servers), refer to Chapter 2.

As a way of reducing network traffic, changes do not occur right away. The default delay is five minutes (this is known as *replication latency*). The DS knows about each server within its site because it gets this data from a cached list. That is to say, because Exchange knows about other servers, it keeps this list in memory so that it may quickly check the list instead of digging up the list from the hard drive. When the replication latency period expires, the local DS notifies all known servers one at a time. It waits 30 seconds for changes to occur before calling the next server (see Knowledge Base article Q137203 in TechNet or the Microsoft Web site).

The remote server uses an internal unique number to determine the last time it was updated. Each update bumps this number by one. Armed with this knowledge, the server can tell what has changed since the last call. The remote DS

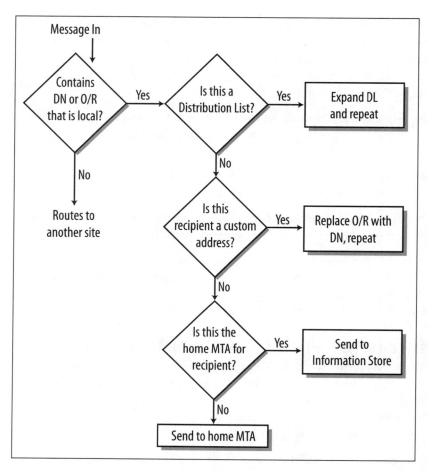

Figure 4.2 A flow chart of the decision points for an incoming message.

then requests all changes. Any local DS that has the changes connects to the remote DS (via RPC) and changes the remote server, which updates its local directory. Within a single site, the IS sends the data directly to the MTA. Should this cached information get out of sync, you can use the IS/DS Consistency Checker to correct this. For more information on the Knowledge Consistency Checker, refer to Chapter 14.

Information Stores

There are two Information Stores—public and private. Both folders containing the actual data your users will desire are located in the IS. A private IS typically exists for individual end users. When you send a message to a user whose mailbox resides on a different server, the MTA determines the destination server and queues it up for that location. The MTA gets mail that needs to be delivered from the IS and then connects to the destination MTA (via RPC). Once again, it retains this connection for five minutes, waiting for activity before closing.

The second storage area is the public folder. It looks a little different because this folder needs a public folder hierarchy and the public folder replicas. The hierarchy must be displayed to clients, because not every item of data may be on any single server. Replicas are used to copy data from one server to another. When either of these items change, the IS informs the MTA about the changes made.

System Attendant

The System Attendant has more than one duty. One of the services it checks is the link monitor, testing the connection between the servers using the MTA. The SA will create a message destined for the SA on the remote server. If the remote server is foreign, you should create an autoresponder to inform you of any (usually bad) changes. For more information about the SA, please refer to Chapter 2.

Connectors

Exchange is supplied with a number of connectors, and many third-party connectors are available. The number of connectors that come built in differs between the standard version of Exchange and the Enterprise edition. Determine which connectors you require before deciding which edition to purchase. It's usually more cost-effective to buy the Enterprise edition on the front end, as opposed to purchasing additional connectors for the standard edition.

Connectors can function at these levels:

➤ Server

➤ Site

➤ Third party

Microsoft has the Exchange Development Kit (EDK) for the following connectors:

➤ Internet Mail Service

➤ Lotus cc:Mail

➤ Lotus Notes

➤ Third party

MS Mail connectors can forward messages directly to the MTA. If the mail is local to the server, the MTA sends the message to the IS. If it's remote, it is passed to the MTA on the other server. This is the only connector to behave this way. MTA considers the Exchange site and X.400 Connectors to be part of itself, not separate connectors.

DirSync manages information with both MS Mail types—PC and Macintosh. It's also responsible for foreign mail. In the event the DirSync is on a remote server, its communications are done on behalf of the services of the MTA. This is covered in more detail in Chapter 2.

All services, such as IS (both public and private), SA, and DirSync for MS Mail, communicate through the MTA. The only exception to this is the Directory Service, which talks directly to the other DS. Keep this in mind if you're troubleshooting your Exchange site.

Communication among all servers within a site is critical and must be maintained. As Exchange traffic increases, the point will come when you have to add a server to a site.

Directory replication (DR) performs the tasks of passing data and provides an easy way to add a server. DR uses the Knowledge Consistency Checker (KCC) to accomplish this.

New Server Setup

Adding a server to a site requires some setup information; you must identify any server within the site. Once you've added a server, it will then get the data it needs to become part of the site. Here are the steps involved in adding a new server:

1. The server adds itself to the directory on the remote server.

2. It then copies the data in the directory from the DS in a specific order. All containers, with the exception of the recipients, are copied to the new server.

3. The new server, using the new information, informs the other servers to begin directory replication. This occurs immediately.

The KCC uses a stub directory to speed up this expansion exercise. Lacking a stub directory, the entire directory will need to be replicated before setup can be completed. By using only a stub directory, setup can complete, reducing the time needed to join the site. The new server can now engage in regular replication and message transfer to finish becoming part of the site.

The KCC performs the following functions:

1. It attaches to the first remote server.

2. It asks the first server to check what servers it thinks are in the site.

3. It connects to another remote server and compares that data to the information from the first server.

4. It updates any differences between the servers. This process continues until the entire site is checked.

Out of the box, the KCC runs every three hours. You can perform a manual check by clicking on the Directory Service object inside the local server container.

Replication List Maintenance

It's the function of the replication link to tell when a Directory Service is set between two servers. Because data flows two ways, two lists maintain this link. These lists are Reps-To and Reps-From, and they include any new server added to the list. Each server knows about the other servers, which it gets from its cached list. This being the case, each list is unique to that server. A unique list cannot be replicated to other servers.

Directory Management

At the time a replication occurs, a unique number is assigned to the replication. This unique number is known as the *update sequence number (USN)*. Each time a replication occurs, the USN is raised by one. In this fashion, each server can query all the other servers to confirm directory changes.

Note that if multiple changes occur on multiple servers of the same object, a conflict occurs. Only the last changes are recorded.

A local DS finds out if changes have occurred by following these steps:

1. It requests a USN from a remote server, which sends its most current value.

2. If the USN is higher, the local DS copies all changes made from the previous USN.

3. The USN is then updated on the local server.

Exam Prep Questions

Question 1

> Whenever two MTAs are communicating with each other, the communication must be in the form of which of the following?
>
> ○ a. A message
>
> ○ b. A USN
>
> ○ c. A distinguished name
>
> ○ d. A relative distinguished name

Answer a is correct. All Exchange Server services communicate via messages. If a service is not capable of creating a message, it relies on the IS to create the message. A USN is used to determine the last time a server has obtained information from another server; therefore, answer b is incorrect. A distinguished name is used in addressing, and a relative distinguished name is a subset of the DN; therefore, answers c and d are incorrect.

Question 2

> What is USN an abbreviation for?
>
> ○ a. Unique serial number
>
> ○ b. United States Navy
>
> ○ c. Update sequence number
>
> ○ d. Uniform source name

USN stands for update sequence number; therefore, the correct answer is c. In a way, a USN is a unique serial number; however, this is not the Microsoft term for it, so answer a is incorrect. USN is also the abbreviation for the United States Navy, but because this is an Exchange test, answer b is incorrect. Uniform source name is a fictitious answer and is incorrect.

Question 3

> By default, how many associations does Exchange create?
>
> ○ a. 1
> ○ b. 240
> ○ c. 40
> ○ d. 20

The default number of associations created by Exchange is 40; answer c is correct. You can have one association (a single association), but this is not the default; therefore, answer a is incorrect. 240 associations is the maximum, so answer b is incorrect. 20 is the minimum that the MTA uses; answer d is incorrect.

Question 4

> Which of the following are the names of the services that transfer all mail within an Exchange site? [Check all correct answers]
>
> ❑ a. Message Transfer Agent
> ❑ b. Directory Service
> ❑ c. Domain Name Service
> ❑ d. WinSock Proxy Service

The correct answers are a and b. The Message Transfer Agent and Directory Service transfer all mail within an Exchange site. The Domain Name Service and WinSock Proxy Service are not responsible for this type of transfer; therefore, answers c and d are incorrect.

Question 5

> A replication list is used to send and receive updates from other servers. What are the names for this list? [Check all correct answers]
>
> ❑ a. Reps-To
> ❑ b. Reps-From
> ❑ c. Reps-In
> ❑ d. Reps-Out

The correct answers are a and b. The replication lists referred to are called Reps-For and Reps-From. Reps-In and Reps-Out do not exist; therefore, answers c and d are incorrect.

Question 6

> Which of the following performs link monitoring?
>
> ○ a. Message Transfer Agent (MTA)
>
> ○ b. Information Store (IS)
>
> ○ c. System Attendant (SA)
>
> ○ d. Domain Name Service (DNS)

The System Attendant performs link monitoring; therefore, answer c is correct. The MTA, IS, and DNS do not perform this function and are incorrect answers.

Question 7

> Which of the following Exchange Server services does not communicate via mail messages within the same site?
>
> ○ a. Directory Service (DS)
>
> ○ b. Information Store (IS)
>
> ○ c. System Attendant (SA)
>
> ○ d. DirSync

The correct answer is a. The Directory Service is the only Exchange Server service that does not communicate via messages, but rather, it communicates directly with other Directory Services within the same site. Intersite directory messages are transported by the MTA. All the other services listed communicate via mail messages; therefore, answers b, c, and d are incorrect.

Question 8

> Which of the following is included with connectors based on Exchange Development Kit (EDK)?
>
> ○ a. Internet Mail Server
>
> ○ b. Third-party connectors
>
> ○ c. Lotus connectors for cc:Mail and Lotus Notes
>
> ○ d. All of the above

The correct answer is d. The Internet Mail Server, third-party connectors, and Lotus connectors for cc:Mail and Lotus Notes are all examples of EDK connectors.

Question 9

> Before changes are made to an object, such as a DL, there's a delay of five minutes. What is this is called?
>
> ○ a. Synchronization delay
>
> ○ b. Directory update
>
> ○ c. Backup sync time
>
> ○ d. Replication latency

The correct answer is d. Replication latency causes a delay when objects are updated. Although the other answers sound correct, they are fictitious and are therefore incorrect.

Question 10

> Replication latency has a delay of five minutes. This cannot be changed. True or False?
>
> ○ a. True
>
> ○ b. False

This statement is false; answer b is correct. Replication latency can be modified in either the MTA Site Configuration dialog box or the Advanced tab of a connector.

Question 11

> How many types of data can be replicated in the Public Information Store?
>
> ○ a. 1
>
> ○ b. 2
>
> ○ c. 3
>
> ○ d. 4

Answer b is correct. Only two types of data can be replicated in the Public Information Store: public folder hierarchy and public folder replication. Therefore, answers a, c, and d are incorrect.

Question 12

Which type(s) of data might an Exchange server need to send?
[Check all correct answers]

❑ a. Transaction logs

❑ b. Public folder hierarchy

❑ c. Public folder replicas

❑ d. Directory updates

The correct answers are b and c. Transaction logs are checkpoints for checking what has been committed to the IS; therefore, answer a is incorrect. Directory updates is a fictitious answer, so answer d is incorrect.

Question 13

Which of the following interfaces is used by servers within a site?

○ a. Remote Access Service (RAS)

○ b. Interprocess Communications (IPC)

○ c. Remote Procedure Call (RPC)

○ d. Message Transfer Agent (MTA)

The correct answer is c. RAS would not work because it's used for dial-up, nonpermanent connections; therefore, answer a is incorrect. IPC communicates between computers, but it's not a process that is done in the same way as RPC; therefore, answer b is incorrect. The MTA is a conductor for messages; therefore, answer d is incorrect.

Question 14

When you're working with Exchange servers within a single site, no special connectors are required. True or False?

○ a. True

○ b. False

Answer a is correct. Connectors between sites can use direct or indirect communications.

Question 15

A client has sent a message to a distribution list. This message will route directly to each recipient without expansion because the DL is maintained on each Exchange server. True or False?

○ a. True

○ b. False

The correct answer is b. This statement is false.

Question 16

You recently had a server go offline, and now this server no longer exists to Exchange. You had a number of public folders set up to replicate onto your current server. What is the best way to get rid of them without bringing the old server back online, reestablishing the site connector, and either removing them or turning off folder replication on the box where they were originally created?

○ a. Remove Exchange and reinstall

○ b. Copy the REPS-TO and REPS-FROM data files

○ c. Call PSS

○ d. Run Network Monitor

○ e. Run the IS/DS Knowledge Consistency Checker on every other server in the site

The correct answer is e. Run the IS/DS Knowledge Consistency Checker on every other server in the site. This may have to be performed several times to get all the servers back in sync. Answer a could work, but it's hardly your most efficient solution; therefore answer a is incorrect. Copying the REPS-TO and REPS-FROM data files may be a grand idea, but it does not have the supporting code to fix your configuration error; therefore, answer b is incorrect. You could call PSS, but you'll be several hundred dollars poorer, and they will tell you to run the IS/DS KCC; therefore, answer c is incorrect. Running Network Monitor will tell you about your network, but it will not assist you in getting your Exchange servers back in sync; therefore, answer d is incorrect.

Need To Know More?

 Gerber, Barry. *Mastering Microsoft Exchange Server 5.5 for Windows NT*, 3rd Edition. Alameda, CA: Sybex Press, 1998. ISBN: 0-7821-2237-X. With more than 1,000 pages, this offering is excellent for those new to Exchange. The author creates a fictional company that makes the Enter key for keyboards and then displays a masterful use of Exchange, based on real-life experience. He also manages to keep the deep subject of Exchange on the fun side.

 TechNet. Each month, Microsoft ships a series of CD-ROMs that contain both Knowledge Base articles and whitepapers.

 Exchange 5.5 CD-ROM. This is an option when you install Exchange. You may choose to install it at a later date if you did not do so with your initial installation.

 Visit www.msexchange.org. This is where the world masters of MS Exchange live. This list has very heavy traffic, averaging hundreds of messages a day. You're strongly urged to subscribe and read without posting. Archives are available at the site. Posting a previously asked question or asking a "newbie" question will have, at a minimum, a strongly worded and negative response. It's not advisable to upset the masters of the Exchange universe. Who knows what evil things they might do to your mailbox!

 Visit www.microsoft.com/exchange/default.asp. This is the official site for Exchange. At the time of this writing, it was possible to download an evaluation version of Exchange version 5.5 for your study.

5

Message Recipients

Terms you'll need to understand:

√ Custom recipients

√ Deleted message retention

√ Distribution list

√ Home server

√ Internet Locator Server

√ Mailbox

√ Trust level

Techniques you'll need to master:

√ Understanding the differences between mailboxes, distribution lists, and custom recipients

√ Using the Microsoft Exchange Server import/export tools

√ Understanding how to manage recipient objects

Microsoft Exchange Server relies on message recipients (also known as *recipient objects*) to transfer messages. Without recipients, the transfer of messages would not occur. You can think of a recipient object as a person's phone number. If you attempt to contact this person when you do not have the phone number, communication between the two of you will not occur. Similarly, you do not have any way of contacting a user who does not have a mailbox accessible through the Microsoft Exchange Server.

Recipient Objects Explored And Explained

A *recipient* is a Microsoft Exchange object that can receive a message. One of an Exchange administrator's most important roles is the creation and management of recipient objects. Recipients include mailboxes, distribution lists, custom recipients, and public folders, as described in the following list:

➤ **Mailboxes** A *mailbox* is a storage location on the Microsoft Exchange Server computer that allows information to be sent, received, and stored. Email messages, file attachments, and forms are some common types of information that can be sent to a mailbox. Each user who is to receive messages through Exchange must have a mailbox.

➤ **Distribution lists** A *distribution list (DL)* is a logical grouping of recipients created to simplify bulk mailing of messages. All the members of the distribution list will receive messages sent to that list.

➤ **Custom recipients** A *custom recipient* is a pointer to a foreign address or a recipient outside the organization. For example, if you have an employee who works in a different city (using a local Internet Service Provider for email), this user may not have access to your Microsoft Exchange Server. In this case, you can list his or her foreign email address in the Exchange Address Book so that all employees can email that user without having to know his or her email address.

➤ **Public folders** A *public folder* is a repository for many different types of information, such as files and messages, that can be shared by a number of different users. Public folders make custom applications, such as customer tracking systems, possible. Public folders are covered in detail in Chapter 10.

Understanding Common Recipient Object Properties

The different recipient objects have similar properties. These properties will be covered in this section. Table 5.1 lists all the properties and shows which recipient objects the properties belong to.

Table 5.1   Common recipient object properties.

Property	Mailbox	Distribution List	Custom Recipient
General			
First Name	X		X
Initial	X		X
Last Name	X		X
Display Name	X	X	X
Alias Name	X	X	X
Address	X		X
City	X		X
State	X		X
Country	X		X
ZIP Code	X		X
Title	X		X
Company	X		X
Department	X		X
Office	X		X
Assistant	X		X
Phone	X		X
Primary NT Account	X		X
Email			X
Owner		X	
Expansion Server		X	
Members		X	

(continued)

Property	Mailbox	Distribution List	Custom Recipient
Table 5.1 Common recipient object properties _(continued)_.			
Organization	X		X
Limits	X		
Phone/Notes	X		X
Distribution List	X	X	X
Email Addresses	X	X	X
Delivery Restrictions	X	X	X
Delivery Options	X		
Protocols	X		X
Permissions	X	X	X
Custom Attributes	X	X	X
Advanced			
Simple Display Name	X		X
Directory Name	X	X	X
Trust Level	X	X	
Online Listing	X		
Home Server	X		
Hide From DL	X		
Outlook Web Access	X		
Container Name	X	X	X
Downgrade X.400	X		
Message Size		X	
Distribution List Options		X	
Custom Recipient Options			X

Note: The bolded text within the table indicates the property pages, whereas normal text indicates individual properties within the page. Also, although both mailboxes and custom recipients have a primary Windows NT account assigned to them, the location at which this is set differs between the two objects. The primary NT account is assigned in the General property page for mailboxes and in the Advanced property page for custom recipients.

The following properties are shared among mailboxes, distribution lists, and custom recipients:

➤ **General** The display and alias names are shared among all three recipient objects.

➤ **Display Name** The display name appears in the Administrator window and the Address Book, and it is automatically generated by combining a user's first and last name. For example, a user with the first name Joe and the last name Smith will have the display name Joe Smith. The administrator can change this manually. There is a limit of 256 characters in the Display field.

➤ **Alias Name** Another name used to identify the mailbox that is usually used to generate foreign email addresses for the mailbox. By default, the alias name is automatically generated by combining the user's first name and the first initial of the user's last name. For example, Joe Smith would have the alias JoeS. This, too, can be manually changed by the administrator. There is a limit of 64 characters in the Display field.

➤ **Distribution Lists** This property page specifies the distribution lists to which the recipient object belongs.

➤ **Email Addresses** When a recipient object is created, several non-Exchange email addresses are also created (also known as *proxy* or *foreign addresses*). This allows Microsoft Exchange to communicate with foreign mail systems. By default, Microsoft Exchange generates mail addresses for the following foreign mail systems:

➤ Lotus cc:Mail

➤ Microsoft Mail

➤ Internet Mail (SMTP)

➤ X.400

➤ **Delivery Restrictions** This property page allows you to accept or reject messages from any sender listed in the Microsoft Exchange Server directory. By default, messages are accepted from everyone (All) and rejected from nobody (None).

➤ **Permissions** This property page allows you to specify which users and/or groups are granted access to the recipient object. Sometimes it makes sense to have one owner for a mailbox or a distribution list. For example, the sales department may want all its employees to have access to the sales mailbox.

By default, the Permissions property page is hidden; to enable it, select Options from the Tools menu and then select Show Permissions Page For All Objects from the Permission tab.

➤ **Custom Attributes** This property page allows you to enter custom information, such as employee number, employee start date, or employee birthday.

Note: The Custom Attributes property page for the Directory Service (DS) site contains 10 unique, customizable attribute fields.

➤ **Configuration** An object in the Exchange Administrator program.

➤ **Directory Name** The name used to distinguish the recipient object in the Directory service. This is a read-only field.

➤ **Container Name** This is the name of the container in which a recipient object resides. This is a read-only field.

Working With Mailboxes

As a rule, all users accessing your Microsoft Exchange Server will require a mailbox. The mailbox is a location on a Microsoft Exchange Server where messages and attachments are stored and organized. Mailboxes can contain messages created by the user, sent from users within the organization, or from users outside the organization. Although the mailbox resides on the Exchange Server, the user must use a client email application, such as Microsoft Outlook, to access the mailbox information. Normally, a mailbox will have only one user associated with it. You can, however, assign multiple users to the same mailbox. There are several different ways of creating mailboxes:

➤ The Windows NT User Manager For Domains

➤ The Microsoft Exchange Administrator program

➤ The Microsoft Exchange export and import tools

Using User Manager For Domains

When you install Microsoft Exchange Server, the application installs a User Manager For Domains extension called MAILUMX.DLL. This is a dynamic link library (DLL) that links the Exchange Administrator program's Mailbox property page to the User Manager For Domains. Any time an account is created with User Manager For Domains, a mailbox can also be created. If you delete a user account, you can also delete the corresponding mailbox.

Using The Exchange Administrator Program

When you create a new Microsoft Exchange mailbox, you need to associate it with one or more NT user accounts. These accounts may be existing accounts (from the current or a trusted domain) or new accounts created by the Exchange Administrator program. The Exchange Administrator program can create NT user accounts by directly accessing the NT domain SAM (Security Accounts Manager).

Using The Exchange Export And Import Tools

The Exchange export and import tools work in tandem to create mailboxes. The export tools gather information about user accounts, and the import tools use this extracted information to create the mailboxes. Here are the two mail extraction tools available with Microsoft Exchange:

➤ **Extract Windows NT Account List** This tool extracts user account information from existing Windows NT servers or an NT or LAN Manager domain and prepares this data for the creation of Exchange objects. To execute this command, you must be logged into the NT domain from which the user account information is to be extracted. This tool is available from the Administrator program by selecting the Extract Windows NT Account List option from the Tools menu or from the command line.

➤ **Extract NetWare Accounts List** This tool extracts user account information from existing Novell NetWare 2.x, 3.x, or 4.x servers, as long as the Novell server is running bindery emulation. To use this tool, you must be logged into the NetWare server with supervisor rights. This tool is available from the Administrator program by selecting the Extract NetWare Account List option from the Tools menu.

Once an extraction tool is executed, the import tool can create Exchange recipients using the extracted data. You access the import tool by selecting the Directory Import option from the Tools menu. The import tool may also be used to modify existing recipients.

To make a major change (such as changing an area code in the entire Exchange site), you must export the directory, search and replace the area code in the text file, and import the directory back into Exchange.

Mailbox Properties

Like other objects, mailboxes have properties. These properties may be viewed and configured through the mailbox's property pages and can be accessed in one of two ways. One method is to highlight the mailbox to be configured and select the Properties option from the File menu. The other method is to double-click on the desired mailbox. Many of the object properties are straightforward and do not require any explanation (for example, Address). Each property page and the important properties will be explained in greater detail in the following list:

➤ **General** Within the General property page, you can configure basic user information, such as the user's name and location. You can also assign the primary Windows NT user account to be used with the mailbox. The General page of the Properties dialog box for a mailbox is shown in Figure 5.1. You'll find the following important information on this dialog box:

➤ **Primary Windows NT Account** This is the NT domain account that's associated with the mailbox. You'll be given the option of choosing an existing user account or having a new user account created.

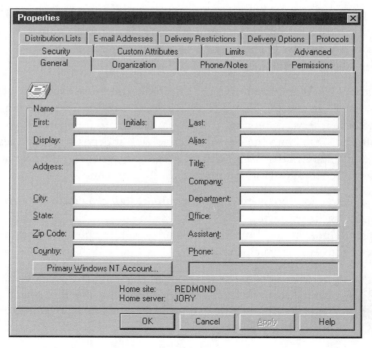

Figure 5.1   The General property page of a mailbox.

➤ **Organization** Within this property page, you can record information about the mailbox owners. You can also report the name of the users' managers or any staff members who report directly to them (also known as *direct reports*).

➤ **Phone/Notes** Within this property page, you can enter detailed telephone information (business, fax, mobile, pager, and so on) and notes for the mailbox. Information on this property page is optional.

➤ **Limits** This property page allows you to set limits on message storage and on the size of incoming and outgoing messages. A new feature in Microsoft Exchange Server 5.5 allows deleted message retention, which is also configured on this page. The Limits property page for a mailbox is shown in Figure 5.2. The following information can be found on the Limits property page:

➤ **Deleted item retention time** Microsoft Exchange Server can be configured to retain messages that are deleted from mailboxes for a specified amount of time before they are permanently deleted. When a user deletes messages, the items are marked as hidden until they are permanently deleted from the private information store (assuming that a delete item retention period has been set). Users

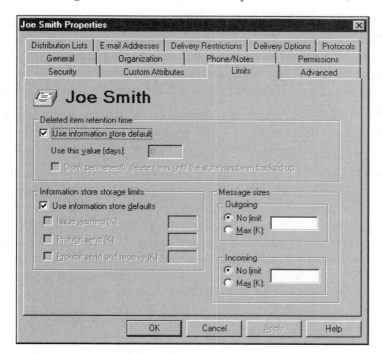

Figure 5.2 The Limits property page of a mailbox.

can recover deleted messages by selecting the Recover Deleted Items command (using Microsoft Outlook version 8.03 or higher) and moving them to a different location. You can set deleted item retention periods on the public and private stores or on individual mailboxes and public folders. Deleted item retention periods set on individual mailboxes supersede the settings on the private information store.

➤ **Information store storage limits** You can set storage limits on how much space a mailbox can use on a server. You can issue an option such as Warnings, Prohibit Send, or Prohibit Send And Receive At Certain Levels.

 The Prohibit Send option cannot be used when messages are sent by the POP3 or IMAP4 protocols, because these protocols do not support this function.

➤ **Message sizes** You can specify a size limit on all incoming or outgoing messages for the mailbox. By default, there is no limit on message size.

➤ **Distribution Lists** This property page specifies the distribution lists to which the mailbox belongs.

➤ **Delivery Options** This property page allows you to give users a "send on behalf of" right for the mailbox. You can also specify an alternate recipient. The alternate recipient can be configured to receive mail instead of the mailbox, or as well as the mailbox.

➤ **Protocols** This property page allows you to enable Internet protocols for individual mailboxes. You can specify the different protocols and character sets. Configuration options include:

➤ **IMAP4** The Message Encoding option determines the format to which the Exchange Server messages are converted when they are retrieved by an IMAP4 client. By default, Exchange enables public folders to be listed for all clients. Clearing the Include All Public Folders When A Folder List Is Requested box can improve performance for clients that have problems listing public folders. You delegate a user to access another user's mailbox and view personal folders in the other user's mailbox.

➤ **NNTP & POP3** Allows you to select either the MIME or UUENCODE protocol for encoding mail messages.

➤ **Advanced** Within this property page, you can set a simple display name and trust levels for directory synchronization, and you can hide the mailbox from the Address Book. The Advanced property page for a mailbox is shown in Figure 5.3. The following information can be found on the Advanced property page:

➤ **Simple display name** This name is used by non-Exchange mail systems that cannot recognize all the characters that can be used in an Exchange mailbox name, such as spaces and foreign (non-ANSI) characters.

➤ **Trust level** Used to specify whether the mailbox is to be replicated to other servers during directory synchronization. If the trust level set for the mailbox is higher than that set for the container, the mailbox information will not be replicated during directory synchronization. Trust levels range between 0 and 100. The Hide From Address Book checkbox must be cleared in order to use this option.

If you do not want a recipient name to be replicated to other servers, set a trust level on the mailbox higher than the trust level set on the container.

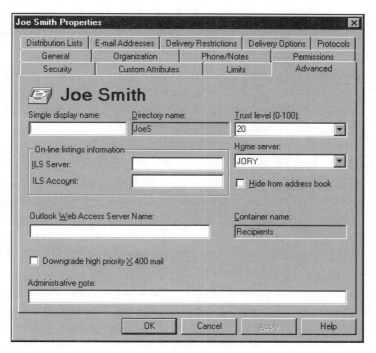

Figure 5.3   The Advanced property page of a mailbox.

➤ **Online listing information** If your organization uses Microsoft NetMeeting, you can specify the Internet Locator Server (ILS) information of individual mailboxes. Doing this enables users using NetMeeting to locate the mailbox owner and set up online meetings.

➤ **Home server** The home server is the Exchange server where the mailbox is physically located. After the mailbox is created, you can move the mailbox to another server by using the Move Mailbox option from the Tools menu.

➤ **Hide from address book** By checking this box, you hide a particular mailbox from the Global Address List. However, even if the mailbox is hidden from the Address Book, you can still send messages to the mailbox if you know the email address.

➤ **Outlook Web Access server name** If an Outlook Web Access Server is specified, the user can use a POP3 or IMAP4 client for email access, as well as the Outlook Web interface for calendaring and custom forms. Meeting requests and custom forms are received in the user's mailbox as messages containing the URL at which the request or forms are located. By default, the Outlook Web Access server specified in the private information store is used if an Outlook Web Access server is not specified for a given mailbox. The messages containing the URLs for meeting requests and custom forms will not be sent if this field is left blank.

➤ **Downgrade high priority X.400 mail** Check this box to downgrade all X.400 messages marked as high priority and send them as normal priority. By default, X.400 messages marked as high priority will be sent as high priority.

Mailbox Roles

As mentioned earlier, you can assign users to mailboxes with specific roles. By default, the Permissions tab is not seen—it is set to Hidden within the Exchange Administrator. To view this tab, select Options from the Tools menu and check the Show Permissions Page For All Objects box under the Permissions tab. The Properties page of the Permissions dialog box for a mailbox is shown in Figure 5.4.

The Permissions tab of the Properties page has two fields. The first field shows the NT accounts with inherited rights to the mailbox. This is a read-only field. The second field shows the NT accounts with permissions to the mailbox, and it allows you to edit the accounts and permissions. You assign permissions to a user or a group by giving them a *role*. Roles are predetermined sets of permis-

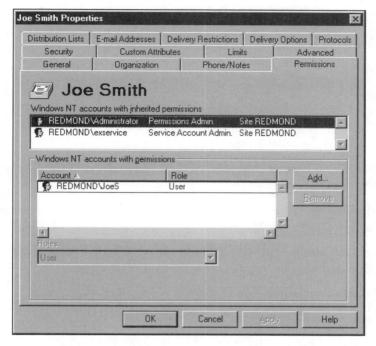

Figure 5.4   The Permissions tab of the Properties page for a mailbox.

sions that specify what activities can be performed on a mailbox. Here's a list of the roles (they are also listed in Table 5.2):

Table 5.2	Directory permissions and roles.				
Permission	**Admin**	**Permissions**	**Search**	**Send As**	**User**
Add Child	X	X			
Modify User Attributes	X	X	X		X
Modify Admin Attributes	X	X			
Modify Permissions		X			
Delete	X	X			
Send As				X	X
Mailbox Owner					X
Logon Rights	X	X			
Replication					
Search			X		

➤ Admin

➤ Permissions Admin

➤ Search

➤ Send As

➤ User

Here's a list of the permissions:

➤ **Add Child** Creates objects below the selected object in the directory hierarchy.

➤ **Modify User Attributes** Modifies user-level attributes associated with an object.

➤ **Modify Admin Attributes** Modifies administrator-level attributes associated with an object.

➤ **Modify Permissions** Modifies permissions on existing objects.

➤ **Delete** Enables users to delete objects.

➤ **Send As** Enables users to send messages with the sender's return address. This permission is also granted for server objects in the directory of the service account so that directory service processes can send messages to each other.

➤ **Mailbox Owner** Enables users to read and delete messages in this mailbox. This permission is also granted for server objects in the directory of the service account so that directory processes can send messages to each other.

➤ **Logon Rights** Enables users and services to access the directory. Users need this permission to use the Administrator program. Services also need this permission.

➤ **Replication** Enables users and services to replicate directory information with other servers. This permission is required by the Microsoft Exchange Server service account to replicate with other servers.

➤ **Search** Enables the selected user account to view the contents of the container. This permission is most useful for restricting access to Address Book View containers.

Working With Distribution Lists

A distribution list (DL) is a logical grouping of recipients created to expedite the mass mailing of messages and other information. A message sent to a distribution list will be sent to all members of the distribution list. Creating a distribution list is easy. In the Microsoft Exchange Administrator program, select the New Distribution List option from the File menu (or Ctrl+D). You'll have property pages to configure similar to those for mailbox configuration.

Distribution List Properties

Many of the property pages have been covered in the previous sections. The General and Advanced property pages deserve more explanation.

The distribution list General property page is used to specify a new distribution list, to modify the distribution list owner and name, and to change the membership of the distribution list. The General property page for a distribution list is shown in Figure 5.5 and contains the following information:

➤ **Owner** The owner of a distribution list is the primary contact for the list. The owner receives any notifications about the distribution list, such as non-delivery reports (NDRs). The owner also has the ability to

Figure 5.5 The General tab of the Managers Properties page of a distribution list.

change the name and the membership of the distribution list. This is all done through the Microsoft Outlook client.

➤ **Expansion server** When a message is sent to a distribution list, the Microsoft Exchange server must expand the list, resolve the names of all the recipients in the list, and find the most efficient route for the message. With a large distribution list, the task of expanding the list can be very processor intensive. This option allows you to specify a server to expand the distribution list, thus reducing the overhead on the main server. The default is that any Exchange Server within the site where a distribution list is located may be used as the expansion server.

➤ **Notes** Allows you to enter additional information about the distribution list (up to 256 characters).

➤ **Members** This is the list of the recipients who are part of a distribution list. All distribution list members, including mailboxes, public folders, other distribution lists, and custom recipients, receive any message sent to the distribution list.

The Advanced property page is used to provide a simple display name, set message transfer limits, specify a trust level for directory synchronization, and determine whether the distribution list is hidden from the Address Book. The Advanced property page for a distribution list is shown in Figure 5.6 and contains the following information:

➤ **Simple display name** The simple display name is a name used with foreign mail systems that cannot handle the Exchange non-ANSI characters.

➤ **Trust level** The trust level determines whether information about the distribution list is replicated to other sites during directory synchronization. If the trust level set for the distribution is higher than that set for the directory synchronization requester, the distribution list information will not be replicated during directory synchronization. Trust levels range between 0 and 100.

➤ **Message size** You can set the size limit for messages that can be sent to and from the distribution list. By default, there is no limit on message size.

➤ **Distribution lists** You can set several options on this tab, including enabling out-of-office messages and hiding the distribution list or distribution list membership from the Address Book.

➤ **Report to distribution list owner** This option sends notification reports to the distribution list owner when a message sent to the

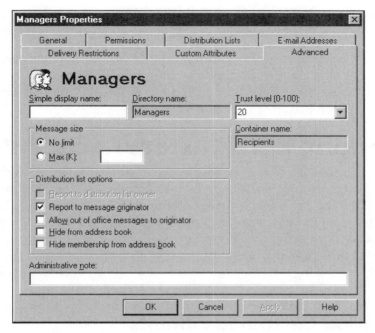

Figure 5.6   The Advanced tab of the Managers Properties page.

distribution list has requested delivery notification or is undeliverable. By default, this is not selected.

➤ **Report to message originator** This option sends notification reports to the message originator that indicate the delivery status for each member of the list when a message sent to the distribution list has requested delivery notification or is undeliverable. When this option is not selected, the message originator receives reports from the list, not notification for each member. By default, this is selected.

➤ **Allow out of office messages to originator** The out-of-office option is a mailbox mechanism that allows the mailbox owner to notify senders that he or she is unavailable to read the messages. If selected, this option sends out-of-office messages from members of the distribution list to the originator on behalf of any member who has enabled his or her out-of-office option. It's not a good idea to activate this option for large distribution lists. By default, this is not selected.

➤ **Hide from address book** If selected, this option hides the distribution list from the Address Book. However, even if the mailbox is hidden from the Address Book, you can send messages to the mailbox if you know the email address. By default, this is not selected.

➤ **Hide membership from address book** If selected, this option hides the recipients that are members of the distribution list from the Address Book, but it does not hide the distribution list. By default, this is not selected.

Working With Custom Recipients

A *custom recipient* is a recipient who resides outside the site, organization, or post office (an example would be an Internet Simple Mail Transfer Protocol recipient). When a custom recipient is created, it appears in the Address Book and can receive messages like any other recipient; however, a custom recipient does not have a mailbox on the local Exchange Server. A custom recipient can be created in one of two ways: using the Exchange Administrator program or using the directory import feature to import custom recipients from other mail systems.

Creating Custom Recipients With Exchange Administrator

You can create a custom recipient from the Exchange Administrator program by selecting the New Custom Recipient option from the File menu (or Ctrl+R). You'll be prompted to select the type of foreign email address to create and provide the actual email address. Here are the types of foreign email addresses available:

➤ cc:Mail Address

➤ Microsoft Mail Address

➤ MacMail Address

➤ Internet Mail Address

➤ X.400 Address

➤ Other Address

Custom Recipient Properties

The properties for a custom recipient are very similar to those of a standard mailbox; the main difference is that you're prompted for the foreign mail address of the custom recipient. The format of this foreign mail address depends on the foreign mail system.

The General property page for a custom recipient is the same as that for a mailbox, except that you can change the custom recipient's email address. The General property page for a custom recipient is shown in Figure 5.7.

The General property page for a custom recipient (Advanced) is shown in Figure 5.8 and is the same as that for a mailbox, except for the following information:

➤ **Custom recipient options** You can select Allow Rich Text In Messages.

➤ **Primary Windows NT Account** This is the NT domain account that is associated with the mailbox. You'll be given the option of choosing an existing user account or having a new user account created.

Managing Recipient Objects

Recipient object management tasks include the following:

➤ Using templates for mailbox creation

➤ Finding a recipient

➤ Moving a mailbox

➤ Cleaning a mailbox

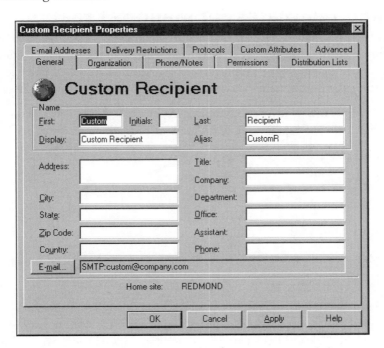

Figure 5.7 The General property page for a custom recipient.

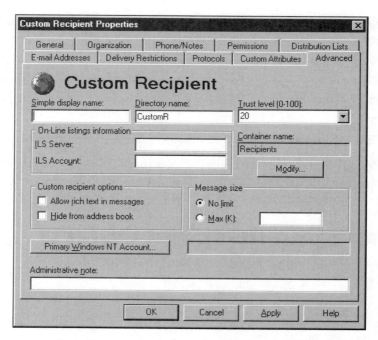

Figure 5.8 The Advanced property page for a custom recipient.

Using Templates For Mailbox Creation

A *template* is a mailbox created for the purpose of using its configuration information to create new mailboxes. You can use the Migration wizard, the Directory Import command, or the Duplicate command to create new mailboxes. You duplicate a template mailbox to create a single mailbox or many mailboxes.

Any mailbox can be used as a template mailbox. However, several configuration items are not copied to the new mailbox or mailboxes:

➤ First name

➤ Last name

➤ Display name

➤ Alias name

➤ Directory name

➤ Email address

The template's name should be something that clearly states the nature of the mailbox it will be used to create. For example, you may want to create a template named "sales" for the creation of users in sales, and you would use this template to create a new mailbox for a new user in the sales department. You may also want to place a pound sign (#) as the first character of the template's name. This causes the templates to be listed at the top of the recipients list. The templates should also be hidden from the Address Book so that mail is not accidentally sent to them.

Finding A Recipient

You can use the Exchange Administrator program to search for recipients anywhere within an organization by selecting the Find Recipients option in the Tools menu. The Find Recipients page is shown in Figure 5.9. You can search for recipients based on several search criteria, including first, last, or display name, department, assistants, and so on.

Moving A Mailbox

Although a mailbox physically resides on a specific server, it is possible to move it to another server within the site. To do this, highlight the desired mailbox in the contents pane (the right window pane) and select the Move Mailbox option from the Tools menu. Any time a user is moved, the client profile is automatically updated and points to the correct server. Mailboxes can also be

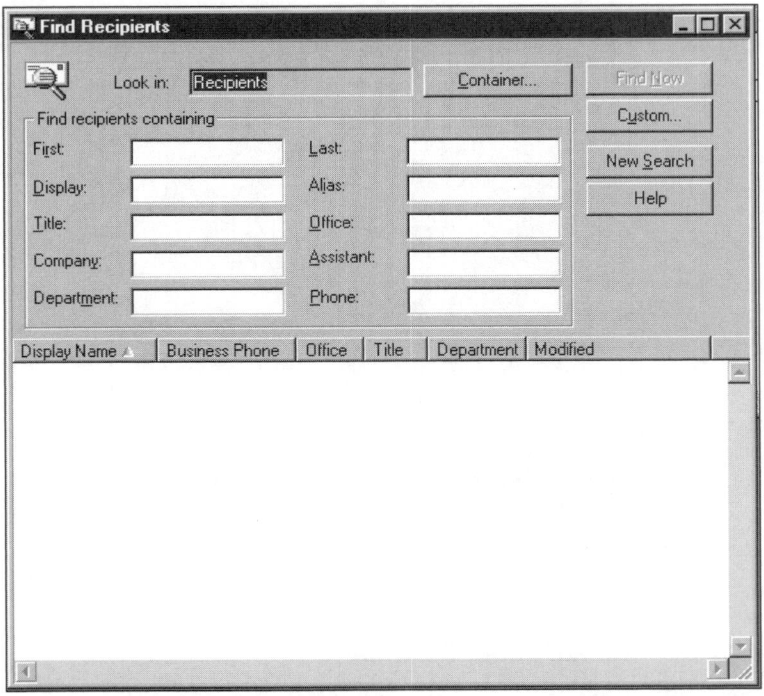

Figure 5.9   The Find Recipients page.

moved using the Home Server field on the Advanced property page of the user's mailbox.

> *Note: When you're moving mailboxes to a new home server, the size of the mailbox contents on the destination server may increase, because when a message is sent to multiple mailboxes on the same server, a single copy of the message is stored and each recipient on that server receives a pointer to that single copy. This is called single-instance storage. When a mailbox is moved to a new server, this pointer must be replaced with a copy of the message, because pointers do not operate between servers.*

> *Note: You can select multiple mailboxes to be moved by holding down the Shift key for contiguous users or the Ctrl key for noncontiguous users.*

Cleaning A Mailbox

Cleaning a mailbox simply means deleting certain messages stored in the mailbox. To clean a mailbox, select the mailbox to be cleaned in the contents pane and then select the Clean Mailbox option from the Tools menu. The Clean Mailbox dialog box appears as shown in Figure 5.10. The Ad-

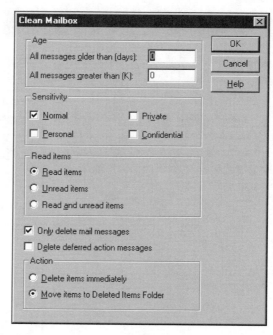

Figure 5.10 The Clean Mailbox dialog box.

ministrator can select predefined criteria for cleaning the mailbox, including the following:

➤ All messages older than (days)

➤ All messages greater than (K)

➤ Normal, personal, private, and confidential messages

➤ Read and unread messages

As an administrator, you also have the option of deleting the messages immediately or having them moved to the Deleted Items folder.

Exam Prep Questions

Question 1

> What does a custom recipient allow Microsoft Exchange Server to do?
>
> ○ a. Create a second name for an existing Microsoft Exchange mailbox
>
> ○ b. Have Microsoft Exchange communicate with a foreign mail system
>
> ○ c. Change a custom mailbox role
>
> ○ d. Have one message sent to the custom recipient be delivered to all its members

The correct answer to this question is b. Custom recipients allow Microsoft Exchange Server to communicate with foreign mail systems. A custom recipient cannot be used to create a second name for an existing mailbox; therefore, answer a is incorrect. A custom mailbox role is set within the Permissions property box of the mailbox; therefore, answer c is incorrect. The role of delivering a message to multiple users is that of a distribution list; therefore, answer d is incorrect.

Question 2

> Which of the following attributes belong to a mailbox? [Check all correct answers]
>
> ❏ a. Alias
>
> ❏ b. Expansion Server
>
> ❏ c. Primary Windows NT Account
>
> ❏ d. Country

Answers a, c, and d are correct. An alias, a primary Windows NT account, and a country value can be assigned to a mailbox. An expansion server is used by a distribution list to expand the list and send out the messages; therefore, answer b is incorrect.

Question 3

> Which of the following is an object that can receive, store, and organize messages?
>
> ○ a. An Exchange mailbox
>
> ○ b. A POP3 account
>
> ○ c. An Exchange distribution list
>
> ○ d. An Exchange custom recipient

The correct answer to this question is a. Microsoft Exchange mailboxes can receive, store, and organize messages. Although a POP3 account will receive and store messages, it does not have the ability to organize these messages; therefore, answer b is incorrect (and the trick in this question). A distribution list is a logical grouping of mailboxes and is used to redirect a message to multiple mailboxes; therefore, answer c is incorrect. A custom recipient is used to redirect a message to a foreign email address. Therefore, answer d is incorrect.

Question 4

> Which of the following tools would you use to selectively delete messages from a mailbox?
>
> ○ a. Move Mailbox
>
> ○ b. Delete Mailbox
>
> ○ c. Clean Mailbox
>
> ○ d. Rename Mailbox

The correct answer to this question is c. Clean Mailbox will allow you to selectively delete messages according to age, size, and so on. Move Mailbox and Rename Mailbox will affect the mailbox without affecting the contents; therefore, answers a and d are incorrect. Deleting a mailbox will delete the entire contents of the mailbox without allowing you to select what is to be deleted; therefore, answer b is incorrect.

Question 5

> How are mailbox permissions controlled?
>
> O a. Distribution lists
>
> O b. Mailbox roles
>
> O c. Windows NT groups
>
> O d. Windows NT permissions

The correct answer to this question is b. By assigning an NT account a role, you specify which permissions that user will have to the mailbox. A distribution list is a logical grouping of mailboxes and has nothing to do with mailbox permissions; therefore, answer a is incorrect. Both Windows NT groups and permissions cannot be used to assign mailbox permissions; therefore, answers c and d are incorrect.

Question 6

> Which of the following advanced attributes are configurable by an administrator? [Check all correct answers]
>
> ❏ a. Simple Display Name
>
> ❏ b. Trust Level
>
> ❏ c. Home Server
>
> ❏ d. Directory Name

The correct answers to this question are a, b, and c, all of which are configurable by the administrator. Directory Name is a read-only field and cannot be configured by the administrator; therefore, answer d is incorrect.

Question 7

> What is the Internet Locator Service used for?
>
> O a. Locating users for online meetings
>
> O b. Locating users for Microsoft Chat
>
> O c. Locating users for Microsoft NetShow
>
> O d. Locating a user's email address in the Exchange site

The correct answer to this question is a. The Internet Locator Service is used to schedule online meetings between users. None of the other answers is correct.

Question 8

> Which program would you use to create mailboxes for NetWare users?
>
> ○ a. NetWare Directory Synchronization
>
> ○ b. Gateway Services For NetWare
>
> ○ c. The Extract NetWare Accounts List tool
>
> ○ d. Client Services For NetWare

The correct answer to this question is c. The Extract NetWare Accounts List tool can be used to migrate users from NetWare to Exchange. NetWare Directory Synchronization is a fictional product; therefore, answer a is incorrect. Gateway Services For NetWare allows a Windows NT Server to act as a gateway to share information from a Novell NetWare server to a Microsoft network; therefore, answer b is incorrect. Client Services For NetWare allows Windows NT Workstation to connect to a Novell NetWare server for services; therefore, answer d is incorrect.

Question 9

> A user has deleted a message and would like to recover it. When would it be possible for the user to recover the deleted message?
>
> ○ a. Whenever the user wants. This is an automatic feature of Microsoft Exchange.
>
> ○ b. When the user is part of the Backup Operators Windows NT group.
>
> ○ c. When the administrator sets a deleted message retention period.
>
> ○ d. Never, once a message is deleted, it is lost forever.

The correct answer to this question is c. A new feature in Microsoft Exchange Server 5.5 is the ability to specify an amount of time that the server waits before permanently deleting a message. This is not an automatic feature and has to be manually configured; therefore, answer a is incorrect. A user who is part of the Backup Operators group can restore from or backup to a tape system but cannot recover the individual message; therefore, answer b is incorrect. By setting a deleted message retention period, the administrator can allow users to recover their own deleted messages; therefore, answer d is incorrect.

Question 10

What would you configure to ease processor usage on a specific Exchange Server when dealing with distribution lists?

○ a. A home server

○ b. An SQL server

○ c. An expansion server

○ d. A distribution server

The correct answer to this question is c. By configuring an expansion server, you take the job of expanding a distribution list and offload it to another server. A home server is where a mailbox is located; therefore, answer a is incorrect. An SQL server is a database server and has nothing to do with distribution list expansion; therefore, answer b is incorrect. There is no such thing as a distribution list server; therefore, answer d is incorrect.

Need To Know More?

 Microsoft Technical Information Network. February, 1998. The technical notes for Exchange Server provide insight into its design and architecture. Search using the keywords "Mailbox," "Distribution Lists," and "Custom Recipients."

 Install the online books from the Microsoft Exchange Server 5.5 CD-ROM. It will yield a wealth of useful information.

 Go to the Microsoft Exchange Server home page at www.microsoft.com/exchange. Many of the documents located here are newer than the ones available on the Microsoft Technical Information Network.

 Go to the Microsoft Knowledge Base and Support home page at www.microsoft.com/kb. Many of the documents located here are newer than the ones available on the Microsoft Technical Information Network.

Configuring Exchange Server

Terms you'll need to understand:

√ ADMIN.EXE

√ Configuration object

√ Connections object

√ Container object

√ CSV files

√ Directory import

√ Exchange Administrator

√ Extract account lists

√ Organization object

√ Server object

√ Server recipients object

√ Site object

Techniques you'll need to master:

√ Understanding the Exchange Administrator

√ Grasping the Exchange hierarchy, as displayed in the Exchange Administrator

√ Grasping the relationship between common objects in the Exchange Administrator

√ Navigating the Exchange hierarchy using the Exchange Administrator

√ Navigating the menus in the Exchange Administrator

This chapter provides a detailed look at the Microsoft Exchange Administrator. The Exchange Administrator is a complex product, and it contains many features and options—so much so, that the number and variety of settings and options can almost seem overwhelming. This chapter discusses the various configuration and management options in Microsoft Exchange.

Exchange Server Management Overview

A Microsoft Exchange administrator's day-to-day duties involve adding mailboxes, setting up address book views, establishing connections to other sites, establishing connections to the Internet, and setting up directory replication between sites. To do all of this—and more—you need to master the Exchange Administrator.

Understanding The Exchange Administrator

The "nerve center" for Microsoft Exchange is the Exchange Administrator. From this control panel, of sorts, an entire Microsoft Exchange organization can be managed—including configuring sites, servers, connections, and protocols. In addition, the Exchange Administrator provides status information for the Information Stores, monitors, connectors, protocols, services, synchronization, and recipients. This versatility comes at a price, however: The many menus and dialog boxes can be confusing and overwhelming to new users. At first, the interface may seem a bit unwieldy, but once you get used to it, you'll appreciate what a good job it does at presenting a wealth of information.

Starting The Exchange Administrator Program

You start the Exchange Administrator by going to the Start menu and selecting Programs|Exchange|Exchange Administrator. This menu item is a shortcut to the ADMIN.EXE file, located in the \ExchSrvr\Bin directory (or wherever you installed Microsoft Exchange). If you're starting Exchange Administrator for the first time, the Connect To Server dialog box will appear (see Figure 6.1). Type the name of the Exchange server you want to connect to, or you can press the Browse button to display a graphical layout of your organization's Exchange servers. If browsing, select an Exchange server to connect to and then click OK to return to the Connect To Server dialog box. The name of the Exchange server you selected appears in the dialog box.

Figure 6.1 The Connect To Server dialog box.

Selecting the Set As Default checkbox tells Exchange Administrator that you want to automatically connect to this Exchange server the next time you start Exchange Administrator. Next, click the OK button. Exchange Administrator then attempts to connect to the specified server. If a connection to the specified server is successful, the Exchange Administrator interface appears.

The Exchange Administrator Interface

Initially, the Exchange Administrator displays only the high-level objects in your Microsoft Exchange organization (see Figure 6.2). By selecting and expanding the objects displayed, you can view your organization at any level of detail you want. The title bar of Exchange Administrator includes the name of the server currently connected to, the name of the site that this server belongs to, and the name of the currently selected object. Below the title bar, menu bar, and toolbar, the left side of the Exchange Administrator window shows your Exchange hierarchy, which displays every object in your Exchange organization. The right side of the Exchange Administrator window displays some of the details of the object currently selected in the left side of the window.

The Exchange Administrator displays your Exchange hierarchy in a directory/file format—similar to Windows Explorer. Rather than directories and files, however, the Exchange Administrator displays container objects and noncontainer objects. Every object displayed in the Exchange Administrator has an associated icon.

Similar to directories in Windows Explorer, *container objects* are objects that "contain," or encompass, other objects—either other container objects or noncontainer objects. Examples of container objects include sites, servers, and connectors. Noncontainer objects are objects that do not contain other objects. Examples of noncontainer objects include a recipient or a specific connector. Obviously, with this type of hierarchy, an object can be a container object as well as be contained within another container object.

For instance, the site object container includes all the objects that are within that site—servers, connectors, recipients, and so forth. However, a server within the site object container is also, itself, an object container.

Figure 6.2 The Exchange Administrator interface.

Plus and minus signs appear to the left of most objects, indicating that the object is a container object (in other words, there are other objects below it). An object without a plus or a minus sign indicates that the object is a noncontainer object (in other words, there's no further detail below the object). Clicking a plus sign expands a container object, whereas clicking a minus sign collapses a container object. When you select a container object in the left side of the window, the objects associated with that container object appear in the right side of the window.

 When Exchange Administrator is first opened, the organization object is selected. The organization object is the topmost object in the Exchange hierarchy.

The name of the organization object was defined when you installed your first Exchange server. With the organization object selected, the right window displays the objects contained in that object: Address Book Views, Folders, Global Address List, and sites (refer to Figure 6.2).

As you initially expand the available container objects, you may not see as many objects in the Exchange hierarchy as you would expect—especially if this is your organization's first Exchange server, or if no connectors have been established with other Exchange servers in your organization. After connectors and other objects are added, however, you'll be able to see much more detail in the Exchange hierarchy.

Microsoft Exchange Object Hierarchy

As you use the Exchange Administrator to traverse the objects in the Exchange hierarchy, it's helpful to keep in mind the basic relationship between the objects:

Organization

    Folders

        Public Folders

        System Folders

            Eforms Registry

                Organization Forms Library

                Events Root

                EventConfig_Server

            Offline Address Book

            Schedule+ Free/Busy

    Global Address List

    Site (one object for each site defined)

        Configuration

            Add-Ins

            Addressing

                Details Templates

                Email Address Generator

                On-Off Address Templates

            Connections

                Connection (one object for each connection defined in the site)

Directory Replication

Monitors

    Monitor (one object for each monitor defined in the site)

(Site) Protocols

    Protocol (one object for each protocol in use in the site)

Servers

    Server (one object for each server defined)

        Private Information Store

        (Server) Protocols

            Protocol (one object for each protocol defined on the server)

        Public Information Store

        Server Recipients

            (Server) Recipient (one object for each recipient defined on the server)

        Directory Service

        Directory Synchronization

        Message Transfer Agent (MTA)

        System Attendant

DS Site Configuration

Information Store Site Configuration

MTA Site Configuration

Site Addressing

Site Encryption Configuration

(Site) Recipients

    (Site) Recipient (one object for each recipient, distribution list, and custom recipient defined in this site)

It's important to know the location of objects (both container and noncontainer), so it's good to keep object relationships in mind.

A brief consideration of each of these objects follows.

As already mentioned, there's only one Organization object in the Exchange hierarchy, and it's always at the top. The Organization object is a container object; all other objects are contained within it. The Organization name is used for message addressing; it cannot be changed after installation (although the display name can be changed).

The Folders object is the container for all organization folder information. Folder information is shared among all sites within the organization. Public folders and system folders are contained within the Folders object.

The Public Folders object contains configuration information for all the organization's public folders. Changes made to a public folder are recorded here, and this information is automatically replicated to every replica of that folder throughout the organization. When the Public Folders object is displayed, all the organization's public folders and replicas are displayed.

The System Folders object contains the following objects: the Eforms Registry, the Offline Address Book, and the Schedule+ Free Busy.

The Eforms Registry object contains all the forms that have been created in the organization. This object is a container for the following objects:

➤ **Organization Forms Library** This object is a public folder containing electronic forms. When a form is saved to a public folder, by default, it's made available to all Microsoft Exchange users.

➤ **Events Root** This object contains folders that maintain event configuration information for all Exchange servers in the organization.

➤ **EventConfig_Server** This object contains folders representing configuration information for specific Exchange servers in the organization.

The Offline Address Book object contains recipient names to which remote users can address messages. This object is a container for multiple Offline Address Book objects. Each site in the organization has its own Offline Address Book object. Remote users can download offline address books and thereafter send mail to any recipient in the Exchange organization.

The Schedule+ Free/Busy object is a container for Schedule+ Free/Busy folders. Each site has its own Schedule+ Free/Busy folder. New mailboxes result in an entry in the Schedule+ Free/Busy Information public folder, including the current Exchange site and the associated Windows NT account. Every time a change is made to a user's Schedule+ data, an update is automatically made in the appropriate site's Schedule+ Free/Busy folder. Using Microsoft

Schedule+, users can set permissions to prevent others from seeing their free/busy information.

The Global Address List object lists all your organization's mailboxes, distribution lists, public folders, and custom recipients.

The Site object (and its child objects) contains most of the information you'll alter when using the Exchange Administrator. Each site in your organization is represented by its own Site object. A site is one or more Exchange servers that have been grouped together. The first site is added to the Exchange hierarchy when the first Exchange server is installed in the organization. The Site object is a container for the following objects: Configuration and Recipients.

The Configuration object contains configuration information about a specific site. The object is a container for the following objects: Add-Ins, Addressing, Connections, Directory Replication, Monitors, Protocols, Servers, DS Site Configuration, Information Store Site Configuration, MTA Site Configuration, Site Addressing, and Site Encryption Configuration.

The Add-Ins object contains third-party services that don't require mailboxes—AppleTalk, for instance.

The Addressing object contains directory entries dealing with Microsoft Exchange address generation. The Addressing object is a container for the following objects:

➤ **Details Templates** This object maintains localized templates that specify how recipient object details are displayed, by language and country.

➤ **Email Address Generator** This object is a container for email generators. Email generators automatically generate email addresses for newly created Exchange recipients. The following email generators are contained in the Email Address Generator object: cc:Mail Email Address Generator, Internet Email Address Generator, Microsoft Mail Address Generator, and X.400 Email Address Generator.

➤ **On-Off Address Templates** This object maintains localized templates used to determine the format of new email addresses entered by the user when the email address is not in his or her global address list or personal address book. Templates are grouped by language and country.

The Connections object contains all the connectors used to link Exchange sites with other Exchange sites, Microsoft Mail systems, and other foreign messaging systems. The Connections object is a container for the following objects:

➤ **cc:Mail Connector** This object is used to configure message transfer with Lotus cc:Mail messaging systems.

➤ **Internet Mail Service** This object configures message transfer with messaging systems based on the Simple Mail Transfer Protocol (SMTP).

➤ **Microsoft Mail Connector** This object configures message transfer with Microsoft Mail (for PC Networks), Microsoft Mail (for AppleTalk Networks), and Microsoft Mail (for third-party gateways).

➤ **Site Connector** This object is used to create links between Microsoft Exchange sites that are on the same physical network.

➤ **X.400 Connector** This object is used to create links between Microsoft Exchange sites over an X.400 network. The connector is also used to establish links to foreign X.400 messaging systems.

➤ **Microsoft Mail Connector for AppleTalk Networks (Quarterdeck Mail)** This object is used to configure message transfer with AppleTalk networks.

➤ **Dynamic RAS (Remote Access Service) Connector** This object is used to create links between Microsoft Exchange sites over a Windows NT RAS connection.

➤ **Directory Exchange Requestor** This object is used by an Exchange server to request directory information from other email systems (for example, Microsoft Mail).

➤ **Directory Exchange Server** This object is used by Exchange Server to perform directory synchronization with external messaging systems.

➤ **DirSync Server** This object processes inbound updates from directory requestors and adds the updates into its own directory as custom recipient objects.

➤ **Remote DirSync Requestor** This object is used by remote directory requestors during directory exchange to authenticate and respond to directory requestors.

The Directory Replication object contains all directory replication connectors for Microsoft Exchange. Directory replication connectors result in two-way exchanging of directory updates. The Directory Replication object is a container for the Directory Replication Connector object, which is used for sharing recipient information between sites.

The Monitors object contains tools that monitor an Exchange organization's servers and the links between those servers. The Monitors object is a container for the following objects:

➤ **Server Monitor** This object monitors the status of an Exchange server's services, providing warnings and alerts if errors occurs.

➤ **Link Monitor** This object monitors the status of messaging connections. It does this by monitoring the amount of time it takes for messages to bounce between Exchange servers. Administrative users can be alerted if the amount of time exceeds the value expected.

The (Site) Protocols object contains all the Internet protocols supported by Microsoft Exchange. It's a container for the following objects:

➤ **IMAP4** IMAP4 stands for the *Internet Message Access Protocol, version 4, revision 1*. Users with an IMAP4rev1 client can access mail in their Exchange Server mailboxes using the IMAP4 object. Clients can also read and post messages to public folders and access other users' mailboxes to which permission has been granted.

➤ **HTTP** HTTP stands for *Hypertext Transfer Protocol*. When used with Windows NT's Active Server Components, the HTTP Connector allows users to access their Exchange Server mailboxes using an Internet browser.

➤ **LDAP** LDAP stands for *Lightweight Directory Access Protocol*—an Internet directory protocol. With the LDAP object, clients with appropriate security permissions can use LDAP-enabled programs to browse, read, and search directories. The LDAP object can be configured to specify authentication forms, permit anonymous access, and permit searching.

➤ **NNTP** NNTP stands for *Network News Transfer Protocol*—an Internet protocol used for newsgroup support. With the NNTP Connector installed, site defaults, message content, time-out options, and so forth, can be configured.

➤ **POP3** POP3 stands for *Post Office Protocol 3*. This connector enables users with POP3 clients to retrieve their messages from their Exchange Server mailboxes.

The Servers object contains all the Exchange servers in the parent site. Numerous Exchange servers can appear in the Servers object.

A Server object represents a specific server in the server list. Each server is, itself, a container for the following objects: Private Information Store, Protocols, Public Information Store, Server Recipients, Directory Service, Directory Synchronization, Message Transfer Agent (MTA), and System Attendant.

The Private Information Store object stores all messages sent to individual mailboxes. The Private Information Store object is a container for the following objects:

➤ **Logons** This object displays information about which users are currently logged on to a mailbox located on the server.

➤ **Mailbox Resources** This object displays detailed resource usage information about each mailbox on the server. For example, from this object, you can see how much disk space an individual user's mailbox is taking up.

The (Server) Protocols object contains configuration dialog boxes for the Internet protocols discussed earlier in the Protocols object. The Protocols object is a container for the IMAP4, LDAP, NNTP, and POP3 objects.

The Public Information Store object stores all public folder messages. The Public Information Store object is a container for the following objects:

➤ **Folder Replication Status** The Folder Replication Status object displays the current status of public folder replication within the current site.

➤ **Logons** The Logons object displays information about who is currently logged on to the public folders located on the server. By viewing the details of this object, you can get a bird's-eye view of who is currently accessing the public folders.

➤ **Public Folder Resources** The Public Folder Resources object displays detailed information about public folder resource usage. For example, from this object, you can see how much disk space an individual public folder is using.

The Server Recipients object is a container for all Exchange recipient objects (for example, mailboxes) located on the server. Mailbox recipient objects appear in both the Server Recipients and (Site) Recipients objects.

A recipient object (when contained in the Server Recipients object) corresponds to an individual Exchange account on the server. Most Recipient objects are mailboxes. There's one recipient object for each mailbox. Mailboxes contain messages.

The Microsoft Schedule+ Free/Busy Connector is a special recipient object that's used for transferring free/busy scheduling information with Schedule+ for Microsoft Mail.

The Directory Service object contains configuration information about how directories are handled within the server's site.

The Directory Synchronization object contains general properties for Exchange directory synchronization. The Directory Synchronization object is also called the *Exchange DXA*.

The Message Transfer Agent (MTA) object is responsible for transferring messages from one server to another, including via external connectors.

The System Attendant object is responsible for managing messaging log files. The System Attendant service starts all other Microsoft Exchange services.

The DS Site Configuration object contains general directory service properties for the server and the site in which the server is contained.

The Information Store Site Configuration object contains general properties for all the Information Stores within the site the server is in.

The MTA Site Configuration object contains general properties for all the Message Transfer Agents in the site the server is in.

The Site Addressing object contains general site addressing information. This information is used to route messages.

The Site Encryption Configuration object is used to configure message encryption. By accessing the properties of this object, advanced security features can be configured.

A (Site) Recipients object is a container for all Exchange recipient objects located on all servers within the site. Mailbox recipient objects appear in both the Server Recipients and (Site) Recipients objects.

A Recipient object—when contained in the (Site) Recipients object—corresponds to an individual Exchange account on a server in the site. Most site recipient objects are mailboxes. There's one recipient object for each mailbox, distribution list, and custom recipient.

Mailbox objects are private containers that contain messaging data.

Distribution lists objects are made up of a group of individual recipients. When a message is sent to the distribution list, everyone in the distribution list receives the message.

Custom recipient objects are for foreign recipients whose mailboxes are not contained on an Exchange server.

Lastly, the Microsoft Schedule+ Free/Busy Connector object is a recipient used for transferring free/busy scheduling information with Schedule+ for Microsoft Mail.

The Exchange Administrator Menu

There are six items on the Exchange Administrator menu: File, Edit, View, Tools, Window, and Help. Menu items can also be quickly accessed by using the configurable toolbar, which appears below the menu.

The File Menu

The File menu is where you'll spend most of your time when administering an Exchange server (see Figure 6.3). From the File menu, you can connect to other servers, create new connections and objects, and modify and view object properties. The options accessed from the File menu are explained in the following paragraphs.

Connect To Server

The Connect To Server menu item is used to connect to another Exchange server. In the Connect To Server dialog box, you can type the name of the Exchange server to which you want to connect. If you press the Browse button, a list of your organization's Exchange servers appears. Select an Exchange server to which to connect and click OK.

Once you're connected to an Exchange server, the view changes to present the Exchange hierarchy—in the context of that particular Exchange server. This view might differ because of the settings, objects, and connectors that are unique to that particular Exchange server.

 You can connect to more than one server while in the Exchange Administrator. Each Exchange server you connect to is presented in its own MDI window. Only one connection can be in the foreground at a time.

Figure 6.3   The File menu.

Exercise care when you're connected to more than one Exchange server. Objects are created on the current (that is, foreground) server. Therefore, verify that you're working with the right server when you create objects.

Close

Use the File menu's Close menu item to close the connection to the current Exchange server. If you're still connected to another Exchange server, the Exchange Administrator changes to display a window for that Exchange server. When there are no more connections to Exchange servers, the Exchange hierarchy view disappears. However, the Exchange Administrator remains open, but with limited menu features—such as connecting to an Exchange server.

New Mailbox

Choose the File menu's New Mailbox menu item to add a new mailbox to the currently selected site. Mailboxes must be created in the recipients container. If the site's recipients container is not selected, the Exchange Administrator offers to expand the site and select the recipients container for you.

The New Mailbox dialog box is displayed in Figure 6.4. Fill in the prompted information, press the Primary Windows NT Account button to select an associated Windows NT account, and then click OK.

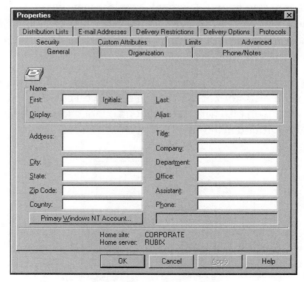

Figure 6.4   The New Mailbox dialog box.

New Distribution List

Select the File menu's New Distribution List menu item to create a new distribution list recipient. As with the New Mailbox menu item, distribution lists must be created in the recipients container.

The New Distribution List dialog box is displayed in Figure 6.5. Fill in the requested information and then click OK.

New Custom Recipient

The File menu's New Custom Recipient menu item is used to create a recipient object for a mailbox that is located on a foreign messaging system—such as cc:Mail, Microsoft Mail, or SMTP.

New Other

Choosing the File menu's New Other menu item opens up another menu that provides choices for creating other types of Microsoft Exchange objects (see Figure 6.6). All the items in this submenu, which represent other types of objects that can be created, are explained in the following paragraphs.

The File menu's New Other|Server Monitor menu item is used when you want to monitor a server's condition. Server monitors can be defined to produce an alert when critical problems occur.

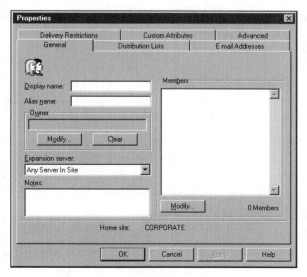

Figure 6.5   The New Distribution List dialog box.

Figure 6.6 The New Other menu.

The File menu's New Other|Link Monitor menu item is used to monitor the messaging connection between Exchange Server sites and servers. Similar to server monitors, link monitors can be configured to generate an alert when serious problems occur.

The File menu's New Other|Recipients Container menu item is used when you want to create another recipients container in the current site. You can create multiple recipients containers, in addition to the default recipients container. For instance, you might add an "Internet Recipients" container to hold the SMTP addresses of custom recipients.

Select the File menu's New Other|Address Book View menu item to configure an address book's view.

Choose the File menu's New Other|Address Book View Container menu item to modify an address book view container's configuration.

The File menu's New Other|MTA Transport Stack menu item is used to define the transport protocol for newly created Dynamic RAS Connectors or X.400 Connectors. Before selecting this menu item, make sure you have all the required transport software properly configured in Windows NT Server.

Select the File menu's New Other|X.400 Connector menu item to define an X.400 connection to either another Microsoft Exchange site or to a foreign system. Before installing an X.400 Connector, you need to define an MTA transport stack. The X.400 Connector requires an MTA transport stack.

Choose the File menu's New Other|Dynamic RAS Connector menu item to establish a part-time remote access connection between two Exchange servers. Dynamic RAS connections can be established via modem, Integrated Services

Digital Network (ISDN), or X.25—assuming the appropriate MTA transport stack has been properly installed.

The File menu's New Other|Site Connector menu item is used to create a connection between two Microsoft Exchange sites. The two sites should be on the same physical network.

Select the File menu's New Other|Directory Replication Connector menu item to share messaging directories between two Microsoft Exchange sites.

Select the File menu's New Other|DirSync Requestor menu item to establish a DirSync requestor (directory synchronization requestor). DirSync requestors are compatible with the MS Mail 3.x directory synchronization protocol and are usually used by a messaging server to request updates from an MS Mail post office that has been configured to be a directory synchronization server. See Chapter 13 for more information.

The File menu's New Other|DirSync Server menu item is used to set up a DirSync server (directory synchronization server). DirSync servers are compatible with the MS Mail 3.x directory synchronization protocol.

Choose the File menu's New Other|Remote DirSync Requestor menu item to tell Exchange Server (the DirSync server) to receive directory requests from a foreign messaging system.

Select the File menu's New Other|Information Store menu item to create a Public or Private Information Store. This menu item is rarely used, because an Information Store can only be created if one doesn't already exist on the selected Exchange server.

The File menu's New Other|Newsfeed menu item starts a wizard that sets up an NNTP newsfeed. To successfully complete this wizard, you need your ISP's Usenet site name, the names (or IP addresses) of your ISP's host servers, and the username and password your Exchange server uses to log on to your ISP's newsfeed server.

Choosing the File menu's New Other|Internet Mail Service menu item launches a wizard that configures the Internet Mail Service to send and receive Internet messages.

Save Window Contents

Choose the File menu's Save Window Contents menu item to save the contents of the object window to a comma-separated text file (with a .CSV extension). You might find this information helpful for organizational documentation purposes.

Properties

The File menu's Properties menu item is used to view (and optionally change) the properties of a particular Microsoft Exchange object or container. Double-clicking many of the objects and containers also brings up the properties; however, you may find that certain objects' properties can only be accessed via this menu item.

Duplicate

The File menu's Duplicate menu item makes a copy of the selected recipient or distribution list. The copy is placed in the same recipients container the original object was located in.

Exit

Choose the File menu's Exit menu item to close all your Exchange Server connections and then exit the Exchange Administrator.

The Edit Menu

From the Edit menu, standard Windows editing tasks can be performed. The following menu items are accessed from the Edit menu: Undo, Cut, Copy, Paste, Delete, and Select All.

Undo

After cutting, copying, or pasting text, select the Edit|Undo menu item to reverse the change. Because most Exchange Administrator text operations occur within dialog boxes, however, this menu item is not very useful. To undo a change in a dialog box, press Ctrl+Z.

Cut, Copy, And Paste

Selecting the Edit menu and then the Cut, Copy, or Paste menu item performs the appropriate standard Windows editing action.

Delete

The Edit|Delete menu item is used to delete the object that's currently selected. Exercise care here, because once an object is deleted, the action cannot be undone.

Select All

When viewing a recipients container's objects, selecting the Edit|Select All menu item automatically selects all the objects in the right side of the Exchange Administrator.

The View Menu

The View menu is used to filter and sort recipients container's objects that are viewed in the Exchange Administrator (see Figure 6.7). Filtering and sorting recipients can be helpful—as the size of your Exchange organization grows, finding a particular recipient can be difficult. The menu items accessed from the View menu are discussed in the following paragraphs.

The View menu's Mailboxes, Distribution Lists, Custom Recipients, Public Folders, and All menu items are used to define which recipient objects are displayed. A checkmark appears next to the recipient objects that are currently being displayed. Choose All to view all the objects in the recipients container.

Recipients

Recipients can be designated as hidden and, as such, do not show up in the Global Address List. Choose the View menu's Hidden Recipients menu item to display hidden recipients.

Columns

Select the View menu's Columns menu item to change the data columns that are displayed in the right side of the Exchange Administrator. A subsequent dialog box lets you add and remove columns (see Figure 6.8). Column widths can also be adjusted from this dialog box, although you'll likely find it easier to change column widths by using your mouse.

Sort By

Choose the View menu's Sort By menu item to sort the objects that are currently displayed in the right side of the Exchange Administrator. Another menu appears, from which you can choose to sort by display name or by last modified date.

Figure 6.7   The View menu.

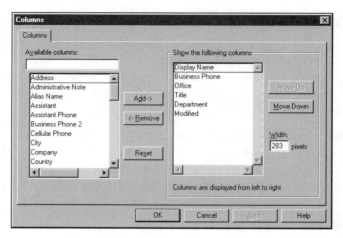

Figure 6.8 The Columns dialog box.

Font

Choosing the View menu's Font menu item brings up the Font dialog box, where you can specify the font used to display Exchange Administrator object information. Changing the font can be particularly useful when viewing the Exchange Administrator output from a distance—from a video projector, for example.

Move Split Bar

Choose the View menu's Move Split Bar menu item to adjust the dividing line between the left and right sides of the Exchange Administrator. The mouse can also be used to move the dividing line.

Status Bar

The View menu's Status Bar menu item is used to toggle the status bar (which appears at the bottom of the Exchange Administrator) on and off. The status bar displays useful information (the number of objects displayed, for instance), so you'll probably want to keep the status bar on.

Toolbar

The View menu's Toolbar menu item toggles the toolbar on and off. The toolbar appears right below the menus.

The Tools Menu

The Tools menu is used to perform various administrative functions (see Figure 6.9). Next to the File menu, the Tools menu is the most often used menu.

Figure 6.9   The Tools menu.

The menu items accessed from the Tools menu are explained in the following paragraphs.

Directory Import

The Exchange Administrator can create or modify recipients by reading the contents of a comma-separated text file. The Tools menu's Directory Import menu item displays a dialog box from which the file name and appropriate options can be specified (see Figure 6.10). Comma-delimited text files can be generated from other messaging systems by using the Microsoft Exchange Migration wizard or by using directory export tools in other messaging systems.

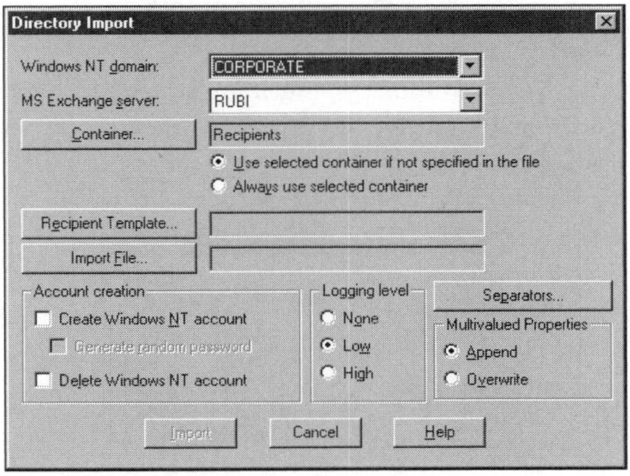

Figure 6.10   The Directory Import dialog box.

Directory Export

Choose the Tools menu's Directory Export menu item to create a text file of the current site's directory information. The contents of this text file can be imported into other messaging systems.

Extract Windows NT Account List

Select the Tools menu's Extract Windows NT Account List menu item to display the Windows NT User Extraction dialog box, from which you can produce a comma-separated file (CSV) containing user information from a Windows NT domain user list (see Figure 6.11). The contents of this CSV file can then be imported into Microsoft Exchange (using the aforementioned Directory Import menu item) to batch create Exchange recipients.

Extract NetWare Account List

Select the Tools menu's Extract NetWare Account List menu item to display the NetWare User Extraction dialog box (see Figure 6.12). From here you can produce a comma-separated file (CSV) containing user information from a Novell NetWare server. The contents of this CSV file can then be imported into Microsoft Exchange (using the aforementioned Directory Import menu item) to batch create Exchange recipients.

Find Recipients

Select the Tools menu's Find Recipients menu item to search your entire orga-nization for a particular recipient. The criteria to search for is entered using the Find Recipients dialog box shown in Figure 6.13.

Move Mailbox

The Tools menu's Move Mailbox menu item is used to move the currently selected mailbox from its current server to another server within the same Microsoft Exchange site.

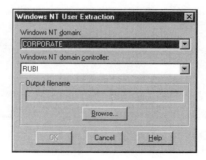

Figure 6.11   The Windows NT User Extraction dialog box.

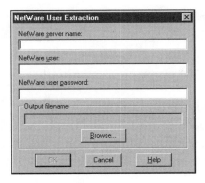

Figure 6.12 The NetWare User Extraction dialog box.

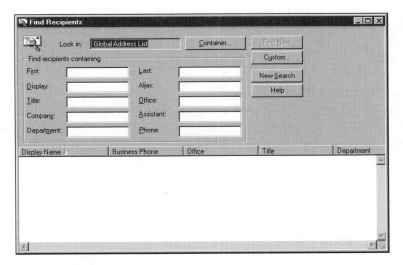

Figure 6.13 The Find Recipients dialog box.

Add To Address Book View

Choose the Tools menu's Add To Address Book View menu item to add the selected recipient to an address book view.

Clean Mailbox

Select the Tools menu's Clean Mailbox menu item to delete messages in the currently selected recipient's mailbox. The criteria for what messages to delete is entered using the Clean Mailbox dialog box.

Start Monitor

After selecting a server monitor or link monitor, selecting the Tools menu's Start Monitor menu item starts the monitor.

Track Message

Choose the Tools menu's Track Message menu item to bring up the Message Tracking Center. The Message Tracking Center is a tool for tracking a message as it travels through an Exchange organization.

Forms Administrator

Choose the Tools menu's Forms Administrator menu item to bring up the Organization Forms Library Administrator. From this dialog box, you can manage forms that were created using the Exchange client's (or Outlook's) form designer tool.

Newsgroup Hierarchies

Choose the Tools menu's Newsgroup Hierarchies menu item to convert an existing Exchange public folder scheme into a hierarchy of newsgroup public folders.

Save Connections On Exit

Select the Tools menu's Save Connections On Exit menu item to save the information about your current Exchange server connections upon exiting the Exchange Administrator. The next time you start Exchange Administrator, the saved connection information is used to reestablish connections to the Exchange servers you were connected to earlier.

Save Connections Now

Select the Tools menu's Save Connections Now menu item to save current Exchange server connection information.

Customize Toolbar

Choose the Tools menu's Customize Toolbar menu item to modify the icons that appear on the toolbar. This is helpful if you want to add or remove icons for your own preferences.

Options

The Tools menu's Options menu item brings up a dialog box of options that affect what information is displayed in the various dialog boxes (see Figure 6.14). The Auto Naming tab is used to specify the format in which you want names to be generated. The Permissions tab is used to specify object-related permission information. Lastly, the File Format tab is used to specify the default file settings for directory import and export functions.

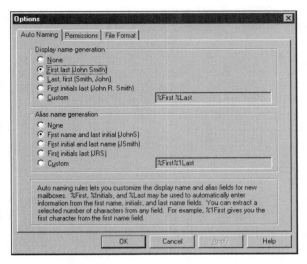

Figure 6.14   The Options dialog box.

The Windows Menu

The Windows menu is the standard Windows menu you're used to seeing. The Refresh menu item is particularly useful, because it requests updated information from the Exchange server and updates the currently displayed information.

The Help Menu

The Help menu is another standard Windows menu. Selecting the Microsoft Exchange Server Help Topics menu item brings up the standard Help information for Microsoft Exchange. Choosing the Books Online menu item launches your Web browser and opens up the official Microsoft Exchange documentation. Lastly, choosing the About Microsoft Exchange Server menu item displays version and copyright information. From the About form, you can click the System Info button to obtain detailed information about the Windows NT computer you're currently using.

Exam Prep Questions

Question 1

> Microsoft Exchange can be managed from a Windows 95 computer.
>
> ○ a. True
>
> ○ b. False

The correct answer to this question is b, False. The Exchange Administrator program is used to manage Exchange Server. The Exchange Administrator does not run on Windows 95; it only runs on Windows NT.

Question 2

> Which of the following are objects (or object containers) in the Exchange hierarchy? [Check all correct answers]
>
> ❑ a. Sites
>
> ❑ b. Servers
>
> ❑ c. Users
>
> ❑ d. Protocols
>
> ❑ e. All of the above

The correct answers to this question are a, b, and d. Sites, servers, and protocols are all Exchange hierarchy objects that can be configured and managed using the Exchange Administrator. Users, though technically considered "objects" from Windows NT's point of view, are not objects in the Exchange hierarchy. Therefore, answers c and e are incorrect.

Question 3

> You can be connected to multiple Exchange servers when in the Exchange Administrator.
>
> ○ a. True
>
> ○ b. False

The correct answer to this question is a, True. Using an MDI interface, the Exchange Administrator can connect to many Exchange servers at the same time. To connect to an additional Exchange server, select the File menu's Connect To Server menu item. Although you can be connected to multiple Exchange servers concurrently, only one connection is considered the current, or *foreground*, server.

Question 4

> Which of the following objects are contained in the (Server) Protocols container object?
>
> ○ a. IMAP4
>
> ○ b. LDAP
>
> ○ c. NNTP
>
> ○ d. POP3
>
> ○ e. All of the above

The correct answer to this question is f. All the listed protocols are contained within the (Server) Protocols container. Each protocol object has its own configuration dialog box.

Question 5

> The Site object is the top item in the Exchange hierarchy.
>
> ○ a. True
>
> ○ b. False

The correct answer to this question is b, False. The Organization object is the top item in the Exchange hierarchy. The Site object is contained within the Organization object.

Question 6

Which object can reveal how much space an individual user's mailbox is taking up?

○ a. Logons

○ b. Private Information Store|Mailbox Resources

○ c. Servers

○ d. Public Information Store|Mailbox Resources

○ e. User mailbox usage cannot be determined in the Exchange Administrator

The correct answer to this question is b. From the Private Information Store|Mailbox Resources object, you can determine how large each user's personal mailbox is—as well as how many items are contained in the mailboxes. The other answers, while informative in themselves, do not represent objects that can reveal mailbox space usage. Therefore, answers a, c, d, and e are incorrect.

Question 7

The Private Information Store's Logons object contains a list of all users who have ever accessed their respective mailboxes.

○ a. True

○ b. False

The correct answer to this question is b, False. The Private Information Store's Logons object displays information about which users are currently logged on to a mailbox located on a server—not whether they have ever accessed their mailboxes.

Question 8

What file formats can be imported into the Exchange Administrator to generate Microsoft Exchange recipients?

○ a. Tab delimited

○ b. Comma separated (CSV)

○ c. EBCDIC

○ d. Word 6.0/95

○ e. All of the above

The correct answer to this question is b. The Exchange Administrator can create or modify recipients by reading the contents of a comma-separated text file. Select the Tools menu's Directory Import menu item. The other file formats listed cannot be imported. Therefore, answers a, c, d, and e are incorrect.

Question 9

> The Servers object represents a specific server in a site.
>
> ○ a. True
>
> ○ b. False

The correct answer to this question is b, False. The Servers object contains all the Exchange servers in the parent site. There can be more than one Exchange server in the Servers object. The Server object (identified by the name of the server) represents a specific server in the server list.

Question 10

> From which messaging systems can the Exchange Administrator extract user lists? [Check all correct answers]
>
> ❏ a. Windows NT
>
> ❏ b. NetWare 3.x
>
> ❏ c. SendMail
>
> ❏ d. LANtastic Messaging System

The correct answers to this question are a and b. By selecting Tools|Extract Windows NT Account List or Tools|Extract NetWare Account List, a comma-separated file (CSV) can be generated that contains user information from a Windows NT or Novell NetWare server. The contents of this CSV file can then be imported into Microsoft Exchange to batch create Exchange recipients. The Exchange Administrator cannot extract user lists from the other systems. Therefore, answers c and d are incorrect.

Question 11

> What actions can be taken on a mailbox, using the Exchange Administrator? [Check all correct answers]
>
> ❑ a. Delete the mailbox
>
> ❑ b. Move the mailbox to another server
>
> ❑ c. Examine the contents of the mailbox
>
> ❑ d. See how many messages are contained in the mailbox
>
> ❑ e. All of the above

The correct answers to this question are a, b, and d. Using the Exchange Administrator, individual mailboxes can be deleted and moved to another server. Mailbox usage—including the total number of messages contained in the mailbox—can also be viewed using the Exchange Administrator. The actual contents of a mailbox cannot be viewed using the Exchange Administrator. Therefore, answers c and e are incorrect.

Question 12

> How can the Microsoft Exchange documentation be accessed online?
>
> ○ a. Insert the Microsoft Exchange CD-ROM and run DOCS.EXE.
>
> ○ b. From the Help|Documentation menu item.
>
> ○ c. It can't; the documentation is not available in electronic format.
>
> ○ d. Insert the Microsoft Exchange Miscellaneous Tools CD-ROM and select the Help|CD Help menu item.
>
> ○ e. None of the above.

The correct answer to this question is e. Microsoft Exchange documentation is in HTML format. To access the documentation online, select the Help menu's Books Online menu item. This launches your Web browser and displays the documentation. The other answers (a, b, c, and d) are incorrect.

Need To Know More?

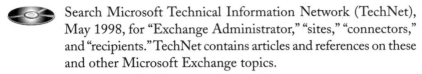

Search Microsoft Technical Information Network (TechNet), May 1998, for "Exchange Administrator," "sites," "connectors," and "recipients." TechNet contains articles and references on these and other Microsoft Exchange topics.

Online Books from the Microsoft Exchange 5.5 CD-ROM contains many references to the subjects discussed in this chapter, including "Operations."

Check out the Microsoft Exchange home page at www.microsoft. com/exchange, where you'll find whitepapers and updated references about managing (configuring, monitoring, and maintaining) Exchange Server.

Visit the Microsoft Knowledge Base and support home page at www.microsoft.com/kb. It contains updated articles on Microsoft Exchange management and monitoring.

Exchange Clients And Client Configuration

7

Terms you'll need to understand:

√ ActiveX, Active Server, and Active Desktop

√ Global Address List (GAL)

√ Hypertext Markup Language (HTML)

√ Hypertext Transfer Protocol (HTTP)

√ Internet Message Access Protocol (IMAP)

√ Lightweight Directory Access Protocol (LDAP)

√ Multipurpose Internet Mail Extensions (MIME)

√ Network News Transfer Protocol (NNTP)

√ Outlook Web Access (OWA)

√ Personal address book (PAB)

√ Personal information manager (PIM)

√ Post Office Protocol (POP)

√ Remote Access Service (RAS)

√ Simple Mail Transfer Protocol (SMTP)

√ Secure Sockets Layer (SSL)

Techniques you'll need to master:

√ Understanding the different ways you can configure Outlook

√ Understanding how to use the Outlook Web Access

Prior to Exchange version 5, there was Exchange the server product and the Exchange client, which shipped with every copy of Windows 95. This greatly confused the end users. With the advent of Exchange 5.5, the word *Exchange* refers to the server product only; Outlook is the name for all client software for Exchange Server. In this chapter, we examine Outlook 98 and its features. We also show you how to use the Outlook Web Access.

Outlook 98

The current version of the client software is Outlook 98, which is as much a personal information manager (PIM) as it is an Exchange client. The Outlook family has an entirely different approach to the email and calendar world with Outlook Express, which has a similar look and feel as the more complex Outlook.

Outlook Express is limited to use for Internet mail only. It wasn't that long ago that Internet mail flexibility came with a price. Internet mail was very simplistic. With the advent of advanced services, such as the Lightweight Directory Access Protocol (LDAP), Internet mail now has almost as many features as a local Exchange server. With LDAP, it's possible to have the equivalent of a really huge Exchange Global Address List (GAL). Of course, the GAL is a separate directory from Internet-based public directories, such as BigFoot and Four11. A second example of upgraded features includes the ability to send Hypertext Markup Language (HTML) inside a message. The cross-platform nature of HTML allows for richer email content across different types of computer systems.

Another Outlook member, Outlook Web Access (OWA), can be installed on the Exchange server, and is the missing link between Exchange and Internet Information Server (IIS). In other words, OWA is the glue that allows the data stored in the Information Store (IS) to be published on the Internet.

First, OWA allows virtually any browser to use public folders (using self-registration) without requiring the user to have an Exchange mailbox. An example of this might be a customer service center that is available to all customers without the need for an Exchange mailbox. From the Exchange mailbox users' viewpoint, OWA can also provide access to the users' calendar data.

Outlook may be installed on the server or on the client machine. Installing on the server greatly increases network traffic; however, it reduces the administrative burden. Wherever you decide to install Outlook, running SETUP.EXE is the first step. If Outlook was installed before Exchange (for example, with Office 97), Outlook will not recognize Exchange and will have to be configured manually. Outlook 98 has two modes. The first is the full Outlook PIM, which lacks the ability to connect to Exchange and is known as the *Internet mode*. A second version has the ability to connect to the Exchange server and is known as the *corporate* or *workgroup mode*. If you need to convert from Internet mode to workgroup mode, go to the Outlook 98 Setup folder and run Setup again; you can choose to upgrade from the CD or the Web.

System Requirements

Here are the Microsoft stated minimum requirements for Outlook 98:

➤ **Processor** 486/66MHz

➤ **Memory** 8MB RAM for Windows 95; 16MB RAM for Windows NT 4.0

➤ **Operating system** Windows 9x or Windows NT 4, Service Pack 3

➤ **Internet Explorer 4.01 installed** (does not have to be the default browser)

Outlook 98 comes with three installation options:

➤ **Minimum** Installs core Outlook 98 files (including Internet Explorer 4.01, Microsoft VM for Java, and multimedia enhancements).

➤ **Standard** Installs the Minimum option plus the Outlook Help files. This is the recommended installation option.

➤ **Full** Installs the Standard option plus database converters, development tools, Microsoft NetMeeting, and Outlook enhancements (Office sounds, animated cursors, and Lotus Organizer converter).

Outlook Client System Requirements

The Outlook client system requires Outlook 98 and Internet Explorer 4.01. If you have Internet Explorer 3 on your computer when you install Outlook 98, it will be automatically upgraded to Internet Explorer 4.01. However, you don't need to use Internet Explorer as your regular browser.

Storage Space Requirements

Table 7.1 shows hard drive sizes for each installation and configuration option. The size of the application on your computer, after you've completed the installation, is called a *footprint*. This number excludes setup and backup files. The last number is the space needed for installation: This is the amount of space necessary on your hard drive to run Setup. This is larger than the final installed disk size because the final footprint uses compression technology.

Table 7.1	Exchange storage requirements for Minimum, Standard, and Full installations.		
Minimum			
What's On Your Computer	**File Size**	**Footprint**	**Space Needed**
IE 4.01 and Outlook 97	15MB	22MB	34MB
IE 4.01 (but not Outlook 97)	15MB	39MB	55MB
No IE 4.01 or Outlook 97	26MB	65MB	102MB
Standard			
What's On Your Computer	**File Size**	**Footprint**	**Space Needed**
IE 4.01 and Outlook 97	16MB	22MB	37MB
IE 4.01 (but not Outlook 97)	16MB	41MB	57MB
No IE 4.01 or Outlook 97	28MB	68MB	104MB
Full			
What's On Your Computer	**File Size**	**Footprint**	**Space Needed**
IE 4.01 and Outlook 97	21MB	32MB	52MB
IE 4.01 (but not Outlook 97)	21MB	53MB	75MB
No IE 4.01 or Outlook 97	33MB	81MB	121MB

Outlook Modes

As Outlook has evolved, there's been more than a little confusion as to what exactly it is, as well as what its place in the computing world is. Outlook 98 can be used in three different ways (or *modes*):

➤ As an Internet client email program with personal information manager (PIM) features. This uses POP3 or IMAP4 for incoming mail, and SMTP for outgoing mail. The name used for this configuration is *Internet mode*.

➤ As a standalone PIM with no email. The name used for this configuration is *standalone mode*.

➤ As an email client/PIM for Microsoft Exchange Server, Microsoft Mail, cc:Mail, Internet mail servers, and other servers with MAPI clients. This is commonly called *corporate* or *workgroup mode*.

Storage

Data can be stored in several ways. For example, if you don't leave mail on the Exchange server, the mail is stored locally in a PST file. The PST file is where mail folders and all the messages within them are stored. When mail folders and messages are stored locally and user profiles are in effect, the PST file is stored in each user's profile subdirectory. Also, if the mail is stored locally and profiles are used, the PST file is stored under the following Profiles subdirectory:

```
D:\WINNT\Profiles\Tcat\Application Data\Microsoft\
Office\8.5\Outlook
```

Experienced Exchange administrators do not store mail in PST files, because this approach leaves it up to clients to back up their personal folders and messages. If personal folders and messages reside on the server, however, the server should be subject to regular and reliable backup, which will protect each user's folders and messages. Sometimes a PST file can be used as an import/export holding bay of sorts, which is useful when you must delete and re-create a user's mailbox and cannot afford to lose the mail. To work with mail, you need to know two file extensions:

➤ **.PAB** The extension for files containing personal address books

➤ **.SCD** The extension for files where Schedule+ information is held

Exchange Profiles

Profiles are very useful for reconfiguring how a user's mail is handled as his or her day changes. Clients using laptops can make liberal use of profiles to suit their sometimes ever-changing environment. You can create a new profile by clicking Start|Settings|Control Panel|Mail. Options for this sample account include working from a LAN or from a dial-up connection (see Figure 7.1).

Laptop users are best served using offline folders. You can configure the use of offline folders by following these steps:

1. Select Start|Settings|Control Panel and then double-click the Mail icon.

2. Choose a profile you want to configure for the offline folder.

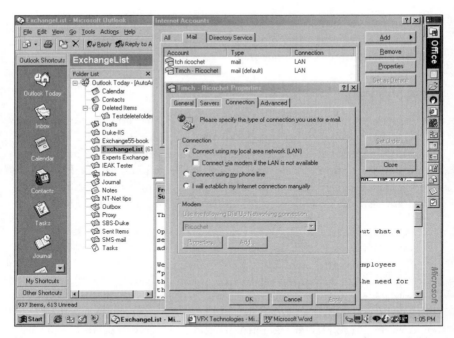

Figure 7.1   Remote users can attempt a LAN connection first and then attempt a RAS connection.

3. Select the Services tab, choose Exchange Server, and click Properties.

4. Select the Advanced tab and click the offline folder setting.

5. In the File box, enter the path and file name of your folder. Click OK.

 Use an OST file on the server as a backup for the user. Exchange currently has no native method for restoring a single mailbox without you restoring the entire Exchange Server Information Store and then copying out the single mailbox of data.

It's easier to create a profile via a wizard. To create a profile, run the Profile wizard:

1. Select Start|Settings|Control Panel and double-click the Mail icon.

2. Click Show Profiles and then the Add button.

3. Select one or more services you would like to apply to this profile. Click Next.

4. Select a name for your profile (for example, Office Connection).

5. Fill in the data to each account.

You must complete each of these steps for your profile to function. Internet accounts will need mail account data, such as where the SMTP and POP servers live. Personal Address Books (PAB files) can be created from scratch or connected to an existing valid path on either the local drive or the server.

Once a profile is created, you can select a particular profile to be the default profile, or you can always select a profile when first entering Exchange. This presto chango method comes in very handy for remote clients. Your roving users can flip from connecting using the LAN to connecting using a dial-up connection.

The ways a user can interact with a profile are not static events. For example, ISPs change; therefore, phone numbers, the Simple Mail Transfer Protocol (SMTP) used, and so on must be updated. As time goes on, a service may need to be added or deleted.

To see what services are installed on a computer, select Start|Settings|Control Panel and then double-click the Mail icon. The Services tab appears. Adding services that are not already listed places them on the hard drive for availability and adds them to the list of choices for setting up a profile.

Adding a service to a profile may require choosing a particular profile first. For example, it wouldn't be wise to add fax services to a profile if the client doesn't have access to a modem. Be careful to distinguish between removing a service from a profile and removing a service from the Services tab. Removing a service from a profile means the profile will not use that service. Removing a service from the Services tab means that the service will not be available on the hard drive. This disables the service.

 It's a good idea to examine all your profiles before removing a service from the Services tab. If you delete any profile, this does not delete the data residing in any PST files when you delete the profile associated with that service.

Multiple Profiles

An Exchange profile determines the way your mail is handled. You must decide how mail will be routed and stored based on user needs. Here are some examples for personal folders:

➤ Single user; network computer (desktop); PST files stored locally (no backup on server)

➤ Multiple users; network computer (desktop); PST files stored locally; use passwords

➤ Roaming profile; network computer (desktop); PST files stored on server

Items that are typically stored in personal folders include personal archives by folder, containing a subject or project (for example, our very active ExchangeList), appointments, and journal entries.

Putting Outlook To Work

The clean look of Outlook 98 hides the deep complexity of the industry's latest personal information manager (PIM). Figure 7.2 shows, in the middle of the screen, the Folder List. It contains all the folders. The folders may contain subfolders. Selecting a folder (in Figure 7.2, it is the msexchange mailing list) displays the messages in the upper-right corner. Finally, the lower-right corner contains the selected message. This way you can see all your mail folders, the messages contained in a specific folder, and a preview of any single message you have selected in that folder all in one screen.

Running down the list of folders, you'll see Outlook Today, which allows you to look at tasks, find a contact, and access the calendar. The Contacts folder is a default folder; it contains the information you need to reach people. You can add contacts to this folder in three ways:

➤ Click File|New|Contact.

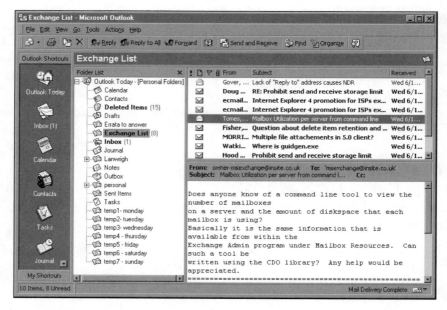

Figure 7.2 A simple view of Outlook.

➤ A "three finger salute" (Ctrl+Shift+C).

➤ Right-click the From area in a mail message and select Add To Contacts from the pop-up menu.

Next on the screen, you'll see a deleted item folder, another default folder. Notice that there's a subfolder under deleted items called TestDeleteFolder. This folder is a custom creation for this particular installation and is used to test rules for mail management. Drafts is another standard folder; it's the home for any work in progress. The rest of the folders, up to the Inbox folder, are custom creations.

 A boldfaced folder name visually indicates that new mail has arrived in that folder.

The next folder is the Inbox folder. This is where all new mail ends up if a rule wizard isn't sending it somewhere else. Finally, the Journal folder is another default folder. Notice that it's possible to track your workflow. The default for tracking workflow is disabled.

Appointments

Electronic appointments have several advantages over appointments written down on paper. Not only are electronic appointments easier to change, it is also easier to distribute changes or to share changes with other workers to determine group scheduling. It's even possible to post an appointment to a Web page.

When you create an appointment, select the start time of the meeting. By default, you're informed of the upcoming event with a 15-minute advance alert. You can invite other members, schedule reoccurring meetings, and even interface with Microsoft NetMeeting for an online discussion.

For detailed information on NetMeeting, refer to *MCSE IE 4 Administration Exam Cram* published by The Coriolis Group. For the purposes of this topic, you only need to know that you can use a LAN or the Internet with NetMeeting. Also, with a sound card and video camera installed, you can have a virtual meeting, complete with audio and video. NetMeeting also includes an electronic whiteboard, a type-based chat area, and the ability to share a computer program.

You can create an appointment in several ways. The most obvious way is to select the calendar from your folder area and click on the day in the calendar. Perhaps a better way to create an appointment is to select a person in the

Contacts folder and then select Actions|New Meeting With Contact. This method allows not only a fast and efficient way to organize a meeting, but also a way to send email to invite the contacts to the meeting.

Because situations change, you may need to change a meeting. There are two methods for changing a meeting time: You can drag-and-drop the appointment or you can double-click to change the time directly. Outlook 98 supports different time zones for traveling users or for scheduling meetings with someone in a different time zone. Simply select Tools|Options from within the calendar to make time zone changes.

Contacts

Contact information can be confusing. This is because Outlook 98 can connect to the Global Address List (GAL) on the Exchange server or to its own Contacts database (if you have multiple places where addresses can be stored).

Protocols

Without protocols, communication is not possible. Outlook 98 supports either IMAP4 or POP3 as the Internet mail protocol. Remember that IMAP4 is a new protocol option that allows a user to leave messages on a server. It can be more efficient than POP3. It's possible to support mail from multiple mail accounts, although each account can have only one protocol.

When Outlook 98 connects to an Exchange server (corporate or workgroup mode), the program receives notification via a remote procedure call. RPCs send commands to another computer that operates on behalf of the requesting computer. This creates a fair amount of network traffic, so an RPC would not be effective with a modem connection. Internet accounts require a connection to the Internet and may have scheduled checking for new messages.

Advanced Features

In this section, we'll look at only one feature: the Organize key. Keep in mind that the Organize key is context sensitive, which means that the button's behavior changes based on where you are. Organize behaves differently, with different options, when you're in Contacts, say, versus when you're mailing messages.

To see how Organize works, look at the mail folder ExchangeList in Figure 7.2. In this window, the folder is full of Exchange-specific messages. Although this is a huge stash of email, it is directly related to the technical discussion of Exchange 5 and Exchange 5.5. To subscribe to this list service, see the "Need

To Know More?" section at the end of this chapter. The average amount of mail from this listserv (a.k.a. Usenet newsgroup) is in excess of 100 messages a day. Attempting to keep track of what is developing based on the time a message was sent is not very efficient, so let's organize a view (see Figure 7.3). To organize a view, follow these steps:

1. Highlight Exchange List.

2. Select Organize.

3. Select Using Views.

4. Scroll down to By Conversation Topic.

To save some time here, we cheated. After Outlook 98 organized the messages by conversation topic, we expanded one of the topics for the screen shown in Figure 7.3. Notice that the originating message has a closed envelope and that the response, which arrived later, is open and flagged.

Here's what happens in this configuration: When a message comes in, the Rules wizard sorts out the traffic so that Exchange mail is separated from another heavily used list for Systems Management Server (SMS) topics. When

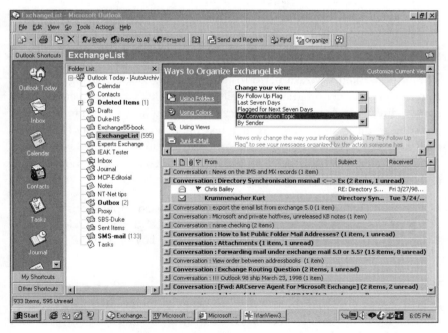

Figure 7.3   Outlook 98 organizes the messages as soon as the By Conversation Topic is selected.

you go into the Exchange mail folder, each message can be checked for importance without actually opening it by viewing the message in the pane. As with many of the messages from this group, the message shown in Figure 7.3 looked like a good question. It was left without being opened to see what subsequent pearls of wisdom showed up. When a good response arrived, it followed the first message according to topic. After being opened, and possibly printed for later study, the message was flagged as a reminder.

 Outlook 98 can flag messages with a variety of different options. Flags can be used for the Read (very useful if flagging and forwarding), Review, For Your Information, Call, Forward, Do Not Forward, No Response Necessary, Reply, and Reply To All options.

Upgrading Outlook

Upgrading from a previous version of Outlook is usually painless. The area of concern, however, involves any rules written with the Rules wizard. Outlook rules need to be re-created in Outlook 98. Rules from previous versions do not function and need to be upgraded. Furthermore, it's possible to create a conflict between rules that are run on the server side and rules that are run on the client side. The user must make a choice which rule set to use—server based or client based.

Importing And Exporting

The Import/Export wizard performs all importing and exporting. Selecting Import from another program or file allows Outlook 98 to import email information directly from other PIMs or text files. If you have a program that does not support direct importing, create a text file in a comma/quote format and then import your data. Outlook imports information from legacy programs with invisible conversion; such programs include Act, ECCO, Lotus Organizer, and SideKick.

 Outlook Express and other Internet-based applications such as Eudora (Lite and Pro), MS Internet Mail and News, and Netscape (Mail and Messenger), are all supported by Outlook 98.

You can export data from Outlook to a variety of Microsoft programs, such as Access, Excel, and FoxPro, as well as to personal folders. You can also send information to dBASE. In addition, mail-merges (comma delineated) are also supported by the wizard.

Deleted Item Recovery

Exchange 5.5 has improved deleted item recovery. To recover a deleted item, follow these steps:

1. On the Outlook Bar, click Outlook.

2. Click Deleted Items.

3. Select the items you want to retrieve.

4. Right-click the selection and then click Move To Folder on the short-cut menu.

5. In the Move The Selected Items To The Folder box, click the folder to which you want to move the items.

For remote users with underpowered laptop computers, Microsoft has released the Outlook Web Access (OWA), which allows Exchange to be accessed with a browser client. This places much of the computing resource needs on the server side.

 When using Outlook Web Access over the Internet, keep Exchange behind a firewall. Otherwise, you open your Exchange system to the world without security.

OWA is an optional program that can be installed when you first install Exchange or added later. If you did not add OWA using the Complete or Custom installation, you can do so later by rerunning the installation program and selecting OWA to be installed.

OWA allows Exchange services such as scheduling and electronic messaging to become available via the Internet. OWA requires Active Desktop, Active Server (IIS with Active Server Pages), and ActiveX. You'll also need a browser that supports frames and JavaScript. This makes it possible to run OWA from a system based on Windows (16 or 32 bit), Unix, or Macintosh, with accessibility to messages, public folders, Global Address Lists, and calendars. The message base may use attachments when using OWA.

It's reasonable to use the Challenge Handshake Authentication Protocol (CHAP) for anything but access to public folders. If you cannot use CHAP, you must ensure security with other measures. Remember, in NT, you have the option of using Dial-Up Networking with Remote Access Service (RAS). One of your security choices is CHAP.

In the event that you have public folders available via a Web browser, you may not want to use CHAP, because self-registration provides the required login to post anonymously. Exchange will use self-registration for the incoming user, eliminating the need to have a mailbox on Exchange. The IIS server communicates to the Exchange server using RPC. As mentioned in Chapter 3, Service Pack 3 (or later) and NT 4 are required.

OWA allows you to use Secure Sockets Layer (SSL). When you do this, the port required for communication moves from port 80 to port 995. To access Exchange via OWA, enter this at the login point:

```
http://[IIS-Server Name]/exchange
```

Exam Prep Questions

Question 1

> You have Exchange 5.5 running on Windows NT 4 with Service Pack 3. Internet Information Server with Active Server Pages is installed. You would like to install Outlook Web Access to the Windows 98-based laptops used by your company's sales team. What do you need to do?
>
> ○ a. Make sure you've installed OWA in Exchange Server by running SETUP.EXE to see if OWA support is installed. If not, install it.
>
> ○ b. Install Personal Web Server on each laptop.
>
> ○ c. Install OWA on each laptop.
>
> ○ d. All of the above.
>
> ○ e. None of the above.

The correct answer is a. If Outlook Web Access is not installed on the server, you must install it. Answers b, c, d, and e are all incorrect.

Question 2

> Your company wants to have public folder access available to all users so they can post questions to your technical support group. What do you need to do?
>
> ○ a. Create a folder shortcut for each folder you want to make public.
>
> ○ b. Order the self-registration CD kit (MS Part #288-0561616).
>
> ○ c. Assign each user an Exchange mailbox when he or she sends in the registration card.
>
> ○ d. All of the above.

The correct answer is a. To make public folder access available to all users, you would create a folder shortcut for each folder you want to make public. There is no self-registration CD; therefore, answer b is incorrect. Answer c would work, in theory, if you had a very small number of users and the users had registration cards to send in. However, it would be very impractical, if not impossible, to get a large number of users to send in registration cards and to give each of them an Exchange mailbox; therefore, answer c is incorrect. Performing the tasks listed in answers a, b, and c would not make public folder access available to all users; therefore, answer d is incorrect.

Question 3

> You have a new employee who recently joined your firm. The new employee already has a personal laptop and uses Outlook 98. When this person joined the firm, you created a mailbox for the new user. You cannot find a way to have Outlook use Exchange. Why?
>
> ○ a. Outlook 98 is not used with Exchange.
>
> ○ b. The installation of Outlook 98 is incomplete. Rerun setup from the Outlook Setup folder.
>
> ○ c. The new employee needs to use Outlook Web Access.
>
> ○ d. None of the above.

Answer b is correct. Outlook 98 has two modes, Internet mode and corporate or workgroup mode. When the user installed Outlook 98, Setup didn't find an Exchange server, so the software for workgroup or corporate mode wasn't installed. Answer a is incorrect because Outlook is the family name for all Exchange clients, beginning with version 5. Answer c would allow limited use of Exchange, but the user would only get access to mail and his personal calendar; therefore, answer c is incorrect. Finally, answer d is incorrect because the choices include the correct response in this case.

Question 4

> Once you configure an offline folder, you cannot synchronize it with the server.
>
> ○ a. True
>
> ○ b. False

The answer is b, False. An offline folder enables a user to connect to an Exchange server, update all data, and get offline, thus reducing connection costs.

Question 5

There are ____ ways to change a meeting time for an event that is already created.

- ○ a. 0 (Once a meeting is created, you must honor your agreements.)
- ○ b. 1
- ○ c. 2
- ○ d. 3
- ○ e. 4

Answer c is correct. You can double-click the appointment time and edit it, or you can view an appointment and drag the start time or end time, or both. Answer a, zero is incorrect, because not being able to change a meeting time would greatly limit the usefulness of Exchange. Answer b is not correct, in keeping with the design concepts of most Microsoft products, which dictate that a user should have at least two choices, wherever possible. Choices d or e are also incorrect.

Question 6

From what source can Outlook 98 retrieve contact information?

- ○ a. Global Address List
- ○ b. Stub directory
- ○ c. Knowledge Consistency Checker
- ○ d. Information Store

Answer a is correct. Outlook 98 can retrieve contact information from the Global Address List. The stub directory can be thought of as a seed or framework for setting up a new server within a site, which will replicate data from another server (but that is not what the question asked for); therefore, answer b is incorrect. Answer c is incorrect because the KCC is used to check the database for data. Finally, the Information Store is used to hold messages, both public and private; therefore, answer d is incorrect.

Question 7

> Which version of Internet Explorer is required by Outlook 98?
>
> ○　a. IE 2
>
> ○　b. IE 3
>
> ○　c. IE 4
>
> ○　d. IE 4.01

The correct choice is d, Internet Explorer 4.01. None of the previous versions of IE will work with Outlook 98; therefore, answers a, b, and c are incorrect.

Question 8

> What is the minimum processor requirement for Outlook 98?
>
> ○　a. 486/33MHz
>
> ○　b. 486/66MHz
>
> ○　c. 486/100MHz
>
> ○　d. Pentium

Choice b is correct. Keep in mind that 66MHz is the minimum Outlook 98 will support. Its performance in the real world, however, might not be acceptable. A 486/33MHz processor simply does not have the horsepower to run Outlook 98; therefore, answer a is incorrect. Answers c and d are incorrect because they are not the minimum requirement asked for in the question.

Question 9

> What is the minimum amount of RAM required for Outlook 98 when using Windows NT?
>
> ○　a. 8MB
>
> ○　b. 12MB
>
> ○　c. 16MB
>
> ○　d. 24MB

The correct answer is c. Because the question asked for the minimum amount of RAM, which is 16MB, answers a, b, and d are incorrect.

Question 10

Outlook Web Access supports which of the following? [Check all correct answers]

❑ a. Calendar

❑ b. Public folders

❑ c. Exchange Private Mailbox

❑ d. Directory replication

Choices a, b, and c are correct. Outlook Web Access does not support directory replication; therefore, answer d is incorrect.

Question 11

Because Outlook Web Access is a "light" program, it's not possible to have message attachments.

○ a. True

○ b. False

The correct answer is b, False. Outlook Web Access does support mail attachments.

Question 12

Your sales force travels frequently. They use laptops so they can connect both to the Exchange server when in the office and to an ISP when traveling in the field. You are not using Outlook Web Access. One of your sales staff has come to you complaining that their laptop "ate" critical contact information, needed for a proposal. What happened to the contact information?

○ a. The laptop corrupted the contact information, and it is now lost.

○ b. The user didn't save the contact information. More training of that user is required.

○ c. The user was in Internet mode, so the contact information is in the PST file.

○ d. None of the above.

The correct answer is c, the user was in Internet mode, and therefore contact information has been stored in the PST file. This is a common challenge facing you as the Exchange administrator. Users frequently are not aware of the fact that information can be stored in two different places. When not connected to an Exchange server, Internet mode is used in place of corporate or workgroup mode. This frequently leads users to the belief that the data is somehow gone. Although it is possible for a PST file to become corrupt, we have no indication that this has happened, therefore choice a is incorrect. Choice b is not valid because it is difficult to enter information into contacts and exit without saving. A user would be prompted to save changes first, if they choose File|Exit. Answer d is incorrect because we have a valid answer.

Question 13

> Experienced Exchange administrators ask users to store data in PST folders to keep network traffic down.
>
> O a. True
> O b. False

The correct answer is b, False. A PST file is useful for standalone use, such as connecting to the Internet and collecting mail from a personal account. A PST folder is sometimes used by Exchange administrators for moving information from a user's mailbox while that mailbox is moved or deleted and re-created. Experienced administrators prefer not to use PST files because they place the requirement of backups on the shoulders of the users. If a PST file is lost, the data is gone. If an Exchange system is lacking performance due to network traffic, reconfiguration of the Exchange system and/or a faster network is needed. Data can only be backed up if it's on the Exchange server.

Question 14

> How many profiles are supported by Outlook 98?
>
> O a. 1
> O b. 2
> O c. 3
> O d. Unlimited

The correct choice is d, Unlimited. A user may have as many profiles as the situation warrants. Each profile can have as many or as few services per profile as needed. It's also possible for a profile to have multiple versions of one service. Care should be taken not to create an excess volume of profiles. Because the number of profiles is unlimited, answers a, b, and c are incorrect.

Question 15

Time zones can be changed in Outlook 98 for which reasons? [Check all correct answers]

❏ a. To find out what time it is in another city

❏ b. To schedule a meeting with a contact in a different city

❏ c. To change the time zone Outlook 98 is using when you're traveling with a laptop

❏ d. To change when a reminder timer should alert a user

Answers b and c are correct. A user may need to contact someone in a different time zone for a meeting time, or a user may be traveling with a laptop and need to correct the time his or her schedule is using. Answer a is incorrect because you're better served by selecting the clock in the lower-right corner of the desktop. Reminder warnings are not part of the time zone configuration; therefore, answer d is incorrect.

Question 16

You've recently converted from Outlook version 8.02 to Outlook 98. Your users are having some trouble getting incoming messages to sort correctly to different folders. You did not have this trouble before. What is wrong?

○ a. Folders need to be re-created for Outlook 98.

○ b. The rules from Outlook need to be regenerated with the Rules wizard.

○ c. Rules need to be regenerated for the Exchange server.

○ d. None of the above.

For this situation, answer b is correct. The rules from Outlook need to be regenerated with the Rules wizard. The rules in previous versions of Outlook do not seem to work well with Outlook 98. Remember that it's possible to create two different sets of rule wizards—client based and server based. Because of this, it's possible to create a conflict between server-based rules and client-based rules. That makes answer c tempting. However, you have no indication that rules on the server were causing a challenge; therefore, answer c is incorrect. When you're installing Outlook 98, all folders that existed follow forward; therefore, answer a is incorrect. The final answer, d, is incorrect because a valid answer exists.

Question 17

The Organize key's behavior changes depending on where you are in Outlook 98.

○ a. True

○ b. False

The answer is a, True. Outlook 98 is context sensitive. When you're at the Inbox, for example, an option in Organize is to create a rule for filing, deleting, and so on. When you're viewing Contacts, the Organize button allows you to change the view, just like with mail messages, but instead of a rule wizard option for where to store mail, it offers you the ability to create different categories of contacts.

Need To Know More?

 Gerber, Barry. *Mastering Microsoft Exchange Server 5.5 for Windows NT*, 3rd Edition. Alameda, CA: Sybex Publishing, 1998. ISBN: 0-7821-2237-X. With more than 1,000 pages, this book is excellent for those new to Exchange.

 Visit www.slipstick.com is one of the best Exchange client-side Web sites available. It includes numerous links and subfolders of Outlook add-ins (freeware and shareware). Most of the latest tips and tricks for Outlook begin life here.

 Visit www.msexchange.org is where the world masters of MS Exchange live. The list has heavy traffic, averaging hundreds of messages per day. You are strongly urged to subscribe, and to read, without posting.

 Visit www.microsoft.com/exchange/default.asp is the official site for Exchange. At the time of this writing, it was possible to download an evaluation version of Exchange 5.5 for your study.

Intersite Connectors

8

Terms you'll need to understand:

√ Bridgehead server

√ Connector cost

√ Dynamic RAS Connector

√ Gateway address routing table (GWART)

√ Internet Mail Service

√ Site Connector

√ Target server

√ X.400 Connector

Techniques you'll need to master:

√ Understanding how Exchange communicates between sites

√ Configuring the Site Connector between two sites

√ Understanding when to use the X.400 Connector to communicate between sites

√ Understanding the configuration options available for the Internet Mail Service

√ Establishing a connection between two remote sites using the Dynamic RAS Connector

√ Understanding how Exchange routes messages across multiple connectors

It's not uncommon for an organization to have multiple sites within its network; often this is due to geographic limitations, network infrastructure, or administrative needs. When two sites are connected and information is transferred between them, this is known as *intersite communication*, as opposed to communication within a site (or *intrasite communication*).

With intrasite communication, servers communicate directly with each other using either the Message Transfer Agent (MTA) or the Directory Service (DS). Messages are delivered through MTA-to-MTA communication and directory information is delivered through DS-to-DS communication; both use the remote procedure call (RPC) protocol to communicate. All intrasite configuration is done automatically by the Exchange servers. Within a site, it's assumed that the availability and speed of the network is high and the servers can communicate directly with each other. Between sites, however, high speed communication isn't always guaranteed. This chapter focuses on the intersite communication and the connectors that make intersite email communication possible.

Intersite Communication Explored And Explained

Intersite communication is more complex and requires some manual configuration. High-speed connections between the sites are not necessary. An Exchange component, called a *connector*, must be installed at each site in order for information to pass between the sites. In a multiple-site situation, the MTA transfers all information, regardless of type. Instead of the DS directly transferring directory-related information to the other DS, it places the directory-related information in a mail message and uses the MTA to deliver the data.

There are two types of connectors: messaging connectors and the Directory Replication Connector. Here are the four main messaging connectors:

➤ Site Connector

➤ X.400 Connector

➤ Internet Mail Service

➤ Dynamic RAS Connector

The Directory Replication Connector transfers directory information between sites. The Directory Replication Connector is different from the other connectors because it can use any of the messaging connectors to relay directory information between the servers.

Some of the connectors can be used to provide communication between foreign (Exchange and non-Exchange) systems. Examples of foreign systems include the Internet Mail Service and the X.400 Connector. When used to communicate with foreign systems, the connector can take an Exchange message and translate it into the format of the foreign system, allowing the foreign client to read it. The reverse is also true; the connector can take a foreign message and translate it into the Exchange format so that Exchange users can read it.

Common Connector Properties

Two connector properties—the address space and the connector cost—are common to all the connectors. When a connector is created outside the site, a logical path must be created to allow the MTA to determine how to get the messages to their final destination. This logical path is the address space, and it must be unique for each recipient. The format of the address space depends on the format of the remote messaging system. For example, if you're sending a message to a Simple Mail Transfer Protocol (SMTP) network, the SMTP address space will be used. Some sample address space entries are shown in Table 8.1.

 Think of address space as an email address less the recipient name.

A connector does not only have an address space for its own messaging system; it can have address space entries for different messaging systems, as well. For example, the X.400 Connector can be used to send messages to a remote Internet mail system as well as to a remote X.400 mail system.

You can create multiple connectors between two sites. The connectors can be the same type (for example, both IMS Connectors) or different types (for example, an IMS Connector and an X.400 Connector). The only exception to this rule is the Site Connector, which allows only one connector between two sites. Using multiple connectors balances the load and increases fault tolerance in your Exchange organization. As long as one of the connectors is operating, messages will be delivered between sites.

Table 8.1 Sample address space entries.		
System	**Address**	**Address Space**
X.400	g=Bill;s=Gates;p=microsoft;c=us	c=us;p=microsoft...
MS Mail	MS:Microsoft/Redmond/Bgates	Microsoft/Redmond
IMS	bgates@microsoft.com	microsoft.com

The MTA checks the cost of the connector when choosing which connector to use. You can specify a cost value of 1 to 100. The lower the cost, the more frequently the MTA will use the connector. For example, you can install a Site Connector with a cost of 1 and a Dynamic RAS Connector with a cost of 50 for fault tolerance. If the MTA cannot send messages using the Site Connector, it will attempt to use the Dynamic RAS Connector. If your sites are in different geographic locations, you wouldn't want the Dynamic RAS Connector to be used all the time due to long distance charges. Assigning it a higher cost guarantees that it will only be used in emergencies. Cost connectors are shown in Figure 8.1.

The Site Connector

The Site Connector, which tells the MTA component of Exchange how to transfer messages to a remote site, is the easiest way to configure two sites for

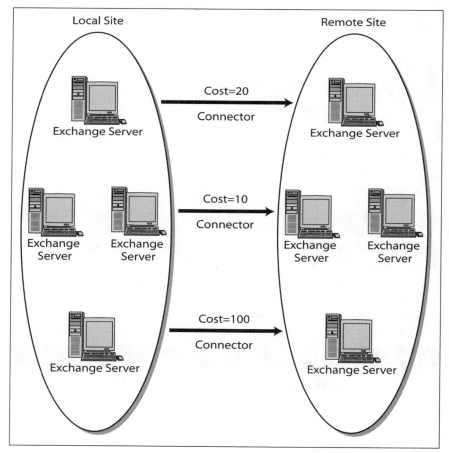

Figure 8.1   Connector costs.

communication. With the Site Connector installed, the MTA can handle intersite as well as intrasite communication. The Site Connector maintains a list of target servers in the remote site. A *target server* is a server in the remote site that the local MTA can use to send intersite messages. Any server within the remote site can be used as a target server. How the Site Connector works is illustrated in Figure 8.2.

When the local MTA needs to transfer a message to a remote site, it selects a target server from the target list and delivers the message to that server. The remote server is not necessarily the final destination of the message; the target server may need to transfer the message to another remote server. This occurs until the message is delivered to its final destination. There's a maximum of one hop for any message being delivered to a remote site. The concept of Site Connector bridgehead servers is illustrated in Figure 8.3.

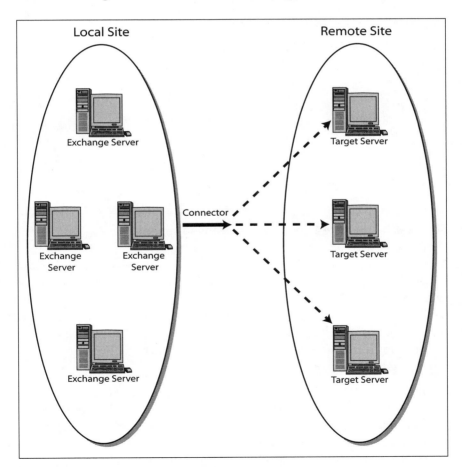

Figure 8.2   The Site Connector target servers.

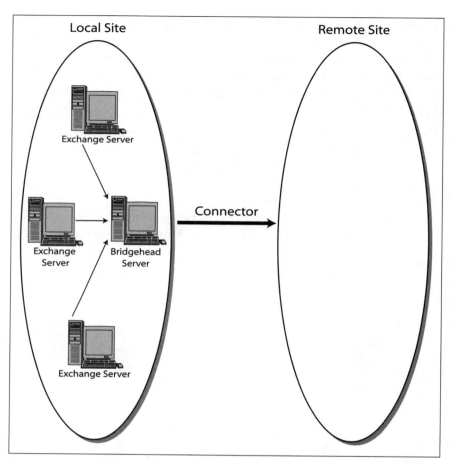

Figure 8.3 The Site Connector bridgehead servers.

You can also configure the Site Connector to work with messaging bridgehead servers. You can think of the messaging bridgehead server as a gateway for the site. A messaging bridgehead server receives mail from servers within a site and delivers those messages to either a messaging bridgehead server or a target server in the remote site. This enables you to specify which server will be used to communicate between sites, and it offloads some of the message transfer processing to another server.

Because the Site Connector uses RPC for intersite communications, it requires a permanent, high-speed connection (128Kbps ISDN or higher is recommended) between the sites. The Site Connector can use any network protocol that supports RPCs, such as NetBEUI, TCP/IP, or IPX/SPX. Keep in mind, however, NetBEUI is not a routable protocol.

In order to transfer messages to a remote site, the local MTA must authenticate itself on the remote site server using a service account. The account that is used for this process depends on the configuration of the two sites. Here are some of the common configurations:

➤ **A single account in a single domain or two domains with a two-way trust** If both Exchange sites are in the same Windows NT domain, both sites can use the same service account. If the two sites are in different Windows NT domains, the service account can be used only if a two-way trust relationship is in place.

➤ **A single account in two domains with a one-way trust** If two sites are in different Windows NT domains, you can create a remote account with the same permissions as the service account in the local site. The local site must then trust the remote site's Windows NT domain.

➤ **A specific remote service account in two domains with no trust** Using the Override page, you can specify a remote service account to be used in the remote Windows NT domain. You may want to do this if you do not want to set up trust relationships.

 The Site Connector is the most efficient connector that ships with Microsoft Exchange. It's approximately 20 percent faster than the X.400 Connector, due to the fact that no message translation is required when transferring messages to the remote site. Another nice feature of the Site Connector is that it provides automatic configuration for the remote side of the connection.

Here are the five property pages for the Site Connector:

➤ **General** Identifies the target site and allows you to specify a connection cost to the connector. You can also specify either any server or a specific server as the local messaging bridgehead server. If a specific server is not selected as the messaging bridgehead, any server in the local site can send messages to the remote site using the Site Connector.

➤ **Permissions** You set permissions on the Site Connector the same way you would any other object permissions. You must have sufficient authority to set the permissions.

➤ **Target Servers** Identifies which server will receive the incoming messages to the site and the cost associated with the server. This can be used for load-balancing and fault tolerance. The server with the lowest cost receives all the mail, unless it's unavailable.

➤ **Address Space** Identifies the X.400 address for the remote site. You can also add, edit, or remove any address. A different cost can be specified for each address space to facilitate the selection of an address space to use.

➤ **Override** Allows you to enter information about the service account of the remote site. Use this property page if the service account in the remote site is different than the service account in the local site.

Each target server can be assigned a cost. The costs assigned to the target servers are different from the cost assigned to the Site Connector itself. When Exchange transfers information between sites, the lowest-cost connector will always be used. The costs assigned to the target servers act more as a load-balancing option. The cost values range from 0 to 100, where a value of 0 means the server will be used 100 percent of the time and a value of 100 means that the server will be used only if other paths are not available.

The X.400 Connector

The X.400 Connector is based on the CCITT X.400 standard and is similar to the Site Connector in that it can use messaging bridgehead servers to route mail traffic. It cannot, however, use target servers; the X.400 Connector always uses messaging bridgehead servers for its message transfer. The X.400 Connector allows you, as the administrator, to restrict times for the connector to be operating and to specify which users can send mail to the remote site. Two sites connected by an X.400 Connector are shown in Figure 8.4.

With a Site Connector, the MTA of the local site connects with the MTA of the remote site to transfer the information. With an X.400 Connector, each server must pass its information to the messaging bridgehead server. The messaging bridgehead server then connects to its partner bridgehead server in the remote site and transfers the information. If necessary, the remote messaging bridgehead server then passes the information to the final destination.

The X.400 Connector requires less bandwidth than the Site Connector (low to medium bandwidth). Because all information must be converted to messages before information can be transferred, the connector tends to slow down. Also, the X.400 Connector is more complex to configure than the Site Connector (eight property pages versus the Site Connector's five). Because all mail must flow through the messaging bridgehead servers, messaging bottlenecks can result, slowing down intersite communication.

There are some benefits to using the X.400 Connector. For example, it's the most generic Exchange connector and can be used to connect to any X.400

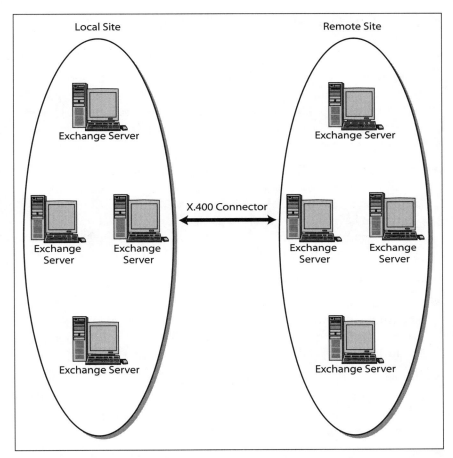

Figure 8.4   The X.400 Connector.

system. Also, the X.400 Connector allows you to restrict message size and user access.

The X.400 Connector requires more configuration than does the Site Connector. You must perform two steps in order to install the X.400 Connector. First, you install the MTA transport stack, and then you install the X.400 Connector.

The MTA transport stack configures Microsoft Exchange to use the network transport used by the Windows NT server. You must configure one of the appropriate network transports before the connector is configured. Here are the available network transports for the X.400 Connector:

➤ **TCP/IP** The Exchange server uses the Windows NT TCP/IP services. The MTA uses port 102 to communicate.

➤ **TP4/CLNP** The Exchange server has an interface that allows it to work with the Windows NT TP4 driver. This interface is used to communicate with remote systems using TP4 for message transport. In CLNP, data is transferred without using a connection request; TP4 is designed for use in a connectionless mode network. The server running the transport stack determines TP4 network address information.

➤ **TP0/X.25** TP0/X.25 provides both dial-up and direct communication. X.25 network software must be installed and running on the server before you install the MTA transport stack. Multiple X.25 transport stacks can be installed on a server, and you can install multiple X.25 port adapters on one server. Be aware, however, that a separate MTA transport stack is required for each X.25 port on an adapter.

Here are the X.400 Connector Properties pages:

➤ **General** Allows you to change the display name (the name displayed in the Administrator program), the remote MTA name and password (the same as the information specified in the MTA General Properties page in the other site), and a previously installed transport stack.

➤ **Schedule** You can configure when communication occurs with the Never, Always, and Selected Times (up to 15-minute intervals) options. This schedule affects only the outgoing messages; it does not affect the messages coming in from a remote site.

➤ **Stack** This Properties page allows you to specify additional address information. All the information on this page must match the transport stack configuration of the remote site. The information available on this page is based on which MTA transport stack you install for the X.400 Connector.

➤ **Override** Allows you to override the default MTA attributes for this specific X.400 Connector.

➤ **Connected Sites** The sites that are directly connected should appear on this list. This page is used to ensure that directory replication occurs.

➤ **Address Space** As with the Site Connector, this page allows you to add, edit, or remove address spaces to be used with this connector. You can also associate a cost with each address space.

➤ **Advanced** You can specify X.400 message format and transfer information when sending messages to a remote site. This information does not affect the type of information that the local Exchange server can receive from the remote site.

Finally, note that you must configure each "side" of the X.400 Connector separately before a connection between the two remote sites is made.

Using Internet Mail Service

The Internet Mail Service (IMS) can be installed within Microsoft Exchange to allow the server to send and receive mail from computers that use the Simple Mail Transfer Protocol (SMTP). Many of today's Internet mail systems use SMTP, and installing SMTP almost guarantees a connection between your network and the Internet. An example of how you can use the Internet Mail Service to connect remote sites is illustrated in Figure 8.5.

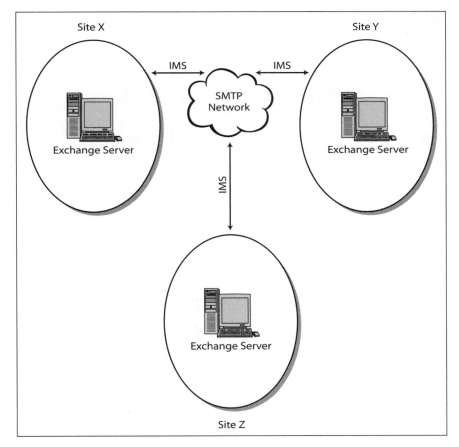

Figure 8.5　The Internet Mail Service.

SMTP is a universal protocol that specifies the procedure for transferring mail between two computers running the TCP/IP protocol stack. TCP/IP must be installed and configured on the Windows NT Server running Microsoft Exchange for the Internet Mail Service to work.

 Any time a client application is to send email to the Internet, you need SMTP and, therefore, the Internet Mail Service.

The IMS has many of the same Properties pages as the other connectors, including address space, connector costs, and delivery restrictions. There are disadvantages to using the IMS. For example, all data must be translated from the Exchange message format to the SMTP format and then retranslated back at the remote side of the connector. These data translations can slow down Exchange Server performance. Also, IMS supports only the scheduling of connections if you use a dial-up connection.

The Internet Mail Service is covered in greater detail in Chapter 9.

The Dynamic RAS Connector

The Dynamic RAS Connector uses Microsoft's Remote Access Service (RAS) to provide message transport between sites that have no permanent connection. RAS supports modem connections over normal telephone lines, Integrated Services Digital Network (ISDN), and X.25. The Dynamic RAS Connector can be set up to automatically activate a RAS connection on a scheduled basis.

Before you can use a RAS connection, the following items need to be configured:

➤ The RAS network software installed and configured on the Exchange Server computer

➤ The service account or a Windows NT account with Send As and Mailbox Owner permissions for the Servers or Configuration containers in the remote site

➤ The name to use for the MTA transport stack

➤ The name of the remote server

➤ The phonebook entry for the remote server (including the name of the server and the phone number)

➤ The name you want to use for the Dynamic RAS Connector

As with the X.400 Connector, you need to install the MTA transport stack (for RAS) before installing the Dynamic RAS Connector. A typical Dynamic RAS Connector installation is shown in Figure 8.6.

Because RAS can require additional processing to answer calls and handle communications, you may want to configure a calling server to dial a dedicated RAS server instead of having the Exchange server deal with these connections.

The Dynamic RAS Connector also uses the messaging bridgehead server to concentrate traffic between two remote sites. This requires only one RAS connection between the two sites. If this were not true, you would have to configure

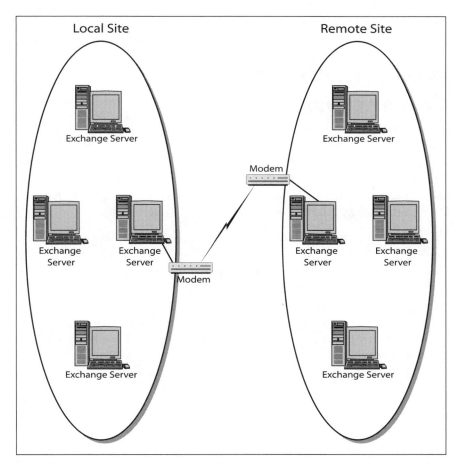

Figure 8.6   The Dynamic RAS Connector.

multiple modems, multiple RAS entries, and multiple phone lines, which would make the connector very inefficient.

The Dynamic RAS Connector has many of the same features as the Site Connector and the X.400 Connector, including address space and connector cost. Like the X.400 Connector, the Dynamic RAS Connector has the ability to restrict which users have access to it.

The connector has a feature called MTA Callback for added security. If you enable this feature, the local server will initiate the RAS connection to the remote server. When the remote server answers the call, the local server will terminate the connection and wait for the remote server to call back. The remote server uses the phone number specified in the MTA Callback Number field. To use this option, RAS Callback must be enabled on the RAS server.

Working With Multiple Connectors

You can install multiple connectors between sites; this method provides load-balancing as well as redundancy. The connectors you install can be of the same type (if you use a single transport) or they can be of different types (if you have multiple transports). For example, you may want to configure an X.400 Connector as the main transport between two sites and then configure a Dynamic RAS Connector as a backup in case the X.400 Connector fails.

You can assign a cost number to each connector, which allows you to control the importance of the message connectors. The cost value ranges from 1 to 100. The connector with the lowest cost will be used over connectors with higher costs. You can use costs to identify the primary and backup paths for message transfer to occur. It's common to assign the cost based on the real cost of the connection. If the Dynamic RAS Connector in the earlier example requires connecting over a long-distance phone line, you'll want to limit how this connector is used.

The Microsoft Exchange MTA is the service responsible for delivering all messages to recipients on any Exchange server (excluding the server where the sender is located). When the MTA receives a message for delivery to a recipient outside the site, it must determine how to deliver the message to its final destination. It does this by using *message routing*, which determines how to deal with mail sent by the MTA to an MTA in a remote site by using one of the following connectors:

➤ Site Connector

➤ Dynamic RAS Connector

➤ X.400 Connector

➤ External connectors, such as the IMS or the Microsoft Mail Connector

Note that the MTA will always perform message routing independent of the number of connectors between the two sites.

Every connector has an address space (or spaces) associated with it, which is the set of addresses that can be reached through this connector. The System Attendant collects this address space information from all the connectors and creates a route table known as the gateway address routing table (GWART). Each Exchange server has its own GWART. When the MTA needs to send a message to a remote site, it compares the recipient of the message to the GWART to determine which connectors can deliver the message. This search provides the MTA with a list of connectors that it can use to deliver the message, and the MTA then selects a connector from the list based on the lowest cost.

A GWART has three major sections; each section is associated with an address type that Exchange can use to send mail. The different address types are shown in Table 8.2.

The GWART is stored in a text file in the Exchsrvr\Mtadata directory. When server routing is updated, the GWART is also updated and a single backup copy is kept. The most recent copy of the GWART is stored in the GWART0.MTA file and the previous GWART is stored in the GWART1.MTA file. You can use a regular text editor to edit these files.

The Role Of Directory Replication

Once you configure a messaging connector between two sites (Site Connector, X.400 Connector, or Dynamic RAS Connector), you can also configure a Directory Replication Connector. This connector will replicate directory

Table 8.2 The GWART address types.	
Address	**Description**
Distinguished name (DN)	The native Exchange address format. Type EX.
Domain defined attribute (DDA)	The format used for custom recipient storage. Type MS or SMTP.
Originator/recipient (O/R) address	The native X.400 format. Type X.400.

information between local and remote sites. Figure 8.7 shows how directory replication works.

When you configure a Directory Replication Connector between two sites, you need to specify one server to control the replication for that connector. This server is known as the *directory replication bridgehead*. You can have multiple directory replication bridgeheads within a site, but only one can be responsible for any connection to a remote site. Also, a site cannot have two directory replication paths to a remote site. In Figure 8.7, all three connectors are valid, but all three cannot be combined at one time because this would create more than one path for the directory replication to take (in other words, Site X can connect to Site Z directly or through Site Y). Table 8.3 explains this further.

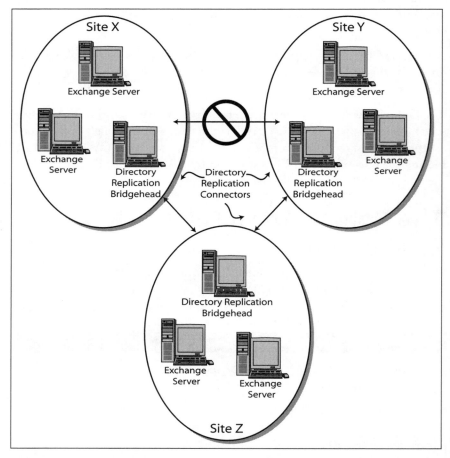

Figure 8.7 The directory replication bridgehead.

Table 8.3   Multiple directory replication bridgeheads.

Connector	From	To
A	Site X	Site Z
B	Site Z	Site Y
C	Site Y	Site X

The directory replication bridgeheads always request the directory replication information. This information is never "pushed"; it must be requested. The directory replication bridgehead requests this information based on a replication schedule. When a change is made in the directory, a notification message is sent out notifying the replication bridgeheads. The directory replication bridgeheads then request that the changes be sent to it.

When three sites are joined with two connectors and directory replication is configured between them, the connection between the two most distant sites is said to be *transitive*. For example, in Figure 8.8, Site X and Site Z are connected, and Site Y and Site Z are connected. Due to this connection, Site X has a transitive connection to Site Y through Site Z.

Connector Comparison

As an additional point of reference, we've included Table 8.4. It compares each of the major connectors by measurements such as bandwidth requirements and supported protocols.

Table 8.4   Connector comparison.

Option	Site	X.400	IMS	Dynamic RAS
Bandwidth	>128K	64K – 2M	64K – 2M	<64K
Automatic remote site configuration	Optional	No	No	No
Service account override option?	Yes	Yes	Yes	Yes
Supported protocols	RPC protocols	TCP/IP TP0/X.25 TP4/CLNP	TCP/IP	TCP/IP IPX/SPX NetBEUI
Delivery mechanism	RPC	Messages	Messages	Messages

(continued)

Table 8.4	Connector comparison *(continued)*.			
Option	**Site**	**X.400**	**IMS**	**Dynamic RAS**
Message format	Exchange	X.400	SMTP	X.400
Connector cost	Yes	Yes	Yes	Yes
Bridgehead server support	Optional	Required	Yes	Yes
Target server support	Optional	Yes	Yes	N/A
Scheduling	No	Yes	No	Yes
User access restrictions	No	Yes	Yes	Yes
Maximum message size restrictions	No	Yes	Yes	Yes

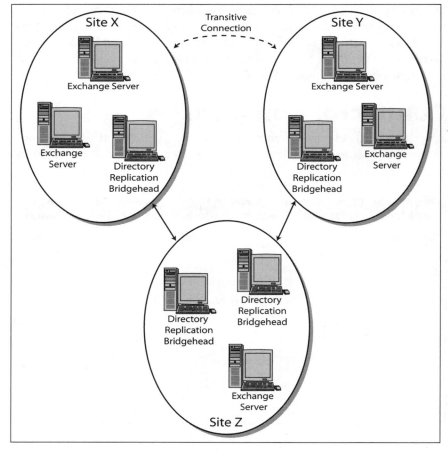

Figure 8.8 Transitive connections.

Exam Prep Questions

Question 1

Which Exchange component makes all routing decisions?

○ a. Directory Service

○ b. Remote Access Service

○ c. Message Transfer Agent

○ d. System Agent

The correct answer to this question is c. The MTA makes all routing decisions in an Exchange server. The DS places directory-related information in a mail message and uses the MTA to deliver the data; therefore, answer a is incorrect. RAS is a service that allows network access over a modem link; therefore, answer b is incorrect. The System Agent is a monitoring and scheduling program; therefore, answer d is incorrect.

Question 2

Why would you configure multiple connectors between two Microsoft Exchange sites? [Check all correct answers]

❑ a. To set up fault tolerance for your site

❑ b. To load-balance your messaging requirements

❑ c. You have to have multiple connectors installed to replicate information between servers

❑ d. None of the above

The correct answers to this question are a and b. Setting up multiple connectors between two or more Exchange sites will balance the message load across the connectors and will enable communications to continue should one of the connectors fail. You do not require more than one connector for information replication; therefore, answer c is incorrect. Because answers are available for the question, answer d is incorrect.

Question 3

Which of the following statements are true for the Site Connector? [Check all correct answers]

- ❑ a. You can automatically configure the remote side of the connector.
- ❑ b. It's the most efficient connector in Microsoft Exchange Server.
- ❑ c. You can control which users have access to it.
- ❑ d. You can limit the message size transferred by the Site Connector.

The correct answers to this question are a and b. The Site Connector is the only connector that allows you to auto-configure both ends, and it's about 20 percent faster than the X.400 Connector because it doesn't have to translate the Exchange messages to X.400 messages. All the connectors, except for the Site Connector, allow you to control both user access and maximum message size; therefore, answers c and d are incorrect.

Question 4

Which of the following statements are true about the X.400 Connector? [Check all correct answers]

- ❑ a. It's the most efficient connector.
- ❑ b. You can limit the message size transferred by it.
- ❑ c. You can control which users will have access to it.
- ❑ d. You can configure the remote side of the connector automatically.

The correct answers to this question are b and c. All the connectors, except for the Site Connector, can control both user access and maximum message size. The Site Connector is the most efficient connector; therefore, answer a is incorrect. Only the Site Connector will auto-configure the remote site; therefore, answer d is incorrect.

Question 5

You must establish a connection between the Microsoft Exchange Server computer in your company's main office and multiple Unix SMTP hosts in remote branches. What type of connector would you use?

○ a. A Dynamic RAS Connector

○ b. An Internet Mail Service (IMS)

○ c. A Site Connector

○ d. An X.400 Connector

The correct answer to this question is b. The Internet Mail Service uses the SMTP protocol, which allows mail servers to communicate over the Internet. The Dynamic RAS Connector, the X.400 Connector, and the Site Connector allow two Exchange sites to communicate rather than multiple Unix systems; therefore, answers a, c, and d are incorrect.

Question 6

A Dynamic RAS Connector connects two of your sites. How can you maintain a continuous dial-up connection?

○ a. Edit the Dial-Up Networking Phonebook entry for the connection.

○ b. This can only be done with an X.400 Connector.

○ c. Change the connector to the IMS.

○ d. Create a schedule for the Dynamic RAS Connector.

The correct answer to this question is d. By configuring a schedule for the Dynamic RAS Connector, you can control the times at which the connector is to operate. Editing the Phonebook entry configures only what information the connector will use to connect, not the times; therefore, answer a is incorrect. The X.400 Connector and the Dynamic RAS Connector can both be scheduled; therefore, answer b is incorrect. The Internet Mail Service cannot be scheduled, unless you configure a Dynamic RAS Connector; therefore, answer c is incorrect.

Question 7

> You have several connectors installed between two of your sites.
> You would like the Site Connector to be used always unless it is
> unavailable. What must you do?
>
> ○ a. Assign it a cost of 1 and the other connectors a cost of
>   100
>
> ○ b. Assign it a cost of 100 and the other connectors a cost of 1
>
> ○ c. Do not assign it a cost
>
> ○ d. Assign all the connectors a cost of 1

The correct answer to this question is a. The lower the cost, the more often the
connector will be used. Assigning the Site Connector a cost of 100 will configure Exchange to use it only if no other connectors are available; therefore,
answer b is incorrect. If you do not assign it a cost, the connectors will be used
equally; therefore, answer c is incorrect. Assigning all connectors a cost of 1
will force Exchange to use all the connectors equally; therefore, answer d is
incorrect.

Question 8

> You would like to connect two of your sites. They are on the same
> high-speed LAN. Which connector would you use?
>
> ○ a. A Dynamic RAS Connector
>
> ○ b. An Internet Mail Service (IMS)
>
> ○ c. A Site Connector
>
> ○ d. An X.400 Connector

The correct answer to this question is c. The Site Connector is designed to
operate on high-speed connections. The other three connectors will work over
the high-speed LAN, but the Site Connector is the most efficient connector
and is the *best* choice; therefore, answers a, b, and d are incorrect.

Question 9

> Your server's GWART is corrupt. How would you recover it?
>
> ○ a. You can't. You must reinstall.
>
> ○ b. Copy GWART0.MTA from another Exchange server.
>
> ○ c. Copy GWART1.MTA from another Exchange server.
>
> ○ d. Copy GWART1.MTA to GWART0.MTA on the server
>   where the GWART is corrupt.

The correct answer to this question is d. The GWART1.MTA file is the previous version of the gateway address routing table. Copying it over the corrupt file will restore the older version. By copying the older version of the GWART, you can recover it; therefore, answer a is incorrect. The GWART on one Exchange server is different than the GWART on another; therefore, answers b and c are incorrect.

Question 10

> You have a Site Connector installed. You would like to install a backup connector that will use a modem to connect to the remote site. Which connector would you use?
>
> ○ a. A Dynamic RAS Connector
>
> ○ b. An Internet Mail Service (IMS)
>
> ○ c. A Site Connector
>
> ○ d. An X.400 Connector

The correct answer to this question is a. The Dynamic RAS Connector uses a modem to connect to a remote site. Although IMS can use the Dynamic RAS Connector, it cannot use a modem to connect; therefore, answer b is incorrect. The Site Connector requires a high-speed connection and cannot use a modem; therefore, answer c is incorrect. The X.400 Connector cannot directly use a modem to connect; therefore, answer d is incorrect.

Need To Know More?

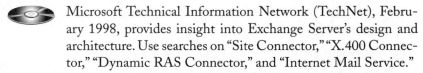

Microsoft Technical Information Network (TechNet), February 1998, provides insight into Exchange Server's design and architecture. Use searches on "Site Connector," "X.400 Connector," "Dynamic RAS Connector," and "Internet Mail Service."

Install Online Books from the Microsoft Exchange 5.5 CD-ROM. It will yield a wealth of useful information.

Go to the Microsoft Exchange Server home page at www.microsoft.com/exchange. Many of the documents located here are newer than the ones available on the Microsoft Technical Information Network.

Go to the Microsoft Knowledge Base and support home page at www.microsoft.com/kb. Many of the documents located here are newer than the ones available on the Microsoft Technical Information Network.

The Internet Mail Service And Protocols

· ·

Terms you'll need to understand:

- √ Domain Name System (DNS)
- √ Fully Qualified Domain Name (FQDN)
- √ Internet Message Access Protocol version 4 (IMAP4)
- √ Inbound Newsfeed
- √ Internet Mail and News services
- √ Lightweight Directory Access Protocol (LDAP)

- √ Outbound Newsfeed
- √ Outlook Web Access
- √ Post Office Protocol 3 (POP3)
- √ Pull feed and push feed
- √ Resolver
- √ Simple Mail Transfer Protocol (SMTP)

Techniques you'll need to master:

- √ Understanding how the DNS and SMTP work
- √ Using the Internet Mail Service wizard
- √ Installing and configuring the Internet Mail Service
- √ Understanding the features and options available from the Internet Mail Service

- √ Scheduling the Internet Mail Service to receive mail from remote sites using Remote Access Service connections
- √ Configuring POP3
- √ Configuring IMAP
- √ Configuring LDAP
- √ Configuring the Network News Transfer Protocol (NNTP)
- √ Configuring Microsoft Outlook Web Access

The Internet has become a part of every network administrator's life. Many businesses rely on the Internet for commerce, product delivery, advertising, and, most importantly, messaging. The Internet has allowed us to communicate with individuals and businesses that we would have never had access to in the past. For example, you can easily and securely purchase products from anywhere in the world without actually "talking" to a real person.

Microsoft realized this need to connect to the "Net" when it developed Exchange. Microsoft Exchange Server with the Internet Mail Service allows you to connect your site to literally millions of other sites and users. This chapter details the installation and configuration of the Internet Mail Service component of Microsoft Exchange Server.

Microsoft Exchange Server has several of the most popular Internet protocols available for you to use to connect your users to the Internet and to the server itself. These include mail protocols (POP3 and IMAP4), a directory access protocol (LDAP), a Usenet protocol (NNTP), and the Hypertext Transfer Protocol (HTTP).

Both the Post Office Protocol 3 (POP3) and Internet Message Access Protocol version 4 (IMAP4) allow users to connect to the Exchange server to access their mailboxes remotely (from home or from anywhere on the Internet). IMAP4 also allows users to read from and post to public folders located on your Exchange server. The Lightweight Directory Access Protocol (LDAP) allows you to share your Microsoft Exchange Address Book information with your remote users or with anonymous Internet users. Using the Network News Transfer Protocol (NNTP), you can connect your Exchange server to the Usenet to receive or publish information. Finally, HTTP allows your users to gain complete access to their mailboxes, public folders, and scheduling information. HTTP also grants anonymous users access to specific public folders you want to share.

Internet Mail Service Explored And Explained

The Internet Mail Service (IMS) is an integrated component of Microsoft Exchange that uses the Simple Mail Transfer Protocol (SMTP), the Transmission Control Protocol/Internet Protocol (TCP/IP) suite, and the Domain Name System (DNS) to route messages to the Internet or directly to an SMTP host.

IMS is a Windows NT service that is optionally installed on an Exchange Server computer. Installing this service allows the Exchange server to function as an SMTP server. An Exchange server with IMS installed can send and receive SMTP messages from any computer that supports SMTP. Figure 9.1 illustrates how Microsoft Exchange Server can communicate on the Internet.

SMTP is a protocol that specifies the procedure for transferring mail messages between two systems. You accomplish this by specifying how the message will be formatted as well as the method that will be used to deliver the message from the sending host to the receiving host.

The Windows NT TCP/IP suite must be installed and configured on a system running Microsoft Exchange to allow the IMS to function. TCP/IP and SMTP work in tandem to allow for the transmission of messages over the Internet or between SMTP hosts.

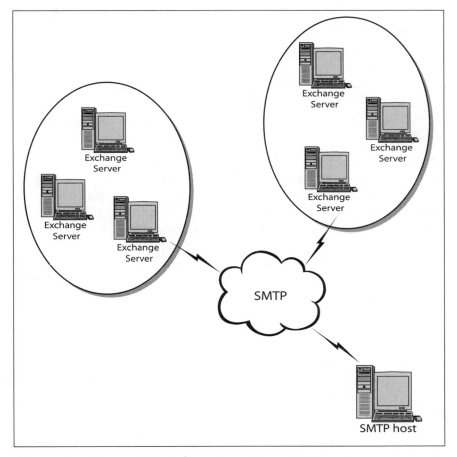

Figure 9.1   Microsoft Exchange Server in an SMTP environment.

Internet Mail Service Protocols And Services

IMS relies on several components to function properly. These components are discussed in the following sections.

Domain Name System (DNS)

In a TCP/IP environment, every computer requires a unique numerical identifier in the form of an IP address (for example, 192.168.23.34). For a user to contact a server on the network, the IP address of that system must be known. In a small network, it would be fairly easy to remember a few IP addresses. In a large network, however, this becomes a very difficult task. For this reason, each computer on the network can also be assigned an easy-to-remember name, such as jory.corp.com.

DNS is a distributed database that provides a hierarchical naming system for identifying systems on the Internet or an intranet. DNS is made up of two components: the server and the client. The server component of DNS maintains a database of domain and computer names, whereas the client component of DNS (also known as a *resolver*) generates the queries against the database on the server.

The DNS database is a hierarchical tree structure called the *domain name space*. Don't be confused by the similar names. The Domain Name System uses the structure called the domain name space. Each node in the tree structure is known as a *domain*, and each node below that is known as a *subdomain*. To better understand this, let's compare it to a file system. A file system has a root folder that can contain subfolders. Also, as with a file system, the root of the DNS tree is at the top and is known as a *top-level* (or *root*) *domain*. Figure 9.2 is a comparison of the DNS tree structure and the file system tree structure.

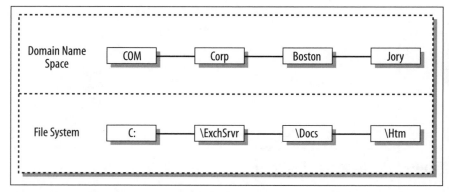

Figure 9.2 A comparison of the DNS tree and file system tree structures.

Here are some examples of top-level domains:

➤ **EDU** An educational institution

➤ **GOV** A governmental organization

➤ **COM** A commercial site

The full domain name (from bottom to top) is called the *Fully Qualified Domain Name (FQDN)*. As shown in Figure 9.3, an example of an FQDN would be jory.boston.corp.com.

The main function of DNS is to resolve FQDNs to IP addresses and IP addresses to FQDNs. This is known as *name resolution*. The actual name resolution process is as follows:

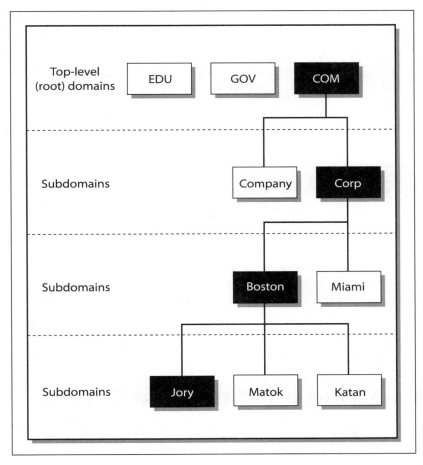

Figure 9.3 The domain name space.

1. A client passes a query to the local name server (either IP to FQDN or FQDN to IP).

2. If the local name server does not have the required information, it will act the part of the client and query a remote name server for the name on behalf of the client.

3. If necessary, the local name server will start at the top of the DNS tree, query one of the root name servers, and work its way down until all the requested data is found.

Simple Mail Transfer Protocol

The Simple Mail Transfer Protocol (SMTP) is used to send messages from one host on the Internet to another using the Transmission Control Protocol (TCP) port 25. When one host sends an email message to another, the process is as follows:

1. The SMTP *sender* (client) establishes a connection to the SMTP *receiver* (server). The client requests an SMTP session by sending a **HELO** command. Before the client can continue, the server must send back an OK message to indicate that it will accept the session request.

2. The client then uses the **MAIL FROM** command to tell the server who is sending the message. The server then returns an OK message (if the user is authorized to send mail to it).

3. The client now sends the server a list of the recipient(s) of the message using the **RCPT TO** command. A **RCPT TO** command is issued for each recipient separately. The server must then acknowledge the command by returning an OK message.

4. The client then uses the **DATA** command to request to send the actual message body. The server must reply with an OK for the client to send the message; the client then sends the message body information to the server.

5. When the message has been sent successfully, the client sends a **QUIT** command to close the connection. The client can send another message by repeating steps 2 through 4 before issuing the **QUIT** command.

Installing Internet Mail Service

Before you install IMS, you need to make sure TCP/IP is installed and configured on the Windows NT Server that is running IMS. To install TCP/IP, follow these steps:

1. Right-click the Network Neighborhood icon and select Properties from the drop-down menu.

2. Select the Protocol tab, click the Add button, and select TCP/IP from the list. Click OK.

3. Enter your TCP/IP address, subnet mask, and default gateway.

4. Select the DNS tab.

5. Type in the host name and domain name of the computer. Together these will be the FQDN of the system.

6. Type in one or more of the DNS server IP addresses.

Microsoft Exchange 5.5 has an installation wizard for installing IMS. To start the wizard, select File|New Other|Internet Mail Service. Figure 9.4 shows the first Internet Mail Wizard screen.

The following list is what Microsoft recommends you review to ensure that you have your system configured correctly to install IMS:

➤ For improved security and performance, you should run IMS on a Windows NT Server machine using the Windows NT File System (NTFS) rather than a File Allocation Table (FAT) file system.

➤ Know the addressing scheme for your organization.

➤ Determine the SMTP address for the site.

➤ Determine the address space the Internet Mail Service will service.

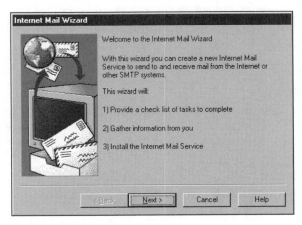

Figure 9.4   The Internet Mail Wizard.

➤ Identify a recipient who will receive notifications if the Internet Mail Service fails (a postmaster).

➤ Obtain the host name and domain name of the computer on which the Internet Mail Service will be installed.

➤ Determine whether Domain Name System (DNS) will be used to provide address resolution for host and domain names to the Internet Protocol (IP).

➤ Obtain the IP address of DNS servers or the SMTP hosts that will service the Internet Mail Service.

Starting And Configuring Internet Mail Service

You can configure the Internet Mail Service using various Properties tabs. Be aware that you must restart IMS for any changes to take place. To access the IMS Properties tabs, select the connections option in the left pane and double-click the IMS to be modified in the right pane. The IMS tabs are shown in Figure 9.5.

The IMS Properties Tabs

The following sections detail each of the IMS Properties tabs.

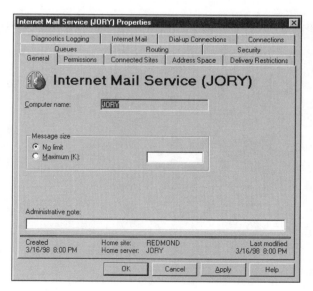

Figure 9.5   The IMS Properties tabs.

General

Within the General tab you have the ability to view the computer name (this is a read-only field) and enter an administrative note to distinguish this IMS connector from any other IMS connectors that you may have installed. You also have the ability to limit the message size handled by this connector to a specified number of kilobytes.

Permissions

This tab has two sections to it. The first section is a read-only section that lists the users with inherited rights to this connector; the second section allows you to assign specific roles and rights to individual users and/or groups. You can assign any or all of the following roles:

➤ Admin

➤ Permissions Admin

➤ Search

Also, you can assign one or more of the following rights:

➤ Modify User Attributes

➤ Modify Admin Attributes

➤ Delete

➤ Modify Permissions

➤ Search

> Note: For more information on user roles and rights, refer to Chapter 5.

Connected Sites

Within the Connected Sites tab, you have the ability to specify connections to existing Microsoft Exchange Server sites. This information is used to verify that directory replication takes place and that other connectors in the organization are accessed.

When you click the New button, the dialog box shown in Figure 9.6 appears. The Properties dialog box has two separate tabs: General and Routing Address. In the General tab, you must enter the organization name and the name of the site to be connected. In the Routing Address tab, you're required to enter the type of address to be used (for example, SMTP), the routing cost involved with this connection, and the email address to use for the site.

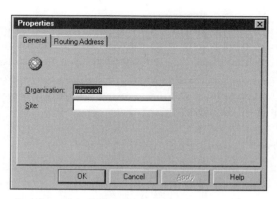

Figure 9.6 Adding a connected site.

Address Space

When a connector is created outside the site, a logical path must be created to allow the Message Transfer Agent (MTA) to determine how to get the messages to the final destination. This logical path, the address space, must be unique for each recipient. A connector must have at least one address space entry to operate properly. The format of the address space depends on the format of the remote messaging system. For example, if you're sending a message to an SMTP network, use the SMTP address space.

 If you have multiple routes to a destination, the IMS uses only the lowest cost route. The only time that IMS uses a route with a higher cost is when the lowest cost route is not available. You can use MX records in your DNS server to override this feature and to allow for the forwarding of incoming mail to a secondary route.

Delivery Restrictions

This tab is used to either accept or reject outbound messages from any recipient within the Microsoft Exchange site. The message is returned to the originator if a recipient is listed in the Reject Messages box or is not listed in the Accept Messages From box. You cannot use this tab to control inbound messages, but you can control outbound messages.

Queues

The Queues tab allows you to view important information about messages in the queues. Although you can view details about specific queued messages and delete problem messages, you cannot reorder the messages in the queues. You can also use the Queues tab to determine the number of messages in each queue. Four different queues can be viewed:

➤ **Inbound messages awaiting conversion** Queues any incoming messages that need to be either converted or rerouted to the IMS and then delivered to the Information Store (IS).

➤ **Inbound messages awaiting delivery** Queues any converted incoming messages that need to be delivered to the recipient.

➤ **Outbound messages awaiting conversion** Queues any outgoing messages received by the IMS from the MTA that are waiting to be converted by the IMS.

➤ **Outbound messages awaiting delivery** Queues any converted outgoing messages that need to be delivered by the IMS scheduler.

Outbound messages are received by the MTA (stored in the Exchsrvr\ Imcdata\Out folder) and moved into the IMS's MTS-OUT (Message Transport System-OUT) queue in the Information Store. The IMS then converts the messages and moves them into the Out queue until they are delivered. When inbound Internet messages arrive, the IMS stores them in its In queue (stored in the Exchsrvr\Imcdata\In folder) until they can be converted and moved to the MTS-IN queue in the Information Store.

You have the ability to view extra details about messages stored in one of the four IMS queues. To do this, either double-click the message on which you want more information or select it and click the Details button. The information includes the following message details:

➤ **Originator** The address of the user who sent the message.

➤ **MTS-ID** A unique identifier that includes the originating server's name, the date and time the message was sent, and a hexadecimal identifier. This field is not available (that is, it's blank) in the In and Out queues.

➤ **Message ID** A unique identifier given to a message by the Exchange server that remains with the message from start to finish. This field is not available (that is, it's blank) in the MTS-OUT queue.

➤ **Destination Host** The name of the server to which the message is to be delivered.

➤ **Submit Time** The time the message arrived in the queue.

➤ **Size** The size of the message (in bytes).

➤ **Next Retry Time** The scheduled time for resending the message. (This is only if previous attempts were unsuccessful.)

➤ **Retries** The number of times IMS has tried to deliver the message.

➤ **Expiration** The time when message retries will be stopped and a non-delivery report (NDR) will be sent to the originator.

➤ **Recipients** The addresses to which the message is to be delivered, including a status of attempts made to deliver the message.

Several other options are available to you under the Queues tab. Be aware, however, that the information in the queues' windows is the status of the queues when you accessed the Queues tab. In other words, this information is static, not dynamic. Therefore, you need to click the Refresh button to refresh the queue. You delete a message by highlighting the message and clicking the Delete button. You can delete messages in all the queues except for the MTS-IN queue. Finally, you can force IMS to retry sending a message. This is handy if you've made some configuration changes to try to solve a problem and you want to know if your solution worked. To do this, click the Retry Now button.

Routing

Use this tab to intercept any inbound messages from SMTP hosts or POP3 and IMAP4 clients, as well as to reroute these messages to other SMTP hosts before the IMS processes them.

You have the following options:

➤ Not reroute incoming SMTP mail

➤ Reroute incoming SMTP mail (required for POP3/IMAP4 support)

When you add a routing address, you can specify whether the addresses should be accepted as inbound or should be rerouted to a specific domain.

Security

The Security tab is used to enable security on outbound connections to other mail systems. You can also encrypt or authenticate message transfers from an Exchange server to a remote SMTP host. Three types of security are available for connections to other systems in the Security tab: Simple Authentication and Security Layer (SASL), Secure Sockets Layer (SSL), and Windows NT Security.

Here are the security options:

➤ **No authentication or encryption** No security features are enabled.

➤ **SASL authentication/SSL encryption** Allows you to choose SASL/AUTH, SSL encryption, or both.

➤ **SASL/AUTH clear text password authentication** Sends the clear text account and password information on outbound connections using the AUTH LOGIN ESMTP extension.

➤ **SSL encryption** Uses SSL encryption.

➤ **Windows NT Challenge/Response Authentication and encryption** Uses Windows NT Challenge/Response Authentication to encrypt account and password information.

Diagnostic Logging

You can set the logging levels for this connector using the Diagnostic Logging tab. You can log the following items:

➤ Initialization/termination

➤ Addressing

➤ Message transfer

➤ SMTP interface events

➤ Internal processing

➤ SMTP protocol logs

➤ Message archival

You can select four different levels to log:

➤ **None** Only critical or error events, as well as events with a logging level of zero are logged. This is the default level.

➤ **Minimum** Events with a logging level of one or lower are logged.

➤ **Medium** Events with a logging level of three or lower are logged.

➤ **Maximum** Events with a logging level of five or lower are logged.

Internet Mail

The Internet Mail tab allows you to configure the administrator's mailbox, message content, and message tracking.

The administrator's mailbox receives any error notifications sent out by IMS as well as any messages sent to the postmaster. To select a recipient to act as the administrator for this IMS, click the Change button and select a recipient from the list. You can either select an individual recipient or a distribution list.

You have the ability to configure under what circumstances IMS will notify the administrator when NDRs are generated. To configure this, click the Notifications button. Notifications can be configured to always be sent or only be sent for specific NDRs, including the following:

➤ Email address could not be found.

➤ Multiple matches for an email occurred.

➤ Destination host could not be found.

➤ Protocol error occurred.

➤ Message timeout exceeded.

The remaining configuration options include the following:

➤ **Attachments (outbound)** Allows you to specify either MIME (plain text or HTML) or UUEncode (BinHex) attachments.

➤ **Character sets** Allows you to specify a default character set for either MIME or non-MIME messages.

➤ **Email domain** Click the Email Domain button to use different encoding methods, character sets, and message sizes for each domain that you host on your Microsoft Exchange Server machine. For example, you may want to use the MIME encoding method for your domain corp.com and the UUEncode encoding method for the boston.corp.com subdomain. To do this, you're required to list the subdomain before the domain.

➤ **Advanced** Allows you to disable out-of-office responses to the Internet, to disable automatic replies to the Internet, and to disable sending display names to the Internet.

➤ **Message tracking** Prompts the MTA to create a daily log file that contains all routing information about all the processed messages. Use this log file to track specific messages using the Message Tracking Center.

Dial-Up Connections

You can use the Dial-up Connections tab to configure connection and schedule information. IMS can be configured to use the Windows NT Remote Access Service (RAS) to connect to an Internet Service Provider (ISP) or to a remote Microsoft Exchange site. You can use a dial-up connection with IMS if a permanent one does not exist, or you can use a dial-up connection for fault tolerance if the permanent connection goes down.

To add dial-up connections to IMS, you must first configure one or more RAS entries in the RAS Phonebook. If you have multiple RAS entries in the RAS Phonebook, only the entries selected in the Available Connections window are used.

Some ISPs require your system to issue a command to identify itself to the provider and to notify it that messages can be sent. You can configure your system to use ETRN (an SMTP extension that causes the remote host to send stored messages), to use TURN (an SMTP extension that causes the remote host to send stored messages requiring authentication), to issue a custom command, or not to send any retrieval messages.

You also have the ability to specify a default timeout period (in minutes) to keep the RAS connection open, the logon information for your ISP, and either a daily or weekly schedule for how frequently IMS should connect to the remote host to receive email.

Connections

Within the Connections tab, you can configure the transfer mode, message delivery, connection acceptance, service message queue information, and security features.

In the Transfer Mode area, your options are as follows:

➤ **Inbound & Outbound** Accept inbound messages and send outbound messages.

➤ **Inbound only** Accept only inbound messages.

➤ **Outbound only** Send only outbound messages.

➤ **None (flush queues)** Do not accept inbound or outbound messages.

➤ **Advanced** Allows you to specify the maximum number of inbound connections, outbound connections, connections to a single host, and messages in a connection.

In the Message Delivery area, your options are as follows:

➤ **Use Domain Name System (DNS)** Use DNS to resolve all remote domains.

➤ **Forward all messages to host** Use a specific host to resolve and deliver all remote mail.

➤ **Dial using** Use a RAS connection to connect to a remote host.

➤ **Email domain** Allows you to specify how different domains will deliver their messages.

In the Accept Connections area, your options are as follows:

➤ **From any host (secure or nonsecure)** Messages from any host not explicitly listed are accepted.

➤ **Only from hosts using** Specify whether the connection will use authentication, encryption, or both.

➤ **Hosts** Allows you to override the default for specific hosts.

In the Service Message Queues area, your options are as follows:

➤ **Retry Interval (hrs)** Specifies the amount of time (in hours) that IMS will attempt to reconnect to a remote host if the initial connection failed. To specify different intervals, separate them with commas. For example, to try after 15 minutes, then 1 hour, and then 5 hours, you would enter ".25, 1, 5".

➤ **Time-outs** Allows you to specify different timeouts for urgent, normal, or nonurgent messages.

Your options in the Other area are as follows:

➤ **Clients can only submit if homed on this server** Allows a client to submit messages only if he or she has a mailbox on the Exchange server in which the IMS is located.

➤ **Clients can only submit if authentication account matches submission address** Allows a client to submit messages only if his or her Windows NT account matches the information in the From field in the message.

Overview Of IP Messaging Protocols

The Internet is a network of networks that all communicate using a common language. This language is the Transmission Control Protocol/Internet Protocol (TCP/IP). An Internet protocol is a set of standards or rules that is designed to enable one computer on the Internet to communicate with another and to exchange information. This allows for different computer platforms (for example, a Windows NT Server and a Unix server) to communicate and exchange information.

In addition to supporting the Simple Mail Transfer Protocol (SMTP), Microsoft Exchange Server also supports the following protocols:

➤ Post Office Protocol 3 (POP3)

➤ Internet Message Access Protocol version 4 rev1 (IMAP4rev1)

➤ Lightweight Directory Access Protocol (LDAP)

➤ Network News Transfer Protocol (NNTP)

➤ Hypertext Transfer Protocol (HTTP)

Each site and server has a container associated with it called *Protocols*. This container stores configuration objects for each of the Internet protocols. You have the ability to configure the default settings that apply to all the protocols in the site using the site Protocols container. On the other hand, you can configure settings that would apply only to individual servers. If you configure default settings for protocols at the site level, those settings apply to all the servers in the site but do not replicate to other sites. Figure 9.7 shows the Internet protocol objects in the site and server containers.

 All the Protocol objects, with the exception of the HTTP protocol, can be controlled from three different locations: the site level, the server level, and the mailbox level. The HTTP protocol can be controlled from the site level and the mailbox level, but not the server level.

By default, the protocols are enabled in all locations. As an administrator, you can enable/disable the protocols to provide different functionality. For example, you can use the following protocol configurations:

➤ **Disabled at the site level and enabled on a per-server basis** This allows clients to connect only to the servers that have the protocol enabled.

➤ **Enabled at the site level and disabled on a per-server basis** This allows clients to connect only to the servers that do not have the protocol disabled.

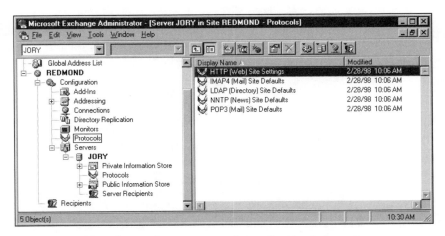

Figure 9.7 The site and server containers for the Internet protocol objects.

➤ **Enabled at the site level and the server level but disabled at the mailbox level** This allows clients who do not have the protocol disabled to connect to the server.

Note: If you disable the protocol at the server level, the setting on the mailbox has no effect.

The Protocols container has four different tabs associated with it. These tabs are described in the following sections. The Protocols Properties dialog box is shown in Figure 9.8.

General

The General tab is used to set the defaults for all the servers in the site. These default settings are:

➤ **Display Name** This is the name that's displayed in the Microsoft Exchange Administrator program for these protocols. This field can have a maximum of 256 characters in it.

➤ **Directory Name** This is a read-only field that's defined during the installation process.

 Within the Internet protocol properties in the Server container, you can select the Use Site Defaults For All Properties checkbox. This ensures that the configuration made to the protocols in the Site container is true in the Server container.

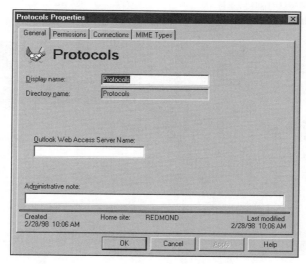

Figure 9.8 The Protocols Properties dialog box.

Permissions

The Permissions tab is used to specify which objects in the Protocols container a user has access to. You grant permissions to a user (or group) by assigning the user a role. These roles are very similar to those in the recipient objects. You can set permissions on each protocol object in the site and server Protocols container only if you have configured the Exchange Administrator program to display the Permission tabs for all objects.

 If you need to use Secure Sockets Layer (SSL) encryption with POP3, IMAP4, LDAP, and NNTP, you must grant the Exchange Server service account the Administrator permissions for the local computer.

Connections

The Connections tab is used to accept or reject POP3, IMAP4, LDAP, or NNTP access based on a client's IP address. By default, all connections are allowed.

 These settings do not apply to HTTP. To restrict HTTP connections, you must configure the Advanced tab in the Microsoft Internet Information Server Internet Service Manager.

MIME Types

The MIME Types tab is used to assign appropriate file extensions for inbound attachments. The Multipurpose Internet Mail Extensions (MIME) content type and the corresponding file extensions are defined in this tab and are used by Microsoft Exchange to assign the file extensions to inbound attachments.

> *Note: Duplicate entries are allowed for both content type and file extensions. However, if multiple entries exist, the first occurrence in the list is used as the mapping.*

In addition to being able to control protocols at the site level, all protocols (except for LDAP) can also be controlled at the mailbox level. Even though LDAP appears under the protocols tab of the properties of a mailbox, the protocol cannot be modified. As the administrator, you can control the individual users accessing the server.

Post Office Protocol 3 (POP3)

The Post Office Protocol 3 (POP3) enables users with POP3 clients to retrieve mail messages from the Exchange Inbox. Because Microsoft Exchange uses this standard, any email client application that supports POP3 can be used to connect to a Microsoft Exchange Server machine and access the user's messages.

POP3 is known as a *mail-drop service*, which is a service that can hold email messages until the client requests the messages be sent to it.

By default, when you install Microsoft Exchange Server, the POP3 protocol is also installed. This allows POP3 clients to retrieve their email as soon as the server is set up. You must configure the IMS before the clients can send email, because the client uses the POP3 protocol to retrieve messages and the SMTP protocol to send messages.

The POP3 protocol can be configured at three different levels:

➤ **Site level** These protocol settings are default values that are inherited by the servers.

➤ **Server level** These tabs allow you to use either the site defaults or to configure different options on each server.

➤ **Mailbox level** These tabs allow you to use either the server defaults or to configure different options on a mailbox-by-mailbox basis. It's important to note that if you disable POP3 at the server level, all the mailboxes on that server are disabled, even if you enable the mailboxes individually.

POP3 Site And Server Properties

You can configure five POP3 tabs at the site level. These include General, Permissions, Authentication, Message Format, and Idle Time-out. The POP3 Site Defaults Properties page is shown in Figure 9.9.

General

The General tab is used to enable or disable the protocol. Also, you can change the display name of the protocol (the name that appears in the Administrator program). The directory name is displayed in a read-only field.

Authentication

This tab is used to specify the methods of authentication that POP3 clients must use to connect to the Exchange server. You can select one of six different methods of authentication (or any combination of them). These methods are listed in Table 9.1.

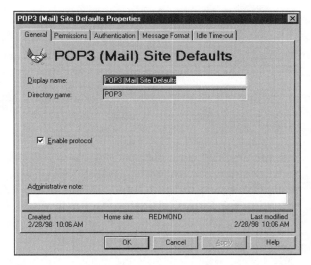

Figure 9.9 The POP3 Site Defaults Properties configuration dialog box.

Table 9.1 POP3 authentication methods.	
Option	**Description**
Basic (Clear Text)	Use authentication through an unencrypted username and password. Most POP3 clients support this method of authentication.
Basic (Clear Text) Using SSL	Uses the SSL protocol to encrypt clear text usernames and passwords. This method uses port 995.
NT Challenge/Response	Uses authentication through Windows NT security and an encrypted password.
NT Challenge/Response Using SSL	Uses the SSL protocol to authenticate through Windows NT security. This method uses port 995.
MCIS Membership System	Uses Windows NT security authentication through the Microsoft Commercial Internet Server (MCIS) Membership System.
MCIS Membership System Using SSL	Uses the SSL protocol to authenticate through the Microsoft Commercial Internet Server Membership System using Windows NT security. This method uses port 995.

Message Format

This tab is used to control the message content encoding and character set. You can select MIME or UUEncode content encoding, as well as rich text format.

Idle Time-Out

This tab is used to set the amount of time POP3 needs to be idle before closing a connection. You can select to either not close idle connections or to close idle connections after a specified amount of time (measured in minutes).

You have an extra tab available to you when configuring POP3 at the server level—Diagnostic Logging. Diagnostic logging allows you to set logging levels for several Microsoft Exchange Server events.

 To configure POP3 on a mailbox level, select the POP3 protocol and click Settings in the Protocols tab of the mailbox. Any changes you make on this tab override the server level properties, unless the protocol is disabled for the server.

POP3 Client Configuration

To connect a POP3 client to an Exchange server, you must specify the following information:

➤ **POP3 Account Name** The alias name of a Microsoft Exchange Server mailbox that supports POP3.

➤ **POP3 Email Address** The SMTP email address that Internet users will use to send messages.

➤ **POP3 Server Name** The computer name of the Microsoft Exchange Server computer that has the POP3 mailbox account on it.

➤ **SMTP Server Name** The name of the computer running the Internet Mail Service that provides SMTP services for the POP3 client.

Note: Because each POP3 client is different, the steps for configuring each of these clients to connect to a Microsoft Server POP3 computer are different.

Internet Message Access Protocol (IMAP)

The Internet Message Access Protocol (IMAP) enables users with any IMAP4-compliant client to access mail stored in their Exchange mailbox. The users can also read and post messages to public folders or access another user's mailbox if they have been granted the right to do so.

By default, when you install Microsoft Exchange Server, the IMAP4 protocol is also installed. This allows IMAP4 clients to retrieve their email as soon as the server is set up. You must configure IMS before the clients can send email, because the client uses the IMAP4 protocol to retrieve messages and the SMTP protocol to send messages.

The IMAP4 protocol can be configured at three different levels:

➤ **Site level** These protocol settings are default values that are inherited by the servers.

➤ **Server level** These tabs allow you to use either the site defaults or to configure different options on each server.

➤ **Mailbox level** These tabs allow you to use either the server defaults or to configure different options on a mailbox-by-mailbox basis. It's important to note that if you disable IMAP4 at the server level, all the mailboxes on that server are disabled, even if you enable the mailboxes individually.

IMAP4 Site And Server Properties

You can configure six IMAP4 tabs at the site level. These include General, Permissions, Authentication, Anonymous, Message Format, and Idle Time-out. The IMAP4 Site Defaults Properties page is shown in Figure 9.10.

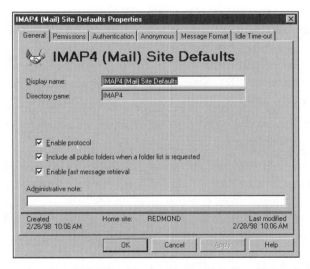

Figure 9.10   The IMAP4 Site Defaults Properties configuration dialog box.

General

This tab is used to enable or disable the protocol. Also, you can change the display name of the protocol (the name that appears in the Administrator program). The Directory name is displayed in a read-only field.

Authentication

This tab is used to specify the same methods of authentication as POP3 that IMAP4 clients must use to connect to the Exchange Server machine. You can select one of six different methods of authentication (or any combination of them). These methods are listed in Table 9.1.

Anonymous Connections

This tab is used to specify whether IMAP4 clients can connect to the Exchange server anonymously. Sometimes it makes sense to allow certain public folders to be accessible to users outside the organization. To make this possible, check the box next to Allow Anonymous Connections. Once you enable anonymous access, IMAP4 clients can access information on the Exchange server without requiring a Windows NT user account.

Message Format

This tab is used to control the message content encoding and character set. You can select MIME or UUEncode content encoding, as well as rich text format.

Idle Time-Out

This tab is used to set the amount of time IMAP4 needs to be idle before closing a connection. You can select to either not close idle connections or to close idle connections after a specified amount of time (measured in minutes).

Similar to the POP3 server-level properties, the IMAP4 server-level configuration has a Diagnostic Logging tab, which allows you to set logging levels for several Microsoft Exchange Server events.

To configure IMAP4 on a mailbox level, select the IMAP4 protocol and click Settings in the Protocols tab of the mailbox. Any changes you make in this tab override the server-level properties, unless the protocol is disabled for the server. Figure 9.11 shows what you see when you configure IMAP4 at the mailbox level.

IMAP4 Mailbox Configuration

Three extra options are available for you to configure in the Mailbox page:

➤ **Include all public folders when a folder list is requested** Some IMAP4 clients show poor performance when they display a large number of

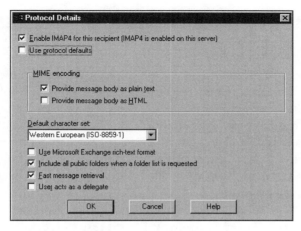

Figure 9.11   The mailbox-level IMAP4 page.

public folders. By default, public folders are listed for all clients. Clear this option to specify that this particular mailbox will not receive the public folder listing to improve client performance.

➤ **Fast message retrieval** This option allows you to specify slow IMAP4 clients so that message headers are sent. The user can then select which messages to download.

➤ **User acts as a delegate** You can use this option to allow an IMAP4 delegate user to access another user's mailbox to view personal folders contained within the other user's mailbox.

To connect an IMAP4 client to an Exchange server, you must specify the following information:

➤ **IMAP4 Account Name** The alias name of a Microsoft Exchange Server mailbox that supports IMAP4.

➤ **IMAP4 Email Address** The SMTP email address that Internet users will use to send messages.

➤ **IMAP4 Server Name** The name of the Microsoft Exchange Server computer that has the IMAP4 mailbox account on it.

➤ **SMTP Server Name** The name of the computer running IMS that provides SMTP services for the IMAP4 clients.

Note: Because each IMAP4 client is different, the steps for configuring each of these clients to connect to a Microsoft Server IMAP4 computer are different.

Lightweight Directory Access Protocol (LDAP)

The Lightweight Directory Access Protocol is an Internet protocol that enables LDAP clients to access directory information on your Microsoft Exchange Server machine. Given the correct permissions, these clients can browse, read, search, and write directory listing information to the Microsoft Exchange Server directory. Many LDAP clients can access your Exchange server and perform directory queries (including user names and phone numbers). If you assign the correct permissions, the users can modify Exchange directory information, such as changing phone numbers.

LDAP Site And Server Properties

To configure LDAP, you use the Microsoft Exchange Administrator program. The Protocols container stores the configuration parameters for the LDAP object. The LDAP Site Defaults Properties page is shown in Figure 9.12.

General

You use this page to enable or disable the protocol. Also, you can change the display name of the protocol (the name that appears in the Administrator program). The directory name is displayed in a read-only field.

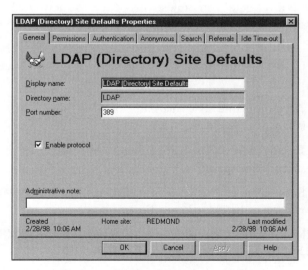

Figure 9.12 The LDAP Site Defaults Properties page.

Authentication

Use this property page to specify the same methods of authentication as POP3 that LDAP clients must use to connect to the Exchange server. You can select one of six different methods of authentication (or any combination of them). These methods are listed in Table 9.1.

Anonymous

Use this tab to specify whether LDAP clients can connect to the Exchange server anonymously.

Search

LDAP allows clients to perform searches on the directory. The LDAP search can perform three types of substring searches:

➤ **Initial substring search** The user specifies an attribute in the directory. The directory then matches the substring to the beginning of the attribute. "Initial" substring searches tend to be faster than the other types of substring searches.

➤ **Final substring search** The user specifies an attribute in the directory. The directory then matches the substring to the end of the attribute. "Final" substring searches tend to be slower than initial substring searches.

➤ **Any substring search** The user specifies an attribute in the directory. The directory then matches the substring to any portion of the attribute. "Any" substring searches are the slowest of the substring searches.

Referrals

Sometimes an LDAP client will request information that your Exchange server does not have access to. Therefore, you can configure your Exchange server to refer to another server that can fulfill the request. Be aware, however, that clients can only be referred to servers outside the local Exchange organization.

Idle Time-Out

Use this tab to set the amount of time LDAP needs to be idle before closing a connection. You can select to either not close idle connections or to close idle connections after a specified amount of time (measured in minutes).

Network News Transfer Protocol (NNTP) And Newsfeeds

The Internet News Service is a method for your organization to connect to a Usenet host to exchange information with Usenet. The Internet News Service is a Windows NT service that allows you to configure both unidirectional (read-only or write-only) and bi-directional (read and write) newsfeeds. This allows your clients to send messages to and receive messages from the Internet. If you have several Exchange servers in your site, only one of them needs to be configured with the Internet News Service. NNTP clients are still able to access newsgroup public servers on the server running the Internet News Service.

The Internet News Service integrates tightly with the IS to provide newsgroups as public folders. The service connects to Usenet hosts on a scheduled basis (one that you set). It connects to the remote hosts using a push feed or a pull feed. (The different types of newsfeeds are discussed later in this section.)

The Internet News Service can operate with either a dedicated or a dial-up connection to the Internet. Microsoft Outlook or any other NNTP-compatible client can access the newsgroup public folders. As far as the third-party newsreaders are concerned, they are communicating with a standard NNTP server.

A nice feature about the Internet News Service is its ability to communicate with multiple sources on multiple newsfeeds. It can perform these newsfeeds from one or more Microsoft Exchange Server computers.

Newsfeeds

The Internet News Service uses one of two different methods to establish newsfeeds with a remote NNTP host—a push feed or a pull feed.

With a *push feed*, your provider's host computer initiates a newsfeed to your Exchange Server computer and then "pushes" the news article to your computer. A push feed is best for a large newsfeed, but it does require you to interact with your newsfeed provider, because the provider controls which newsgroups you receive. A push feed is illustrated in Figure 9.13.

With a *pull feed*, your Microsoft Exchange Server computer initiates the connection with your provider's NNTP host and delivers any new messages to the host. The pull feed then checks for any news messages and retrieves them. Pull feeds work well when you only require a small feed, and they work well over a dial-up connection. A pull feed is illustrated in Figure 9.14.

You can also configure inbound and outbound newsfeeds. An *inbound newsfeed* allows you to pull messages from your provider's NNTP host computer, and it

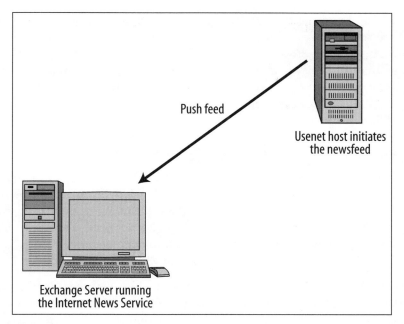

Figure 9.13   A push feed.

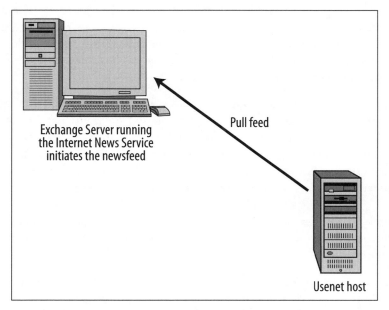

Figure 9.14   A pull feed.

allows you to accept messages that your provider's host pushes to your Exchange server. An *outbound newsfeed* allows you to push (or send) messages posted by your users to a newsgroup public folder to your provider's host computer. If a remote host computer needs to pull messages from your Exchange server, you would need to configure your computer with only NNTP client support. This allows the host computer to pull messages and act as if it's an NNTP newsreader.

Newsgroup Public Folders

You have the ability to designate any public folder in your site as a newsgroup public folder. These folders are accessible to NNTP clients and are used to send and receive items in a newsfeed. Outlook clients access these newsgroup public folders in the same way they would access any other Exchange public folder. However, with these newsgroup public folders, your users can exchange information with people all over the world or within your organization.

By default, when you set up the Internet News Service, it creates a public folder named Internet News. You have the ability to rename or move the Internet News public folder, but you do not have the option to delete it. Also, you can create other public folders that will contain newsgroup public folders.

A newsgroup public folder is just like any other public folder in Microsoft Exchange. As the administrator, you can set permissions on these public folders to control who can have access to the newsgroup. These folders are replicated with an organization using Exchange public folder replication, just like any other public folder.

How you name newsgroup public folders is important. You have to assign newsgroup public folders names that are based on their location in the newsgroup hierarchy. A newsgroup folder inherits a portion of the parent folder in which it resides. The full newsgroup folder name is the combination of the public folder's name and the name of its parent folders. Each of these names is separated by a period, similar to Internet domain names. For example, in Figure 9.15, if the newsgroup public folder named ActiveX is in the microsoft.public hierarchy, the newsgroup name of the ActiveX newsgroup public folder would be microsoft.public.activex. An example of newsgroup public folders is shown in Figure 9.15.

Because periods are used to separate the newsgroup public folder names, you cannot use periods in the name of a public folder. For example, you cannot have a newsgroup public folder named activex.components. If you use an unsupported character (such as a period) in the newsgroup public folder name, Microsoft Exchange automatically replaces it with a dash.

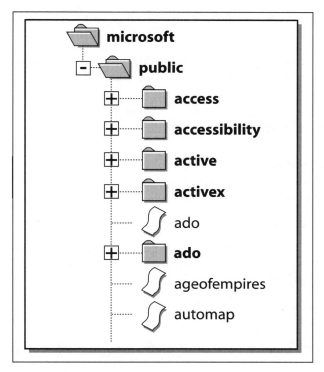

Figure 9.15   Newsgroup public folders naming conventions.

Newsgroups are either moderated or not. When a newsgroup is moderated, all items posted to that newsgroup are first mailed to a designated individual (known as the *moderator*). The designated moderator decides whether to accept or reject the posting based on its content. Any messages sent to a moderated newsgroup public folder do not appear in the public folder until the moderator has accepted the posts. To assign a moderator to a newsgroup public folder, use Microsoft Outlook.

Configuring An NNTP Newsfeed

To configure the Internet News Service, run the Newsfeed Configuration wizard. The wizard makes it easy for you to create one or more newsfeeds on an Exchange Server machine. You need to provide the wizard with the following information:

➤   The site name of the newsfeed provider that will be supplying your site with the newsfeed. Normally, this is the FQDN of the host computer sending the newsfeed.

➤ The mailbox name of the administrator that will be able to add and remove newsgroup public folders.

➤ The name and location of the active file if it will not be downloaded from the newsfeed provider upon installation.

Note: The active file is a text file that contains all the newsgroups that your newsfeed provider receives into its NNTP host.

To get the active file, you need to download it from your provider, or you can use the Windows NT **Telnet** command to create a text file with your provider's active newsgroups. To create the active text file, use the following procedure:

1. On the news server computer, click Start and then Run.

2. Type "Telnet [*server_name*] 119", where *server_name* is the name of the NNTP server that will be sending you your newsfeed, and 119 is the IP port used by NNTP.

3. In the Telnet application, select Start Logging from the Terminal menu; then specify a location for the active file you're creating to be stored.

4. From the Terminal menu, select Preferences and then select the Local Echo checkbox.

5. Type "list active" to capture a list of active newsgroups. Wait for the newsgroup directory list to be completed.

6. From the Terminal menu, select Stop Logging; then exit out of the Telnet application.

7. Using a text editor (such as Notepad), remove the first two lines and the last line (a period). You may also want to remove any newsgroups that you do not want in your newsgroup directory.

An example of an active file is shown in the following code:

```
microsoft.public.exchange.admin 42953 27481 y
microsoft.public.exchange.applications 9740 6310 y
microsoft.public.exchange.clients 24037 18134 y
microsoft.public.exchange.connectivity 24218 16773 y
microsoft.public.exchange.misc 21661 15846 y
microsoft.public.exchange.setup 23771 16560 y
microsoft.public.mail.admin 4030 3041 y
microsoft.public.mail.connectivity 3016 2359 y
microsoft.public.mail.misc 4721 3643 y
microsoft.public.outlook 424 1 y
microsoft.public.outlook.configuration 89 1 y
```

Configuring Newsfeed Properties

Once a newsfeed is created, you have the option to set additional NNTP properties. Figure 9.16 shows the tabs used to configure the newsfeed provider.

General

The General tab is used to enable the selected newsfeed, specify a display name, and change the administrator's mailbox. These options are as follows:

➤ **Display Name** The name displayed in the Exchange Administrator program. This field can be a maximum or 256 alphanumeric characters (which can include spaces and special characters).

➤ **Directory Name** A read-only field that displays the directory name specified during the installation.

➤ **Enable Newsfeed** Check this box to enable the selected newsfeed to send or receive newsgroup items.

➤ **Administrator's Mailbox** Use this option to assign an administrator that will have the right to add and remove newsgroup public folders from the selected newsfeed. Click the Change button to select the mailbox.

Messages

Use the Messages tab to specify the maximum size of all incoming and outgoing messages in the selected newsfeed. You can specify either no limit or a maximum limit (in kilobytes) for both outgoing and incoming messages.

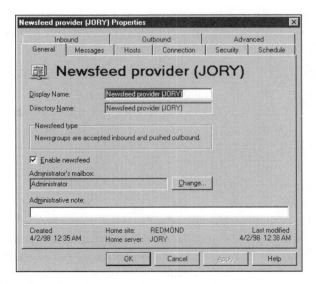

Figure 9.16 The Newsfeed Provider Properties page.

Hosts

Use the Hosts tab to configure the NNTP computers supplied by your newsfeed provider. Normally, you have an inbound host configured to receive messages from and an outbound host configured to send messages to. One host can act as both the inbound and outbound host.

If your Microsoft Exchange computer initiates and then connects, you must specify the remote Usenet site and host names. Your Internet News Service can then either push messages to the remote site or accept push messages from the site.

You can also configure additional inbound hosts by host names or IP addresses. You are only required to use this option if your newsfeed provider is pushing messages to you from multiple hosts.

Connection

The Connection tab is used to specify whether the selected newsfeed is to use a dedicated (LAN) connection or a dial-up connection.

If you're using a dial-up connection with IMS on the same computer as the Internet News Service, then the following connection information can be shared:

➤ **Connection** Select an existing RAS Phonebook entry as the dial-up connection you would like to use.

➤ **Refresh List** Click this button to update the Connection drop-down menu with the most current connections.

➤ **New Connection** Allows you to create a news dial-up connection (RAS Phonebook entry). After adding a new connection, you should choose Refresh List to update the connection list.

➤ **Account** This is the account name for the dial-up connection. This is an optional field.

➤ **Password** This is the password for the dial-up connection. This is an optional field. Reenter the password in the Confirm Password field to verify that the password is correct.

Security

By default, security is not enabled for NNTP newsfeeds. However, you can use this tab to specify that the select newsfeed is to use Secure Sockets Layer (SSL) when connecting to remote servers. This encrypts all data sent between your Microsoft Exchange Server computer and the remote NNTP host computer. You can also specify the account and password required to log on to the remote NNTP host computer. These options are explained as follows:

➤ **Require secure connection (SSL)** Check this box to enable SSL encryption for message transfer.

➤ **Outbound Connections** Your Exchange computer uses the username (the Log In To Remote Servers As: option) and the password for all outbound host connections. Your newsfeed provider supplies this account name and password to you. These are case-sensitive fields.

➤ **Inbound Connections** You can specify an Exchange mailbox or custom recipient that your newsfeed provider's host computer will use to log in to your Exchange server. The password for inbound host connections is a case-sensitive field.

Schedule

The Schedule tab is used to define when your Exchange server is to connect to your newsfeed provider's remote host to send and receive Usenet messages.

You can specify to connect never, always, or at selected times. If you choose the Selected Times option, you must also specify when the connections will take place (in either 1 hour or 15 minute intervals).

Inbound

The Inbound tab lists all the newsgroups that are available in the active file. You can configure both pull and push newsfeeds depending on how you configured the newsfeed through the Newsfeed Configuration wizard.

Outbound

If your Internet News Service is configured to send outbound newsfeeds to your provider, you can select which newsgroups your Exchange server will send in the newsfeeds.

Advanced

Use the Advanced tab to flush queued messages.

Click the Mark All As Delivered button to flush the queue of messages waiting to be processed. This allows your Exchange server or another host to catch up on the most recent newsgroup posts.

Setting Up Properties For NNTP

To send and receive Usenet newsfeeds, you must configure the newsfeed and the NNTP properties. You can set the NNTP object properties at both the site and server levels. Site-level properties apply to all the servers in the site, whereas server-level properties apply to the specified server only. The NNTP Site Defaults Properties page is shown in Figure 9.17.

General

This tab is used to enable or disable the protocol. Also, you can change the display name of the protocol (the name that appears in the Administrator program). The directory name is displayed in a read-only field. You can also enable or disable client access.

Newsfeeds

You can view the configuration properties of a newsfeed from either the site or server level. These configuration properties are the ones covered in the previous section.

Control Messages

Control messages are used to control how new newsgroups are created and how old ones are deleted. All control messages received by the Internet News Service are queued here until you (as the administrator) decide whether to accept or reject the messages. If for some reason you do not trust a particular Usenet host, you can choose to delete the control message without accepting its changes.

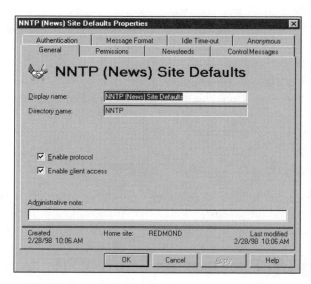

Figure 9.17 The NNTP Site Defaults Properties page.

Authentication

Use this tab to specify the same methods of authentication as POP3 and IMAP4 that NNTP clients must use to connect to the Exchange Server machine. You can select one of six different methods of authentication (or any combination of them). These methods are listed in Table 9.1.

Message Format

Use this tab to control the message content encoding and character set. You can select MIME or UUEncode content encoding, as well as rich text format.

Idle Time-Out

Use this tab to set the amount of time IMAP4 needs to be idle before closing a connection. You can select to either not close idle connections or to close idle connections after a specified amount of time (measured in minutes).

Anonymous

Use this tab to specify whether NNTP clients can connect to the Exchange server anonymously.

Microsoft Outlook Web Access

Microsoft Outlook Web Access allows users to access data on your Exchange server using an Internet Web browser from a Macintosh, Unix, or Windows-based computer. You can also use it to provide Global Address List information and to access any public folders you may have on your Exchange server. Users who have access (a mailbox) to your Exchange server can log in to their personal accounts to read and send private messages. Users also have the ability to publish information to the Internet without having to convert their documents to HTML format.

The Outlook Web Access works in conjunction with a client's Web browser. The browser communicates with Microsoft Exchange through Microsoft Internet Information Server (IIS) to provide the interface to the user's mailbox information. Use this feature of Microsoft Exchange Server to grant your users access to company and personal information from anywhere in the world via the Internet.

Outlook Web Access Installation

You have the option to install the Outlook Web Access files during the Microsoft Exchange Server setup. Outlook Web Access uses Active Server Pages (ASP files), to provide dynamically changing Web pages, and HTML, to provide static Web pages. IIS can be installed on the same Windows NT Server computer as Microsoft Exchange, or it can be installed on a different Microsoft Windows Server computer that can be accessed by the server on which Outlook Web Access is installed. When installing Outlook Web Access and Microsoft Exchange Server on the same computer, you must make sure the WWW service in IIS is enabled and running.

IIS version 2 can be installed when you install Microsoft Windows NT 4. The Active Server Pages component of IIS is only available in IIS version 3 or higher. If you have IIS 2 installed, you must upgrade it to IIS 3 or higher for Outlook Web Access to function. The Active Server component of IIS acts as a connector between Outlook Web Access and the Web browser (such as Microsoft Internet Explorer or Netscape Navigator). Active Server dynamically generates Web pages using a combination of HTML, server-executed scripts, and remote procedure calls (RPCs). You have the option to customize the default .ASP files for your organization. For example, you can add your organization's logo to Outlook Web Access.

Outlook Web Access Operations

When users want to access their Microsoft Exchange Server computer, they need to start their Web browser and specify the URL of their Active Server. The Web browser then displays a welcome page that allows the users to log on to the Exchange server using their mailbox names. Users must enter their Microsoft Exchange Server mailbox aliases in the Log On dialog box and either press Enter or click the "Click Here" hyperlink. The Outlook Web Access welcome page is shown in Figure 9.18.

The Enter Network Password dialog box appears and prompts users to enter their Windows NT usernames and passwords. If logging onto a certain domain, users must type in their domain names and Windows NT usernames in the Username box in the format

```
Domain\Windows NT username
```

followed by their Windows NT passwords in the Password box. The login dialog box is shown in Figure 9.19.

 A user's Exchange Server mailbox alias and Windows NT user account name may be different, because Windows NT User Manager For Domains and the Exchange Administrator program allow you to create a mailbox with a different name for a specific Windows NT account.

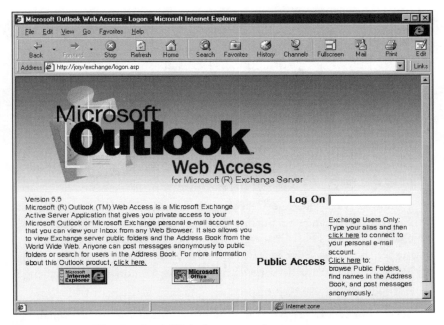

Figure 9.18   The Outlook Web Access welcome page.

Figure 9.19   The Enter Network Password dialog box.

Authentication

Users can access your Microsoft Exchange Server computer via the Internet using secure connections to log on as either validated users or anonymous users. When users log on to your Microsoft Exchange server, secure and encrypted sessions are established between the users' Web browser and the IIS computer. Before users are granted access to their Exchange information, their Windows NT domain account password must be validated with the Windows NT domain. IIS then logs users on to the Exchange Server computer.

Remember that IIS authenticates the user in the Windows NT domain, not Exchange Server. It's also important to note that the different security levels available to you are configured in the WWW service of IIS, because IIS established the secure connection between itself and the user's Web browser.

Several different levels of security are available to you for authentication of Internet or intranet users:

➤ **Basic Authentication** This is the lowest level of security available for Internet and intranet users. When you set up basic authentication, you must also set up the Log On Locally permission on the IIS computer.

➤ **Windows NT Challenge/Response Authentication** If you have IIS and Microsoft Exchange Server installed on the same computer, you can enable Windows NT Challenge/Response Authentication to offer a higher level of security. If IIS is installed on a different computer than Microsoft Exchange Server, you must disable Windows NT Challenge/Response Authentication.

➤ **Secure Sockets Layer** You can establish additional security by enabling Secure Sockets Layer (SSL), which is used to encrypt all data transferred between the Web browser and IIS. Don't forget that this feature can only be used with Web browsers that support SSL (such as Microsoft Internet Explorer 3.02 or Netscape Navigator 3.01). To enable SSL, you must obtain a security certificate.

Outlook Web Access uses Windows NT authentication to grant access to a user's mailbox. To be granted access, the user must enter his or her Windows NT user account name, password, and mailbox name. After a user has been validated, he or she will have the same permissions as when he or she logs on to a computer directly connected to the network.

An anonymous user is a nonvalidated user and is not recognized by Microsoft Exchange Server. When users log on to the Exchange server anonymously, they are restricted to viewing and accessing only the published public folders and address lists. You can control which folders and address lists are published using the Exchange Administrator program.

Outlook Web Access Configuration

To configure Outlook Web Access, use the Exchange Server Administrator program. You can determine which public folders and Global Address Lists anonymous users can view. The public folder that's available to all Internet users is known as a *published public folder* and is configured in the Folders Short-cuts tab. Once you have configured Outlook Web Access, users can access it with the following URL:

```
http://<IIS Server name>/exchange
```

Figure 9.20 shows the General tab of Outlook's HTTP Web Site Settings Properties page.

 The user's Web browser must support both JavaScript and frames.

General

Use the General tab to specify a display name, enable the protocol, and grant anonymous users access to published public folders. The options are explained as follows:

➤ **Display Name** The name displayed in the Exchange Administrator program. This field can be a maximum of 256 alphanumeric characters (which can include spaces and special characters).

Figure 9.20 The General tab of Outlook's HTTP Web Site Settings Properties page.

➤ **Directory Name** A read-only field that displays the directory name specified during the installation.

➤ **Enable HTTP** Allows you to enable or disable HTTP access to the site.

Folder Shortcuts

Folder shortcuts are links to the Microsoft Exchange Server published public folders. Use this tab to select which public folders can be accessed by anonymous users when they connect to your Exchange server from the Internet.

Advanced

This tab allows you to set the number of address book entries that will be returned to the users. The default is set at 50 entries.

Exam Prep Questions

Question 1

You have a single Microsoft Exchange Server computer in your organization. Joe complains that he cannot access his Inbox from home using his POP3 application, whereas other employees can. You verify that Joe is entering the correct configuration information into his POP3 application and that other users can access their mailboxes. Joe can access his mailbox at the office using Microsoft Outlook. What is the most likely problem?

○ a. POP3 is disabled for the site.

○ b. POP3 is disabled for the server.

○ c. POP3 is disabled for Joe's mailbox.

○ d. There's insufficient information to find a solution.

The correct answer to this question is c. If Joe cannot access his mailbox using POP3 and other users can, his mailbox access for POP3 must be disabled. Other users can access their mailboxes using POP3; therefore, answers a, b, and d are incorrect.

Question 2

Your company upgrades one of your Microsoft Exchange Server computers from version 4 to version 5.5. You enable POP3 support on the newly upgraded server. Your users complain that they cannot access their mailbox information using the POP3 protocol. What is the problem?

○ a. The Exchange Service account is set up incorrectly.

○ b. POP3 is disabled for the server.

○ c. The clients are using the wrong POP3 client.

○ d. Windows NT Challenge/Response Authentication is disabled.

The correct answer to this question is a. The service account must be able to "act as the operating system"; this is not required in Exchange 4. If POP3 was disabled on the server, none of your users would be able to access the server. Therefore, answer b is incorrect. Basically, a POP3 client is a POP3 client is a POP3 client. Some may have extra bells and whistles, but they still use the POP3 protocol to receive messages. Therefore, answer c is incorrect. Windows NT Challenge/Response is not used with POP3. Therefore, answer d is incorrect.

Question 3

> Which client component would you use to resolve a domain name to an IP address?
>
> ○ a. DNS
>
> ○ b. IMS
>
> ○ c. Microsoft Outlook
>
> ○ d. A resolver program

The correct answer to this question is d. The client portion of DNS is called the *resolver*. It passes any name resolution requests to the DNS server. DNS is the server component of Internet name-to-IP address resolution. Therefore, answer a is incorrect. IMS is the Internet Mail Service. It's used to connect an Exchange server or site to the Internet using the SMTP protocol. Therefore, answer b is incorrect. Microsoft Outlook is the client portion of Microsoft Exchange Server. Therefore, answer c is incorrect.

Question 4

> To connect to the Internet via a modem using the Internet Mail Service, which components must be installed? [Check all correct answers]
>
> ❑ a. RAS
>
> ❑ b. A valid RAS Phonebook entry must be created
>
> ❑ c. NetBEUI
>
> ❑ d. TCP/IP

The correct answers to this question are a, b, and d. RAS is the component that establishes the connection using the Phonebook entry over TCP/IP. Although NetBEUI is a valid RAS protocol, it's not required for connection to the Internet. Furthermore, it's not routable. Therefore, answer c is incorrect.

Question 5

> You would like to receive a small number of newsgroups from your newsfeed provider. Which is the best way to configure your newsfeed?
>
> ○ a. An inbound push
>
> ○ b. An inbound push, outbound pull
>
> ○ c. An inbound pull, outbound push
>
> ○ d. An inbound pull

The correct answer to this question is d. To receive only a small number of newsgroups, you must pull the specific newsgroups. An inbound push will send all the newsgroups to your server. Therefore, answers a and b are incorrect. An outbound push will send all the newsgroups to your provider's host computer; therefore, answer c is incorrect.

Question 6

> Which components allow you to send and receive Internet mail using a POP3 client? [Check all correct answers]
>
> ❏ a. IMAP4
>
> ❏ b. POP3
>
> ❏ c. SMTP
>
> ❏ d. NNTP

The correct answers to this question are b and c. The POP3 protocol is used to receive messages from the Internet, and the SMTP protocol is used to send messages to the Internet. IMAP4 would only be a correct answer if an IMAP4-compliant mailer were used. Therefore, answer a is incorrect. The NNTP protocol is used for Usenet information, not for the sending and receiving of Internet mail. Therefore, answer d is incorrect.

Question 7

> What must you do to your Exchange server to be able to share
> some newsgroups as public folders?
>
> ○ a. Install a newsreader client on the server and share its data.
>
> ○ b. Install and configure the Internet News Service.
>
> ○ c. Install newsreader client software on each of your user's
> desktops.
>
> ○ d. This cannot be done with Microsoft Exchange Server.

The correct answer to this question is b. The Internet News Service has the
ability to share newsgroup information in public folders. A newsreader cannot
share its information. It can only read information from a news server. Therefore, answer a is incorrect. Installing a newsreader client on your users' desktops
will allow them to connect to an NNTP server to receive newsgroup information, but it will store newsgroups in private folders. Therefore, answer c is
incorrect. Answer d is incorrect because this can be done with Exchange.

Need To Know More?

 Search the Microsoft Technical Information Network (TechNet) CD-ROM. The technical notes for Exchange Server provide insight into its design and architecture. Use searches on "Internet Mail Service," "Internet News Service," "POP3," "IMAP4," "Active Server Pages," and "LDAP."

 Install Online Books from the Microsoft Exchange 5.5 CD-ROM. It contains a wealth of useful information.

 Go to the Microsoft Exchange Server home page at www.microsoft.com/exchange. Many of the documents located here are newer than the ones available on the Microsoft Technical Information Network (TechNet) CD-ROM.

 Go to the Microsoft Knowledge Base and support home page at www.microsoft.com/kb. Many of the documents located here are newer than the ones available on the Microsoft Technical Information Network (TechNet) CD-ROM.

Exchange Server Security

Terms you'll need to understand:

- ✓ Backfill
- ✓ Change message
- ✓ Granularity
- ✓ Key Management Server (KM Server)
- ✓ Master encryption key
- ✓ Private and public keys
- ✓ Public folders
- ✓ Public folder replication agent (PFRA)
- ✓ Replica
- ✓ Sealing
- ✓ Secret key
- ✓ Signing
- ✓ Time stamp
- ✓ Top-level public folders

Techniques you'll need to master:

- ✓ Understanding and configuring the public folder architecture and replication
- ✓ Understanding the difference between hierarchy and contents replication
- ✓ Understanding the Microsoft Exchange advanced security features
- ✓ Configuring and maintaining Key Management Servers

One of the most powerful features Microsoft Exchange Server provides you is the ability to configure and maintain public folders. Public folders can store message items, such as email messages and word processing documents, and have forms attached to them. Public folders can also be configured to replicate themselves to other servers within a site or organization. This allows users from anywhere in the organization to access public folder information without having to cross wide area network (WAN) links to communicate with remote servers.

Also, with Microsoft Exchange Server's advanced security, you can allow users to digitally sign and seal their mail messages.

Public Folders Explored And Explained

Using public folders is a way to share information among users within a site or organization. Public folders can contain several different types of information:

➤ Mail messages

➤ Word processing documents

➤ Graphic files

➤ Spreadsheets

With Exchange public folders, you have the ability to create custom applications using custom forms and views. Some of these custom applications may include the following:

➤ Customer tracking systems

➤ Help desk applications

➤ Vacation time request forms

➤ Expense forms

➤ Automated time tracking

Microsoft Exchange public folders are stored in the Public Information Store (IS), located in a file called named PUB.EDB in the Exchsrvr\Mdbdata\ directory. You can choose to replicate your public folder to one or more remote Microsoft Exchange servers.

Public folders are made up of two parts: the public folder hierarchy and the public folder contents.

Public Folder Hierarchy

When public folders are created, they take on a tree structure. The structure is similar to that of a directory tree, with the root (or top-level) folders at the top and the subfolders below them. This structure is called the *public folder hierarchy*. The public folder hierarchy appears as a series of folders in the left pane of the Microsoft Outlook client user interface, as is shown in Figure 10.1.

The Information Store on the public folder server supplies the information required to build the hierarchy structure.

 The public folder hierarchy is replicated to all Public Information Stores within an organization automatically. Public folder content is not replicated unless folder replication is configured.

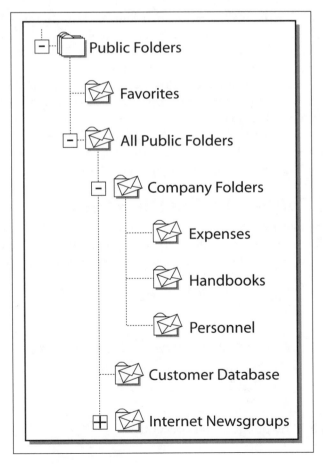

Figure 10.1   The public folder hierarchy.

The highest level in the hierarchy is called the *root* or *top level*. By default, all users can create folders at this level. You can, however, use the Microsoft Exchange Administrator program to modify the list of users who have permissions to create top-level folders. If you do not restrict the number of users who can create at this top level, the hierarchy will become cluttered with everyone's public folders, and it will be difficult to locate specific information.

Subfolders can be created within the top-level folders. As with a directory tree, subfolders can be created within subfolders, which can be created within subfolders, and so on. By default, the folder's owner (the user who created the folder) controls who gets access to navigate the subfolders as well as to create new subfolders.

Public Folder Contents

The contents of a public folder are the messages (made up of the message headers and the bodies with attachments) contained within the public folder hierarchy. The public folder contents are stored in one or more Microsoft Exchange Server computers (as long as the server has a Public Information Store). Note that even though the hierarchy is stored on all public folder servers, the contents are stored only on some of these servers. The location of the content is automatically selected when a user creates a public folder, or the administrator can control this location. For example, if Joe creates a public folder named *Joe's Private Folder*, and Joe's mailbox resides on the server named *Jory*, the public folder contents will automatically be located in Jory's Information Store. The public folder's contents are shown in Figure 10.2.

Public Folders In The Directory

Every public folder created by a user automatically has an entry in the Directory (the Microsoft Exchange Directory) and can also appear as a recipient. In other words, when a user creates a public folder, the public folder can receive

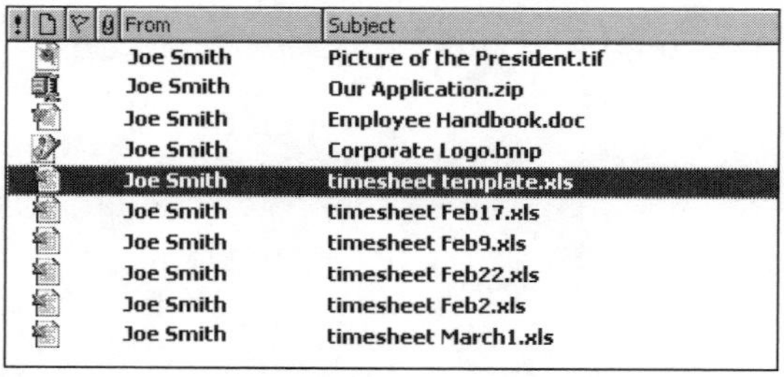

!	D	▽	ℓ	From	Subject
				Joe Smith	Picture of the President.tif
				Joe Smith	Our Application.zip
				Joe Smith	Employee Handbook.doc
				Joe Smith	Corporate Logo.bmp
				Joe Smith	timesheet template.xls
				Joe Smith	timesheet Feb17.xls
				Joe Smith	timesheet Feb9.xls
				Joe Smith	timesheet Feb22.xls
				Joe Smith	timesheet Feb2.xls
				Joe Smith	timesheet March1.xls

Figure 10.2 The public folder contents.

messages just like any other Exchange recipient. By default, all public folders are hidden recipients and cannot be viewed in the recipients container in the Exchange Administrator program. To display these hidden recipients, select the Hidden Recipients option from the View menu while in the recipients container. You can also have a public folder appear in the Global Address List by clearing the Hide From Address Book checkbox in the Advanced property page of the public folder. The correlation between public folders and Exchange Directory entries is shown in Figure 10.3.

Directory Store Latency Problems

A public folder can possibly appear in the hierarchy of a remote server before the recipient appears in the address book or the Administrator program, because the replication of the public folder hierarchy can occur faster than directory information replication.

On the flip side, a public folder can possibly appear as a recipient in the Administrator program, yet any attempts to obtain its property pages fail because the Information Store has not yet replicated the public folder in the hierarchy. This occurs when directory replication takes place faster than Information Store (and public folder hierarchy) replication.

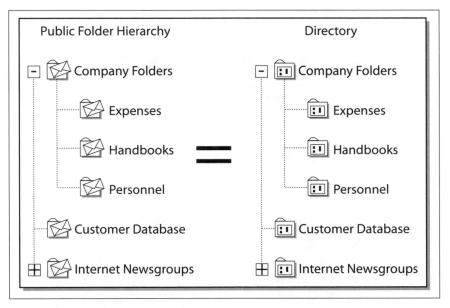

Figure 10.3   How public folders correspond with Exchange
Directory entries.

Configuring The Information Store

The site configuration properties are used to control public folders. These properties are controlled through the site configuration object in the configuration container of the site. Figure 10.4 displays the Information Store Site Configuration property page.

From the Information Store Site Configuration property page, you, as the administrator, can configure several property pages:

➤ **General** This property page allows you to configure the following information:

➤ **Display name** A name given to the Information Store that will identify it in the Exchange Administrator program. This field can be up to 256 characters long.

➤ **Directory name** A read-only field that displays the directory name.

➤ **Public folder container** Allows you to select where the public folder container will be located.

➤ **Enable message tracking** Allows you to enable or disable message tracking in the Information Store.

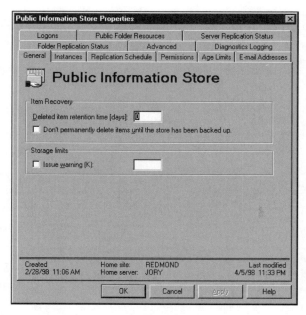

Figure 10.4 The Server Public Information Store Properties page.

➤ **Top-Level Folder Creation** You, as the administrator, control who in the organization can create top-level (or root) public folders. By default, all users are allowed to create top-level public folders.

➤ **Storage Warnings** This property page is used to specify the times at which notification messages are to be sent to mailbox owners or public folder contacts when the folders or mailboxes have exceeded the maximum amount of storage space assigned to them. Quota limits can be set for public folders in two locations: the General property page for the Public Information Store and the Limits page under properties of a selected public folder.

➤ **Public Folder Affinity** Sometimes the contents of a public folder are not located on a server within the site but instead are found on one or more servers in other sites. If this situation occurs, site affinity must be configured to allow clients access to these folders (or replicas) in the remote site. This is known as *public folder site affinity*. The client needs to be able to connect to the server in the remote site using a remote procedure call (RPC) as well as have an affinity value set.

You can use public folder site affinity to specify a preference for one site over another for the client to connect to the remote public folder servers. By default, no public folder site affinity is set, and it is only necessary when folders/replicas are located in different remote sites. The client will not connect to a server containing a replica in a site without having an affinity value. Public folder site affinity is a cost value assigned to a connection between sites and is similar to that of the site connector cost value.

 Public folder affinity values can be set only between sites and not between servers within the site or servers in a remote site.

The site with the lowest affinity value is attempted first; if a connection cannot be made, the site with the next lowest affinity value will be attempted, and so on. For example, if a site can connect to four remote sites with public folder affinity values of 1, 20, 50, and 80 assigned to them, the site with the affinity value of 1 will be attempted, followed by the site with the value of 20, and so on.

Similar to trust relationships in a Windows NT enterprise environment, affinity values are one way. That is to say that if a remote site has an affinity value of 30 with respect to your local site, this does not mean your local site automatically has an affinity value of 30 with respect to the remote site. You must configure the affinity values in the remote site independently.

Creating And Handling Public Folders

The user can access property pages to set general configuration items for a folder, as well as views, permissions, and forms.

Using The Microsoft Exchange Client To Create A Public Folder

To create a new public folder using the Microsoft Exchange client, select New Folder from the File menu. A dialog box will appear requesting you to enter a name. The public folder is then created, and you are prompted to use the properties.

 Be aware of the following name change. The original Microsoft Exchange client no longer exists. Microsoft now calls the client side of the Microsoft Exchange Server "Outlook" and the server side of the Microsoft Exchange Server "Exchange." This becomes apparent when you notice that Microsoft's email clients are called Outlook, Outlook Express, and Outlook Web Access.

Using The Microsoft Outlook Client To Create A Public Folder

You can create a public folder using Outlook by selecting the Create Subfolder option in the File|Folder menu. A dialog box will appear requesting that you enter in a folder name. It also allows you to select a type of folder to create.

Public Folder Permissions

For users to access a public folder, they must have the appropriate permissions. Microsoft Exchange provides you with some predefined roles as an easy way to group required user permissions. Eight permissions are set for each role, and these roles are set in the public Folders Permissions Properties page, shown in Figure 10.5. These permissions are described in Table 10.1.

Table 10.2 describes the permissions granted to the following predefined roles:

➤ Owner

➤ Publishing Editor

➤ Editor

➤ Publishing Author

➤ Author

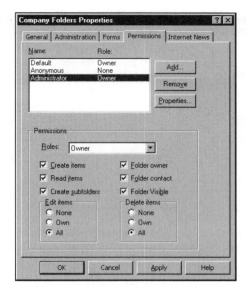

Figure 10.5   The public Folders Permissions Properties page.

Table 10.1	Public folder permissions.
Permission	**Description**
Create Items	Creates new items in a folder.
Read Items	Opens and reads items in a folder.
Create Subfolders	Creates subfolders within a folder.
Edit Items	Modifies items in a folder.
Folder Owner	Performs administrative tasks on the folder and changes permissions of the folder.
Folder Contact	Any email messages specific to this folder are sent to the contact. These notifications might include storage limit notifications or replication conflicts.
Folder Visible	Specifies whether this folder is visible to the user in the public folder hierarchical tree.
Delete Item	Deletes items from a folder.

➤ Nonediting Author

➤ Reviewer

➤ Contributor

➤ None

Role	Folder Owner	Create Items	Create Sub-folders	Edit Items	Delete Items	Read Items	Folder Contact	Folder Visible
Table 10.2	**Predefined roles and their corresponding permissions.**							
Owner	✓	✓	✓	✓(all)	✓(all)	✓	✓	✓
Publishing Editor		✓	✓	✓(all)	✓(all)	✓		✓
Editor		✓		✓(all)	✓(all)	✓		✓
Publishing Author		✓	✓	✓(own)	✓(own)	✓		✓
Author		✓		✓(own)	✓(own)	✓		✓
Nonediting Author		✓			✓(own)	✓		✓
Reviewer						✓		✓
Contributor		✓						✓
None								✓

If one of the predefined roles does not meet the needs of your organization, you can grant custom permissions using any combination of permissions.

To prevent users from viewing and reading the contents of a specific public folder (including subfolders), you can remove the Read Items permission. You can remove any name (except the default name and the name of the folder owner) by selecting the name and clicking the Remove button. If you remove the default name or the name of the folder owner, it will reappear the next time the Permissions property page is viewed, because a public folder must always have an owner assigned to it.

For a folder that contains private or sensitive information, you can hide it from most users by clearing the Folder Visible checkbox in the Permissions property page of the public folder.

Users can create and use what are called *public folder favorites*. Public folder favorites are links to public folders within the hierarchy and are used as short-cuts to gain quick access to folders. The favorites are stored in the user's Favorite folder. The links open the public folder without having to open all the public folders in the hierarchy. This can bypass any permission you set on the top-level folders of the linked folder. To prevent this from happening, change the permissions on all folders and subfolders to those set on the higher-level folder. You can accomplish this by selecting the Propagate These Properties To All Subfolders checkbox in the General property page of the top-level public folder (in the Exchange Administrator program).

Naming And Situating Public Folders

By default, the contents of a public folder are stored on a single public folder server, assuming no public folder replication has been established. Having one copy of the public folder contents has both its advantages and disadvantages.

Single Copy Advantages

The advantages to having a single copy include the following:

➤ No Exchange Server overhead is required for replicating the public folder's contents to other public folder servers.

➤ No latency (delay) is involved for replicating the public folder's contents to other public folder servers.

Single Copy Disadvantages

The disadvantages to having a single copy include the following:

➤ If many users need to access specific contents on a specific public folder server, the server may be overloaded with these requests. This can cause a bottleneck when these folders are accessed.

➤ If you take the public folder server down for maintenance or the public folder server goes offline unexpectedly, the public folder's contents will not be available for users to access.

You can configure public folders to replicate to other servers within your organization. You can choose to place the replicated public folder contents on another server in the same site or on a server in a remote site.

 Know the advantages and disadvantages of having a single copy as well as having replicas. Also be aware of some of the extra overhead required when using replicas.

Replica Advantages

Replicating public folder contents to other servers within the local site or a remote site is beneficial in the following situations:

➤ When trying to balance the user access load among several public folder servers within the organization.

➤ When scheduling public folder replication to remote sites to control the use of the available network bandwidth. For example, you might not want your users in a remote site accessing your local public folder server for contents information, because your WAN link is slow or is billed by the amount of data transferred on it.

Replica Disadvantages

Deciding when it is advantageous to replicate public folders can be difficult. If the amount of bandwidth needed to replicate public folders is greater than the amount of bandwidth that would be consumed if all users accessed the folders from a single server, replicating may not be advantageous.

Understanding Public Folder Replication

Public folder replication is achieved through two steps: public folder contents replication and public folder hierarchy replication. Each component of the public folder (contents and hierarchy) is replicated and managed separately.

➤ **Public folder contents replication** Copies of all messages within a public folder that is to be replicated are transferred as mail messages to all servers participating in the replication. You can control public folder contents replication on a folder by folder basis.

➤ **Public folder hierarchy replication** Propagates all top-level and subfolder hierarchical information to all servers in the organization as mail messages. This process cannot be prevented.

Public Folder Replication Advantages

Using public folder replication provides you with the following advantages:

➤ Fault tolerance is provided for your public folder contents should your primary server be unavailable.

➤ You can distribute the load of users accessing the public folder server. You can also improve the response time in accessing public folder information because information is accessed locally rather than remotely.

➤ The amount of information transferred over your WAN links between your public folder server and your clients is reduced.

Public Folder Contents Replication

You need to know who will be accessing your replicas and which server or sites these replicas will be accessed from. Here are some issues you should be aware of when configuring public folder contents replication:

➤ Each message with a replica folder is copied to all servers that store replicas.

➤ You can schedule when the replication will occur.

➤ You must manually specify which servers are to partake in a specific public folder's replication.

➤ Setting up folder replication to remote sites allows clients who normally cannot access the public folders server (because they lack RPC access) a method for accessing the public folders.

Public folder contents replication deals with two levels of granularity. *Granularity* is defined as a computer activity or feature in terms of the size of the units it handles. For example, if the feature is screen resolution, the size will be measured in pixels.

Here are the two levels of granularity:

➤ **Granularity of replication** Measured at the message level. Any changes to a message property or to an attachment contained within the message will cause the message to be replicated to all the other public folder instances.

➤ **Granularity of configuration** Measured at the folder level. If multiple messages are to be replicated, Exchange Server will group these messages into a large message and replicate the single message. The size of the combined message is specified by the maximum message size property.

Public Folder Hierarchy Replication

The public folder hierarchy is replicated using mail messages to all public folders in the organization. These messages are transferred using the Message Transfer Agent (MTA). The public folder hierarchy is replicated to all public folder servers in the Exchange organization automatically. Note that public folder hierarchy replication cannot be scheduled. Instead it is replicated at a set interval configured in the Registry.

The default hierarchy replication interval is set to 60 seconds. Therefore, any public folder hierarchy changes will be replicated to all the public folder servers in the organization every 60 seconds. You can control the hierarchy replication interval by changing the following Registry setting (in seconds):

```
HKEY_LOCAL_MACHINE\SYSTEM
  \CurrentControl Set
    \Services
      \MSExchangeIS
        \ParametersPublic
          \Replication Send Folder Tree
```

Configuring Public Folder Replication

You configure the public folder replication from the Exchange Administrator program. In order to replicate a specific public folder, you must follow this procedure:

1. Select the public folder to be replicated from the Organization container.

2. Select the Properties option from the File menu.

You will use the following three property pages to replicate public folders:

➤ **Replicas** This property page is used to configure which servers within the site or in remote sites will contain the replicas (see Figure 10.6). Any server listed in this property page will have the replicas "pushed" to it.

➤ **Folder Replication Status** This property page displays all the public folder servers that are receiving the replicated folder (see Figure 10.7).

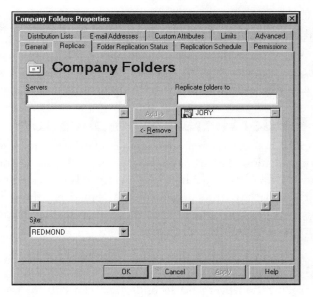

Figure 10.6 The Replicas property page.

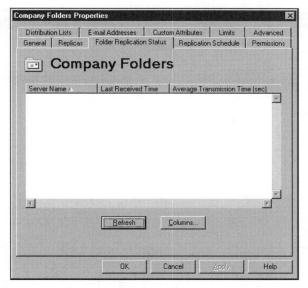

Figure 10.7   The Folder Replication Status property page.

   If you need to troubleshoot a failed replication, the Folder Replication Status property page is the place to go. Replication information stored here is very valuable to you when you need to find a problem with your setup.

By clicking on the Columns button, you can specify which columns of information will be displayed in this property page. The different columns that you can specify are:

➤ **Server name** The name of the server to which the folder was replicated.

➤ **Last received time** The last time the local server received updates from the selected server.

➤ **Average transmission time** The average time it takes to update the selected remote server from the local server.

➤ **Replication status** The status of the replication. The different status categories are listed in Table 10.3.

➤ **Replication Schedule** This property page is used to configure the intervals at which the public folder will be replicated to other public folder servers within the organization. This property page is displayed in Figure 10.8.

Table 10.3	Replication status categories.
Status	**Description**
In Synch	No local public folder has been modified. The remote public folder server is synchronized with the local server.
Local Modified	The local public folder has been modified, but the replicas have not been sent to the remote server.
Last Received Time	The last time the local server has received updates from the remote server.
Average Transmission Time	The average time it takes to update the remote server from the local server.
Last Transmission Time (sec)	The amount of time for the last transmission to take place.

If you're replicating over a WAN connection, you may want to configure the Replication Schedule to force the replication to occur during nonpeak times (that is, in the middle of the night or on weekends). This is especially true if you're performing user authentication over the WAN link as well. This same approach should be taken when replicating folders with large amounts of information or large folders containing large files.

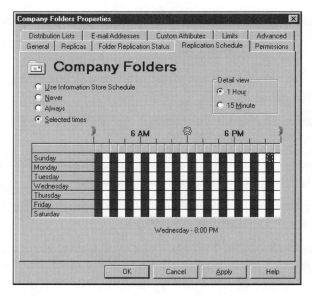

Figure 10.8 The Replication Schedule property page.

You can specify the schedule at which this public folder will be replicated to the rest of the public folder servers using the following options:

➤ **Use Information Store Schedule** This option will use the schedule set in the Public Information Store Replication Schedule property page.

➤ **Never** This option will disable replication for this public folder.

➤ **Always** This option will replicate the public folder every 15 minutes.

➤ **Selected Times** This option allows you to configure specific times to replicate the public folder (in 15 minute or 1 hour intervals).

 If you set a schedule on the folder level for a specific folder, it will override any schedule set at the Information Store level.

Configuring Public Information Store Replication

The following property pages are available to you for the configuration of the Public Information Store:

➤ **Instances** Use this property page to configure which replicas of a specified public folder to "pull" to the Public Information Store.

➤ **Replication Schedule** Use this property page to set the replication schedule.

You can specify the schedule at which this public folder will be replicated to the rest of the public folder servers. You can specify the following options:

➤ **Never** This option will disable replication for this public folder.

➤ **Always** This option will replicate the public folder every 15 minutes.

➤ **Selected Times** This option allows you to configure specific times to replicate the public folder (in 15 minute or 1 hour intervals).

➤ **Folder Replication Status** Displays the public folders that are being replicated and how many servers this folder is being replicated to.

➤ **Advanced** Allows you to specify the frequency at which replication of the Information Store will occur as well as the maximum size of the replication messages.

➤ **Public Folder Resources** Allows you to view the amount of space that is currently being used by the public folders and replicas on this Information Store (see Figure 10.9).

Use the information contained in the Public Folder Resources property page to decide what your replication schedule should be.

➤ **Server Replication Status** Displays the replication information for all the servers in your organization to which this Information Store is being replicated.

Replicating Public Folders

Public folder replication uses the MTA as its replication transport mechanism.

Public Folder Replication Agent

When more than one instance of a public folder exists, the public folder replication agent (PFRA) monitors all modifications, additions, and deletions to the public folder. The PFRA then sends change messages to other Information Stores that store replicated instances.

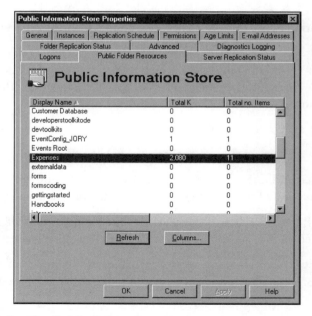

Figure 10.9 The Public Folder Resources property page.

The PFRA uses the following message attributes to ensure that messages are correctly replicated within the organization:

➤ **Change Number** A number created using a globally (organization-wide) unique Information Store identifier and a server-specific change counter. Due to its structure, the change number is Information Store specific and it reflects a sequential change. The change counter is sequential for all folders and messages in the Information Store but not for a single folder or message.

Any time a user makes a change (adds, modifies, or deletes) a message in any public folder on the server, the change counter is incremented. Following any modification to the public folder contents, the PFRA increments the change counter.

➤ **Time Stamp** When messages arrive in a public folder, they are assigned a time stamp. When a message is modified, the PFRA assigns a new time stamp using the greater of either the current system time or the old time stamp.

➤ **Predecessor Change List** The predecessor change list for a specific public folder message is a list of the Information Stores that have made the change and the last change number made by each Information Store. The predecessor change list is used to help identify public folder conflicts.

Out-Of-Sync Public Folders And Backfill

It's assumed that messaging transports will successfully deliver any replication message sent by the originating Information Store. No way exists to confirm that a replication message sent between the originating and the receiving Information Stores has been completed successfully (other than receiving a nondelivery report), because delivery confirmation is a messaging overhead. If an Information Store was to send a confirmation message for every replication message sent, it would be required to add an extra message to each transfer.

If a replication message does not arrive at its intended destination, the Information Store in that location will no longer have an up-to-date copy of the message. Therefore, the public folders on the local and remote computers are no longer synchronized. The originating Information Store assumes that replication has completed successfully, even though this is not the case.

To correct this problem, the Public Information Stores participate in a *backfill* process. The backfill can help the Information Stores recover from the following situations:

➤ Lost replication messages

➤ A public server being restored from a backup

➤ A public server that is being shutdown and then restarted

The backfill process is displayed in Figure 10.10 through Figure 10.13 and occurs as described in the following sections.

Replication To Information Store 2 Fails

Information Store 1 sends out a replication message to Information Store 2 and Information Store 3. Information Store 2 does not receive the replication message. Information Store 1 and Information Store 3 are synchronized, but Information Store 2 has an old version of the message. Information Store 1 and Information Store 3 have a matching change number that is not known to Information Store 2. See Figure 10.10.

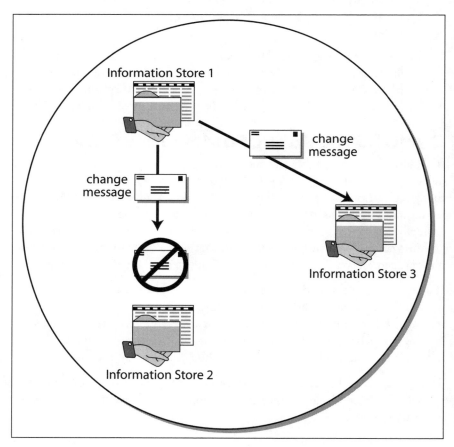

Figure 10.10 Replication to Information Store 2 fails.

Status Messages Sent And Analyzed

Information Store 3 sends out a status message to Information Store 1 and Information Store 2. Information Store 2 will check to see if the change numbers are the same as the ones it has recorded. If the change numbers are the same, Information Store 2 and Information Store 3 are synchronized. However, if the change numbers are not the same, Information Store 2 will determine if there are any higher change numbers in the list of changes for Information Store 3 that are not in the list of changes for Information Store 2. See Figure 10.11.

Backfill Request Sent

When Information Store 2 finds mismatching change numbers, it creates a backfill request for the changes that it has not yet received. This backfill request is sent (in the form of a mail message) to a preferred public folder server (in this case, Information Store 3). See Figure 10.12.

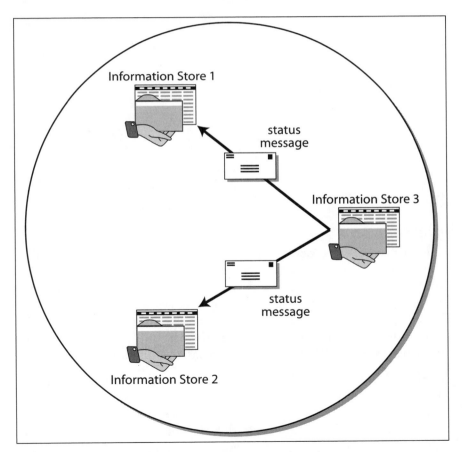

Figure 10.11   Status messages sent and analyzed.

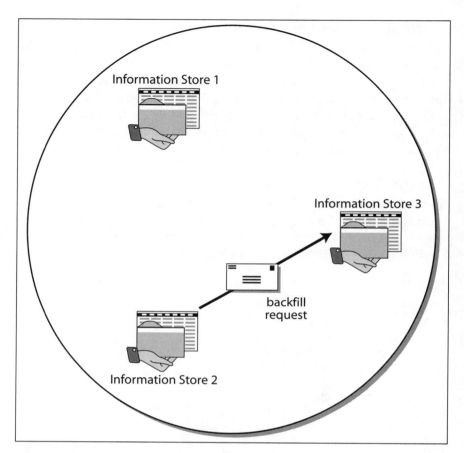

Figure 10.12   Backfill request sent.

Changes Sent

If Information Store 3 does not respond to Information Store 2's backfill request, another Information Store will be selected based on mail transit time and the site affinity values. The Information Store will first attempt to contact all the servers within its own site in the order of average transmission time. If no servers from the local site respond to the backfill request, the Information Store will use site affinity values to pick the next site and then the average transmission time will be used to select an order within the remote site.

In Figure 10.13, Information Store 2 chooses Information Store 3 and sends it the backfill request. Information Store 3 responds to the backfill request by sending the missing changes to Information Store 2, which then modifies its public folders to reflect these changes. Information Store 1, Information Store 2, and Information Store 3 are now synchronized.

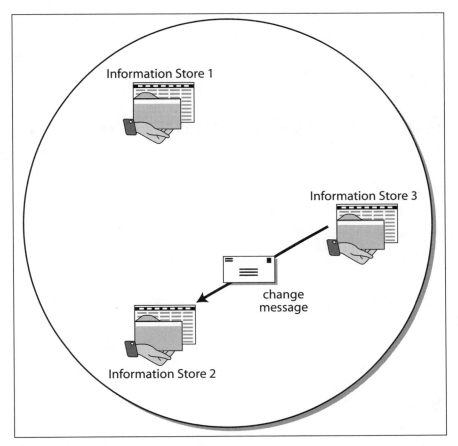

Figure 10.13 Changes sent.

Content Conflict Resolution

A conflict occurs under the following situation: A user modifies an item in a public folder, and before the changes can be replicated, another user modifies the same item on another Exchange computer. A conflict will now occur, when both servers attempt to replicate the change.

When such a conflict occurs, the public folder contact and the users involved in the conflict will receive a notification message of the conflict. The only users who can resolve such a conflict are:

➤ The public folder contact

➤ The public folder owner

➤ Any user with "edit all items" permission to the public folder

Another conflict can occur when two public folder owners modify a public folder design at the same time. In this type of a conflict, the design change that took place last will overwrite the previous changes. No message will be displayed in the public folder, but the public folder contacts (or the public folder owner) will receive notification of the conflict.

An Advanced Security Overview

Microsoft Exchange Server provides your organization with protection and verification of messages. It accomplishes this by using message encryption and key technology.

Exchange Server offers advanced security when used with the following clients:

➤ Microsoft Windows 3.x-based Microsoft Exchange clients

➤ Microsoft Windows 95-based Microsoft Outlook or Microsoft Exchange clients

➤ Microsoft Windows NT-based Microsoft Outlook or Microsoft Exchange clients

➤ Macintosh Microsoft Exchange clients

 Microsoft Exchange Server advanced security is not available to you if you are running the MS-DOS-based Microsoft Exchange client.

Advanced security supports both the signing (signatures) and the sealing (encryption) of any message generated by either Microsoft Outlook or an Exchange client. With signing, the user places a signature on the message. This enables the message recipient to verify that the message did in fact originate from the expected user. With sealing, the sender encrypts the message and any attachments, effectively locking the message. The message can only be unsealed (or unlocked) using the correct key.

Key Technology

To allow users to sign and seal their messages, Microsoft Exchange Server uses an industry standard encryption technology known as *public/private key technology*. Each mailbox is assigned a key pair; one key is publicly known, and only the user knows the other key.

Public Key

A *public key* is a fixed-length security string that is made available to all users. The advanced security features of Exchange use two public keys to perform the following tasks:

➤ **Seal the message** One of the public keys is used to encrypt the message, thus sealing the message.

➤ **Verify the message** The other public key is used to verify the sender of an encrypted (or sealed) message.

Private Key

Each user has an encrypted security file on his or her computer that contains a fixed-length string. The advanced security features of Exchange use two private keys to perform the following tasks:

➤ **Sign a message** One of the private keys is used to sign the message, thus securing it.

➤ **Unseal a message** The other private key is used to unseal a sealed message that was received by the user.

Secret Key

This method uses an algorithm (using a single key) to encrypt and decrypt messages. Both the sender and the recipient use a secret key. This is a more efficient method of encrypting large amounts of data.

The Key Management Server (KM Server)

To manage the different security keys, Microsoft Exchange Server uses a service called the *Key Management Server (KM Server)*. To enable and use the advanced security features of Microsoft Exchange, you must install the Key Management service separately.

The Exchange advanced security features use several components to implement the security. Some of these components are server based, whereas others are client based.

The server-based components of Microsoft Exchange Server's advanced security must reside on a Windows NT computer running Microsoft Exchange

Server. This computer can be located anywhere in the organization. Here's a list of the server-based components:

➤ **A Windows NT service** This service, known as the *Key Management service*, is the main component of advanced security. This service allows the KM Server to function as a certification authority (CA). The CA creates and assigns keys, maintains the certification revocation list (CRL) in the Exchange directory database, and creates and manages the KM database that stores all the users' public keys.

➤ **A Dynamic Link Library (DLL)** This DLL, the KM Security DLL (SECKM.DLL), allows for communication between the client and the server to take place. When a client makes a request for a new key, a function in this DLL is called and the key request is passed on to the KM service.

➤ **A storage database** This database, the KM database, manages advanced security information for the Exchange organization.

A person who manages the KM Server is known as the KM administrator. The KM administrator is not necessarily the same person as the Exchange administrator (although usually they are both the same person). The KM administrator must have access to the Exchange Administrator program.

 There can only ever be one KM Server per Exchange organization.

Two other components are installed during the KM setup process: the client security DLL and the security administration DLL.

The client security DLL resides on the client computer and is used to sign/verify and seal/unseal advanced security messages. Two different DLLs are involved (depending on your Windows operating system): ETEXCH.DLL is used with 16-bit Windows operating systems, and ETEXCH32.DLL is used with 32-bit Windows operating systems.

The security administration DLL resides on the Exchange administrator's workstation. It's used by the Exchange Administrator program whenever advanced security is being configured for a user's account.

Installing KM Server

KM Server is installed by the administrator from the Microsoft Exchange Server CD-ROM. It must be installed onto one of the Exchange Server computers in the organization.

The setup program performs the following events:

➤ Checks for a previous installation of KM Server within the site

➤ Checks for a previous installation of KM Server within the organization

➤ Copies the necessary files from the CD-ROM

➤ Creates the Microsoft Exchange Key Management service

➤ Creates two objects, the CA and encryption, in the directory related to Key Management services under the configuration container of the site

➤ Creates a password for the KM Server

Once the setup process is complete, you must start the Microsoft Exchange Key Management service from Windows NT's Control Panel|Services.

You can select either to create the KM Server password on a floppy disk or to display it on the screen for you to note. When you restart the KM Server, one of two things will happen. If you selected to create the password on a floppy disk, KM Server will attempt to search for the password and the floppy disk. If the disk is not in the server's floppy drive, KM Server startup will fail. If you selected to make a note of the KM password yourself, you'll be prompted to enter the password before the KM Server will start.

KM Server Key And Password Functions

All keys stored within the database are encrypted using a master encryption key. This key maintains the security of the information contained within the file. This master encryption key is encrypted using passwords from each service that uses the KM Server database.

During the KM Server setup process, a password is created that will be used by the KM server to perform the following tasks:

➤ **Start the Key Management service** This password must be provided at startup either manually or via a floppy disk.

➤ **Access the Key Management database** This password is used to decrypt the lockbox and to gain access to the KM database.

➤ **Restrict password entry** Normally the startup password is placed in a local file called KMSPWD.INI and is written to a floppy disk. You may, however, choose not to use the floppy disk and to enter in the password manually. Therefore, be aware that the KM Server startup may not be fully automated because you'll have to either supply the password floppy disk or enter the password in manually.

➤ **Encrypt the master encryption key** An additional password is used to encrypt the master key, which becomes a lockbox, for each KM Server administrator.

Different countries in the world have different encryption laws. Due to this fact, KM Server is able to provide some control over which encryption algorithm is used to sign and seal messages. The encryption algorithm options are controlled by the encryption object under the configuration container. These options are shown in Table 10.4.

Implementing Advanced Security

The creation and management of advanced security—such as public and private signing keys, public and private sealing keys, security tokens, and signing and sealing certificates—take place in two distinct steps:

Step 1 The administrator's step

Step 2 The client's step

Step 1: The Administrator's Step

The administrator must use the Microsoft Exchange Administrator program to enable mailbox advanced security for a specific user or users. This involves generating and implementing a private and public sealing key and a security token.

The following steps are completed to enable advanced security for the mailbox:

1. Select the Enable Advanced Security button under the Advanced Security property page for each user.

2. The security administration DLL retrieves the KM Server location and uses this information to pass the user's name and administrator's password to the Key Management service.

Table 10.4	Location-specific encryption algorithms.
Location	**Algorithm**
North America	CAST-64 (default)
	DES
International	CAST-40
	Plain text (if not using advanced security)

3. The Key Management service generates a sealing key pair. This key pair is stored in the KM database.

4. The KM service generates a random 12-character security token and encrypts it using the administrator's password. This token is then passed to the security administration DLL on the administrator's computer.

5. The security administration DLL finally decrypts the security token and displays it in a dialog box on the administrator's computer.

Step 2: The Client's Step

The user submits the security token to the KM Server, which, in return, issues the sealing keys generated by the administrator back to the client.

The following steps are completed to enable advanced security:

1. The KM administrator gives the user the access token via a secure method.

2. The user enables advanced security by selecting Set Up Advanced Security in the Security property page. The client enters in the security token received from the KM administrator.

3. The security DLL generates a public and private signing key pair for the user. The public signing key is encrypted (using the security token) and then mailed to the hidden mailbox of the System Attendant.

4. This message is transferred to the Exchange Server computer running KM Server, and the user is notified of the successful submission.

5. The message is then extracted by the Windows NT System Attendant service and is passed to the Key Manager service through the KM security DLL.

6. The KM service decrypts the message, retrieves the public signing key, and places the signing key in the KM database.

7. The KM service generates two certificates—one for sealing and the other for signing—and then generates a message addressed to the user.

8. This message is delivered to the user's mailbox, which prompts the user to enter his or her unique password. This password is used to verify the identity of the user.

9. The security DLL extracts the public sealing certificate and submits it to the local directory service for storage and replication.

Here are the four main storage areas for security information in Microsoft Exchange Server:

➤ Directory store

➤ Security file

➤ KM database

➤ X.509 certificate

Table 10.5 describes the type of information kept in each storage area. Figure 10.14 illustrates digital signing and encryption of a message.

Sending A Sealed Message

For a sealed message to be sent, the following steps take place:

1. The recipient's public key is retrieved from the directory.

2. A bulk encryption key is generated and is used to encrypt the contents of the message.

Table 10.5 Security information storage locations for Microsoft Exchange Server.				
Security Information	**Directory Store**	**Security File (.EPF)**	**KM Database**	**X.509 Certificate**
CA's certificate		✓		
CA's directory name				✓
CA's signature				✓
Certificate expiration date				✓
Certificate serial number				✓
Private sealing key	✓		✓	
Private signing key		✓		
Public sealing key				✓
Public signing key			✓	✓
Sealing certificate	✓	✓		
Signing certificate		✓		
User's directory name				✓

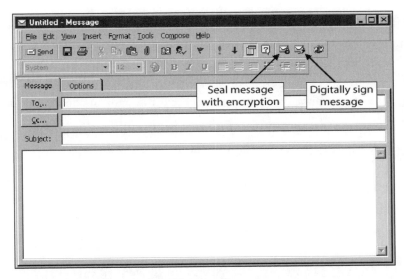

Figure 10.14   Sealing and signing mail messages.

3. A lockbox is created using the public sealing key to encrypt the bulk encryption key.

4. The encrypted message and a lockbox are sent to the Information Store for delivery.

Unsealing A Sealed Message

To unseal a message, the recipient must decrypt the lockbox with his or her private sealing key; the original bulk encryption key can now be accessed and used to decrypt the message.

Sending A Signed Message

When a user wants to sign a message, the client uses the sender's private signing key as well as a technique known as *hashing* to prevent message tampering. Hashing reduces a message of any length to a unique 128-bit result known as a *message digest*. For a message to be signed, the following steps take place:

1. The original message is hashed to obtain a unique message digest.

2. The user is prompted to enter his or her security profile password. The EPF file is decrypted, and the private signing key is extracted out of it.

3. The message digest is encrypted with the sender's private signing key. This step creates the digital signature.

4. The client sends a copy of the sender's signing certificate, the digital signature, and the message to the Information Store for delivery.

Verifying A Signed Message

To verify that a message has been sealed, you use a process that recalculates the message digest and verifies that the hash is the same as the one contained in the message digest included with the message. The following steps take place:

1. The user displays the message and checks the signature on the message.

2. The client prompts the user for his or her security profile password.

3. Using the certificate enclosed in the message, the sender's public signing key is extracted and used to decrypt the digital signature. The original message digest is then decrypted from the signature.

4. The client performs a hash on the original message.

5. Both digests are compared to ensure that they are identical.

Managing Multiple KM Servers Across Multiple Sites

There can only be one KM Server in the organization that manages all CA activities. The KM Server setup program, however, needs to be run on one server within each site. This does not actually install another KM Server; instead, it creates an entry linking the directory structure to the KM Server.

 You must replicate the existence of the KM Server to the remote site before you can run the setup on that site. If replication has not taken place, the setup will attempt to install a KM Server.

Key And Certificate Management

Normally, the keys and certificates maintained by the KM Server require no management. Sometimes, however, you'll need to perform some management-related duties such as those outlined in the following list. As an administrator, you may be required to revoke a user's ability to send signed and sealed messages or to recover a forgotten or corrupted key pair and certificate. You'll also have to update security information that is about to expire.

➤ **Revocation** To revoke advanced security keys and certificates from a mailbox, a KM administrator uses the Exchange Administrator program to perform step 1 in the following list. The remaining steps are completed automatically:

1. For the mailbox from which you want to revoke advanced security, click the Revoke Advanced Security button on the Security property page.

2. The security DLL locates the KM Server and informs it which mailbox is to have its security configuration revoked.

3. The KM Server adds the user's signing and sealing keys to its revocation list.

4. The KM Server informs the directory service to add the user's sealing certificate to the CRL. The user can no longer sign or seal messages.

5. A dialog box will appear to let you know that the task is complete.

Revoking does not delete keys from the KM database, rather they become unusable for future sealing. However, they can be used by a KM administrator to unseal any messages still signed and sealed by those keys.

➤ **Recovery** If a user forgets his or her password, or the password becomes corrupt or is accidentally deleted, the KM administrator can perform a recovery. A recovery is similar to enabling advanced security. The KM administrator clicks the Recover Security Key button in the Security property page. The KM Server then sends the user a history of the keys associated with the mailbox, and the user must then reconfigure advanced security on his or her computer to create a new EPF file.

➤ **Renewal** New certificates are only valid for 18 months. After this period, the certificate must be renewed, or *rolled over*. Before a certificate has expired, the Exchange client software will send a renewal message.

Exam Prep Questions

Question 1

> What is the public folder replication agent?
>
> ○ a. A Dynamic Link Library that is used when advanced security is being configured for a user account.
>
> ○ b. The Microsoft Exchange component responsible for the successful replication of public folder information.
>
> ○ c. A Dynamic Link Library used to sign/verify and seal/unseal advanced security messages.
>
> ○ d. A Dynamic Link Library that responds to any advanced security configuration requests from users and then submits them to the Key Management service.

The correct answer to this question is b. The public folder replication agent is responsible for the replication of public folder information. The Dynamic Link Library files are not used for public folder replication. Therefore, answers a, c, and d are incorrect.

Question 2

> You have just set up a Key Management Server without creating the startup disk. When you reboot, an error message appears. What is causing this?
>
> ○ a. Key Management Server is not installed.
>
> ○ b. The Key Management service is not installed.
>
> ○ c. You're missing the startup disk.
>
> ○ d. The Key Management password is not found or invalid.

The correct answer to this question is d. The Key Management Server cannot start without the password. Therefore, if a startup disk was not created, you must enter in the password manually before the KM Server will start. If Key Management Server was not installed, the error message would not appear, because KM Server issues the error. Therefore, answer a is incorrect. The Key Management service is installed when you install KM Server. If KM Server is installed, so is the service. Therefore, answer b is incorrect. Because you did not create a startup password disk, the KM Server will not search for it. Therefore, answer c is incorrect.

Question 3

> What must you do to hide a subfolder from a particular recipient?
>
> ○ a. Select the Hide From option on the Security property page.
>
> ○ b. Highlight the subfolder in Exchange Administrator and click the Hide button.
>
> ○ c. Revoke the read items permission from the recipient at the parent folder.
>
> ○ d. Revoke the read items permission from the recipient at the top-level folder.

The correct answer to this question is c. The only valid answer is to revoke the read items permission from the recipient at the parent folder. The other answers are invalid. Therefore, answers a, b, and d are incorrect.

Question 4

> What is a secret key?
>
> ○ a. A cryptography key that encrypts or decrypts messages using an algorithm.
>
> ○ b. A fixed-length security string that's used to seal or verify a message.
>
> ○ c. A fixed-length security string that's used to unseal or sign a message.
>
> ○ d. A 128-bit message digest.

The correct answer to this question is a. A secret key is a cryptography key used to encrypt or decrypt messages. A fixed-length security string that's used to seal or verify a message is a public key. Therefore, answer b is incorrect. A fixed–length security string used to unseal or sign a message is a private key. Therefore, answer c is incorrect. Although the 128-bit message digest deals with encryption, it is actually the algorithm that's used to encrypt and decrypt messages. Therefore, answer d is incorrect.

Question 5

What is a private key?

○ a. A cryptography key that encrypts or decrypts messages using an algorithm.

○ b. A fixed-length security string that's used to seal or verify a message.

○ c. A fixed-length security string that's used to unseal or sign a message.

○ d. A 128-bit message digest.

The correct answer to this question is c. A private key is a fixed-length security string that's used to unseal or sign a message. A cryptography key used to encrypt or decrypt messages is a secret key. Therefore, answer a is incorrect. A fixed-length security string that's used to seal or verify a message is a public key. Therefore, answer b is incorrect. Although the 128-bit message digest deals with encryption, it is actually the algorithm that's used to encrypt and decrypt messages. Therefore, answer d is incorrect.

Question 6

What is a public key?

○ a. A cryptography key that encrypts or decrypts messages using an algorithm.

○ b. A fixed-length security string that's used to seal or verify a message.

○ c. A fixed-length security string that's used to unseal or sign a message.

○ d. A 128-bit message digest.

The correct answer to this question is b. A public key is a fixed-length security string that's used to seal or verify a message. A cryptography key that encrypts or decrypts messages using an algorithm is a secret key. Therefore, answer a is incorrect. A fixed-length security string that's used to unseal or sign a message is a private key. Therefore, answer c is incorrect. Although the 128-bit message digest deals with encryption, it is actually the algorithm that's used to encrypt and decrypt messages. Therefore, answer d is incorrect.

Question 7

What is the client security DLL?

○ a. A Dynamic Link Library that's used when advanced
security is being configured for a user account.

○ b. The Microsoft Exchange component responsible for the
successful replication of public folder information.

○ c. A Dynamic Link Library used to sign/verify and seal/
unseal advanced security messages.

○ d. A Dynamic Link Library that responds to any advanced
security configuration requests from users and then
submits them to the Key Management service.

The correct answer to this question is c. The client security DLL is used to
sign/verify or seal/unseal advanced security messages. It's not used to configure advanced security for user accounts, and it's not used for the replication of
public folder information. Also, it doesn't respond to advanced security configuration requests. Therefore, answers a, b, and d are incorrect.

Question 8

What is the Key Manager security DLL?

○ a. A Dynamic Link Library that's used when advanced
security is being configured for a user account.

○ b. The Microsoft Exchange component responsible for the
successful replication of public folder information.

○ c. A Dynamic Link Library used to sign/verify and seal/
unseal advanced security messages.

○ d. A Dynamic Link Library that responds to any advanced
security configuration requests from users and then
submits them to the Key Management service.

The correct answer to this question is d. The Key Management security DLL
responds to advanced configuration requests from users and then submits them
to the Key Management service. It is not used to configure a user account, to
replicate public folder information, or to sign/verify or seal/unseal messages.
Therefore, answers a, b, and c are incorrect.

Question 9

> What are predefined groups of public folder permissions called?
>
> ○ a. Groups
>
> ○ b. Roles
>
> ○ c. Sets
>
> ○ d. Clusters

The correct answer to this question is b. The predefined groups of public folder permissions are called roles. The other answers are invalid. Therefore, answers a, c, and d are incorrect.

Question 10

> What is the security administration DLL?
>
> ○ a. A Dynamic Link Library that's used when advanced security is being configured for a user account.
>
> ○ b. The Microsoft Exchange component responsible for the successful replication of public folder information.
>
> ○ c. A Dynamic Link Library used to sign/verify and seal/unseal advanced security messages.
>
> ○ d. A Dynamic Link Library that responds to any advanced security configuration requests from users and then submits them to the Key Management service.

The correct answer to this question is a. The security administration DLL is a Dynamic Link Library that's used to configure advanced security on a user account. This DLL has nothing to do with the successful replication of public folder information or the signing or sealing of advanced security messages. Therefore, answers b, c, and d are incorrect.

Need To Know More?

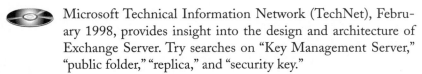

Microsoft Technical Information Network (TechNet), February 1998, provides insight into the design and architecture of Exchange Server. Try searches on "Key Management Server," "public folder," "replica," and "security key."

Install the online books from the Microsoft Exchange 5.5 CD-ROM. They will yield a wealth of useful information.

Go to the Microsoft Exchange Server home page at www.microsoft.com/exchange. Many of the documents located here are newer than the ones available on the TechNet.

Go to the Microsoft Knowledge Base and support home page at www.microsoft.com/kb. Many of the documents located here are newer than the ones available on the TechNet.

Monitoring And Maintaining Exchange Server

11

Terms you'll need to understand:

- √ Circular logging
- √ Copy, differential, incremental, and normal backups
- √ Defragmentation
- √ Directory synchronization database
- √ ESEUTIL
- √ Exchange Performance Optimizer
- √ Information Store (private and public)
- √ ISNTEG
- √ Key Management Server
- √ Load Simulator
- √ MTACHECK
- √ Objects and counters
- √ Redundant Array of Inexpensive Disks (RAID)
- √ Transaction log
- √ Uninterruptible power supply (UPS)

Techniques you'll need to master:

- √ Understanding the process of maintaining and monitoring Exchange Server
- √ Understanding the process of creating and verifying backups
- √ Understanding the importance of planning for disaster recovery

Exchange Server includes two important components: Information Store (IS) and Directory Service (DS). The IS is a repository that stores information users create. The IS can store heterogeneous types of data including emails, forms, attachments, voice messages, and so on. IS includes two folders: private and public. The private folder stores mailboxes for the users; the public folder includes information for all the Exchange clients. PRIV.EDB and PUB.EDB represent the Information Store private and public databases, respectively. These databases reside within the C:\Exchsrvr\Mdbdata directory on the server. In addition to the Information Store databases, files with the extensions .PST (personal message store), .OST (offline message store), and .PAB (personal address book), as well as the transaction logs, contain user data.

The Exchange Server directory provides a unified view of all the users and resources within the organization. You can use the DS to replicate the Exchange Server directory databases between the different servers within a site and across different sites. DIR.EDB represents the directory database. This database resides within the C:\Exchsrvr\Dsadata directory on the server. The DIR.EDB database contains Exchange Server configuration data.

Microsoft Exchange Server automatically compacts the Information Store and Directory databases without interruption to messaging.

Monitoring Exchange Server includes monitoring these different server objects, their counters, and values of the counters, and taking appropriate actions based on the values. The section "Monitoring Exchange Server," later in this chapter, discusses the different Exchange Server objects and their counters. That section also discusses the different performance charts you can use to monitor the server's health.

Maintaining Exchange Server

To derive the best performance from Exchange Server and to make sure the server is running at optimal condition, you must perform a set of maintenance chores on the server at regular intervals. Note that monitoring is different than maintaining. Maintaining includes performing a predefined set of tasks on a predefined schedule. Monitoring includes keeping an eye on the server to identify any unusual behavior or activity on the server and then taking the appropriate action(s) to remedy the situation. The next section discusses monitoring Exchange Server.

The responsibility of maintaining and monitoring the Exchange server falls on the administrator. A number of utilities that come with Exchange Server, combined with the use of Windows NT Performance Monitor, make the life of an

Exchange Server administrator a lot easier. You learn about these utilities and the Windows NT Performance Monitor in this chapter.

The regular chores for maintaining Exchange Server include the following tasks:

➤ **Define the maintenance window** A maintenance window is a period of time when you execute the routine maintenance chores. A number of such chores require the users to be off the server. Ideally, you should schedule routine maintenance chores during off or non-peak hours. Make sure you publish this maintenance schedule and alert all your users to these times. Perform the following chores within the maintenance window:

➤ Install service packs and upgrades

➤ Defragment the database

➤ Check for errors

➤ **Record configuration changes** Recording the changes you make to Windows NT settings, Exchange Server connector configurations, protocol addresses, path information, and so on is very important.

Exchange Server Database Utilities

In addition to the regular chores, you can use the following utilities to maintain consistency of information within the Exchange Server databases:

➤ **ISNTEG** Checks the consistency of the Information Store database at a database level. You can also direct ISNTEG to fix errors, if any. The ISNTEG file exists within the \Exchsrvr\Bin directory. You can run ISNTEG from the command prompt.

➤ **ESEUTIL** This file exists within the \Exchsrvr\Bin directory. You can run ESEUTIL from the command prompt, and you can use it to perform the following tasks:

➤ Check the consistency of the Information Store database and directory databases

➤ Defragment these databases

➤ Repair any inconsistencies

➤ **MTACHECK** Checks the data the Message Transfer Agent (MTA) stores within the DAT files. This utility also automatically repairs errors, if any. The MTACHECK utility exists within the \Exchsrvr\Mtadata\ MTACHECK.OUT directory.

Note the difference between ESEUTIL and ISNTEG. ESEUTIL helps you check for any inconsistency within the Information Store and directory databases. If any inconsistencies exist, ESEUTIL repairs them. ESEUTIL also helps defragment the Information Store and directory databases. On the other hand, the ISINTEG utility only checks the database at a higher level, which corresponds with the message store.

Exchange Server Performance Optimizer

To improve the performance of Exchange Server, especially if you upgrade the hardware (such as adding more memory to the server), use the Microsoft Exchange Performance Optimizer. The Performance Optimizer uses a wizard-style approach to improving the Exchange server's performance.

To optimize the Exchange server, follow these steps:

1. Click Start|Programs|Microsoft Exchange|Exchange Server Optimizer. Windows NT displays the Microsoft Exchange Performance Optimizer dialog box, as shown in Figure 11.1.

2. To begin the optimization process, click on the Next button. The Performance Optimizer stops all Exchange Server services that are running. These may include the following:

➤ Microsoft Exchange Directory

➤ Microsoft Exchange Event Service

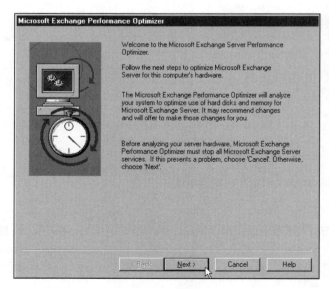

Figure 11.1   The Microsoft Exchange Performance Optimizer.

➤ Microsoft Exchange Information Store

➤ Microsoft Exchange Message Transfer Agent

➤ Microsoft Exchange System Attendant

3. The Performance Optimizer displays the dialog box shown in Figure 11.2. In this dialog box, you specify system parameter information. These include the number of users on the server that you want to optimize, the total number of users within the organization, and the type of Exchange server. In addition, you can limit the memory this server can use.

4. After specifying the values for these system parameters, click on the Next button. If the system has only one logical drive, the Performance Optimizer displays the warning dialog box shown in Figure 11.3.

Within seconds, the Performance Optimizer indicates it has configured the server for optimal use, as shown in Figure 11.4.

Check the default log file (C:\Winnt\System32\PERFOPT.LOG) for the results of optimization. If the log file already exists, the Performance Optimizer appends the results.

5. To close the Performance Optimizer dialog box, click on Finish. Unless you specify otherwise, the Performance Optimizer restarts the Exchange Server services. Then, the Performance Optimizer saves the parameters and closes the dialog box.

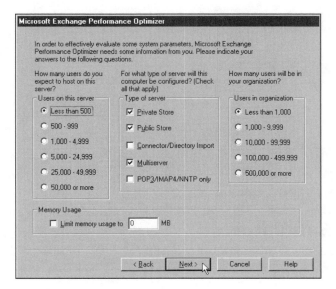

Figure 11.2   Specifying the system parameters.

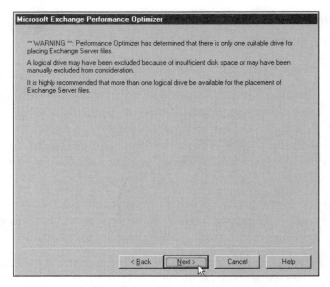

Figure 11.3 Performance Optimizer warns if only one logical drive exists.

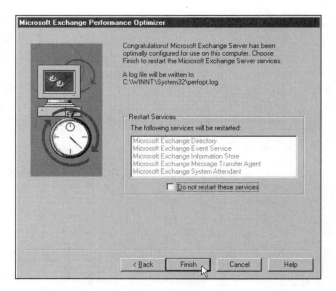

Figure 11.4 The optimization is complete.

Load Simulator

You can use the Load Simulator (LOADSIM.EXE) to identify the bottlenecks within an organization's mail system. The Load Simulator validates a portion of the organization's design by configuring the number of users you hope to support on a particular server configuration. In addition, this utility provides you with valuable information regarding capacity, performance, network bandwidth, and impact analysis.

Monitoring Exchange Server

Monitoring Exchange Server is the other side of the equation. Not only must you create and follow a maintenance schedule, you must also monitor the server for any unexpected problems or errors. Exchange Server comes with a number of utilities you can use to monitor the server's operation. You can also configure the server to alert you of any such problems so you can take appropriate action.

The monitor *monitors* the server for problems. When a problem occurs, the monitor tries to fix the problem. If the monitor fails to fix the problem, it notifies the administrator by any one of the following methods:

➤ **Generating a Windows NT alert** Exchange Server generates and sends a Windows NT alert to a specified computer (for example, a computer at the central monitoring location).

➤ **Launching a process** In the event of a problem, Exchange Server sends a message to the administrator.

➤ **Mailing a message** Exchange Server sends a message to the specified user(s).

Two types of monitors make the life of an Exchange Server administrator easy: server and link monitors. A *server monitor* verifies that certain specified Microsoft Exchange services are running on the specified Microsoft Exchange Server computer. You can use the server monitor to verify any other Windows NT service. To create a server monitor, use the Microsoft Exchange Administrator. A *link monitor* sends messages to the specified servers and other email components, such as a Message Transfer Agent (MTA). To create a link monitor, use the Microsoft Exchange Administrator.

Monitoring Windows NT Counters

You can monitor a number of Windows NT counters to identify potential bottlenecks as well as hardware and software failures. Each counter is associated with a Windows NT object. The counter indicates the object's performance. For example, the Bytes Total/sec counter is an attribute of the Redirector object, the Network Errors/sec counter is another attribute of the Redirector object, the %ProcessorTime counter is an attribute of the Processor object, and so on.

The key is determining if any of the objects listed in Table 11.1 are potential bottlenecks. If they are, they may directly or indirectly affect the Exchange server's performance. Table 11.1 lists the Windows NT objects and their respective counters.

The following sections look at each of these counters and what they mean.

Hard Drive

➤ **%DiskTime** This counter measures the percentage of time the disk is reading or writing. Use this counter to determine if the hard drive is a potential bottleneck.

Note: If the value of this counter is less than 90 for an extended period of time, the hard drive is indeed a potential bottleneck.

Memory

➤ **Pages/sec** This counter measures the paging of memory from or to the virtual memory paging file.

Note: A high average value of Pages/sec indicates you can improve the Windows NT machine's performance by increasing the RAM.

Network

➤ **Bytes Total/sec** This counter measures the total number of bytes the network redirector sends and receives. This counter helps you determine if the network is a potential bottleneck.

Note: To determine whether the network is a potential bottleneck, compare this value with the network card's maximum throughput value.

Table 11.1 Windows NT objects and counters.	
Object	**Counters**
Hard Drive	%DiskTime
Memory	Pages/sec
Network	Bytes Total/sec, Network Errors/sec
Processor	Elapsed Time, %ProcessorTime

➤ **Network Errors/sec** This counter measures the number of errors the network redirector receives.

Note: To determine whether network errors occurred, check to see if this counter's value is greater than zero. For details on network errors, check the system event log.

Processor

➤ **Elapsed Time** This counter measures the number of seconds a process has been running.

➤ **%Processor Time** This counter measures the percentage of time the server's processor is idle.

Note: An average value of less than 20 percent indicates that the server is not in use or the server is down. An average value of greater than 90 percent indicates that the processor is overloaded.

Monitoring Exchange Server Counters

In addition to the Windows NT counters, you must also monitor the counters specific to Exchange Server. Similar to the Windows NT counters, each Exchange Server counter is associated with an Exchange Server object. For example, the Pending Replication Synchronization counter is an attribute of the MSExchangeDS object, the Messages Received counter is an attribute of the MSMI object, the Messages/sec counter is an attribute of the MTA object, and so on. Again, the key is determining if any of the Exchange Server objects are potential bottlenecks.

Note: The Exchange Server objects support a total of 150 Exchange Server counters.

Is Your Server Performing Beyond Expectations?

A significant part of the monitoring process is reviewing the performance of the Exchange server. As the administrator, you're responsible for the server's performance. Whenever your server experiences performance problems, the first thing you must do is evaluate the values of Exchange Server counters. These values help you narrow down the problem. For example, if your server appears to be overloaded, check the values of the following counters: Message Recipients Delivered/min, Message Submitted/min, Adjacent MTA Association, RPC Packets/sec, AB Browses/sec, AB Reads/sec, ExDS Reads/sec, and Replication Updates/sec. In fact, the Server Load Performance chart graphs these values, making it easy for you to monitor the counters.

Table 11.2 lists the Exchange Server performance charts and their respective frequency of update.

The following sections take a closer look at each of these charts.

IMS Queues

What does the inbound queue look like? How is the outbound queue performing? This is what the IMS Queues chart tells you. Table 11.3 lists the counters the IMS Queues chart tracks.

IMS Statistics

What kind of email traffic does the Internet generate? What's the total number of inbound messages since you started the server? What's the total number of outbound messages? This is what you learn from the IMS Statistics chart. Table 11.4 lists the counters the IMS Statistics chart tracks.

IMS Traffic

How is the message flow? How many connections exist to or from the server? You get this information from the IMS Traffic chart. Table 11.5 lists the counters the IMS Traffic chart tracks.

Table 11.2 Exchange Server performance charts.	
Chart	**Frequency Of Update**
IMS Queues	1 sec
IMS Statistics	.5 min
IMS Traffic	1 sec
Server Health	1 sec
Server History	1 min
Server Load	10 sec
Server Queues	10 sec
Server Users	10 sec

Table 11.3 Exchange Server counters measured by the IMS Queues chart.

Counter	Object
Queued Inbound	MSExchangeINC
Queued MTS-IN	MSExchangeINC
Queued MTS-OUT	MSExchangeINC
Queued Outbound	MSExchangeINC

Table 11.4 Exchange Server counters measured by the IMS Statistics chart.

Counter	Object
Inbound Messages	MSExchangeINC
Outbound Messages	MSExchangeINC

Table 11.5 Exchange Server counters measured by the IMS Traffic chart.

Counter	Object
Messages Entering MTS-IN	MSExchangeINC
Messages Entering MTS-OUT	MSExchangeINC
Messages Leaving MTS-OUT	MSExchangeINC
Connections Inbound	MSExchangeINC
Connections Outbound	MSExchangeINC

Server Health

Making sure the server maintains good health at all times is critical to the successful use of its services. So, how do you learn more about the server's health? The answer is the Server Health performance chart. This chart tells you the percentage of processor time each service uses; therefore, you can determine which services are overutilizing the processor and which services cannot really use the processor as much because of the other services. Table 11.6 lists the counters the Server Health chart tracks. Figure 11.5 shows the Server Health chart.

Table 11.6	Exchange Server counters measured by the Server Health chart.
Counter	**Object**
%Total Processor Time	System
%Processor Time	Process
%Pages/sec	Memory

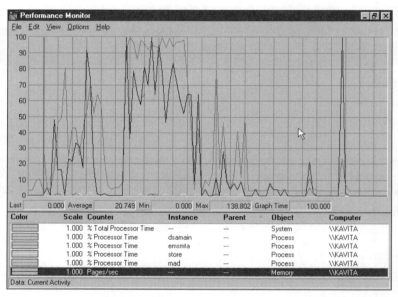

Figure 11.5　The Server Health chart.

Server History

How many messages remain outstanding? How many users have a connection to the server? How many pages does the server process per second? You get all this information from the Server History chart. Table 11.7 lists the counters the Server History chart tracks.

Server Load

How many messages were submitted? How many were actually delivered? To get this type of information, use the Server Load chart. Table 11.8 lists the counters the Server Load chart tracks.

Server Queues

Is the server queue empty? If so, great! Everything is working fine. If not, what is the total number of messages awaiting transmission? Is this number extremely large or small? You can determine this by looking at the Server Queues chart. Table 11.9 lists the counters the Server Queues chart tracks.

Table 11.7	Exchange Server counters measured by the Server History chart.
Counter	**Object**
UserCount	MSExchangeIS
Work Queue Length	MSExchangeITA
Pages/sec	Memory

Table 11.8	Exchange Server counters measured by the Server Load chart.
Counter	**Object**
Message Recipients Delivered/min	MSExchangeIS Public
Message Submitted/min	MSExchangeIS Public
Adjacent MTA Association	MSExchangeMTA
RPC Packets/sec	MSExchangeIS
AB Browses/sec	MSExchangeDS
AB Reads/sec	MSExchangeDS
ExDS Reads/sec	MSExchangeDS
Replication Updates/sec	MSExchangeDS

Table 11.9	Exchange Server counters measured by the Server Queues chart.
Counter	**Object**
Work Queue Length	MSExchangeMTA
Send Queue Size	MSExchangeIS Private
Send Queue Size	MSExchangeIS Public
Receive Queue Size	MSExchangeIS Private
Receive Queue Size	MSExchangeIS Public

Server Users

What is the total number of current users with a connection to the server? The Server Users chart tells you this number. There is only one counter tracked through the Server Users chart, UserCount, which contains one object, MSExchangeIS.

Backups

If you do not perform regular backups of your data, you may experience a number of problems. Here's a list of some of the things you must backup:

➤ **Databases** These include the Information Store and directory databases. You must also backup the Key Management Server and Directory Synchronization databases. The Key Management Server database contains highly sensitive information—all the keys within the database are encrypted with the 64-bit CAST algorithm. Due to the highly sensitive nature of this information, back up this database separately and maintain a high level of security for this backup. The Directory Synchronization database (\Exchsrvr\Dxadata) should be backed up because this database includes information for the directory synchronization process. The recovery process can synchronize the directories quickly from the backup, letting the directory synchronization process proceed from the last backup period.

➤ **Transaction logs** Back up transaction logs on a separate disk. If the drive containing the database fails, the transaction logs still remain intact and available for complete restoration. You must log all the transactions to protect against any system crash and be able to restore the data to the current state before the crash. Circular logging lets you log the transactions and manage disk space by creating and using new log files and purging old log files. The Information Store transaction logs reside within the \Exchsrvr\Mdbdata directory. The Directory Store transaction logs reside within the \Exchsrvr\Dsadata directory.

➤ **The entire Windows NT Server, including the Registry** Use a file-based backup of the entire Windows NT Server. When you do so, make sure none of the services are running, because any files that are open may prevent the backup process. Also, you must remember to back up the Windows NT Registry. If you don't, you may run into unexpected problems when restoring the data.

Maintain backups of your data within two separate physical locations. If one physical location experiences catastrophic loss, chances are the other physical location is intact. You can restore the data from the backup stored at this other location. The probability of two geographically separate physical locations experiencing catastrophic loss at the same time is very low, although it is still possible. Depending on your organization's security policy and procedures, the second location may be within the same organization or at a third-party location.

Backup Strategy

Simply copying files over to a storage disk is not a good backup. For efficient operation, you must create and adopt a backup strategy, because each environment demands a different level of backup and archiving. A backup strategy must include the following:

➤ Creating the backup

➤ Verifying the backup

Creating The Backup

You can create backups in a number of different ways:

➤ **Copy** A *copy* is simply a snapshot of the databases at any given point in time.

➤ **Differential** A *differential* backup includes backing up only a subset of the Information Store and directory databases. In fact, this type of backup includes only the data that has changed since the last normal or incremental backup. The difference between a differential and incremental backup is that only the LOG files are backed up with a differential backup, and they are not purged.

➤ **Incremental** An *incremental* backup is the same as differential backup. The primary difference is that the LOG files are purged within an incremental backup.

➤ **Normal (Full)** A *normal* backup means a complete and full backup. You back up everything, including transaction logs, Information Store databases, and directory databases.

Normally, a combination of backup methods is the preferred approach. For example, you could perform a normal backup initially and then an incremental backup at regular intervals (say, daily).

To create a backup, use the NTBACKUP.EXE utility that comes with Exchange Server. This utility exists within the \Exchsrvr\ directory. Figure 11.6 shows the NTBACKUP utility.

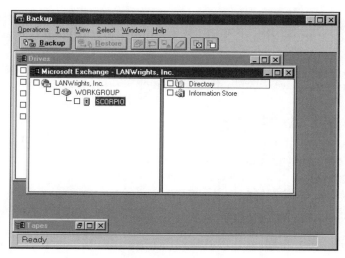

Figure 11.6 Running NTBACKUP.EXE.

Table 11.10 shows the versions of the NTBACKUP.EXE program that in-clude support for Microsoft Exchange Online backup.

Table 11.11 shows the versions of the NTBACKUP.EXE program that do not include the Exchange extensions.

You can create backups online or offline. An online backup requires the IS and DS services to be running. Exchange Server supports online backup without interruption to the messaging system. To perform an offline backup, stop all services and then use NTBACKUP.EXE to implement a file-based backup.

Verifying The Backup

As the saying goes, it's not over 'til it's over. You must verify that the backup was successful and that there will be no problem restoring the data when needed. It is better to be safe than sorry. You can verify the backup in a number of different ways. Microsoft recommends verification at two levels. First, verify that the backup indeed was successful by checking the Windows NT event log or using the backup tool from the Microsoft BackOffice Resource Kit. Then, verify the data by restoring it on another server and making sure the data integrity is intact.

Both creating and verifying backups must be integral parts of your regular maintenance schedule. You should also make users aware of the backup sched-ule by publishing it.

Table 11.10 Versions of the NTBACKUP.EXE program with Exchange extensions.

File	Version (file size/date/time)	Description
NTBACKUP.EXE	716,560 7-15-96 3:30 a	Includes support for Microsoft Exchange Online backup; ships with Microsoft Exchange Server 4.0a (Microsoft Exchange SP2).
NTBACKUP.EXE	716,560 3-8-96 4:00a	Includes support for Microsoft Exchange Online backup; ships with Microsoft Exchange Server 4.

Table 11.11 Versions of the NTBACKUP.EXE program with no Exchange extensions.

File	Version (file size/date/time)	Description
NTBACKUP.EXE	329,777 8-02-96 11:00 p	No Microsoft Exchange extensions; ships with Windows NT Server 4.
NTBACKUP.EXE	675,488 3-8-96 4:00 a	No Microsoft Exchange extensions; ships with Windows NT Service Pack 4.
NTBACKUP.EXE	675,504 9-23-95 10:57 a	No Microsoft Exchange extensions; ships with Windows NT Server 3.51.

Disaster Recovery Plan

Disasters can happen. Although you cannot prevent disasters, you can protect yourself against them by preparing a contingency plan in anticipation. You can protect the Exchange server and all the data associated with it in a number of ways. Some of these are discussed in the following sections.

Using Redundant Array Of Inexpensive Disks (RAID)

RAID provides a high level of fault tolerance. The concept behind RAID is to use an array of inexpensive disks that support multiple I/O in parallel, thus significantly improving the throughput and performance.

There are six common levels of RAID technology: RAID level 0, RAID level 1, RAID level 2, RAID level 3, RAID level 4, and RAID level 5. The more commonly used RAID options are level 1 and level 5. Level 1 provides the highest degree of reliability because this level supports hardware-level disk mirroring, but no data striping. Level 5 uses an independent array with no support for parallel access. The parity information is spread across other disks within the array.

Integrating An Uninterruptible Power Supply (UPS)

Integrating a good UPS with the Windows NT Server provides a second level of safety and security. The primary level is the database engine, which can self-recover from events such as power outages. When a power outage occurs, the UPS lets the server write all the data to the disk and provides a safe and con-trolled shut down of the Exchange Server.

> *Note: Even though the database engine provides a primary level of self-recovery, you should consider integrating a UPS with your Windows NT Server.*

Exam Prep Questions

Question 1

> You want to reformat your Windows NT Server machine and rein-
> stall Windows NT as well as Exchange Server. Before formatting
> your drive, you used the backup feature from Exchange Server
> and backed up the server. To double-check on the backup, you
> want to copy the physical files from the Exchange server. What
> file should you copy?
>
> ○ a. *.LOG
>
> ○ b. *.EDB
>
> ○ c. *.EDP
>
> ○ d. *.XCH

The correct answer to this question is b. You need to copy the *.EDB file that
holds the Exchange database. In case the backup failed, the database file helps
you restore the Exchange server configuration. A LOG file is handy, but of no
assistance in the event of a failed backup; therefore, answer a is incorrect. EDP
stands for electronic data processing and is not a part of the Exchange architecture; therefore, answer c is incorrect. There is no such file type as XCH;
therefore, answer d is incorrect.

Question 2

> You just walked in as a consultant to an organization that needs
> some advice on Exchange's backup features. The system admin-
> istrator asks you to recommend the transaction logging for the
> organization. After studying the hardware setup, you find out that
> the organization is low on free disk space on the server. What kind
> of transaction logging do you recommend?
>
> ○ a. Enable circular logging
>
> ○ b. Disable circular logging
>
> ○ c. Do not log transactions
>
> ○ d. None of the above

The correct answer to this question is a. You must log all the transactions to
protect against any system crash and be able to restore the data to the current
state before the crash. By enabling circular logging, you log the transactions

and manage disk space by creating and using new log files and purging old log files. Answers b, c, and d are incorrect.

Question 3

> What utility can you use to defrag and compact the Information Store and directory databases?
>
> ○ a. ISINTEG
>
> ○ b. ESEUTIL
>
> ○ c. MTACHECK
>
> ○ d. None of the above

The correct answer to this question is b. ESEUTIL helps you check for any inconsistencies in the Information Store and directory databases. If any inconsistencies exist, ESEUTIL repairs them. This utility also helps defragment the Information Store and directory databases. The ISINTEG utility only checks the database at a higher level, which corresponds with the message store. MTACHECK checks the data stored by an MTA within data (DAT) files. Therefore, answers a, c, and d are incorrect.

Question 4

> Which of the following actions help you verify restoration of the Exchange server? [Check all correct answers]
>
>
>
> ❑ a. Review several mailboxes to ensure the Windows NT domain account association and permissions are restored correctly.
>
> ❑ b. Test client connectivity to the Information Store and the directory. You can do this with a version of the client software installed on the same computer or by using another client on the network.
>
> ❑ c. Verify the connector and gateway functionality by sending test messages or by using a server monitor. Several connectors store configuration settings within the Registry files. If the backed-up data is missing in these files, the connectors could be inoperable.
>
> ❑ d. Use the EXVERIFY utility to verify restoration of the Exchange server.

The correct answers to this question are a, b, and c. You must perform all the first three choices to verify the validity of the restoration. There is no such utility as EXVERIFY that does these tasks for you. Therefore, answer d is incorrect.

Question 5

You are the Exchange administrator at XYZ Company. One of the users indicates he has forgotten his password for the PST file. What do you tell him?

○ a. That you, as the administrator, will assume ownership of the PST file and reassign a password.

○ b. The owner of the PST file may assume ownership of the PST file and reassign a password.

○ c. The user can use a third-party decryption utility to recover the data within the PST file.

○ d. The data within the PST file is lost.

The correct answer is d. Because the user sets his own password for the PST file, no utility can help him get his password. It's critical that the user remembers his password for the PST file. Answers a, b, and c are incorrect.

Question 6

You've recently upgraded the hardware for your server. What should you do to increase the Exchange server's efficiency?

○ a. Reinstall Exchange Server

○ b. Run the Exchange Server Performance Optimizer

○ c. Reboot the server

○ d. Make a backup of your Exchange database

○ e. None of the above

The correct answer to this question is b. You can run the Microsoft Exchange Performance Optimizer to take advantage of the upgrade of your hardware and increase your Exchange server's efficiency. You don't need to reinstall Exchange Server. Rebooting the machine does not help you in this scenario. Making a backup of your Exchange server does not improve the server's efficiency. Therefore, answers a, c, d, and e are incorrect.

Question 7

You are the system administrator for an organization with a large client base for Exchange Server. What is the best backup plan?

○ a. Full daily

○ b. Full with differential weekly

○ c. Full with incremental daily

○ d. None of the above

The correct answer to this question is c. A full backup with incremental daily backups provides you with a full backup up to a certain point and all the changes since the last full backup. You can make a full backup on weekends and have an incremental backup on a daily basis. This speeds up your backup process on weekdays as well as maintains available disk space. A full backup on a daily basis is an unacceptable solution for large organizations due to the time it takes to back up the data as well as the disk space required to store such backups. A full with differential backup is also unacceptable because it purges the old backups, and this may be unacceptable at a large organization. Therefore, answers a, b, and d are incorrect.

Question 8

You are a consultant to an organization that wants you to verify the bottlenecks within its mail system and recommend how to resolve them. Assuming the organization uses Microsoft Exchange Server, what tool can help you prepare your recommendation report?

○ a. Link monitor

○ b. Performance Simulator

○ c. Load Simulator

○ d. None of the above

The correct answer to this question is c. The Load Simulator (LOADSIM.EXE) validates a portion of the organization's design by configuring the number of users you hope to support on a particular server configuration and provides you with valuable information regarding capacity, performance, network bandwidth, and impact analysis. A link monitor helps you verify the email links to a particular domain. There is no such utility as Performance Simulator. Therefore, answers a, b, and d are incorrect.

Question 9

> You are brought into an organization as the authority on Exchange
> Server. There are complaints from the users within the organiza-
> tion that it takes a lot of time for the delivery of their messages
> outside the organization. The system administrator for the orga-
> nization does not agree with the users. What Exchange Server
> counter can you use to verify this problem?
>
> ○ a. Microsoft Exchange MTA Work Queue Size
>
> ○ b. Microsoft Exchange IS Message Opens/sec
>
> ○ c. Microsoft Exchange DS Access Violation
>
> ○ d. None of the above

The correct answer to this question is a. Microsoft Exchange MTA Work
Queue Size monitors the number of messages queued within the MTA for
delivery as well as the messages within the incoming queue. Divide this counter's
value by messages/sec to get an approximate estimate of how long the server
takes to deliver a message. A high number indicates a problem, either in performance or in transmitting messages to other servers. Microsoft Exchange IS
Message Opens/sec measures the number of messages stored within the public
folders the users have opened. Microsoft Exchange DS Access Violation measures the number of times the Exchange server refuses to write for a directory
service due to security violations. Therefore, answers b, c, and d are incorrect.

Question 10

> Which Exchange chart helps you track the movement of messages?
>
> ○ a. Microsoft Exchange Server Load
>
> ○ b. Microsoft Exchange IMS Traffic
>
> ○ c. Microsoft Exchange IMS Queues
>
> ○ d. Microsoft Exchange Server History

The correct answer to this question is b. The Microsoft Exchange IMS Traffic
chart tracks the movement of messages as they travel between the MTS-IN
and MTS-OUT internal queues as well as the current number of SMTP sessions established, both inbound and outbound. The Microsoft Exchange Server
Load chart tracks the server load by client activity and adjacent servers. The
Microsoft Exchange IMS Queues chart tracks the number of messages within

the queues, both inbound and outbound. The Microsoft Exchange Server History chart tracks the number of users who have a connection to the server and the number of outstanding messages within the internal queue that have not been processed. Therefore, answers a, c, and d are incorrect.

Need To Know More?

Gerber, Barry. *Mastering Microsoft Exchange Server 5.5*. Alameda, CA: Sybex, 1998. ISBN: 0-78212-237-X. System administrators, power users, consultants, and applications developers are the audience for this comprehensive book. The third edition is essential reading for those within a Windows NT-based corporate networking environment.

Kent Joshi, Tracy Bradley, Tito Del Prado, et al. *Using Microsoft Exchange Server 5.5*. Indianapolis, IN: Que Education & Training, 1998. ISBN: 0-78971-503-1. This book provides the serious Exchange user with details about deploying Microsoft Exchange in the real world. The book probes Exchange administration and configuration details in incredible depth, comprehensively taking on everything from network topology to site management as well as remote access management to connections with all the major networks and protocols.

Redmond, Tony. *Microsoft Exchange Server V5.0: Planning, Design, and Implementation*. Boston: Digital Press, 1997. ISBN: 1-55558-189-7. An excellent resource guide, this book provides in-depth information on POP3, IMS, and X400 connectors, as well as good advice on server design and load balancing. It's a good hands-on guide for administrators looking to implement Exchange Server.

Todd, Greg. *Microsoft Exchange Server 5.5 Unleashed*. Indianapolis, IN: Sams Publishing, 1998. ISBN: 0-67231-283-2. This book is a reference for Microsoft Exchange Server that contains all the information you need to properly install, configure, and maintain an Exchange Server system. This book includes extensive coverage of integrating multiple email subsystems and discusses specific tailoring techniques for the different client workstations. Co-written by members of the Microsoft Exchange Development team, this book contains advanced troubleshooting and optimization techniques and gives insider tips on several advanced functions and features. This book is specifically tailored to cover server administration issues, and it does so in a deep and professional format.

Microsoft Technical Information Network (TechNet), March 1998. The technical notes for Microsoft Exchange Server provide insight into its disaster recovery plans and more.

 Browse product documentation and online help locally on your server or on your CD-ROM. Alternatively, you can download the documentation from the Microsoft Web site at www.microsoft.com/exchange.

 The Microsoft Web site at www.microsoft.com/exchange provides a wealth of information regarding Exchange Server, including data sheets, whitepapers, system requirements, an evaluation copy of Exchange Server, case studies, tips, tricks, and a lot more.

In addition, the Microsoft Web site provides a Frequently Asked Questions (FAQ) and Knowledge Base—an excellent resource.

 The BHS Web site at www.bhs.com is a valuable resource for information on Windows NT and other tools that are dependent on Windows NT, such as Exchange Server.

Exchange Forms

. . . .

Terms you'll need to understand:

√ 16-bit and 32-bit forms

√ Active Server Pages (ASP)

√ Calendar

√ Collaboration

√ Contacts

√ Database

√ Fields

√ Folders

√ Hypertext Transfer Protocol (HTTP)

√ Journal

√ Lightweight Directory Access Protocol (LDAP)

√ Message queues

√ Moderated folders

√ Network News Transfer Protocol (NNTP)

√ Permissions

√ Post Office Protocol 3 (POP3)

√ Simple Mail Transfer Protocol (SMTP)

√ Transaction Server

Techniques you'll need to master:

√ Understanding the form options available to you for use with custom form creation in Outlook 98

√ Understanding the components that allow you to create interactive forms

√ Understanding the roles of permissions

√ Explaining how you can seamlessly create forms that interact between a server and a client machine

√ Modifying existing forms to suit your needs

√ Learning how to create professional-looking and functional forms without programming

317

In this chapter, we explore how to make forms work for you with Outlook 98. Remember that Outlook 97, Outlook Express, and the Exchange Client can all use forms, as well. The methods for creating and using these forms will be similar to those outlined in this chapter. We also tell you what you need to know to make efficient use of some of the programming tools available. Finally, we take an in-depth look at custom forms and teach you how to create them without programming, thus making you an efficiency hero.

Planning Your Forms

A very basic question you may ask yourself is "What are forms and what purpose do they serve?" A *form* is a method for posting and gathering information that might otherwise get lost in a sea of data. Electronic forms are a great choice for replacing paperwork that is used regularly, for information with different security requirements for a group or person, and (with some development effort) for dramatically streamlining paper trails. A classic example of the latter type would be a trouble ticket generated for a help desk.

Before you begin creating your first electronic form, you need to look at the different types of forms and the basis of these forms. The first decision you must make is whether you want to create a form with the Exchange Designer or use Outlook forms. You can use Outlook as the basis for your forms and then modify them to suit your needs. If you go with Exchange forms, the next decision you must make is whether you want to use 16-bit forms or 32-bit forms.

It would be wise to understand the use of 16-bit forms versus 32-bit forms. Remember that Windows 3.1 cannot use 32-bit forms.

Exchange is configured to support the following different types of forms:

➤ **Report forms** These forms are used to automate creating and sending reports.

➤ **Request forms** These forms are useful in streamlining a material request, such as a request for a new set of business cards or a new hard drive for your computer.

➤ **Survey forms** These forms are handy for collecting information from employees or customers. For example, a public folder could be used to query Web site visitors on how likely they are to purchase a new widget from your firm.

When you're planning your forms, the Exchange library of forms has several types of forms you can use:

➤ **Organization forms** These forms are stored on the server and are accessible by all users.

➤ **Personal forms** This type of form is specific to a certain user and is located in the individual's mailbox.

➤ **Folder forms** When placed in a public folder, these forms can be accessed by everyone. The alternative is to store them on a local drive, which makes them available only to users with access to that drive.

In most cases, your forms will be used to communicate information to a group of people. Working with a group is called *collaboration*; therefore, developing forms to fill this need is known as *collaboration development*.

Collaboration Methods

Now that you've seen the types of forms you can use, it's time to break your needs out another way. Your collaboration requirements might be realtime, such as a virtual meeting with NetMeeting, or not realtime. Realtime collaboration uses synchronous communication, while collaboration that does not take place in realtime uses asynchronous communication. An example of the latter would be an electronic phone message taken while someone is out to lunch that is posted to that person's email account. This would be the electronic equivalent of a paper "While You Were Out" message. The major difference is that the person's office could be in Redmond, Wash., and you could be in Philadelphia, Pa.

Components Of Collaboration

An electronic form is actually made up of a number of separate components. In most cases, all your forms will share the following components:

➤ **Folders** Without at least a public or a private folder in which to store your data, your forms would be nothing more than pretty pictures on the screen. It's a good idea to test any public form from a private folder area to make sure it performs correctly. Failure of your first public form may deter management from extending Exchange. Correctly designed public forms greatly improve communication speed and accuracy.

➤ **Views** The various elements of data in a form can represent different things to different users. For example, a help desk form would need to detail the trouble a user is experiencing, along with who is working the trouble ticket and who sent it. A supervisor would only need an overview of who is working what tickets to check on workflow and to verify closure of trouble tickets in a timely manner.

➤ **Fields** A field holds data elements. As in the trouble ticket example, a data element could be the name of the individual working the trouble ticket. This field would be used by the sender of the trouble ticket, as well as the supervisor. Some other examples include Sender First Name, Sender Last Name, Location, and so on.

➤ **Forms** This is the actual "physical" form that defines how data flows in and out of your Exchange database. If you've ever sent email, you used a form to enter data elements in the To field (the From field is usually filled in for you) and to enter a message in the Message field. If you think about it, you use forms all the time. Work life would be rather messy without them.

➤ **Databases** In many cases, Exchange is your database. However, you can link other databases to your forms. Using the Open Database Connectivity (ODBC) Connector, you can check other databases; for example, you could check a SQL database for a part you need to keep your customer's widget running.

Outlook Instant Collaboration

In Chapter 7, we took a good look at Outlook 98 and examined several of its built-in components—Calendar, Tasks, Notes, Contacts, and Journal. Copying one of these modules into a public folder creates an instant public collaboration application. If you enjoy working with Visual Basic (VB), you can combine the Outlook Forms Designer with VBScript to create some powerful and impressive applications.

If you place the Calendar component in a public folder, users can share, post, and update to this folder. When you have several projects going on—for example, the company softball team and the planned rollout of the new deluxe widget—be sure to create a public folder for each topic; otherwise, the usefulness of your public calendar will be a quick exercise in confusion and frustration. The same would also apply to the Outlook Task component. It may be copied to a public folder where a team may collaborate and demonstrate the progress of a task, and a supervisor could quickly track the progress. The sales staff getting the clients ready for your deluxe widget rollout could access a shared contact list from a public folder. This is very handy if someone has to cover for the sales rep who joined you in Philadelphia for lunch, because all contacts are located in the same folder, to which everyone has access. A public Journal component may prove useful as an Exchange form; for example, you can post feedback from the beta testers of the deluxe widget. Finally, Notes can be used both publicly and privately as the electronic equivalent of "sticky notes." A public electronic sticky note can be forwarded as a message.

Collaboration Applications Platform

The collaboration platform is based on Internet standards. Because these standards are open standards, you can use both NT and Windows 9x for your collaboration needs. Because you have open standards, there's no single right way to plan and execute a form rollout. The "right" way is whatever way fits the requirements of the challenge you're attempting to streamline or solve. In our case, we're using NT Server with Exchange as the "database," which, as mentioned previously, can also extend to other databases such as SQL. To make our collaboration as easy as possible to use, we could also use Internet Information Server (IIS). Keep in mind that Exchange offers the Simple Mail Transfer Protocol (SMTP), Post Office Protocol 3 (POP3), as well as Lightweight Directory Access Protocol (LDAP), Network News Transfer Protocol (NNTP), and finally, public and private folders. All of these can be used to incorporate your collaboration forms. If you use IIS, remember that Index Server is available to your users, making short work of locating the needed information. On the client side, Internet Explorer 4 supports the latest version of Hypertext Transfer Protocol (version 1.1). Also, with some programming background, you can use VBScript to extend the programming power of Active Server Pages (ASP).

Outlook Collaboration Applications Environment

Using Outlook 98 for creating collaboration forms gives you a number of advantages over the earlier options. Some benefits include the following:

➤ **32-bit forms** Outlook 98 forms are completely 32 bit. Form definitions are less than 15K in most cases. This gives you quick performance and fast updating.

➤ **Rapid Application Development (RAD)** Developing collaboration forms is a joy when you can quickly switch back and forth between designing your form and testing it, without compiling your work.

➤ **Portable custom forms** Users of your forms can email them to other users who may not have them installed. It's also possible to embed a form in other applications.

➤ **Advanced views and fields** In Chapter 7 when we examined Outlook 98, you saw how easy it is to organize your views. This can be applied to your collaboration forms as well. Furthermore, you can include algebra or other numeric calculations.

Application Development Using Outlook 98

Using Outlook 98 as your design platform greatly enhances your design features over the tools offered in the Exchange client. Besides having the Outlook 98 Forms Designer at your fingertips, you have the VB Scripting tools and the VB Expression service.

To reach your Outlook 98 Forms Designer, simply click Tools|Forms|Design A Form (this is slightly different than in other versions of Outlook). The resulting Design Form dialog box is shown in Figure 12.1.

Another difference between Outlook 98 and earlier versions is the flexibility in the types of forms that you have. This is most easily recognized through the Save As dialog box, which is shown in Figure 12.2. Previously, forms were saved as OFT files. Now you have options such as Rich Text Format and Outlook Template, as well as others.

Visual Basic

Before Outlook 98, if you wanted to design a form for collaboration, you needed to know a bit about Visual Basic to perform some tasks. Although Visual Basic

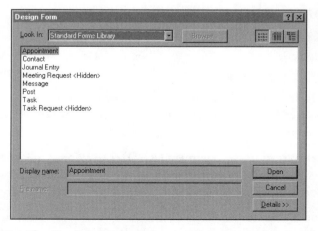

Figure 12.1 The Design Form dialog box is accessed through the Tools|Forms|Design A Form menu item.

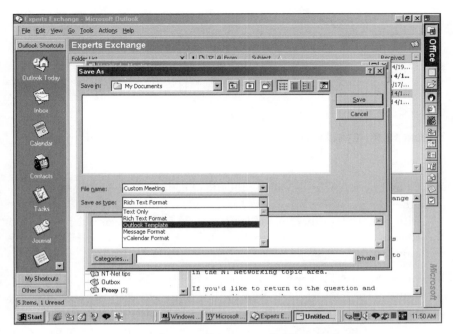

Figure 12.2   Forms can be saved in several different formats.

is still available, the toolbox gives you the ability to create professional-looking forms without knowledge of VB. Notice the options available to you through the toolbox, which is shown in Figure 12.3.

Active Server And Active Desktop Components

By using code and tools common to both the client and the server, both communications and the mechanisms that create the "look and feel" of your collaboration forms are invisible to the end user (and virtually painless for you as the developer). Here's a list of some of the components you have at your disposal:

➤ **HTML** Because HTML can be used with Active Desktop as well as with forms, the view to the end user is the same. This greatly reduces training time.

➤ **Scripting** With ASP offering both VBScript and JavaScript (JScript), the choice of scripting tools is yours. VBScript currently provides more powerful choices, whereas JScript gives you a method to perform the task at hand without concern for the operating system (OS) on which the user is based.

Figure 12.3 Checkboxes, radio buttons, picture inserts, and more can easily be added to a form through the toolbox.

➤ **Components** ASP also allows the use of components developed in other programming languages. Server-side scripting can provide you with support for other human languages. You can provide a user with content in his or her native tongue, based on input from the HTML browser.

➤ **Active Server** This option became available in IIS versions 3 and 4. Some of the features, aside from ASP, include Transaction Server and Message Queues. These offerings ensure the health and safety of your data, and they keep the logic of running the form separate from the display information (such as the language).

➤ **Transaction Server (TS)** Microsoft recently moved from offering TS as a separate product, to making it available without charge to authorized users of NT and IIS. TS can eliminate quite a bit of the program logic required to ensure the accuracy of data. For example, if you had a form that sold a widget part from your inventory, TS would not allow the part to be removed permanently from inventory until the transaction is complete. All you have to know as a developer is two lines of code: Commit and Rollback.

➤ **Message Queues** This is a newer offering from Redmond that is based on transaction messages. For example, suppose your Exchange server is not available because AT&T has a frame relay service failure. Now you need to communicate with a server that is not available. With Message Queue, the message destined for the unavailable Exchange server is stored in a queue until AT&T restores your frame relay service; then the message is delivered to the Exchange server.

Creating Folders With Outlook

In Outlook 98, folders are used to automatically share information from your computer with other computers on the network. Outlook 98 uses two folder types:

➤ **File system folders** These folders behave just like a folder in the
Explorer program. This means you have all the properties of any folder
created by the OS. Outlook 98 or the OS can use these folders.

➤ **Outlook Item folders** These folders are called Outlook folders because
they can only be seen within Outlook 98. You can create a new folder, or
you can duplicate and change the design of one of six folders: Appointments, Contacts, Journal, Message, Post, and Tasks.

Usually, you create an Outlook 98 Item folder when you don't have a good
design to follow, or if you only need standard options. The normal use for a
folder of this type is a discussion folder, a reference folder, or perhaps a tracking folder. You can create a new Outlook 98 Item folder by following these steps:

1. Select File|New|New Folder from the main Outlook screen. The Create
   New Folder dialog box appears, as shown in Figure 12.4.

2. Enter the name for your folder.

3. Through the Folder Contains drop-down list, select the type of items
   that will be stored in the folder. Available options are Appointment
   Items, Contact Items, Journal Items, Mail Items, Note Items, and
   Task Items.

4. From the tree displayed in the Select Where To Place This Folder
   window, define where the folder will be located. It may be a top-level
   folder, or located in any subfolders.

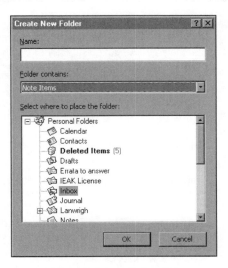

Figure 12.4   The Create New Folder dialog box.

5. Click the OK button.

6. The next choice you need to make is whether you want a shortcut placed on the left-most bar of Outlook 98. The default is No. Select No at this time.

Viewing Folder Permissions

You can view the permissions of any folder by highlighting the folder, right-clicking, selecting Properties, and then clicking the Permissions tab. The default is to allow all Exchange users to read and write to a public folder. This would not be the case in a private folder, which would deny access to everyone but the owner.

Folder Permissions

Outlook 98, in concert with Exchange Server, gives you predefined folder permissions. The default permission of a folder is used if a folder does not have other permissions set. Table 12.1 lists the standard set of permissions for a folder.

Outlook 98 allows one user to assign rights for another user. For example, you could assign a user the right to schedule appointments and meetings on your behalf—in effect allowing that user to be your assistant. Granting this right is called *delegate access*. The delegate access feature of Outlook 98 only shows up

Table 12.1	Standard folder permissions.
Role	**Rights**
Owner	Create, read, modify, and delete all files/items. Allow creation of subfolders. When creating subfolders or using existing folders, the owner can determine who has access to these folders.
Publishing Editor	Create, read, modify, and delete all files/items. Can create subfolders.
Editor	Create, read, modify, and delete all files/items.
Author	Create and read files/items. Modify or delete files/items created by the author.
Nonediting Author	Create and read items; no access to editing files/items.
Reviewer	Read files/items only.
Contributor	Create items and files only. The contents of the folder are not shown.
Custom	Whatever the folder owner defines.
None	Cannot open the folder. Equivalent to NT's No Access.

when using Exchange Server. Naturally, this means you need a connection to the Exchange server with the delegate access feature installed.

Moderated Folders

If a public folder (or for that matter, a listserv or bulletin board) is moderated, you can send a message to that system, but it will not be displayed until a reviewer chooses to accept the posting. You may see notices stating that lists are lightly moderated or heavily moderated. In the case of Exchange, an event service looks for postings to a moderated public folder and transparently forwards the new posting to the Exchange user who has been assigned this task, without modifying the contents. This person then determines the merit of the posting, and, if found in his or her judgment to be suitable to the public folder, must then copy it to the folder in question.

To create a moderated folder, select Moderated Folder and then select the Set Folder As A Moderated Folder checkbox. At this point, the choices on your new folder are as follows:

➤ **Forwarding location** Defines the forwarding location to which all postings (other than the moderator's postings) will be forwarded. Any person with a listing either in the Global Address List (GAL) or the personal address book (PAB) can be a valid moderator. Be careful if you select more than one moderator. If you do this, each person would get a copy of the posting, and this could result in both moderators posting the same message. A better idea is to send the message to a secure public folder, available only to the group of moderators; then, once the posting is accepted, any of the folks with this task can copy the posting to the moderated public folder.

➤ **Send an automated reply message following a posting** If you select this option, either a standard or a custom form can be used. Watch out for the gotcha of not having Send On Behalf Of turned on by the owner of the folder. This is required for a custom template reply.

➤ **Identify the moderators** When you select the moderator(s) for a folder, you have granted a role that allows them to post to the folder.

Message Flow

The following steps show how a message works its way through Exchange when a person posts a message:

1. A rule on the folder (discussed in the next section) checks to see if the sender is a moderator.

2. For purposes of this example, let's assume the sender is not on the list of moderators. The message is forwarded to the location you previously selected, without any changes to the message.

3. The message is deleted from the folder it first landed in.

4. If the folder owner has selected that an auto-responder inform the sender that the message has been received, this happens now. Remember that moderators generating a message bypass the rules, so they may post directly.

5. The moderator reviews the message and passes judgment on the validity of the message. If it fails to meet the list's standards, the moderator deletes the message. Otherwise, the moderator posts the message to the folder.

Roles And Rules

The rule for the moderator is found in the list of rules on the folder. Look for Moderated Folder Rule, which is found in the Conditions column. Also, check the Actions column for Forward To Moderator and Moderate Message. You need to edit these rules with the Moderated Folder button found in the Administration tab. An owner can rearrange the rules up or down the chain, which affects the order of execution. If you do not learn from this text to carefully and fully test your rules *before* live deployment, you'll learn from painful real-world experience (from your first disaster forward).

Cloning And Morphing Folders

Before you begin altering forms, you need owner permissions. If you're not sure of the current status, highlight the folder and right-click it. Select Properties to view the Permissions tab. Also, when you're working with a folder design, the components of the source folder are merged with the parts of the destination folder.

When you are modifying a folder that's in use, you should make only minor changes that don't disrupt the workflow of the users. Some examples of this would be adding a view, changing a contact, or perhaps updating permissions. Remember that any changes in permissions do not take effect for a user already logged in until that user logs out and logs back in again.

To affect more serious changes—for example, changing rules or actually modifying the form—copy the design of the folder in question to a different folder, implement what changes are needed, and then test, test, and test some more. Finally, copy the modified design back to the original folder.

Before we discuss merging folder designs, another word to the wise. If you have conflicting properties between the source folder and the destination folder, the rules to remember are:

➤ The source folder will replace the properties on the destination folder.

➤ You should always double-check permissions.

Planning And Organizing

Regardless of the final role of a folder, Microsoft offers 10 guidelines as planning principles. You should implement the following guidelines:

➤ Identify folder users and requirements.

➤ Create a designer in charge (a lead) who will plan, design, and implement the project folder.

➤ Form a design plan that pinpoints the challenges to be solved and how the folder will overcome the challenge in question. Be sure to include preliminary graphics of the views and windows that will be needed.

➤ Choose where your design work will take place. If you have a group giving input and feedback, be sure to put it in a public folder. Early concept and design stages may be better off in a personal PST folder or Outlook mailbox.

➤ Create or choose a folder. Choices include creating a new folder, directly modifying an existing folder, or copying a folder design.

➤ Publish forms in the folder. You might need to publish the form in either the Standard Forms Library or in another folder.

➤ Design the folder views. To assist your users, create folder views with elements such as Columns, Filters, Sorting, and so forth. Alternatively, create a new view from the start.

➤ Test the folder thoroughly. Be sure to include all views and expressions. Double-check the folder's availability and secure any items that should not be changed.

➤ Copy the folder from the test bed to the appropriate public folder. Test some more, on a limited basis.

➤ Release the form for real work by changing permissions.

Personal Folders (PSTs)

PST files, or *personal folders*, are located on the user's local hard disk. Usually, they are used to archive information. Sometimes a clever administrator will use the user PST as a temporary storage area to hold data when moving a user's mailbox from one Exchange site to another. A PST file has the same properties as any other file. This means it can be renamed, copied, and deleted like any other file. Personal folders support password protection and two levels of encryption. No more than one user at a time can access a PST file. Remember that once a PST is in use on a local hard drive, you are no longer backing up the data with the Exchange server. The burden of backups is moved to the local hard drive. A PST folder can contain the same types of information found on the Exchange Server Information Store.

Testing And Releasing A Folder

By now, you should have made the words "test, test, test" your mantra. After you're comfortable with the way your folder is behaving, ask a few of your users to test your efforts. When seeking guinea pigs for your experiment, be sure to include both advanced users, who can easily communicate feedback on a more technical level, as well as novices, who can more easily be confused. Be sure to set your permissions to "owners" only while in the testing phase. When all changes have been made, go to the Folder Properties dialog box, select the Administration tab, and then pick All Users With Access Permission. Finally, observe carefully that all users have appropriate access.

Folder Rules And Views

Rules are the machinery that makes collaborations behave. Using rules customizes the engine that reduces labor and, once thoroughly tested, eliminates mistakes. Rules that are not thoroughly tested can produce errors faster than rabbits produce bunnies. Rules can also be used to alert users to messages or to create auto-responder messages. Rules are created and managed through the Rules wizard, which is shown in Figure 12.5.

Views assist in the management and use of folders in ways that benefit the user. Views allow advanced sorting, filtering, and manipulation. To review some of the advanced features of views and sorting, refer back to Chapter 7, paying particular attention to the Advanced Features section that deals with the Organize key. With this overview in mind, let's drill down into the use of rules.

You will use rules to perform the following tasks:

➤ Select the specific types of items that are returned to the sender automatically.

Figure 12.5   The Rules wizard is accessed through the Tools menu in Outlook.

➤ Delete unwanted items based on specified conditions. Careful use of a rule here can make unwanted mail (*spam*) nothing more than a bad memory.

➤ Reply automatically to specific kinds of items with a reply template.

➤ Manage, for each machine, the way messages are handled (that is, forwarded, copied, or moved to folders or other users).

Rules perform based on two concepts:

➤ **Conditions** This is the judgment part of a rule. Think of the simplest form of programming—if this, then do that; or, if this, then do other, else third choice.

➤ **Actions** If a rule is met, what is the action step to take? Referring back to Chapter 7, a rule is in place that says, "If the From field contains the mail header from the Exchange list, move the mail message to the Exchange List folder."

Let's look at how rules are applied. Simply put, rules work in a "top down" fashion. Rules are placed with the Inbox Assistant or an Out of Office Assistant. In Outlook 98, you'll find easy assistance with the Rules wizard, which is accessed under the Tools menu.

As a message comes in, the rules are applied to the message starting with the rule at the top of the list. If a rule is found to apply, the action step is taken. If the rule does not apply, the next rule makes a judgment to see if it has anything it can do to the message. Like all well-written judgments, the rule is very exact in what it is looking for. It's possible to use a rule to take a message from the CEO, for example, and have it copied to all department heads.

There are a couple specific conditions that will stop a rule in its tracks. One method is to select the Stop Processing More Rules option, which is available through the rule's properties. Another showstopper is deleting a message. If you're going to use the Delete rule, be sure to place it last. If you decide not to use the Delete rule, a good method for making spam a nonissue is to place some filters before forwarding the mail from the ISP. Then, using the Rule wizard, you can create a rule that forwards mail not meeting other conditions to a folder that's intended to capture any spam that slipped through. Now, before affecting a wholesale permanent delete from this folder, a quick scan of subject and message headers ensures that you don't throw out a legitimate message.

A final thought on applying rules: Sometimes the logic flow takes a bit more effort at first glance, or you may have rules for which you want to create a plan B over a plan A.

To do this, create both rules separately. Select the rule and move it up or down, so the new plan B is in place over plan A. For example, you may have Administrative alerts set up so that if you have a hard drive failure on your RAID disk subsystem, an SMTP message is created and mailed to you. Plan A would see the incoming mail from your NT system, and your plan A rule is to forward this message to your desktop, with high importance. For the weekend, plan B would be to route this message to your home system and call your pager.

This example is only one way of keeping you on top of what's going on. Another idea is to make more complex conditions. In the preceding example, there's only one condition: "If it's from the NT system, track me down." For a rule to function, you must have at least one condition. Remember, of course, you can apply rules to almost any field within your message (for example, From, Subject, Importance, and so forth).

Specifying An Action

Part of designing rules for operation on your system is defining what action will be taken. Table 12.2 shows the types of action that can be taken using Outlook 98.

If none of your rules can be satisfied with these actions, you can create a custom rule. To create a custom rule set, use the CRARUN application on the BackOffice CD-ROM. Although this can be fun and exciting, it's really

Table 12.2 Rule actions.	
Action	**Description**
Alert	Choose to be notified with a sound or a dialog box.
Delete	Delete the item. (Be careful when using this option.)
Move/Copy to folder	Move or copy to designated folder. If you have multiple actions, this occurs multiple times.
Forward to	Forward the message to a new recipient.
Reply using template	Send an automatic reply to the sender.

beyond the scope of this book. Refer to the Outlook and Exchange Server documentation for more information.

Folder Views

Views are simply different ways to see information stored in a folder. As you saw in Chapter 7, you can change the view for messages, contacts, journal entries, and forms. Every folder in Outlook 98 has a set of standard views. The view type varies with the type of folder in which you're holding the information. Let's look at creating a new view. To do this, select View|Current View|Define Views to open the Define Views dialog box.

At this point, you can either change an existing view by using the Modify button or define a new view by clicking New. This opens the Create A New View dialog box, which is shown in Figure 12.6.

The options available in the Create A New View dialog box are explained in Table 12.3.

Figure 12.6 Several options are available when creating a new view.

Table 12.3	View options.
View Type	**Description**
Table	Displays items in a grid of rows and columns. Each row contains one item. A row may be a list of contacts, for example. The column would contain a field of information. In the case of contacts, it may be an email address.
Timeline	Displays items in a chronological order from left to right, oldest to newest. This is handy if you don't remember the name of an item, but you remember, for example, that it happened on that *really bad* Monday morning.
Card	Displays items as individual cards. This is the default for Contacts.
Day/Week/Month	Displays items on the calendar. Views include weekly agenda, multiday format, or monthly.
Icon	Indicates files and items by icon. This is the default view for Notes.

Using The Field Chooser

You can modify or create new fields to view, to add custom fields, or to select from an almost limitless variety of options on your existing fields to suit your needs. These features were available in other versions of Outlook, but unless you knew to look for them, they were invisible to end users. With Outlook 98, the Organize button gives the end user the ability to access some of these features in a less confusing way. Although using the Organizer is simpler, it removes some of the features that are available. Let's look at some of the more common choices that most users find boost productivity:

➤ **Sorting Items** Items in a field can be sorted in an ascending or descending order. When you organize your messages from the Exchange list using Organize, you sort by subject, by default. It's possible to order by any number of fields, including From and Received.

➤ **Grouping Items** Grouping can be useful to hide items when collapsed. If you arrange by a common field, you can get a better overview without drowning in data. One caution is in order here: It's not possible to create groups from custom formulas or combination fields.

➤ **Other Views** Besides the two more common uses listed previously, it's also possible to organize in the following ways:

➤ AutoPreview

➤ Best Fit

➤ Column Alignment

➤ Editable or Noneditable views

With Outlook 98, the Office wizard is standing by to assist you in your customization efforts. Finally, when you or your users are drowning in data, you can use a filter to reduce some of the clutter, as well as to drill down from an overview point to find what you're looking for in a logical manner without being swamped. Filters work in much the same way as views and rules, and they are created through View|Current View|Customize Current View menu item. Speaking of drowning in data, now is a good time to look at how not to do just that. Let's move on to custom views.

Custom View Options

As you can see in Figure 12.7, Outlook 98 provides several standard views for each folder through the Views|Current View menu item. The default views are Messages, Messages With AutoPreview, By Follow Up Flag, Last Seven Days, Flagged For Next Seven Days, By Conversation Topic, By Sender, Unread Messages, Sent To, and Message Timeline. If you've added a custom view, it will also appear in this menu.

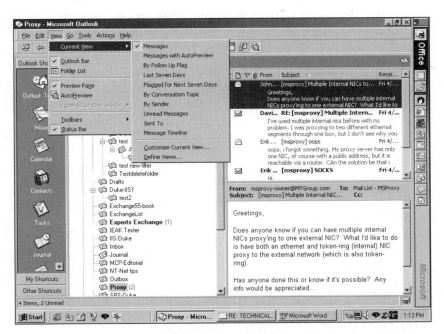

Figure 12.7 Outlook 98 gives you 10 different default views for the messages stored in this folder.

Each of these view options presents the items in the folder in a different way. The default view for most folders is Messages. However, changing the view to Message Timeline, for example, can display the messages in a manner that makes it easier to follow a particular conversation or determine what you did all day.

Creating Forms

Now that we have successfully modified some existing views and forms, it's time to look at building some new ones. Outlook 98 offers several basic forms that can easily be customized. You can leverage these forms to quickly get functionality from them. For that reason, rather than starting with a brand-new form, let's look at some of the forms you have to start with.

Mail Message Forms

You can build forms that automatically handle information to make your job easier. By combining mail message forms with other features of Exchange, such as distribution lists, you can easily convert a manual system to an automated one. Some examples would include the following:

➤ **Request forms** These are used to create items such as a vacation request form, an order form for business cards, or a purchase request form (for that new hard drive for your growing Exchange database).

➤ **Survey or feedback forms** Examples of these forms would be surveys requesting information about how your clients think you're doing in making a widget as a productivity tool, or what they would like to see in Widget Deluxe before you release it.

➤ **Report forms** These are useful in the distribution of information. Examples of these forms might be status reports, travel expense reports, or time sheets.

Post Forms

Typically, post forms are used for threaded conversations. This permits the viewer to conduct and view online conversations. Listservs would be well suited to this type of data. Refer back to the huge pile of messages we have from the MsExchange list in Chapter 7 for an example.

Office 97 Document Forms

These would be forms that are either postings or messages that are embedded in an Office 97 application, such as Excel, Word, PowerPoint, or even Access.

Using an Outlook 98 form as a "wrapper" combines the power of the application in an Outlook 98 form. Suppose you wanted to simplify productivity for your outbound sales force. Combining an Excel spreadsheet with an expense report form would not only simplify the lives of the sales force, it would assist accounting as well.

Built-In Forms

Outlook 98 has some functionality built in. You have seen this in Chapter 7 when working with the various Exchange clients: Calendar, Contacts, Tasks, Journal, and Notes. Each of these has a specific function. It's possible to customize the basics and to add specific forms and controls. Note that the first page of the built-in forms cannot be modified, because some controls are available only on the first page. A case in point is Tasks in the calendar. Tasks will always sit on the first page of the calendar (and remain there).

Outlook 98 Forms Designer

The Outlook 98 Forms Designer uses 32-bit development tools that are provided with Outlook 98. You can get to the Forms Designer by selecting Tools|Forms|Design A Form, which opens the Design Form dialog box shown in Figure 12.8.

The Field Chooser, shown in Figure 12.9, enables you to quickly use your existing fields by simply dragging and dropping them wherever you want on

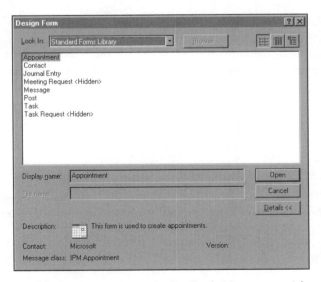

Figure 12.8 The Forms Designer in Outlook 98 comes with predefined forms to jump-start your custom forms.

Figure 12.9 The Field Chooser displays fields that are already defined in Outlook 98.

the form. Depending on the type of form you use as your base, the Field Chooser might not be available. If it is available, it will open automatically when you begin to design the form.

It's very easy to view different fields by selecting a specific category through the drop-down list at the top of the Field Chooser. One of your choices is to create a new field. To do this, select User-Defined Fields Folder from the Field Chooser and click New. You'll be presented with a dialog box similar to the one shown in Figure 12.10. Enter the name of your field, the type of field (Yes/No, Integer, Date/Time, and so on) and the format for your field (which depends on the type of field you're using). Once you've defined your new field, you can drag it onto your custom form and publish the form. Frankly, we wouldn't do any of this in front of your coworkers or supervisor. Let them think you worked for hours (not a few seconds) creating your form.

Figure 12.10 A custom field is easily created using the Field Chooser.

Exam Prep Questions

Question 1

> Outlook 98 produces which of the following types of forms?
>
> ○ a. 64 bit
> ○ b. 32 bit
> ○ c. 16 bit
> ○ d. 8 bit

The correct answer to this question is b. Windows 95/98 use 32-bit forms. Answer a is incorrect because currently no 64-bit computers run a 64-bit form. Answer c is incorrect because this applies to older Exchange forms, which are used in Windows 3.1 environments. Answer d is incorrect because forms have long since outgrown eight bits.

Question 2

> In how many different ways can collaboration occur?
>
> ○ a. 1
> ○ b. 2
> ○ c. 3
> ○ d. 4

The correct answer to this question is c. The types of collaboration are report forms (used to automate the creating and sending of reports), request forms (useful in streamlining a material request), and survey forms (handy in collecting information from employees or customers). The other answers are incorrect.

Question 3

> Outlook 98 can connect to outside databases using MTAs.
>
> ○ a. True
> ○ b. False

The correct answer to this question is b, False. In many cases, Exchange is the database. It's possible to link other databases to a form using the Open Database Connectivity (ODBC) Connector. However, this is not a function of the Message Transfer Agent, so answer a is incorrect.

Question 4

> When creating a collaboration form, which of the following built-in Outlook 98 modules can be used? [Check all correct answers]
>
> ❑ a. Calendar module
>
> ❑ b. Tasks module
>
> ❑ c. Contacts module
>
> ❑ d. Journal module

The correct answers to this question are a, b, c, and d. Each of these modules can be used to create a custom collaboration. Therefore, all answers are correct.

Question 5

> Outlook 98 forms can be extended with which of the following Microsoft developer tools? [Check all correct answers]
>
> ❑ a. VBScript
>
> ❑ b. JScript
>
> ❑ c. COBOL
>
> ❑ d. C++

The correct answers to this question are a and b. VBScript and JScript can both be used to extend an application. Although, you can use C++ to extend an application's development with a suite such as Visual Studio, this is not a native language for extending Exchange forms. Therefore, answer d is incorrect. Data files that use COBOL as an engine can have data extended to Exchange forms using ODBC. Therefore, answer c is incorrect.

Question 6

> When designing an application in Outlook 98, you have selected a mission-critical application that cannot get out of synchronization on your database of information concerning parts for widgets. Which of the following should you also install on the server side?
>
> ○ a. Message Queues
>
> ○ b. Global Address List
>
> ○ c. Knowledge Consistency Checker
>
> ○ d. Transaction Server

The correct answer to this question is d. A developer only needs to "commit" the custom code to be completely satisfied that all databases have been updated or to "rollback" (undo) all changes made in all databases; the Transaction Server manages both of these functions. Message Queues are used to ensure that all email is delivered after a communication link has been restored. Therefore, answer a is incorrect. The Global Address List is used to store a large list of addresses on a global scale. Therefore, answer b is incorrect. The Knowledge Consistency Checker is used to repair an Exchange system that is out of sync. Therefore, answer c is incorrect.

Question 7

> 32-bit forms can be used on a Windows 3.x computer, but they will run slowly. This is okay in a light-use situation in an office.
>
> ○ a. True
>
> ○ b. False

The correct answer to this question is b, False. Because Windows 3.x is a 16-bit operating system, only 16-bit forms can be used. Therefore, answer a is incorrect.

Question 8

> Which two factors come into play when creating a rule set? [Check only two answers]
>
> ❑ a. Moderators
>
> ❑ b. Wizards
>
> ❑ c. Conditions
>
> ❑ d. Action

The correct answers to this question are c and d. To perform an event, first a condition must be met. Then and only then can an action be performed. For example, if email from Hints@examcram.com comes into the inbox, it would be possible to move this mail to a Hints folder. Answers a and b are both fictitious and are therefore incorrect.

Question 9

A form must be created for collaboration.

○ a. True

○ b. False

The correct answer to this question is a, True. For your users to have something to work with, the collaboration requires a form. Therefore, answer b is incorrect.

Question 10

When creating a form for collaboration, you can switch between development and testing without the need for compiling the form.

○ a. True

○ b. False

The correct answer to this question is a, True. Outlook has a VB-based form generator built in. Because VB runs in an interpreted environment, it's possible to write some code and then test it. This is commonly called *Rapid Application Development* (or *RAD*). Therefore, answer b is incorrect.

Question 11

How many steps are there in planning the rollout of a custom collaboration form?

○ a. 1

○ b. 3

○ c. 5

○ d. 10

The correct answer to this question is d. Here are the 10 steps:

1. Identify folder users and requirements.

2. Assign a designer to be in charge (a lead).

3. Form a design plan.

4. Choose where your design work will take place.

5. Create or choose a folder.

6. Publish forms in the folder.

7. Design folder views.

8. Test the folder thoroughly.

9. Copy the folder from the test bed to the appropriate public folder.

10. Release the form for real work by changing permissions.

The other answers are all incorrect.

Question 12

> How many parts does a rule have?
>
> ○ a. 1
>
> ○ b. 2
>
> ○ c. 3
>
> ○ d. 4

The correct answer to this question is a. This question is tricky. A rule may contain many conditions, but there's only one part. For example, "if from Hints@examcram.com and importance is set to high, take some action step." This is only one rule; however, it has a compound condition to meet. Because a rule can only have one part, answers b, c, and d are incorrect.

Question 13

> When setting up a moderated public folder, you must create text for an auto-responder.
>
> ○ a. True
>
> ○ b. False

The correct answer to this question is a, True. You can create a condition that informs the sender that his or her message has been sent to a moderator. Hopefully, this prevents a message sender from sending multiple postings on the same topic, because he or she has not seen the message in the public folder—it's awaiting judgment from a moderator. Answer b is incorrect.

Question 14

Which of the following is the correct term used to describe a field that is made up of several different fields?

○ a. Custom field

○ b. Combination field

○ c. Formula field

○ d. None of the above

The correct answer to this question is b. A custom field is something you create; therefore, answer a is incorrect. A formula field is used for calculations; therefore, answer c is incorrect. Answer d is incorrect because a valid choice is available.

Question 15

Combination fields can be grouped in a view.

○ a. True

○ b. False

The correct answer to this question is b, False. Although you can create combination fields for your view, you can only group on singular fields.

Question 16

When you're merging a collaboration form from a test bed to a live server, in which direction do properties flow?

○ a. Properties flow from the source folder to the destination folder.

○ b. Properties flow from the destination folder to the source folder.

The correct answer to this question is a. When you're working with a folder design, the components of the source folder are merged with the parts of the destination folder. Therefore, answer b is incorrect.

Need To Know More?

 Search the Microsoft Technical Information Network (TechNet) CD-ROM. The technical notes for Exchange Server provide insight into its design and architecture. A search on "exchange forms," brings up an extensive list of resources, including the "Exchange Forms Designer Fundamentals" document.

 Install Online Books from the Microsoft Exchange 5.5 CD-ROM. It contains a wealth of useful information.

 Go to the Microsoft Exchange Server home page at www.microsoft.com/exchange. Many of the documents located here are newer than those available on the Microsoft TechNet CD-ROM.

 Go to the Microsoft Knowledge Base and support home page at www.microsoft.com/kb. Many of the documents located here are newer than those available on the Microsoft TechNet CD-ROM.

Exchange Server Interoperability

13

Terms you'll need to understand:

√ AdminSch account

√ Directory synchronization

√ DirSync

√ IMPORT.EXE and EXPORT.EXE programs

√ Microsoft Exchange Connector for Lotus cc:Mail

√ Microsoft Mail Connector

√ Microsoft Schedule+ Free/Busy Connector

√ MS Mail External MTA program

√ Remote DirSync Requestor

Techniques you'll need to master:

√ Understanding how messages flow between Microsoft Exchange Server and the Microsoft Mail and Lotus cc:Mail post offices

√ Establishing the Microsoft Mail Connector and the Microsoft Exchange Connector for Lotus cc:Mail

√ Configuring directory synchronization between Microsoft Exchange and both Microsoft Mail and Lotus cc:Mail

√ Understanding how Microsoft Schedule+ information is shared between Microsoft Mail and Microsoft Exchange

√ Configuring the Microsoft Schedule+ Free/Busy Connector

√ Understanding how Microsoft Exchange works in a NetWare environment

√ Troubleshooting problems that may occur when the Microsoft Exchange client is running on a NetWare client computer

Connectors Explored
And Explained

It's not uncommon for organizations to have multiple email systems in use on their networks. This happens because different organizational departments may implement their own email systems, instead of one central department being responsible for deciding upon, implementing, and supporting one email system.

Organizations require—and expect—that any new email system (including Microsoft Exchange) be compatible with any existing email systems, at least until that new system is adopted by all users in the organization. To address this need, Exchange uses connectors to communicate with other email systems.

Through a core architecture software component known as a *connector*, Microsoft Exchange has the ability to communicate and transfer messages with the most popular messaging systems in use today. Once a connector is installed and configured properly, messages are automatically transferred between Microsoft Exchange and other messaging platforms.

 Although you need to understand all connectors, it's a good idea to focus on the Microsoft Mail for PC Networks Connector and the Lotus cc:Mail Connector.

Microsoft Mail For PC
Networks Connector

Messages can be exchanged between Microsoft Exchange and one or more Microsoft Mail (MS Mail) For PC Networks systems using the Microsoft Mail Connector. The two messaging systems can be on the same LAN, an asynchronous (RAS) connection, or an X.25 connection. Once the connector is installed and configured, Microsoft Exchange and MS Mail messaging systems can exchange messages and synchronize directories.

The Microsoft Mail Connector makes MS Mail 3.x post offices appear like Microsoft Exchange post offices to Microsoft Exchange, and it makes Microsoft Exchange post offices appear like MS Mail post offices to MS Mail.

The Microsoft Mail Connector runs as a Windows NT Server service. The connector is multithreaded, which enables high capacity and excellent response times. The connector uses a flexible polling scheme to exchange messages.

There can be more than one Microsoft Mail Connector at each site; however, each Exchange Server computer in the site can only have one such connector installed.

The Microsoft Mail Connector has three components that work together to transfer mail between MS Mail post offices and Microsoft Exchange:

➤ **Post Office** A temporary Information Store for inbound and outbound messages. It's also referred to as a *gateway post office* or *shadow post office*. Its sole purpose is to transfer messages, so even though it's referred to as a post office, it has no local mailboxes.

➤ **Interchange** A Windows NT Server service that routes and transfers messages between Microsoft Exchange and the Microsoft Mail Connector Post Office. When an outbound message is sent from an Exchange Server user to an MS Mail recipient, the Exchange Server Message Transfer Agent (MTA) passes the message to the Microsoft Mail Connector Interchange. The Interchange component then converts the message to MS Mail format and transfers the message to the connector post office.

The Interchange component also scans the connector post office for inbound messages from MS Mail users that are sent to Microsoft Exchange recipients. It transfers these messages to the Exchange Server MTA, which then delivers the messages to the appropriate Exchange Server recipients.

➤ **MTA** Another Windows NT Server service that connects to and transfers mail between the Microsoft Mail Connector Post Office and one or more MS Mail post offices. It watches for messages deposited in the connector post office (sent to MS Mail recipients from Microsoft Exchange users) and then copies these messages to the appropriate MS Mail post office. The MTA service must run on an Exchange Server computer.

The MTA component also delivers messages from MS Mail users to Exchange Server recipients and places them in the connector post office.

It's not uncommon to have more than one instance (copy) of the Microsoft Mail Connector MTA in use; one Exchange server can have up to 10 instances of it running at once. Each instance is named and registered as a Windows NT service.

Microsoft recommends that a different instance be used to service one primary type of connection, such as a LAN, asynchronous (RAS), or X.25 connection. MS Mail post offices should be grouped together based on the type of connection used. You should create a separate instance of the connector MTA to service each group.

Understanding Message Flow Between MS Mail And Microsoft Exchange

When a message is sent to an MS Mail recipient, Microsoft Exchange submits the message to the Exchange Server MTA; the MTA then transfers the message to the Mail Connector Interchange. The Interchange converts the message to MS Mail format, converts any attachments, and then places the message in the Microsoft Mail Connector Post Office. How a message proceeds to be delivered depends on the physical connection.

A message addressed to a mailbox on an MS Mail post office that exists on the same LAN connection is retrieved and delivered to the appropriate destination post office by the MTA. Note that the MTA component of the Microsoft Mail Connector combines the features of a gateway post office and the MS Mail External MTA program—including message delivery and distribution to recipients on MS Mail post offices located on the same LAN. Therefore, setting up the MS Mail External MTA program on LAN-based MS Mail post offices isn't necessary.

 A message addressed to a mailbox on an MS Mail post office over an asynchronous (RAS) or X.25 connection is processed and delivered by the MS Mail External MTA program.

An instance of the MS Mail External MTA program must be set up at each remote post office, because the connector MTA can only deliver and distribute a message to an MS Mail post office if it's on the same LAN connection.

The MS Mail External MTA program is usually only required for non-LAN environments; in LAN environments, its functionality is performed by the Microsoft Mail Connector MTA component. However, situations may arise when it might be wise to continue to use an existing MS Mail External MTA program to perform some of the functions provided by the Microsoft Mail Connector MTA component. For example, when you're migrating from MS Mail, it may be easier to integrate the Microsoft Mail Connector into the MS Mail system using the existing MS Mail External MTA program. In addition, if remote clients exist within the MS Mail system, you must continue to use the MS Mail External MTA program, because all mail transfers between a remote client and an MS Mail post office are processed by the MS Mail External MTA program. The Microsoft Mail Connector itself cannot perform this function.

When a message is addressed to a mailbox on an MS Mail post office that exists on the same LAN connection, the Exchange Server MTA passes the mail to the Microsoft Mail Connector Interchange, which then transfers the mail to the Microsoft Mail Connector Post Office. Then, the Microsoft Mail Connector MTA picks up the mail in the connector post office and copies it to the appropriate MS Mail post office. The message is then delivered.

When a message is addressed to an MS Mail post office over an asynchronous (RAS) or X.25 connection, the Exchange Server MTA passes the mail to the Microsoft Mail Connector Interchange, which then transfers the mail to the Microsoft Mail Connector Post Office. Then, the MS Mail External MTA program picks up the mail in the connector post office and delivers it to the appropriate mailbox.

Installing And Configuring The Microsoft Mail Connector

The Microsoft Mail Connector is installed, by default, when a Complete installation of Microsoft Exchange is performed. The connector must be installed before it can be configured.

The Exchange Administrator is used to configure the connector. In the Administrator window, choose the site in which the connector is installed, choose the Connections container, and then double-click the MS Mail Connector. Here are some points to keep in mind when configuring the connector to communicate with MS Mail post offices:

➤ The Administrator's mailbox, primary client language, OLE-compatibility, and message tracking are all configured on the Configure The Connector Interchange Properties page.

MS Mail 3.x only supports earlier versions of OLE. To enable such users to view saved or embedded objects sent from Microsoft Exchange users, select the Maximize MS Mail 3.x Compatibility checkbox. Note that selecting this option effectively doubles the size of any OLE message. If this option is not selected, MS Mail 3.x clients are not able to view or save embedded objects sent from Microsoft Exchange users.

➤ The Configure The Connector's General tab allows users to specify limits for message size transfer between Microsoft Exchange and MS Mail.

 If a maximum message size to be passed through the connector is entered and a message exceeds this size, the message is returned to the sender in the form of a non-delivery report.

➤ When you set up an MS Mail post office connection, you only need to know the network path to the post office directory. The Microsoft Mail Connector extracts the network and post office name from the post office.

➤ LAN connections to MS Mail post offices are created and viewed in the Connections tab. From that tab, you can specify that the Microsoft Mail Connector indirectly access any MS Mail post offices with which a LAN-connected MS Mail post office exchanges mail. Note that if the MS Mail post office resides on a NetWare server, Gateway Services For NetWare must be running on the Exchange Server machine.

➤ The Connector MTAs tab is used to define and configure the connector MTA. More than one connector MTA can be established; each connector MTA is defined here and becomes a separate Windows NT Server service. Use the Control Panel to start or stop Connector MTAs individually.

 If the MS Mail post office resides on a NetWare server, before you create and configure the connector MTA, verify that the Windows NT Server is running Gateway Services For NetWare.

➤ After creating a Microsoft Mail Connector MTA service, you can configure additional options. Options for controlling how the connector MTA will handle special MS Mail post office features—such as Mail Dispatch and NetBIOS notification—are enabled. Also, the connector MTA service can be set to start with system startup or to be started manually.

➤ Maximum message size, shut down and restart disk space thresholds, NetBIOS notification, and system startup settings are all configured on the connector MTA's Options dialog box.

➤ The Verify Connector Post Office Configuration tab allows users to view (and optionally, change) the connector post office (also known as the *shadow post office*).

The information displayed in the following list is needed to configure the real MS Mail post offices so that they will be able to access the shadow post office:

➤ **Start the connector MTA service** Launch the Services applet from Control Panel. Scroll down the list to find the new Microsoft Mail Connector MTA service that was created. Change the startup mode to Automatic. Click the Start button to start the service. Also, verify that the MS Mail Connector Interchange service is running.

➤ **Configure the MS Mail Post Office** Each MS Mail post office that was identified must be configured to access the shadow post office. For each MS Mail post office, use the MS Mail DOS Administrator program to create an external post office listing for the Exchange server with which to communicate. Use the External-Admin menu option to create a new entry. Refer to the post office (shadow) and network name of the Microsoft Mail Connector from the Local Post Office tab.

➤ **Test the configuration** Send a message from the Exchange Server side (using the Exchange client or the Outlook client) to the MS Mail side; then send a new message the other way (using the MS Mail DOS client or the MS Mail Windows client). Do this until directory synchronization is established. The recipient names need to be typed in manually; the address lists will not be populated yet.

If everything has been set up properly, messages should be exchanged between the two mail systems.

Managing Directory Synchronization With MS Mail

If you're using another messaging system in addition to Microsoft Exchange, another directory needs to be maintained. Microsoft Exchange uses directory synchronization to maintain address information with other messaging systems.

 Directory synchronization (also known as *DirSync*) is the process of exchanging address information between a Microsoft Exchange organization and any other messaging system that uses the MS Mail directory synchronization protocol.

The directory synchronization process uses system messages to send address change updates between the messaging systems.

Microsoft Exchange implements directory synchronization in a way similar to that of MS Mail. The MS Mail directory synchronization protocol automatically synchronizes the directories on all post offices in an MS Mail system—whether those post offices reside on the same LAN, are connected asynchronously (RAS), or are connected by a gateway. A change or update to an address on one post office is automatically sent to other post offices in the MS Mail system.

The MS Mail directory synchronization protocol has two components:

➤ **Directory server post office** Maintains a central database of directory changes. There can be only one directory server post office.

➤ **Directory requestor post office** Submits directory changes to the directory server post office and requests directory updates that other directory requestor post offices have submitted. The directory synchronization agent handles this activity.

Each post office in an MS Mail system is either a directory server post office or a directory requestor post office. One computer in the MS Mail system must be designated as the directory server post office. The directory server post office records all address updates received from the directory requestor post offices.

Directory updates occur at scheduled times. This schedule can be modified as needed. At the scheduled time, the directory requestor post office's directory synchronization agent sends any updates to the directory server post office. The directory server post office combines these changes and, in turn, sends the updates to each requestor post office. The MS Mail DISPATCH.EXE program processes the updates into the requestor post offices' address list.

Microsoft Exchange uses a similar, but enhanced, implementation of the MS Mail directory synchronization protocol. As with MS Mail, an Exchange server is designated as either a directory synchronization requestor or a directory synchronization server.

 When an MS Mail system is already in place (with one of the MS Mail post offices designated as a directory server), the Exchange server is usually set up as a directory synchronization requestor.

Directory synchronization roles are set up using the Exchange Administrator. Also, an Exchange Server directory synchronization requestor works just like an MS Mail directory synchronization requestor, as follows:

➤ Address updates are sent from the directory synchronization requestor to the MS Mail directory server.

➤ The MS Mail directory server integrates these changes into its own Global Address List and sends recent changes to the Exchange Server directory synchronization requestor, which integrates the changes into its own Global Address List.

Alternatively, an Exchange server can be set up to be the directory synchronization server instead. In this case, all MS Mail post offices need to be set up to be directory synchronization requestors. In addition, each of these MS Mail post offices needs to be defined as a Remote DirSync Requestor in the Exchange Server Administrator.

If an Exchange server has been set up as a directory synchronization server, a directory synchronization requestor (remote or otherwise) is not needed on that system. The directory synchronization server handles requestor functions inherently.

Configuring Directory Synchronization With MS Mail

An Exchange server can be set up as either a directory synchronization requestor or a directory synchronization server.

To install and configure a directory synchronization requestor, choose the Connections container in the Exchange Administrator. From the File menu, choose New Other; then choose DirSync Requestor. Select the directory synchronization server from the list of MS Mail post offices. In the Exchange Administrator, choose the Connections container and double-click the DirSync requestor. A dialog box with the following five tabs is displayed:

➤ **General** This is where basic properties for the directory synchronization requestor are set. A display name can be specified, as well as the different address types that should be exchanged during directory synchronization. A DirSync server mailbox can be specified for sending and receiving system messages.

➤ **Import Container** This is where the import container (used to store imported addresses sent from the MS Mail directory server) is specified. A trust level can be assigned to objects being imported. If no container is specified, addresses are placed in the Global Address List. (MS Mail and other messaging systems do not have directory objects, nor do they use trust levels. Imported recipient addresses are created with the trust level, which is specified in the Import container's trust level value.)

➤ **Export Container** This is where the Exchange Server recipient containers that should be exported to the MS Mail directory server are specified. By default, the Exchange Server directory exchange requestor does not export any recipient containers. A trust level can be specified so that only certain recipients are exported.

➤ **Settings** This tab provides a means to enter a DirSync password (which must be the same as that on the DirSync server). It also provides a means to specify whether the Exchange Server DirSync requestor will send address updates, receive address updates, send local template information, or receive template information.

➤ **Schedule** An MS Mail directory server only processes directory updates once a day. Updates should be scheduled so that they are sent to the DirSync server before the DirSync server processes updates. This tab is used to set the DirSync requestor schedule so that it coincides with the schedule on the MS Mail directory server.

The MS Mail directory synchronization server must also be configured so that it recognizes the Exchange server as a directory requestor. Use the MS Mail Administrator program to register the Exchange Server DirSync requestor. The Microsoft Mail Connector Post Office network, post office, and password will all need to be entered; these can be viewed in the Microsoft Mail Connector Local Post Office Properties page. The last step to be performed is to start the directory synchronization service on the Exchange server that is serving as the DirSync requestor.

To install and configure a directory synchronization server, choose the Connections container in the Exchange Administrator. From the File menu, choose New Other; then choose DirSync Server. In the Exchange Administrator program, double click the Connections container, click the DirSync server, and select Properties form the File menu:

➤ **General** This is where basic directory synchronization server properties are set. A display name as well as a DirSync administrator mailbox to receive copies of incoming and outgoing DirSync system messages can be specified.

➤ **Schedule** This is where the time that the Exchange Server DirSync server should send master address updates to MS Mail remote DirSync requestors is specified.

Note: If you have enabled "Show Permissions page for all objects" under the Site Container Properties, a third tab called "Permissions" will also appear.

Next, install and configure a remote directory synchronization requestor. If an Exchange server is set up as a DirSync server, each MS Mail post office must be defined as a remote DirSync requestor. In the Exchange Administrator, choose the Connections container. From the File menu, choose New Other; then choose Remote DirSync Requestor. Select the directory synchronization requestor from the list of MS Mail post offices. In the Exchange Administrator again, choose the Connections container and double-click the remote directory synchronization requestor. A dialog box with four tabs is displayed:

➤ **General** This is where primary remote directory synchronization requestor properties are set. The following items can be specified: a display name, a DirSync requestor mailbox (for sending and receiving system messages), a password for the remote directory requestor, and the requestor address type ("MS" for an MS Mail post office).

➤ **Permissions** This is where permissions for the remote DirSync requestor object are assigned. Explicit permissions to a user (a directory synchronization administrator, for example) for the DirSync requestor object can be assigned. For example, a user could be assigned Administrator permissions for a remote DirSync requestor object, but not assigned User permissions for the Configuration container. The user will have permissions to the remote DirSync requestor only.

➤ **Import Container** This is where the Import container (used to store imported addresses sent from the MS Mail directory requestor) is specified. A trust level can also be assigned to objects being imported. (MS Mail and other messaging systems do not have directory objects, nor do they use trust levels. Imported recipient addresses are created with the trust level specified in the Import container's trust level value.)

➤ **Export Container** This is where the Exchange Server recipient containers that will be exported to MS Mail directory requestors are specified. By default, the Exchange Server directory exchange server does not export any recipient containers. A trust level can be assigned so that only certain recipients are exported.

After installing one or more Exchange Server remote directory synchronization requestor post offices on the directory synchronization server, the MS Mail directory synchronization requestor post offices themselves must be configured. Using the MS Mail Administrator program, follow the same process for setting up a directory synchronization requestor as for an MS Mail directory synchronization server.

Microsoft Schedule+ Free/Busy Connector

The Microsoft Schedule+ Free/Busy Connector—an extension of the Microsoft Mail Connector—lets MS Mail and Microsoft Exchange share Microsoft

Schedule+ information. Microsoft Schedule+ is a messaging-enabled program that lets users access other users' schedules and reserve meeting times with those users. The program also serves as a tool to manage personal contact information.

Microsoft Schedule+ is compatible with both MS Mail and Microsoft Exchange. It stores scheduling data in hidden folders on both messaging systems. If a company uses both types of messaging systems, scheduling data needs to be shared between those messaging systems—hence the existence of the Microsoft Schedule+ Free/Busy Connector.

Configuring The Microsoft Schedule+ Free/Busy Connector

After you've installed the Microsoft Mail Connector, the configuration of the Microsoft Schedule+ Free/Busy Connector involves five steps. Once it's configured correctly, you can share schedule data between MS Mail recipients and Exchange Server recipients. The steps are as follows:

1. **Create an AdminSch account on all post offices that will participate in sharing Microsoft Schedule+ data.** MS Mail and Microsoft Exchange use the AdminSch account to share Microsoft Schedule+ data. Therefore, every MS Mail post office and Exchange server that needs to share Microsoft Schedule+ data must have an AdminSch account defined. As part of the Microsoft Schedule+ Free/Busy Connector installation process, an AdminSch account is automatically created on the Exchange Server computer. Verify that this account exists on all applicable MS Mail post offices. Once this has been done, run directory synchronization between the Exchange server and the MS Mail post offices to distribute all AdminSch accounts across the systems.

2. **Install the Microsoft Schedule+ program files on at least one MS Mail post office server.** If multiple MS Mail post offices are in use and Microsoft Schedule+ users need to share schedule data with other MS Mail post offices, the Microsoft Schedule+ program files must be installed on at least one of the MS Mail post office servers. If only one MS Mail post office exists, the program files do not need to be installed on the post office server.

3. **Install and configure the Microsoft Schedule+ Administrator program (ADMINSCH.EXE).** Once the Administrator program is installed, you can use it to configure the Microsoft Schedule+ system, specifying schedule storage duration and network schedule sharing information.

The Microsoft Schedule+ Administrator program must be run from a Windows-based computer that is connected to the MS Mail post office that contains the Schedule+ program files.

4. **Configure schedule data distribution.** The MS Mail SCHDIST.EXE program performs the actual schedule data distribution. The program sends users' free and busy times and resources between MS Mail and Microsoft Exchange. A few options in the program need to be configured before it will distribute schedule data properly. See the MS Mail documentation for more details.

5. **Configure the Microsoft Schedule+ Free/Busy Connector.** When the Microsoft Schedule+ Free/Busy Connector is installed, Microsoft Exchange creates an object with the name "Microsoft Schedule+ Free/Busy Connector *server name*". The object is stored in the Recipients container with the alias name AdminSch, and it's configured using the Exchange Administrator. Microsoft Schedule+ Free/Busy Connector configuration settings are changed from this object.

The Schedule+ Free/Busy Connector Options Properties page is where Microsoft Exchange is configured to exchange Microsoft Schedule+ free and busy information between Microsoft Exchange and MS Mail. The Administrator's mailbox and the Schedule+ distribution list, as well as manual export, update frequency, and logging level options are all configured on this property page.

 The Update Frequency value should be equal to the polling interval for the SCHDIST.EXE program in the MS Mail system.

The General tab is where the Microsoft Schedule+ Free/Busy Connector's display name and alias name are specified. The display name, alias name, and any relevant notes are configured on this tab.

 The Microsoft Schedule+ Free/Busy Connector object's alias name must be AdminSch. Make sure you do not change it!

Once these steps have been performed, Microsoft Schedule+ users should be able to access the schedules of other users—regardless of the messaging system to which those users' mailboxes belong (MS Mail or Microsoft Exchange).

Microsoft Exchange Connector For Lotus cc:Mail

The Microsoft Exchange Connector for Lotus cc:Mail (hereafter referred to as the Lotus cc:Mail Connector) handles messaging connectivity between Microsoft Exchange and Lotus cc:Mail. The following two versions of Lotus cc:Mail software combinations are supported:

➤ Lotus cc:Mail Post Office Database version 6 and cc:Mail Import version 5.15 and Export version 5.14

➤ Lotus cc:Mail Post Office Database version 8 and cc:Mail Import/ Export version 6.

Depending on the messaging environment, one or more Lotus cc:Mail Connectors can be used to transfer messages and to synchronize directories. Each Exchange server can run one instance of the Lotus cc:Mail Connector, and this connector can directly service one cc:Mail post office. The two messaging systems must be on the same LAN. Once the connector is installed and configured, Microsoft Exchange and Lotus cc:Mail will automatically transfer messages and synchronize directories. (Although a Lotus cc:Mail Connector can service only one cc:Mail post office, other Exchange servers operating separate connector instances can be used to service additional cc:Mail post offices.)

The Lotus cc:Mail Connector runs as a Windows NT Server service. The connector has three components that work together to enable Lotus cc:Mail and Microsoft Exchange to communicate:

➤ **Connector For Lotus cc:Mail Service** A Windows NT Server service that performs the actual transferring of messages between Microsoft Exchange and Lotus cc:Mail. In addition, the service also synchronizes the Microsoft Exchange Global Address List with the Lotus cc:Mail directory.

➤ **Lotus Connector For cc:Mail Store** A group of directories on the Exchange Server used for messages in transit.

➤ **Lotus cc:Mail Import/Export programs** Used to import Microsoft Exchange messages and directory entries into Lotus cc:Mail, as well as to export Lotus cc:Mail messages and directory entries into Microsoft Exchange. The import and export programs come with Lotus cc:Mail. Access to a licensed copy of these programs is required for every Exchange Server computer with a Lotus cc:Mail Connector installed. Licensed copies of the programs should be copied to a directory in the Exchange server's system path.

Understanding Message Flow Between Lotus cc:Mail And Microsoft Exchange

When a message is sent to a Lotus cc:Mail recipient, Microsoft Exchange submits the message to the Exchange Server MTA; the MTA then transfers the message to the Connector For Lotus cc:Mail Service. The connector proceeds to convert the message to ASCII format, converts any attachments, and finally places the message in the Lotus Connector For cc:Mail Store. The Lotus cc:Mail Import program then attempts to deliver the message, which produces a non-delivery report to the sender if the message cannot be delivered.

Sending a message to a Microsoft Exchange recipient is similar. The Connector For Lotus cc:Mail Service calls the Lotus cc:Mail Export program to export messages to the Lotus Connector For cc:Mail Store. The connector then retrieves the message and passes it on to the Microsoft Exchange Information Store.

Installing And Configuring The Lotus cc:Mail Connector

The Lotus cc:Mail Connector is installed by default when a Complete installation of Microsoft Exchange is performed. The connector must be installed before it can be configured.

The Exchange Administrator is used to configure the Lotus cc:Mail Connector. In the Administrator window, choose the site in which the connector is installed, choose the Connections container, and then double-click Connector For cc:Mail. Here are the steps necessary for configuring the connector to communicate with cc:Mail post offices:

1. **Verify that the Import and Export programs are in the system path.**
   If not already present in the system path, IMPORT.EXE and EXPORT.EXE should be copied from the cc:Mail Administrator's directory (\Lotus\CCAdmin, by default) to the \WinNT\System32 directory of the Exchange server where the connector is installed. If you're using cc:Mail Database version 8 with Import/Export version 6, the file IE.RI must also be present in the system path. If necessary, copy IE.RI from the cc:Mail Data directory (\Lotus\CCData, by default) to the \WinNT\System32 directory.

To determine the version of Import/Export, type the program name followed by /? at the comment prompt.

2. **Configure the connector Post Office Properties page.** The Administrator's mailbox, cc:Mail post office name, password, path, import/export version, and message tracking options are among the properties configured on this property page.

 If the Lotus cc:Mail post office resides on a NetWare server, Gateway Services For NetWare must be running on the Exchange server. Also, use the Universal Naming Convention (UNC) format to refer to the post office (that is, \\servername\sharename\path for a Windows NT Server and \\servername\volumename\path for a NetWare server).

3. **Configure the connector's General tab.** Limits for message size transfer between Microsoft Exchange and Lotus cc:Mail post offices are specified on this tab.

 If a maximum message size to be passed through the connector is entered and a message exceeds this size, the message is returned to the sender in the form of a non-delivery report. Regardless, if the body of a message exceeds 20K, Lotus cc:Mail converts the message body to a text attachment.

4. **Configure the connector's Export Containers tab.** Mailboxes, public folders, distribution lists, and custom recipients can be exported via directory synchronization. By default, Microsoft Exchange does not export any recipient containers. The site, recipient containers, and trust level are among the properties that are configured on this tab.

5. **Configure the connector's Import Containers tab.** User names, bulletin board names, and mailing lists are imported from cc:Mail to Microsoft Exchange. Import container, filtering options, and manual DirSync buttons are available on this tab.

6. **Configure the connector's DirSync Schedule tab.** This is where the times when Microsoft Exchange and cc:Mail send address list updates to each other are scheduled. Scheduling options can be set to Never Synchronize, Always Synchronize (performed every 15 minutes), or Selected (customized times).

7. **Configure the connector's Address Space tab.** This tab is used to enter information about the addresses that the connector is to process. To route all messages through the connector, add an address with type CCMAIL, an asterisk for the address, and a cost of one. By default, no address types are defined.

8. **Start the Connector For cc:Mail Service.** Launch the Services applet from the Control Panel. Scroll down the list to find the service. Change the startup mode to Automatic. Click the Start button to start the service.

9. **Test the connection.** Send a message from a Microsoft Exchange recipient to a cc:Mail recipient. To ensure a successful configuration, send a message from a cc:Mail client to a Microsoft Exchange recipient.

Managing Directory Synchronization With Lotus cc:Mail

The directory synchronization method used by cc:Mail is not directly compatible with the Microsoft Mail 3.x DirSync protocol. Lotus cc:Mail uses similar terms to describe DirSync features, but the process is quite different. Once configured, however, directory synchronization runs as a scheduled process, seamlessly performing appropriate synchronization of the cc:Mail directory with the Microsoft Exchange directory. Microsoft Exchange uses the Lotus cc:Mail Import and Export programs in the following ways:

➤ **Synchronizing Lotus cc:Mail addresses to Microsoft Exchange** Whether at the scheduled time or when initiated manually, the Lotus cc:Mail Connector Service launches the cc:Mail Export process (EXPORT.EXE). This extracts all available cc:Mail recipient addresses from the cc:Mail post office. The Lotus cc:Mail connector store serves as a temporary storage location for this information. The Lotus cc:Mail Connector Service then retrieves the information and processes it into the Microsoft Exchange directory. The addresses are placed in the Import container that was specified when the connector was configured.

➤ **Synchronizing Microsoft Exchange addresses to Lotus cc:Mail** Whether at the scheduled time or when initiated manually, the Lotus cc:Mail Connector Service retrieves all Microsoft Exchange recipient information (which has been made available through the specified Export containers) from the Directory Service; it then places that information in the Lotus cc:Mail connector store. The connector then launches the cc:Mail IMPORT.EXE program to import this information in the cc:Mail directory.

Configuring Directory Synchronization With Lotus cc:Mail

Configuring directory synchronization between Lotus cc:Mail and Microsoft Exchange is fairly straightforward; however, there are two things to keep in mind:

➤ **Trust levels** When Export containers are specified in the Lotus cc:Mail Connector Service, the specified trust levels are used during directory synchronization. Only those objects in the Microsoft Exchange directory with the same, or less than the connector's trust level, are exported to the cc:Mail post office. If an object's trust level increases above the connector's trust level—either by the object's trust level or the connector's trust level changing—the object will automatically be removed from the Lotus cc:Mail directory.

➤ **Filtering** The Lotus cc:Mail Export process extracts all addresses from the cc:Mail directory. The Lotus cc:Mail Connector Service controls which addresses will end up appearing in the Microsoft Exchange directory. This is specified using the filtering features on the Import Container tab of the connector.

Understanding Exchange Server In A NetWare Environment

Microsoft Exchange must run on a Windows NT Server computer. However, the rest of the servers and workstations in the network can run other operating systems—including Novell NetWare. In a NetWare environment, users can access the Exchange server even if they are on a different LAN.

Microsoft Exchange can coexist seamlessly in a NetWare environment, as long as a few guidelines are followed:

➤ **The SAP agent must be installed** The Service Access Point (SAP) agent must be installed and running on the Exchange server for a NetWare client to access it. This agent is not necessary if a NetWare server is on the same LAN as the Exchange server.

➤ **NetBIOS must be installed** Network Basic Input/Output (NetBIOS) must be supported on the Exchange server. Otherwise, clients are not able to communicate with the Exchange server.

➤ **Ethernet frame types must be configured properly** It's not uncommon to configure multiple frame types for the Windows NT NWLink protocol. If this is the case—or if more than one network card is installed in the Exchange server—the internal network number must be set to a unique number greater than zero.

➤ **File Scan must be enabled on the appropriate NetWare servers** If users will be storing schedule backups or archives, File Scan must be enabled on the NetWare shares in which the data is to be stored. Otherwise, information such as Microsoft Outlook calendar data will not be accessible to users, because the Microsoft Outlook calendar does not support certain types of file operations on NetWare servers that have File Scan disabled.

➤ **Gateway Services For NetWare and Client Services For NetWare must be installed** These services should be installed on the Exchange server to optimize mail delivery performance on servers using the Internetwork Packet Exchange/Sequenced Packet Exchange (IPX/SPX). Add these services via Network Properties, which is accessible from the Control Panel.

NetWare Clients And Microsoft Exchange

When configured properly, a Windows 95 or Windows NT workstation running a NetWare client can access an Exchange server without difficulty. In addition to NetWare client software, workstations need to run client software that provides access to the Exchange server (Windows 95 computers use Client For Microsoft Networks; Windows NT computers use the Windows NT Workstation service).

Once domain validation is performed on the Windows network, the computer is able to access an Exchange server.

Troubleshooting NetWare-Exchange Clients

If NetWare clients are set up correctly, not much can prevent them from accessing Exchange Server. Most problems that do arise deal with issues at the Exchange Server level, which is covered earlier. If problems are still encountered, verify the following:

➤ On Windows 95 clients, in addition to the Client For Novell NetWare, the Client For Microsoft Networks must be installed. On Windows NT clients, in addition to the Client Service For NetWare, the Windows NT Workstation service must be installed.

➤ The NetWare client must be validated on the NT domain on which Exchange Server resides.

➤ The frame type in the Link Driver section of the NET.CFG file on the client must match the frame type on the server.

Exam Prep Questions

Question 1

What are the three primary components of the Microsoft Mail (For PC Networks) Connector? [Check all correct answers]

❑ a. Microsoft Mail Connector Post Office

❑ b. MS Mail External MTA

❑ c. Microsoft Mail Connector Interchange

❑ d. Microsoft Mail Connector MTA

The correct answers to this question are a, c, and d. Each of these components must be configured correctly before messages can be exchanged between MS Mail and Microsoft Exchange. The MS Mail External MTA is an application that ships with MS Mail, not Microsoft Exchange. Therefore, answer b is incorrect.

Question 2

MS Mail and Microsoft Exchange can communicate over which type of connections? [Check all correct answers]

❑ a. LDAP

❑ b. Asynchronous

❑ c. LAN

❑ d. X.25

The correct answers to this question are b, c, and d. MS Mail and Microsoft Exchange can communicate using any of these three connections. Asynchronous and X.25 connections require the MS Mail External MTA program for message delivery. LDAP is an acronym for the Lightweight Directory Access Protocol. Therefore, answer a is incorrect.

Question 3

> What does the Microsoft Mail Connector Interchange do?
>
> ○ a. It routes and transfers messages between Lotus cc:Mail and Microsoft Exchange.
>
> ○ b. It routes and transfers messages between Microsoft Mail and SNADS.
>
> ○ c. It routes and transfers messages between Microsoft Mail and Novell GroupWise.
>
> ○ d. None of the above.

The correct answer to this question is d. The Microsoft Mail Connector Interchange is a Windows NT Server service that routes and transfers messages between Exchange Server and the Microsoft Mail Connector Post Office. Therefore, answers a, b, and c are incorrect.

Question 4

> How many instances of the Microsoft Mail Connector MTA can be installed and configured with each Microsoft Mail Connector?
>
> ○ a. 1
>
> ○ b. 2
>
> ○ c. 5
>
> ○ d. 10

The correct answer to this question is d. There can be up to 10 instances of the Microsoft Mail Connector MTA installed and configured with each Microsoft Mail Connector. Each Connector MTA is a separate Windows NT Server service, controllable via the Services applet in the Control Panel. Answers a, b, and c are incorrect.

Question 5

> What should be noted before enabling the Maximize MS Mail 3.x Compatibility option in the Microsoft Mail Connector?
>
> ○ a. Selecting this option prevents directory synchronization.
>
> ○ b. Selecting this option doubles the storage requirements of any OLE attachments in the message.
>
> ○ c. Selecting this option adversely affects the directory synchronization schedule that has been established.
>
> ○ d. Selecting this option prevents messages composed in Microsoft Outlook from being deliverable to MS Mail recipients.

The correct answer to this question is b. MS Mail 3.x only supports versions of OLE that precede Microsoft Exchange. To enable MS Mail 3.x users to view saved or embedded objects sent from Microsoft Exchange users, select this option. Select it with caution because this effectively doubles the size of all OLE messages. Answers a, c, and d are incorrect.

Question 6

> Which types of directory synchronization (DirSync) objects does Microsoft Exchange use? [Check all correct answers]
>
> ❑ a. Directory synchronization requestor post office
>
> ❑ b. Directory synchronization server post office
>
> ❑ c. Shadow post office
>
> ❑ d. Remote directory synchronization requestor post office

The correct answers to this question are a, b, and d. A directory synchronization requestor post office submits directory changes to the directory synchronization server post office; directory synchronization requestor post offices also request directory updates that other directory synchronization requestor post offices have submitted. Also, if an Exchange server is set up as a directory synchronization server post office, each MS Mail post office must be defined as a remote directory synchronization requestor. A shadow post office is another name for a temporary information store (post office) for inbound and outbound messages. Therefore, answer c is incorrect.

Question 7

> By default, how many recipient containers does the DirSync Requestor export?
>
> ○ a. One
>
> ○ b. All
>
> ○ c. Five
>
> ○ d. None

The correct answer to this question is d. By default, the Microsoft Exchange DirSync Requestor does not export any recipient containers. Using the Exchange Administrator, the recipient containers that should be exported to the MS Mail directory server can be specified. A trust level can be specified so that only certain recipients are exported. Answers a, b, and c are incorrect.

Question 8

> How can you determine if messages sent from an Exchange server to an address on an MS Mail post office are being delivered?
>
> ○ a. Examine the Connector MTAs tab in the Microsoft Mail Connector.
>
> ○ b. Check the contents of the ..\Delivered folder on the Exchange server.
>
> ○ c. Check the contents of the ..\Delivered folder on the MS Mail post office computer.
>
> ○ d. All of the above.

The correct answer to this question is a. The Connector MTAs tab in the Microsoft Mail Connector provides message delivery status information. There is no ..\Delivered directory (by default, anyway) on an Exchange server nor on an MS Mail post office computer. Therefore, answers b, c, and d are incorrect.

Question 9

> Which account must be available on all post offices that need to participate in sharing Microsoft Schedule+ data?
>
> ○ a. SchedAdmin
>
> ○ b. The domain administrator
>
> ○ c. AdminSch
>
> ○ d. All of the above

The correct answer to this question is c. MS Mail and Microsoft Exchange use the AdminSch account to share Microsoft Schedule+ data. Therefore, every MS Mail post office and Exchange server that needs to share Microsoft Schedule+ data must have access to an AdminSch account. Answers a, b, and d are incorrect.

Question 10

> Which versions of Lotus cc:Mail does the Microsoft Exchange Connector For Lotus cc:Mail work with?
>
> ○ a. Database version 8 and Import version 5.15, Export version 5.14; or Database version 6 and Import/Export version 6.
>
> ○ b. Database version 8 and Import/Export version 8.
>
> ○ c. Database version 6 and Import version 5.15, Export version 5.14; or Database version 8 and Import/Export version 6.
>
> ○ d. Database version 6 and Import/Export version 6; or Database version 8 and Import/Export version 8.

The correct answer to this question is c. Microsoft Exchange will not work with any other combinations of Database versions and the Import/Export programs. Therefore, answers a, b, and d are incorrect.

Question 11

How many Lotus cc:Mail post offices can one Microsoft Exchange Connector for Lotus cc:Mail service?

○ a. Unlimited

○ b. 1

○ c. 2

○ d. 10

The correct answer to this question is b. One Lotus cc:Mail Connector can service only one cc:Mail post office. However, other Exchange servers operating separate Lotus cc:Mail Connector instances can be used to service additional Lotus cc:Mail post offices. Answers a, c, and d are incorrect.

Question 12

The Connector For Lotus cc:Mail Service uses which Lotus cc:Mail programs? [Check all correct answers]

❏ a. IMPORT.EXE

❏ b. DISPATCH.EXE

❏ c. EXPORT.EXE

❏ d. All of the above

The correct answers to this question are a and c. IMPORT.EXE is used to import Microsoft Exchange messages and directory entries into Lotus cc:Mail post offices. EXPORT.EXE is used to export Lotus cc:Mail messages and directory entries into Microsoft Exchange. IMPORT.EXE and EXPORT.EXE ship with Lotus cc:Mail; access to a licensed copy of these programs is required for every Exchange Server computer with a Lotus cc:Mail Connector installed. The programs should be copied to a directory in the Exchange server's system path. Answers b and d are incorrect.

Need To Know More?

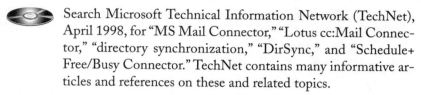 Search Microsoft Technical Information Network (TechNet), April 1998, for "MS Mail Connector," "Lotus cc:Mail Connector," "directory synchronization," "DirSync," and "Schedule+ Free/Busy Connector." TechNet contains many informative articles and references on these and related topics.

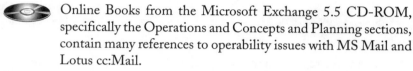 Online Books from the Microsoft Exchange 5.5 CD-ROM, specifically the Operations and Concepts and Planning sections, contain many references to operability issues with MS Mail and Lotus cc:Mail.

Visit the Microsoft Exchange Server home page at www.microsoft.com/exchange. There are numerous whitepapers and updated references about interoperability with Microsoft Exchange.

Visit the Microsoft Knowledge Base and support home page at www.microsoft.com/kb. There are numerous updated articles on Microsoft Exchange interoperability with MS Mail and Lotus cc:Mail.

Maintenance, Trouble- shooting, And Performance

14

Terms you'll need to understand:

√ Defragmentation

√ Diagnostic logging

√ ESEUTIL.EXE

√ ISINTEG.EXE

√ Link monitor

√ Message tracking

√ MTACHECK.EXE

√ Performance Optimizer

√ Server monitor

Techniques you'll need to master:

√ Understanding how to handle common Microsoft Exchange installation and upgrade issues and problems

√ Understanding how the Microsoft Exchange upgrade process works

√ Maintaining the Microsoft Exchange Information Store

√ Using Microsoft Exchange tools to resolve problems

√ Knowing how to improve an Exchange server's performance

√ Understanding how to migrate users from other messaging systems

This chapter provides comprehensive information about maintaining, monitoring, troubleshooting, and optimizing Microsoft Exchange. Although Exchange is a robust messaging platform, periodic maintenance is required to ensure that the system performs optimally. Exchange ships with tools that allow you to monitor its performance. Troubleshooting may also be necessary to keep the performance of your Exchange server at satisfactory levels. Finally, this chapter discusses some useful tools for Microsoft Exchange and Windows NT.

Microsoft Exchange Installation Issues

Before successfully installing Microsoft Exchange Server, you must have properly installed Windows NT Server, including proper NT domain configuration, and, if appropriate, established domain trusts. Assuming that Windows NT Server has been installed and configured properly, you need to keep some additional items in mind to ensure a successful Microsoft Exchange installation:

➤ Microsoft Exchange 5.5 requires Windows NT Server 4 (or a later version). You must also apply Service Pack 3 for Windows NT before installing Microsoft Exchange.

➤ You must be logged onto the Microsoft Windows NT domain as a member of the Administrator group.

➤ To use Microsoft Exchange's Internet Mail Service, TCP/IP must be installed and configured first. Specifically, the steps discussed in Chapter 9 must be followed.

➤ You must install Microsoft Internet Information Server (IIS) version 3 (or a later version) and Active Server Pages if you intend to install Outlook Web Access. Outlook Web Access is the portion of Microsoft Exchange that provides Web browser access to mailboxes over the Internet or an intranet. Note that if you do not install Active Server Pages before Microsoft Exchange, you might encounter a fatal error during Exchange installation.

➤ A Microsoft Exchange Server computer should have at least 24MB of RAM (32MB is recommended). There should also be enough disk space for users' email and public folder information, as well as for the Windows NT Server page file. Even more RAM should be installed if the computer is being used for other tasks (for example, as a domain controller, for other BackOffice components, and so on).

➤ If you're adding an Exchange server to an existing site, verify that enough space exists on the new server's hard disk to import the site directory. Otherwise, the new server may run out of disk space when directory replication occurs. To determine the size of the site directory, view the properties of the DIR.EDB file (located in the \ExchSrvr\ DSAData folder) residing on another server within the site.

➤ When you add a new site to an organization, be sure to use the same spelling for the organization name. If you don't do this, Microsoft Exchange Setup will see this as a new organization/site, which prevents the server/site from communicating with the intended organization.

➤ Microsoft Exchange uses numerous NT services that start and periodically perform routine maintenance using an NT domain service account of your choice. When you install Microsoft Exchange, the Setup program prompts you for the NT account name and password, using the Administrator account by default. Use a different, dedicated NT domain account for this. This way, the Administrator password can be changed without interfering with Microsoft Exchange service account access. Create the Microsoft Exchange service account before running Setup; then select this account when prompted for the name of the service account during the Microsoft Exchange Setup. Create an NT account called SrvcExchange (for *Service-Microsoft Exchange*). After selecting the service account, Microsoft Exchange Setup assigns the proper rights and permissions to the account. This service account should be used for all Exchange Server computers in a site.

➤ Verify that the Windows NT Server Primary Domain Controller (PDC) is accessible before you attempt to install Microsoft Exchange. The installation process needs to query the PDC; if the computer cannot communicate with the PDC, the installation will fail.

➤ If you're upgrading from an earlier version of Microsoft Exchange, shut down any existing server or link monitors, as well as other NT programs that might be accessing Microsoft Exchange, such as Performance Monitor and Event Viewer.

 Before installing and configuring Microsoft Exchange, establish the name of the organization, site, and servers. The only way to change this information later is by reinstalling the product.

After installing Microsoft Exchange, you should verify that the product is working properly. Open Control Panel, select Services, and then verify that the following services are started:

➤ Microsoft Exchange System Attendant

➤ Microsoft Exchange Directory

➤ Microsoft Exchange Information Store

➤ Microsoft Exchange Message Transfer Agent

If any of these services are not running, Exchange Server is probably not working properly. See the "Tools And Techniques For Resolving Microsoft Exchange Problems" section, later in this chapter.

Microsoft Exchange Upgrade Issues

Although Microsoft Exchange 5.5 can coexist in the same site with version 4 or 5 servers, it makes sense to have everything operating under the same version of Exchange. The Setup program for Microsoft Exchange 5.5 upgrades version 4 servers and version 5 servers to version 5.5. The version 5.5 upgrade procedure modifies the underlying Microsoft Exchange database structure. The Setup program checks for any Exchange Server components that have already been installed on the computer and presents different options depending on the version already installed. You can determine which Microsoft Exchange version and Service Pack are currently installed on the computer by using the Exchange Administrator program to view the properties of the server object.

If you're upgrading to Microsoft Exchange 5.5 from an earlier version of Microsoft Exchange, here are some important items to keep in mind:

➤ Before upgrading an Exchange Server computer, turn off all server monitors that reference the computer on which Setup is being run.

➤ If you're upgrading to Microsoft Exchange 5.5 on a computer that has Chat Service installed from an earlier version of Microsoft Exchange, stop Chat Service before performing the upgrade.

➤ Setup estimates the amount of time it will take to upgrade the existing Information Store. Depending on the size of the Information Store, the process may take a long time—even more than an entire day! Unfortunately, the upgrade process cannot be suspended once started, so don't start the upgrade process unless the specified amount of time (or longer) is available.

➤ If you're upgrading from Microsoft Exchange 4, install Microsoft Exchange Service Pack 2 (or higher) because there have been reports of data corruption when this step is not followed. You can obtain Service

Pack 2 from Microsoft (www.microsoft.com or ftp.microsoft.com). You can also order service packs from Microsoft directly.

The amount of time required to perform the upgrade depends on the number of messages, number of folders, and the total size of the Information Store. Requesting users to reduce the amount of mail they keep in their server mailboxes helps reduce the upgrade time.

How The Upgrade Process Works

During the Microsoft Exchange 5.5 upgrade procedure, the existing Information Store (the central storage facility for all Microsoft Exchange messaging data) is converted into a new file format that is optimized for use with Microsoft Exchange 5.5. The conversion process asks for a database backup location of either Standard Database Upgrade or Fault-Tolerant Upgrade. Despite their names, neither option actually performs a complete backup of the existing Information Store. Therefore, you should perform a full backup of the Information Store before performing the upgrade.

Standard Database Upgrade upgrades the Information Store in its present location.

> *Note: If the conversion process fails, the Information Store will need to be restored from a backup before it can be accessed with the earlier version of Microsoft Exchange or before Setup can be run again.*

Fault-Tolerant Upgrade copies the Information Store to a different, temporary location before upgrading. If the conversion process fails, it's unlikely you'll have to restore the Information Store. Simply reboot the computer and run Setup again. The Fault-Tolerant Upgrade's alternate location must have at least twice the amount of available disk space as the current size of the Information Store. The alternate location cannot be a network drive.

 If you're upgrading from Microsoft Exchange 4, the Fault-Tolerant Upgrade option is not available. To perform a fault-tolerant upgrade on an Exchange Server 4 computer, the Information Store must first be upgraded to Microsoft Exchange 5 format, using the Microsoft Exchange 5 Setup program. Then, the Information Store can be successfully upgraded to Microsoft Exchange 5.5 format.

After the version 5.5 upgrade process is complete, all Microsoft Exchange services will automatically restart and the Information Store will become available to users. You do not have to reboot Windows NT Server when upgrading to Microsoft Exchange 5.5.

Upgrading A Microsoft Exchange 4 Computer In A Multiserver Site

Because of directory schema changes between Microsoft Exchange 4 and later releases, all Exchange Server computers in a site should first be upgraded to Microsoft Exchange 4/Service Pack 2 before they are upgraded to Microsoft Exchange 5.5.

After Microsoft Exchange 5.5 is installed on the first server in the site, the new directory schema will automatically replicate to all the Microsoft Exchange 4 computers. This can take anywhere from a few minutes to a few hours, depending on the number of servers in the site. Check the Windows NT Event Viewer to make sure directory replication has been completed; then restart all Microsoft Exchange 4 computers. After these steps have been followed, you can upgrade the remaining computers to Microsoft Exchange 5.5.

Information Store Maintenance

The Information Store is the central storage facility for all Microsoft Exchange messaging data, and it's made up of the Private Information Store and the Public Information Store. The Microsoft Exchange directory is an extension of the Information Store. Periodic checking and housekeeping of the Information Store can prevent problems from developing. The Microsoft Exchange Administrator program has a number of built-in tools designed to check the Microsoft Exchange Information Store; these are covered in the following sections.

Checking The Private Information Store

The Private Information Store Properties dialog box displays the physical resources used by each mailbox on a particular server. Use this information to determine current and future disk space needs. This dialog box may reveal that mailbox storage limits need to be established or that other actions need to be taken in order to free up resources to keep the server running optimally. Follow these steps to access the Private Information Store Properties dialog box and display the physical resources used by each mailbox on a server:

1. Open the Microsoft Exchange Administrator program.

2. Select and expand the desired site.

3. Select and expand the Configuration container. The site configuration objects appear in the pane on the right.

4. Select and expand the Servers container. This displays all the Exchange servers in the site.

5. Select the server that has the Private Information Store.

6. Select the Private Information Store object and then select Properties from the File menu. This opens the Private Information Store Properties dialog box.

7. Select the Mailbox Resources tab.

The Mailbox Resources tab displays the physical resources used by each mailbox on the server. Pay particular attention to the Total K column—this indicates the total amount of disk space taken up by all the items in each user's mailbox. If disk space on this server becomes an issue, a number of options can be taken. One option is to move one or more mailboxes to another Exchange server within the site. This can help balance disk usage across servers. To move a mailbox to another Exchange server, follow these steps:

1. Open the Microsoft Exchange Administrator program.

2. Select and expand the desired site.

3. Select and expand the Configuration container. The site configuration objects appear in the pane on the right.

4. Select and expand the Servers container. This displays all the Exchange servers in the site.

5. Select and expand the server that contains the mailbox to move. This displays all the mailboxes on this Exchange server.

   a. Double-click on the Server Recipients object.

6. Select the mailbox to move and then select Move Mailbox from the Tools menu. This opens the Move Mailbox dialog box, which displays a list of all Exchange servers within the site (see Figure 14.1).

7. Select the destination Exchange server and click OK. The mailbox is moved. Depending on the amount of data in the mailbox, this may take some time to finish. An interesting side effect of moving a mailbox to a

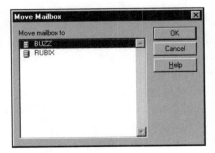

Figure 14.1   The Move Mailbox dialog box.

new server is that the size of the mailbox's contents on the destination server may increase because individual copies of single-instance messages are created for a mailbox moved to another Exchange server.

 Moving a mailbox is usually transparent to the mailbox user. If the server from which the mailbox was moved is available when the user logs in, his or her messaging profiles will be automatically updated to reflect the change to the new server. If the server that the mailbox was moved from is not available when the user logs in, the user will have to update his or her messaging profile manually before he or she can access the mailbox successfully.

Another option is to clean the mailbox. Cleaning a mailbox deletes the mailbox's contents, which increases the space in the server's Private Information Store. You have a good deal of control over what content is actually deleted. To clean a mailbox, follow these steps:

1. Open the Microsoft Exchange Administrator program.

2. Select and expand the desired site.

3. Select and expand the Configuration container. The site configuration objects appear in the pane on the right.

4. Select and expand the Servers container. This displays all the Exchange servers in the site.

5. Select and expand the server that contains the mailbox to clean.

   a. Double-click on the Server Recipients object.

6. Select the mailbox to clean and then select Clean Mailbox from the Tools menu. This opens the Clean Mailbox dialog box, which allows you to specify the content to delete, based on age, size, sensitivity, and read status (see Figure 14.2).

7. Click OK. The content matching the specified criteria is removed from the mailbox. This process may take some time, depending on what data you select to remove.

The final option is to establish mailbox storage limits at either the Information Store level or at the individual mailbox level. Mailbox storage limits at the Information Store level are specified via the Information Store Site Configuration Properties dialog box, which is accessed from a particular site's Configuration container. Storage limits at the individual mailbox level are specified in the Individual Mailbox Properties dialog box, which is accessed from the Server Recipients container, the Servers container, or the Configuration container for a particular site.

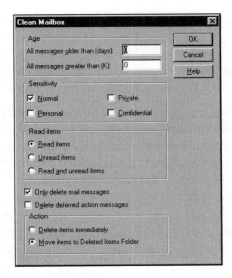

Figure 14.2   The Clean Mailbox dialog box.

Checking The Public Information Store

The Public Information Store Properties dialog box displays the physical resources used by each public folder on a particular server. You can use this information to determine both current and future disk space needs. By checking the Public Information Store, you can determine whether public folders need to be moved to another Exchange Server or perhaps even moderated by a user.

Follow these steps to access the Public Information Store Properties dialog box to display the physical resources used by each public folder on a particular server:

1. Open the Microsoft Exchange Administrator program.

2. Select and expand the desired site.

3. Select and expand the Configuration container. The site configuration objects appear in the pane on the right.

4. Select and expand the Servers container. This displays all the Exchange servers in the site.

5. Select the server that has the public folder(s) to view.

6. Select the Public Information Store object; then select Properties from the File menu. This opens the Public Information Store Properties dialog box.

7. Select the Public Folder Resources tab.

The Public Folder Resources tab displays the physical resources used by each public folder on the server. Again, pay particular attention to the Total K column, because this reveals the total disk space taken up by the items in this folder. If server disk space becomes an issue, move the public folder to another server. An alternative is to limit who can post new items to the public folder.

To move a public folder to another server, first use public folder replication to copy the public folder to another Exchange server; then remove the public folder from the original Exchange server. Use the Exchange client or the Outlook client to assign permissions to public folders. Set the permissions so that only selected users have the ability to post new messages to the public folder but all users have the ability to read messages in the folder.

Compacting The Information Store

Over time, Microsoft Exchange Information Stores tend to become fragmented on the hard disk, which can result in longer response times for users trying to access their mail. Although Microsoft Exchange does a decent job of defragmentation, there may be times when you need to manually defragment the Information Store. The Microsoft Exchange ESEUTIL.EXE utility (an MS-DOS command line program included with Microsoft Exchange) is used to defrag and compact the Information Store. This utility requires you to stop the Information Store service (if you want to defrag the Private and Public Information Stores) or the Directory Service (if you want to defrag the Microsoft Exchange directory). Therefore, you should run the utility when users do not need access to their mailboxes. As an alternative, you can inform users in advance that email will be unavailable during a specified period of time. As a basic rule, it's a good idea to minimize inconvenience to users.

 Manual defragmentation often becomes necessary when the Exchange server is used for SMTP (Simple Mail Transfer Protocol) mail.

Before defragging the Information Store, the Exchange Information Store service must be stopped. To stop the Information Store service, follow these steps:

1. Go to the Exchange server that has the Information Store to defrag.

2. Open Control Panel and select the Services icon.

3. Scroll down the list of services and select Microsoft Exchange Information Store (to defrag the Private and Public Information Stores) or

Microsoft Exchange Directory Service (to defrag the Microsoft Exchange directory).

4. Click the Stop button. This stops the selected service.

After the desired service has been stopped, you can begin defragging the file using the ESEUTIL.EXE utility.

Note: The ESEUTIL.EXE utility (known as EDBUTIL.EXE in earlier versions of Exchange) performs functions other than defragmentation. Some of these other functions are discussed later in this chapter.

Table 14.1 describes the ESEUTIL.EXE options. Here's the syntax for using ESEUTIL.EXE to defrag the Information Store:

```
ESEUTIL /d [/ds | /ispriv | /ispub] [/l[<path>]] [/s[<path>]]
[/b<filename>] [/t[<filename>]] [/p]
```

A simple status bar allows you to keep track of the defragmentation process. After the file has been defragged, you can restart the appropriate Microsoft Exchange service so users can once again access their mailboxes.

Table 14.1   ESEUTIL.EXE options.

Option	Description
/d	Sets ESEUTIL to defrag mode.
/ds	Defrags the directory store.
/ispriv	Defrags the Private Information Store.
/ispub	Defrags the Public Information Store.
/l[<path>]	Specifies the location of the log files. (The default is the current directory.)
/s[<path>]	Specifies the location of the system files. (The default is the current directory.)
/b<filename>	Causes a backup copy of the store to be created using the specified file name.
/t[<filename>]	Sets the temporary database file name. (The default is TEMPDFRG.EDB.)
/p	Leaves the original file uncompacted and writes the compacted file to the temporary database file name.

Tools And Techniques For Resolving Microsoft Exchange Problems

Microsoft Exchange ships with a number of built-in tools and resources that simplify troubleshooting. Many of these tools can even be used to remotely diagnose and fix problems throughout your organization. When a problem arises with Microsoft Exchange, solving it usually involves checking more than one source. The recommended strategy is to consult the items in the following list (not necessarily in order). A network topology or routing map comes in handy as these resources are consulted:

➤ Link monitor display and logs

➤ Server monitor display and logs

➤ Message tracking and logs

➤ Diagnostic logs for connectors and services

➤ Message queues

➤ Windows NT application event log

Link Monitors

Link monitors are used to verify the efficient routing of test (PING) messages. At the specified polling interval, a test message is sent to every server and system configured in the link monitor. Use link monitors to verify that diagnostic messages sent to other servers in the same site or a different site (or even to foreign systems) are being delivered within a specific amount of time—or if they are being delivered at all. To create a link monitor, see Chapter 11. After you create a link monitor, the monitor must be started before it can provide the information needed to resolve problems. The originating server is the one specified when the link monitor was started.

Gathering Link Monitor Information

If you're alerted of a connection problem, check the link monitor display to determine the scope of the problem and which components are affected. Link monitor configurations are stored in the Microsoft Exchange site directory and are therefore available to all Exchange servers in the site. To view a link monitor display, follow these steps:

1. Open the Microsoft Exchange Administrator program.

2. Select and expand the site where the connection problem is expected to be.

3. Select and expand the Configuration container. The site configuration objects appear in the pane on the right.

4. Select the Monitors container. This displays all the monitors in the site.

5. Double-click the link monitor to view (see Figure 14.3).

The link monitor displays the condition of the connections that were set up to be monitored when the link monitor was created. Each line in the link monitor display represents one connection. Sort the connections by clicking the desired column (see Table 14.2).

The Comment column describes the status of the connection based on the thresholds set in the Link Monitor Bounce property page. The comments shown in Table 14.3 can appear in this column.

Double-clicking a connection brings up a property page for the connection that contains status information. Use the link monitor information to analyze where the connection problem might be. Associate the condition of the connections to the network topology map. Using the two resources together can reveal the scope of the problem and point to the source.

> *Note: If the bounce threshold values are set too low, PING messages on fully operational connections will inappropriately go into warning or alert states.*

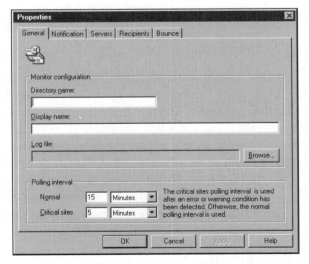

Figure 14.3   The link monitor's Properties dialog box.

Table 14.2	Link monitor columns.
Column	**Description**
<Symbol>	Connection status. The status can be up, down, warning state, or not yet monitored.
Server	The server the PING message was sent to and from which a return PING is expected.
Last Measurement	The time that the last PING message was sent from the originating server.
Last Change	The time that the status of the connection last changed.
Last Time	The amount of time it took for the last PING message to complete.
Comment	The condition of the connection between the originating and receiving server.

Table 14.3	Link monitor comment column values.
Value	**Explanation**
The link is operational	The PING message was returned within the time specified in the bounce threshold.
Bounced mail took (time)	The last PING message was returned, but the bounce time exceeded the warning threshold.
A message was due on (time)	The last PING message has not returned yet, and the elapsed time has exceeded the warning threshold.
Not monitored yet	No PING messages have been returned, and those that were sent are not late yet.

Link monitor log files contain written records of recent connection problems. Each link monitor writes to one log file, even if the link monitor sends PING messages to more than one server. The log file can be examined even if the link monitor is not currently operating. A link monitor log includes all information that the link monitor displays, including time stamps, alerts, warnings, notifications, and dates and times when connections started, slowed, or stopped. This can be a useful addition to other data gathered about connection problems. Log file information can be viewed with any text editor. Link monitor log file names are set in the link monitor's General property page when the link monitor is configured.

Acting On Link Monitor Information

If a link monitor indicates that a communication problem exists, note the number of connections that are having problems. If multiple connections are down, check the network topology map for common features of the problem connections, such as a particular server, router, bridge, gateway, or leased line. If just one connection is down, try to determine why the PING message failed to complete within the specified time. Examine the bounce detail of the PING message in the connection's General property page. A long delay between one hop and the next (or a long delay at the last hop) may indicate a bottleneck or failing connection.

If all PING messages are unsuccessful, use other troubleshooting tools to supplement the data from the link monitor. All PING messages should return eventually unless they are being deleted along the route for some reason. If a particular PING message does not return, check the queues in the Message Transfer Agent (MTA) and the Information Stores of the sending and receiving servers. If message tracking is enabled, the message tracking log can also provide a trace of the PING message.

The Windows NT Event Viewer is also helpful. Search the application event logs on the link monitor's sending and receiving server. Look for warnings and alerts from the MTA, Information Store, and directory.

Here are some additional points to keep in mind about link monitors:

➤ Link monitors must be configured correctly to be useful sources of information about network connectivity.

➤ Configuring and starting link monitors are distinctly separate processes. Link monitors are not operational until they are started, and they function only when they are open. If the link monitor window is closed, the link monitor is stopped; it will no longer send or time PING messages, nor will it write to the link monitor log.

➤ Link monitors assign a status of warning and alerts based on the thresholds established on the link monitor's Bounce property page. If the threshold is not appropriate for every link monitored, the status will not be accurate. If one of the routes requires a longer or shorter threshold, create a separate link monitor for that route.

➤ If an Exchange server's system clock is changed by more than a few minutes, you should restart the link monitors. Otherwise, pending messages will incorrectly appear to be late or connections will appear to be down.

Server Monitors

Server monitors are used to check the condition—including services and clocks—of one or more servers in a site. They use remote procedure calls (RPCs) to do this. Server monitors can also check servers in other sites if those servers are connected with RPCs. Server monitors provide an interface to specify the actions to take when a service or computer has stopped, including restarting servers and services and resetting clocks.

> No special permissions are required to check the state of services on servers in a remote site. However, without the correct permissions on those remote servers, the monitor will not be able to synchronize the clocks or restart services.

If you're alerted to a component failure, check the server monitor display to determine the scope of the problem and the component(s) affected. Before attempting to interpret the display, examine the configuration of the server monitor (using its property page) to learn about its configuration. Server monitor configurations are stored in the Microsoft Exchange site directory and are therefore available to all Exchange servers in the site. To view a server monitor display, follow these steps:

1. Open the Microsoft Exchange Administrator program.

2. Select and expand the site where the connection problem is expected to be.

3. Select and expand the Configuration container. The site configuration objects will appear in the pane on the right.

4. Select the Monitors container. This displays all the monitors in the site.

5. Double-click the server monitor to view the server monitor Properties dialog box (see Figure 14.4).

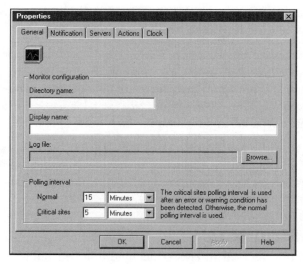

Figure 14.4 The server monitor Properties dialog box.

The server monitor displays the status of servers that were set up to be monitored when the monitor was created. Each line in the server monitor display represents one server. Double-clicking a connection brings up a property page containing status information for the connection. The server monitors can be sorted by clicking the desired column (see Table 14.4).

Server monitor log files contain written records of recent server monitoring events. Each server monitor writes to only one log file, even if the server monitor monitors multiple servers and/or services. The log file can be examined even if the server monitor is not currently operating. A server monitor log includes all information that the server monitor displays, including time stamps, alerts, warnings, notifications, and dates and times when server services started or stopped. Log file information can be viewed with any text editor. Server monitor log file names are set in the server monitor's General property page when the server monitor is configured.

Enabling Message Tracking

Message tracking must be enabled before it can be used for troubleshooting. Messages sent to and from an Exchange server can be tracked to help resolve mail delivery problems. With message tracking, messages can be tracked to locate slow or stopped connections, find lost mail, or determine the delay on each segment of a route (for link monitoring and performance tuning).

Message tracking can be enabled on the Message Transfer Agent (MTA), the Information Store, and the MS Mail Connector. When message tracking is enabled, each component that handles mail records its activities in a log file. The log file serves as a processing trace of each message as the particular component receives, processes, and delivers the message to the next component. By default, message tracking is off, because excessive logging can affect server performance.

Table 14.4 Server monitor columns.	
Column	**Description**
<symbol>	Server component status. If any component is down, the server is considered to be down, as well.
Server	The name of the server being monitored.
Last Measurement	The time the server was last polled.
Last Change	The time the condition of any server component changed.
Comment	The general condition of the server.

All components must be restarted after you enable message tracking before log file writing will take place. For example, if message tracking is enabled on the Information Store, you should restart all Information Store services in the site.

To enable message tracking on the Information Store or the MTA, follow these steps:

1. Open the Microsoft Exchange Administrator program.

2. Select and expand the site where message tracking is to be enabled.

3. Select and expand the Configuration container. The site configuration objects will appear in the pane on the right.

4. Double-click the Information Store site configuration or the MTA site configuration to track messages on.

5. Select the General property page.

6. Select Enable Message Tracking.

7. Click OK.

8. For each server in the site, go to the Control Panel|Services applet and restart the Microsoft Exchange Information Store or the Microsoft Exchange MTA service.

Message tracking must be enabled separately on each MS Mail Connector in a site. To enable message tracking on an MS Mail Connector, follow these steps:

1. Open the Microsoft Exchange Administrator program.

2. Select and expand the site where message tracking is to be enabled.

3. Select and expand the Configuration container. The site configuration objects will appear in the pane on the right.

4. Select and expand the Connections container. The connection objects will appear in the pane on the right.

5. Double-click the MS Mail Connector.

6. Select the Interchange property page.

7. Select Enable Message Tracking.

8. Click OK.

9. Go to the Control Panel|Services applet and restart the MS Mail Connector Interchange service.

Message tracking must be enabled separately on each Internet Mail Service computer in the site. If the site has more than one Internet Mail Service computer, you need to enable message tracking on each. To enable message tracking on the Internet Mail Service, follow these steps:

1. Open the Microsoft Exchange Administrator program.

2. Select and expand the site where message tracking is to be enabled.

3. Select and expand the Configuration container. The site configuration objects will appear in the pane on the right.

4. Select and expand the Connections container. The connection objects will appear in the pane on the right.

5. Double-click the Internet Mail Service.

6. Select the Internet Mail property page.

7. Select Enable Message Tracking.

8. Click OK.

9. Go to the Control Panel|Services applet and restart the Microsoft Exchange Internet Mail Service.

Performing Message Tracking

Once message tracking is enabled, use the resources in the Microsoft Exchange Administrator to track individual messages. The Track Message command (available from the Tools menu) initiates the tracking of a message through the network. Daily tracking logs (generated by each component that has message tracking enabled) are searched for any events having to do with the specified message. Using this approach, messages can be followed through the logs of all Exchange Server computers on the same physical network. Messages can be repeatedly selected and tracked until the source of the problem has been determined.

To track a message, follow these steps:

1. Open the Microsoft Exchange Administrator program.

2. From the Tools menu, choose Track Message.

3. Enter the name of the server to which you want to connect. This displays the Select Message To Track dialog box (see Figure 14.5).

Note: To track a message, first connect to a server to locate the message. Select a server that has the sender or recipient of the message in its Global Address List.

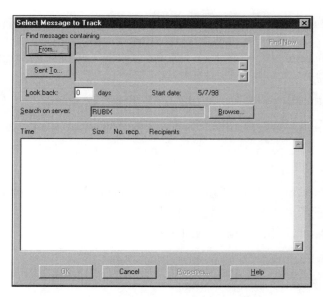

Figure 14.5 The Select Message To Track dialog box.

4. Enter the message criteria using the From, Sent To, and Look Back (How Many Days) controls. The From and Sent To buttons display the Global Address List from which the desired mailbox can be selected. If zero is entered for the Look Back value, only the current day's logs will be searched.

5. Click the Find Now button.

The daily tracking logs are searched for all references to messages matching the specified criteria. All matching message events are displayed in a list below the message criteria information (see Table 14.5).

Table 14.5   Columns for matching events.

Column	Description
<symbol>	The event type.
Time Server	The time and date the message was sent as recorded by the Information Store on the sending server.
Size	The message size in bytes.
No. Recp.	The number of mailboxes to which the message was sent. Distribution lists count as one recipient.
Recipients	The first mailbox in the recipients list. Ellipses indicate the message was sent to more than one recipient.

Access more detail for each matching message event by pressing the Properties button. This brings up the Message Properties dialog box, showing detailed information about the message at the time the event was generated. The Time, Transferred To, and Recipients List information are all particularly useful. Time indicates the time the message was sent or received. Transferred To documents the Exchange Server component that generated this event, and Recipients List itemizes all addresses to which the message was sent.

Once a message is found using the Select Message To Track interface, you can trace its path through the network by using the Message Tracking Center. You'll trace through the logs of all servers that handled the message. At each step, the process determines which service expected to receive the message next. It then searches the logs on that server to find events related to that message. The trace is complete when the message leaves the network or is delivered.

Access the Message Tracking Center from the Select Messages To Track dialog box. Select a message and click OK. The Message Tracking Center dialog box appears, displaying tracking information for the selected message (see Figure 14.6). Click the Track button to activate message tracking. When the search is complete, all matching message tracking events are displayed in the Tracking History list.

To search for a message when either the sender or recipient is not in the Global Address List or to search for messages originating at gateways, use the Message Tracking Center:

Figure 14.6   The Message Tracking Center dialog box.

1. In the Message Tracking Center, choose Advanced Search. The Advanced Search dialog box appears, as shown in Figure 14.7.

2. Select the Transferred Into This Site option and then click OK. The Select Inbound Message To Track dialog box appears.

3. Type the email address of the sender or click the From button to select an entry from the Global Address List.

4. Type the email address of one or more recipients or click the Sent To button to select one or more recipients from the Global Address List.

5. In the Transferred From pull-down menu, select the connector used to transport the message.

6. Modify the Look Back date and server, if appropriate.

7. Click the Find Now button.

The Message Tracking Center displays message tracking results as a hierarchy of the mail-handling events found in the tracking logs. Each line in the list represents one event, and each level in the hierarchy represents a branch in the path of a message—some of which may be concurrent. To get more information, about a particular event, follow these steps:

1. Double-click the event to expand or collapse the underlying hierarchy.

2. Select an event and choose Properties to see more detail about the event.

3. Click the Find Recipient In Tracking History button to search for recipients specified in the message search. Events involving those recipients appear in bold.

To try to resolve a problem message, take one of the following actions: consult the message queues of any affected components, raise the diagnostic logging level of a component or service, consult the Windows NT application event log, or change the configuration of a component.

Figure 14.7 The Message Tracking Center's Advanced Search dialog box.

Diagnostic Logging

Diagnostic logging helps pinpoint messaging problems. Using each component's Diagnostic Logging property page, you can specify the degree of diagnostic logging desired. Diagnostic logs are recorded in the Windows NT event log, where they can be used to resolve messaging problems.

Configure diagnostic logging for Microsoft Exchange components to record only highly significant events (such as an application failure) or moderately important events (such as receipt of messages across a gateway). By default, only critical events are logged.

Diagnostic logging is available for the following Microsoft Exchange components:

➤ MTA

➤ Directory

➤ Information Store

➤ Internet Mail Service

➤ MS Mail Connector

➤ Microsoft Schedule+ Free/Busy Connector

➤ Microsoft Exchange Connector for Lotus cc:Mail

Diagnostic logging levels are set by category—a category is a group of related functions (see Table 14.6). Each category of a Microsoft Exchange component has a diagnostic logging level. When a component generates an event that matches or exceeds the logging level, the event is recorded in the Windows NT application event log.

During normal operation, you can set diagnostic logging to None for every category of every component on every server. Otherwise, too much diagnostic information will be logged. With a diagnostic level of None, only error events and critical error messages are written to the log.

Start diagnostic logging to troubleshoot a problem. Be selective when increasing a logging level. You should increase levels on only those aspects of the component that might be related to the problem.

If a diagnostic level is changed, the respective service must be stopped and restarted for the change to take effect.

Table 14.6	Diagnostic logging levels.
Level	**Description**
None	Only critical and error events are logged. This is the default level.
Minimum	Only high-level events are logged. Use this level to begin trouble-shooting a problem.
Medium	Events dealing with the execution of tasks are logged. Use this level when the problem has been narrowed down to a component or group of categories.
Maximum	All component operations are logged. Use this level only when the problem has been traced to a particular category or categories. This level logs all events, resulting in a large amount of information. This can have a detrimental effect on Exchange Server performance.

Message Queues

You can view and modify Message Transfer Agents (MTAs), the Internet Mail Service, and MS Mail Connector messages. Use the Queues property page for each component to display queues, delete messages, and (in some MTA queues) change the order of the messages in the queue.

When messages are not reaching their destinations, examine the queues. Mail should not normally be retained in the queues. A backed up queue can indicate the following information:

➤ A problem with the physical connection between the servers

➤ A server or MTA configuration error

➤ An improperly configured connector

Use the Queues property page to delete any corrupted messages that are blocking the queues.

Windows NT Event Viewer

Windows NT logs events to its system, security, and application log files. This provides a means to track significant events, such as server reboots, low disk space messages, and so on. The Windows NT Event Viewer can be used to display and search the application event log for problems specific to Microsoft Exchange. Alerts can be set to inform users when problems occur. Because events can differ considerably in their significance, the level of detail for logged events is configured at the component level, using the Diagnostic Logging property page (discussed in the "Diagnostic Logging" section earlier in this chapter). Each Microsoft Exchange component generates different kinds of events based on the functions it performs. Table 14.7 offers a brief overview of Microsoft Exchange events.

Other Troubleshooting Tools

Microsoft Exchange ships with a number of MS-DOS command-line utilities, some of which (ESEUTIL, ISINTEG, and MTACHECK) are designed specifically to analyze and repair the Information Store or related items. There is some overlap among the tools. If you encounter a problem with Exchange Server, use the tool that seems appropriate for the situation.

ESEUTIL

The Microsoft Exchange ESEUTIL.EXE utility is used to perform a number of analysis and recovery actions on Microsoft Exchange databases (the Information Store or the directory store). As we discussed previously, ESEUTIL can be used to defrag and compact the Information Store. ESEUTIL can also be used to (in increasing degrees) perform the following tasks:

➤ Verify the integrity of a Microsoft Exchange database

➤ Upgrade a database created using an earlier release of Microsoft Exchange to the current version

Table 14.7 An overview of Microsoft Exchange events.	
Component	**Typical Events**
All	Component start, failure to start, and stop.
System Attendant	Routing table calculation problems, errors writing to the tracking log.
MTA	Opening and closing connections to other servers, connection errors.
Directory	Replication requests, success and failure messages, changes to security attributes.
Public Information Store	User logons, replication.
Private Information Store	User logons, sending and receiving of messages.
Administrator Program	Configuration of replication features.
Directory Import	Import start and finish, import errors and warnings.
Directory Synchronization	Any errors.
Security Events	Logon, logoff, and privileged use.
Internet Mail Service	Mail connectivity, Internet services, scheduled connection times.

➤ Repair a corrupted or damaged database

➤ Generate formatted output of various database file types (rarely used)

➤ Perform a recovery to bring all databases to a consistent state

ESEUTIL requires that you stop the Information Store service (if working with the Private and Public Information Store) or the directory service (if working with the Microsoft Exchange directory).

After the appropriate service has been stopped, you can proceed to work on the Information Store or directory using the ESEUTIL.EXE utility.

Verifying The Integrity Of A Microsoft Exchange Database

Here's the syntax for using ESEUTIL.EXE to verify a database:

```
ESEUTIL /g [/ds | /ispriv | /ispub] [/t[<filename>]] [/v] [/x]
```

Table 14.8 outlines the ESEUTIL.EXE options you have in integrity verification mode.

When run in verify integrity mode, ESEUTIL performs no recovery; it assumes the database to be in a consistent state, returning an error if this is not the case. As the verify integrity process proceeds, a simple status bar displays. After the integrity of the file has been verified, you should restart the appropriate Microsoft Exchange service so users can once again access their mailboxes.

Table 14.8 Options for ESEUTIL.EXE in verify integrity mode.	
Option	**Description**
/g	Sets ESEUTIL to integrity verification mode.
/ds	Verifies the integrity of the directory store.
/ispriv	Verifies the integrity of the Private Information Store.
/ispub	Verifies the integrity of the Public Information Store.
/t[<filename>]	Sets the temporary database file name. (The default is INTEG.EDB.)
/v	Verbose mode. Provides additional feedback on the integrity verification process.
/x	Provides more information on any error messages encountered.

Upgrading A Database To The Current Version

If you're restoring a Microsoft Exchange database that's in an older format from a backup, it will need to be upgraded to the current version. To upgrade a database to the current version, provide the DLL that shipped with that version of Microsoft Exchange. Here's the syntax for using ESEUTIL.EXE to upgrade a database to the current version:

```
ESEUTIL /u <database name> /d<previous .DLL> [/b[<filename>]]
[/t[<filename>]] [/p]
```

Table 14.9 outlines the ESEUTIL.EXE options for the upgrade database mode.

ESEUTIL should be used to upgrade a database only after an internal database format change has taken place. Before you upgrade the database, it should be in a consistent state. An error will result otherwise. As the upgrade process proceeds, a simple status bar displays. After the database has been upgraded, you should restart the appropriate Microsoft Exchange service so users can once again access their mailboxes.

Repairing A Corrupted Or Damaged Database

If a message in the Windows NT event log indicates that the Microsoft Exchange Information Store is corrupted or damaged, you should attempt to resolve the problem by repairing the database. Here's the syntax for using ESEUTIL.EXE to repair a database:

Table 14.9   Options for ESEUTIL.EXE in upgrade database mode.

Option	Description
/u	Sets ESEUTIL to upgrade database mode.
<database name>	File name of the database to upgrade (for example, PRIV.EDB, PUB.EDB, and DIR.EDB).
/d<previous .DLL>	File name of the DLL that came with the release of Microsoft Exchange and matches the database version.
/b<filename>	Causes a backup copy of the store to be created using the specified file name.
/t[<filename>]	Sets the temporary database file name. (The default is TEMPUPGD.EDB.)
/p	Leaves the original file unconverted and writes the converted file to the temporary database file name.

```
ESEUTIL /p [/ds | /ispriv | /ispub] [/t[<filename>]]
[/d] [/v] [/x]
```

Table 14.10 outlines the ESEUTIL.EXE options in the repair mode.

As the repair database process proceeds, a simple status bar displays. After the database has been repaired, you should restart the appropriate Microsoft Exchange service so users can once again access their mailboxes.

Performing A Recovery To Bring All Databases To A Consistent State

If a message in the Windows NT event log indicates that a Microsoft Exchange database is in an inconsistent state, you should resolve the problem by performing a recovery on the database. Here's the syntax for using ESEUTIL.EXE to perform a recovery on a database:

```
ESEUTIL /r [/ds | /is] [/l[<path>]] [/s[<path>]]
```

Table 14.11 outlines the ESEUTIL.EXE options in recovery mode.

As the recovery process proceeds, a simple status bar displays. After the database has been recovered, you should restart the appropriate Microsoft Exchange service so users can once again access their mailboxes.

ISINTEG

The Microsoft Exchange Information Store Integrity Checker (ISINTEG.EXE) finds and eliminates common Information Store database errors. If the

Table 14.10 Options for ESEUTIL.EXE in repair mode.	
Option	**Description**
/p	Sets ESEUTIL to repair database mode.
/ds	Repairs the directory store.
/ispriv	Repairs the Private Information Store.
/ispub	Repairs the Public Information Store.
/t[<filename>]	Sets the temporary database file name. (The default is REPAIR.EDB.)
/d	Doesn't repair the database, just scans for errors.
/v	Verbose mode. Provides additional feedback on the repair process.
/x	Provides additional information on any error messages encountered.

Table 14.11   Options for ESEUTIL.EXE in recovery mode.

Option	Description
/r	Sets ESEUTIL to recovery mode.
/ds	Recovers the directory store.
/is	Recovers the Information Store (both Private and Public).
/l[<path>]	Location of log files. (The default is the current directory.)
/s[<path>]	Location of system files. (The default is the current directory.)

Microsoft Exchange Information Store service cannot be started or users cannot access their mailboxes, use ISINTEG. Also, use this utility after recovering an Information Store database with software other than the Windows NT backup utility. ISINTEG.EXE is located in the \ExchSrvr\Bin directory.

ISINTEG has three modes of operation:

➤ **Check mode** Check mode searches the Information Store databases for table errors, incorrect reference counts, and any objects that are not referenced. It displays the results and writes them to a log file.

➤ **Check and fix mode** Check and fix mode performs the same tasks as check mode and also attempts to fix any errors it encounters. Select this mode only when instructed by Microsoft Technical Support. Perform a backup first.

➤ **Patch mode** After restoring from an offline backup, the Microsoft Exchange Information Store service will occasionally fail to start. Patch mode usually fixes this problem.

ISINTEG must be run separately on the Public and Private Information Stores; the Information Store must be stopped first. Run ISINTEG from the Windows NT Server command line. See the first ESEUTIL section for instructions on how to stop the Information Store service.

Check Mode And Check And Fix Mode

By default, ISINTEG simply examines the Information Store database tables for errors, displays the results, and reports them to a log file. The fix option instructs ISINTEG to also attempt to repair any errors it finds. Details of all repairs are recorded in a log file (by default, ISINTEG.PRI or ISINTEG.PUB, depending on the whether the Private or Public Information Store was chosen).

Here's the syntax for using ISINTEG.EXE in check mode or check and fix mode:

```
ISINTEG -pri | -pub [-fix] [-verbose] [-l[<filename>]]
[-test<testname>]
```

Table 14.12 outlines the options for ISINTEG.EXE.

As ISINTEG proceeds, a simple status bar displays. Afterward, you should restart the Information Store service so users can once again access their mailboxes.

Patching The Information Store

The Microsoft Exchange Information Store will not start if the globally unique identifier (GUID) for the Information Store does not match the GUID stored in the Windows NT Registry and the Microsoft Exchange directory. This can occur if the Information Store is restored from an offline backup. In this situation, you should use ISINTEG in patch mode.

In patch mode, ISINTEG records consistent GUID entries in the database, directory, and Registry. This allows the Information Store service to start again. Note that ISINTEG patch mode runs on the Information Store as a whole. It cannot be run on only the Public or Private Information Store database. As with check mode and check and fix mode, the Information Store service must be stopped before you run ISINTEG.

 If the Information Store on a server won't start and event ID 2084 appears in the Windows NT application event log, running ISINTEG in patch mode often fixes the problem.

Patch mode and check mode must be run separately; ISINTEG does not perform any database integrity tests when run in patch mode.

Table 14.12 ISINTEG.EXE options.	
Option	**Description**
-pri	Works on the Private Information Store.
-pub	Works on the Public Information Store.
-fix	Specifies that any errors encountered should be fixed.
-verbose	Provides more feedback on the process.
-l[<filename>]	Sets the log file name. (The default is ISINTEG.PRI or ISINTEG.PUB.)
-t<testname>	Performs a specific ISINTEG test. Type **ISINTEG /?** to see a list of available tests.

Here's the syntax for using ISINTEG.EXE in patch mode:

```
ISINTEG -patch
```

As ISINTEG proceeds, a simple status bar displays. Afterward, you should restart the Information Store service so users can once again access their mailboxes. Also, be sure to run ISINTEG in check mode after running it in patch mode.

MTACHECK

The Microsoft Exchange Message Transfer Agent Check utility (MTACHECK.EXE) scans the internal MTA database, looking for damaged objects that might interfere with queue processing. If messages are not being delivered properly, MTACHECK can often resolve the problem. Also, if the Microsoft Exchange MTA service stops and cannot be restarted, MTACHECK can usually get it running again. MTACHECK can also be used for routine checks of the integrity of MTA database queues.

MTACHECK places suspect objects from the queues into files that can be examined later. In addition, MTACHECK rebuilds the queues so the MTA can be restarted and resume processing. Fortunately, most suspect objects removed from the queue by MTACHECK can be recovered. MTACHECK places all suspect objects it considers to be damaged in DB*.DAT files (located in the \ExchSrvr\MTAData\MTACheck.out directory). You should examine these objects and either delete or attempt to repair them.

MTACHECK.EXE is located in the \ExchSrvr\Bin directory, and it can be run only from the command line of the Exchange server having the MTA problem. The MTA service must be stopped before the utility is run. In addition, the MTACheck.out directory (where MTACHECK places suspect objects) must first be emptied or deleted.

Running MTACHECK

MTACHECK displays progress messages as it operates. You have numerous options available for altering the actions that MTACHECK takes. To run MTACHECK, follow these steps:

1. Go to the Exchange server having the MTA problem (or whose queue you want to check).

2. Open Control Panel and select the Services icon.

3. Scroll down the list of services and select Microsoft Exchange Message Transfer Agent.

4. Click the Stop button. This stops the MTA service.

5. Use Explorer to empty the \ExchSrvr\MTAData\MTACheck.out folder.

6. At a command prompt, start MTACHECK with any option switches.

Here's the syntax for using MTACHECK.EXE:

```
MTACHECK [/V] [/F <filename>] [/RD] [/RP]
```

Table 14.13 outlines the MTACHECK.EXE options.

As MTACHECK proceeds, a simple status bar displays. Afterward, a message indicating the results is displayed. You should restart the MTA service so mail will once again be delivered properly.

Interpreting MTACHECK Output

MTACHECK examines each queue in the database. If it finds an error, it reports the name of the queue, the type of error, and the number of messages returned to the rebuilt queue. It then proceeds to examine the actual objects in the queues. If an object is found to be in error, it is removed from the queue and placed in a file in the \ExchSrvr\MTAData\MTACheck.out directory. The object ID, error type, queue name, and the Microsoft Transaction Server (MTS) ID of the corrupted message are all reported.

If message tracking is enabled, you can search the log for the offending object by its message ID. By tracing the path of the offending message, the cause of the problem may be found. You might need to search more than one site's logs to find the complete path of the message.

Improving Exchange Server Performance

A number of techniques can be used for improving the performance of an Exchange server. Some of these techniques are considered in the following sections.

Table 14.13   MTACHECK.EXE options.

Option	Description
/V	Verbose mode. Provides additional feedback on the process.
/F[<filename>]	Saves progress messages to the specified file.
/RD	Repairs the database. This is useful when data integrity is suspect.
/RP	Repairs the post office. This can be used to repair user data, mailboxes, and addresses.

Performance Optimizer

At the end of the installation process, Microsoft Exchange Setup automatically runs Performance Optimizer. Performance Optimizer analyzes and optimizes your hardware so that it performs in the most efficient way. Performance Optimizer also analyzes the server's logical drives and physical memory.

Performance Optimizer can be run at any time. Consider running it on an Exchange server when a connector is added or moved, a server's role within a site is changed, a change or upgrade to any major hardware component occurs, or when migrating a large number of users from a non-Microsoft Exchange messaging system.

For the best performance, optimize your disk subsystem before installing Microsoft Exchange and running the Performance Optimizer. Here's Microsoft's recommended disk configuration for an Exchange Server computer:

➤ One physical disk for the operating system and the page file.

➤ One physical disk for the transaction log files. To increase fault tolerance, mirror this disk.

➤ One stripe set consisting of multiple physical disks for all other Microsoft Exchange components. This allows Microsoft Exchange databases to be accessed in the most efficient manner.

Performance Monitor

Monitor the counter values in Windows NT Performance Monitor to determine how Microsoft Exchange is performing and to track any error conditions. The Performance Monitor counters used for showing system conditions fall into one of two categories: general counters and Exchange-specific counters. Table 14.14 lists a number of relevant Windows NT general Performance Monitor counters.

Table 14.15 lists a number of useful Exchange-related counters. (For a complete list of Performance Monitor counters, see the Microsoft Exchange Resource Guide.)

Migrating From Other Messaging Systems

Microsoft Exchange includes the Migration wizard for migrating users from other messaging systems. Access the Microsoft Exchange Migration wizard from the Microsoft Exchange program group. The Migration wizard provides a migration path for users of the following messaging systems:

Table 14.14 Relevant Windows NT general Performance Monitor counters.

Object	Counter	Problem Indicated
Logical Disk	% Disk Time	A sustained value greater than 90% indicates that the hard drive is experiencing a performance bottleneck.
Memory	Pages/sec	A high average value indicates that the computer needs more memory.
Process	% Process Time	An average value greater than 90% indicates that the processor is experiencing a performance bottleneck.

Table 14.15 Some important Exchange-related Performance Monitor counters.

Object	Counter	Problem Indicated
MSExchangeMTA	Work Queue Length	A high number indicates a problem with the MTA queue.
MSExchangeISPriv	Avg. Time For Delivery	A high value indicates a problem with the Private Information Store MTA.
MSExchangeISPub	Avg. Time For Delivery	A high value indicates a problem with the Public Information Store MTA.
MSExchangeMSMI	Messages Received	If the value remains constant, it might indicate a problem with the MS Mail Connector.
MSExchangePCMTA	File Contentions/Hour	A high value might indicate too much traffic is going through that particular shadow post office.

➤ MS Mail (for PC networks)

➤ Lotus cc:Mail

➤ Novell GroupWise

➤ Collabra Share

Here are the three steps to the migration process:

➤ Use the Migration wizard to create a user list

➤ Modify the user list as needed, removing/adding users

➤ Use the Migration wizard to create mailboxes, migrate messages, and migrate attachments

When mailboxes migrate to Microsoft Exchange, each mailbox's Windows NT user account used to log onto Windows NT Server must also have permissions on the Exchange server. If you're attempting to migrate post office information and the Windows NT account does not have sufficient Exchange Server permissions, the error message "Invalid server specified" will appear.

When you're migrating mailboxes from MS Mail, the default Administrator account (ADMIN) and the Schedule+ Administrator account (ADMINSCH) are automatically skipped and are therefore not migrated. These accounts do not need to be removed from the user list generated by the Migration wizard.

The Exchange server and the Microsoft Exchange post office should not be accessed by any users during the migration. Also, make sure there's at least twice as much space on the Microsoft Exchange computer as the post office being migrated from.

Exam Prep Questions

Question 1

> The name of the organization, sites, or servers can be changed after Microsoft Exchange is installed.
>
> ○ a. True
>
> ○ b. False

The correct answer to this question is b, False. The name of the organization, sites, and servers cannot be changed after Microsoft Exchange is installed.

Question 2

> What are the minimum Exchange-related services that should be started if an Exchange server is installed correctly? [Check all correct answers]
>
> ❑ a. Microsoft Exchange System Attendant
>
> ❑ b. MS Mail Connector Interchange
>
> ❑ c. Microsoft Exchange Directory
>
> ❑ d. Microsoft Exchange Information Store
>
> ❑ e. Microsoft Exchange Message Transfer Agent

The correct answers to this question are a, c, d, and e. After a successful Microsoft Exchange installation, these services (as a minimum) should be started. If one or more of these services is not started, an error has occurred. The MS Mail Connector Interchange service will only be installed and started if the MS Mail (for PC networks) was selected during the installation; therefore, answer b is incorrect.

Question 3

> If an Exchange server is running low on disk space due to a large Private Information Store, what can be done? [Check all correct answers]
>
> ❏ a. Move one or more mailboxes.
>
> ❏ b. Clean one or more mailboxes.
>
> ❏ c. Establish mailbox storage limits.
>
> ❏ d. Compact the Private Information Store.
>
> ❏ e. All of the above.

The correct answer to this question is e. Moving mailboxes to another Exchange server will free up space in the Private Information Store on the original Exchange server. Cleaning mailboxes will reduce the amount of space those mailboxes take up in the Private Information Store. Establishing mailbox storage limits will limit the amount of space the Private Information Store takes up on the Exchange server. Compacting the Private Information Store will reclaim unused space in the Private Information Store, potentially reducing the store's size.

Question 4

> If message transfers fail between Exchange servers, what tools can be used to help resolve the problem? [Check all correct answers]
>
> ❏ a. Link monitors
>
> ❏ b. Server monitors
>
> ❏ c. Disk Administrator
>
> ❏ d. Remote Access Admin
>
> ❏ e. None of the above

The correct answers to this question are a and b. Link monitors are used to verify the efficient routing of test messages between Exchange servers. Server monitors are used to check the condition of one or more servers in a site. Disk Administrator is used to view (and optionally configure) storage devices. Remote Access Admin is used to administer a Remote Access Service (RAS); therefore, answers c, d, and e are incorrect.

Question 5

What does a link monitor display include? [Check all correct answers]

❑ a. The server name to which the PING message was sent

❑ b. The number of physical links between sites

❑ c. The condition of the connection

❑ d. All of the above

The correct answers to this question are a and c. A link monitor displays a good deal of information, including the server name the PING message was sent to as well as the condition of the connection. The number of physical links between sites is not available in a link monitor; therefore, answers b and d are incorrect.

Question 6

A link monitor must be started before it can provide useful diagnostic information.

○ a. True

○ b. False

The correct answer to this question is a, True. A successfully configured link monitor does not actually begin the link monitoring process until the monitor is started using the Start Monitor menu item in the Tools menu.

Question 7

Which action can a server monitor be used for?

○ a. Notification of stopped services

○ b. Resetting server clocks

○ c. Restarting stopped services

○ d. All of the above

The correct answer to this question is d. A server monitor can be configured to notify someone if a service stops, to restart stopped services, and to synchronize server clocks.

Question 8

A backed-up queue might be an indication of what problem? [Check all correct answers]

❏ a. A problem with the physical connection between the servers

❏ b. A server or MTA configuration error

❏ c. The Message Tracking Center was left open

❏ d. An improperly configured connector

❏ e. None of the above

❏ f. All of the above

The correct answers to this question are a, b, and d. A problem with the physical connection between servers can lead to a backed-up message queue. A server or MTA configuration error as well as an improperly configured connector can also lead to this problem. The Message Tracking Center can be left open with no ill effects. Therefore, answers c, e, and f are incorrect.

Question 9

The Performance Optimizer should be run only once on each server.

○ a. True

○ b. False

The correct answer to this question is b, False. The Performance Optimizer can be run at any time, and it should be run whenever a change is made to an Exchange server, such as when a connector is added or removed, when the server's role within a site is changed, when any major hardware component is changed or upgraded, or when a large number of users from a non-Exchange system are migrated.

Question 10

> The Microsoft Exchange Migration wizard can help migrate users from which messaging systems? [Check all correct answers]
>
> ❑ a. MS Mail (for PC networks)
>
> ❑ b. Lotus Notes
>
> ❑ c. Novell GroupWise
>
> ❑ d. Collabra Share

The correct answers to this question are a, c, and d. The Microsoft Exchange Migration wizard provides comprehensive assistance to help migrate users from MS Mail (for PC networks), Novell GroupWise, and Collabra Share. Although the Migration wizard does not include support for migrating users from Lotus Notes, there are other utilities included with Microsoft Exchange 5.5 to help with this process; therefore, answer b is incorrect.

Need To Know More?

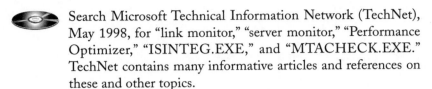

Search Microsoft Technical Information Network (TechNet), May 1998, for "link monitor," "server monitor," "Performance Optimizer," "ISINTEG.EXE," and "MTACHECK.EXE." TechNet contains many informative articles and references on these and other topics.

Online Books from the Microsoft Exchange 5.5 CD-ROM, specifically the Operations section, contains many references to the subjects discussed in this chapter.

Check out the Microsoft Exchange home page at www. microsoft.com/exchange. It contains numerous whitepapers and updated references about maintaining, troubleshooting, and optimizing Microsoft Exchange.

Visit the Microsoft Knowledge Base and support home page at www.microsoft.com/kb. It contains numerous updated articles on Microsoft Exchange maintenance, troubleshooting, and optimization.

Sample Test

In this chapter, we provide a number of pointers to help you develop a successful test-taking strategy, including how to choose proper answers, how to decode ambiguity, how to work within the Microsoft testing framework, how to decide what you need to memorize, and how to prepare for the test. At the end of the chapter, we include 51 questions on subject matter pertinent to Microsoft Exam 70-081: "Implementing And Supporting Microsoft Exchange Server 5.5." Good luck!

Questions, Questions, Questions

There should be no doubt in your mind that you are facing a test full of questions. Currently, this Exchange Server 5.5 test may be a short-form test or an adaptive test. If it is a short-form test, the exam will consist of 30 questions that you must complete in 60 minutes. If it is an adaptive test, it will consist of somewhere between 25 and 50 questions (on average) and take somewhere between 30 and 60 minutes.

Whichever type of test you take, for this exam, questions belong to one of five basic types:

➤ Multiple-choice with a single answer

➤ Multiple-choice with one or more answers

➤ Multipart with a single answer

➤ Multipart with one or more answers

➤ Simulations (that is, operating on a GUI screen capture to simulate using the Exchange Server interface with your mouse and/or your keyboard)

Always take the time to read a question twice before selecting an answer, and always look for an Exhibit button as you examine each question. Exhibits include graphics information related to a question. An exhibit is usually a screen capture of program output or GUI information that you must examine to analyze the question's contents and formulate an answer. Thus, the Exhibit button brings up graphics and charts used to help explain a question, provide additional data, or illustrate page layout or program behavior.

Not every question has only one answer; many questions require multiple answers. Therefore, it's important to read each question carefully, to determine how many answers are necessary or possible, and to look for additional hints or instructions when selecting answers. Such instructions often occur in brackets, immediately following the question itself (as they do for all multiple-choice questions in which one or more answers are possible).

Working Within The Framework

The test questions appear in random order, and many elements or issues that receive mention in one question may also crop up in other questions. It's not uncommon to find that an incorrect answer to one question is the correct answer to another question, or vice-versa. Take the time to read every answer to each question, even if you recognize the correct answer to a question immediately. That extra reading may spark a memory, or remind you about an Exchange Server feature or function, that helps you on another question elsewhere in the exam.

If you're taking a fixed-length test, you can revisit any question as many times as you like. If you're uncertain of the answer to a question, check the box that's provided to mark it for easy return later on. You should also mark questions you think may offer information that you can use to answer other questions. On fixed-length or short-form tests, we usually mark somewhere between 25 and 50 percent of the questions on exams we've taken. The testing software is designed to let you mark every question if you choose; use this framework to your advantage. Everything you will want to see again should be marked; the testing software can then help you return to marked questions quickly and easily.

For fixed-length or short-form tests, we strongly recommend that you first read through the entire test quickly, before getting caught up in answering individual questions. This will help to jog your memory as you review the potential answers and can help identify questions that you want to mark for easy access to their contents. It will also let you identify and mark the really tricky questions for easy return as well. The key is to make a quick pass

> over the territory to begin with, so that you know what you're up against; and then to survey that territory more thoroughly on a second pass, when you can begin to answer all questions systematically and consistently.

If you're taking an adaptive test, and you see something in a question or one of the answers that jogs your memory on a topic, or that you feel you should record if the topic appears in another question, write it down on your piece of paper. Just because you can't go back to a question in an adaptive test doesn't mean you can't take notes on what you see early in the test, in hopes that it might help you later in the test.

> For adaptive tests, don't be afraid to take notes on what you see in various questions. Sometimes, what you record from one question, especially if it's not as familiar as it should be or reminds you of the name or use of some utility or interface details, can help you on other questions later on.

Finally, some Microsoft tests combine 15 to 25 adaptive questions with 10 fixed-length questions. In that case, use our recommended adaptive strategy for the adaptive part, and the recommended fixed-length or short-form strategy for the fixed-length part.

Deciding What To Memorize

The amount of rote memorization you must undertake for an exam depends on how well you remember what you've read, and how well you know the software by heart. If you are a visual thinker, and you can see the drop-down menus and dialog boxes in your head, you won't need to memorize as much as someone who's less visually-oriented. The tests will stretch your recollection of commands and functions of Exchange Server.

At a minimum, you'll want to memorize the following kinds of information:

➤ The upgrade options available for Exchange Server

➤ The mail protocols supported by Exchange

➤ The connectors available for Exchange

If you work your way through this book while sitting at an Exchange Server machine, and try to manipulate this environment's features and functions as they're discussed throughout, you should have little or no difficulty mastering this material. Also, don't forget that The Cram Sheet at the front of the book is designed to capture the material that is most important to memorize; use this to guide your studies as well.

Preparing For The Test

The best way to prepare for the test—after you've studied—is to take at least one practice exam. We've included one here in this chapter for that reason; the test questions are located in the pages that follow (and unlike the preceding chapters in this book, the answers don't follow the questions immediately; you'll have to flip to Chapter 16 to review the answers separately).

Give yourself 90 minutes to take the exam, keep yourself on the honor system, and don't look at earlier text in the book or jump ahead to the answer key. When your time is up, or you've finished the questions, you can check your work in Chapter 16. Pay special attention to the explanations for the incorrect answers; these can also help to reinforce your knowledge of the material. Knowing how to recognize correct answers is good, but understanding why incorrect answers are wrong can be equally valuable.

Taking The Test

Relax. Once you're sitting in front of the testing computer, there's nothing more you can do to increase your knowledge or preparation. Take a deep breath, stretch, and start reading that first question.

There's no need to rush, either. You have plenty of time to complete each question and to return to those questions that you skip or mark for return (if you are taking a fixed-length or short-form test). If you read a question twice and remain clueless, you can mark it if you're taking a fixed-length or short-form test; if you're taking an adaptive test, you'll have to guess and move on. Both easy and difficult questions are intermixed throughout the test in random order. If you're taking a fixed-length or short-form test, don't cheat yourself by spending too much time on a hard question early in the test. If you're taking an adaptive test, don't spend more than five minutes on any single question—if it takes you that long to get nowhere, it's time to guess and move on.

On a fixed-length or short-form test, you can read through the entire test, and before returning to marked questions for a second visit, figure out how much time you've got per question. As you answer each question, remove its mark. Continue to review the remaining marked questions until you run out of time, or you complete the test.

On an adaptive test, watch your time on long or complex questions. Don't deprive yourself of the opportunity to see more questions by taking too long to puzzle over questions, unless you think you can figure out the answer. Otherwise, you're limiting your opportunities to pass.

That's it for pointers. Here are some questions for you to practice on!

Sample Test

Question 1

Your organization has outgrown its Exchange server. You decide to upgrade the Exchange server to a more powerful computer. You complete a full backup of your Exchange server and would like to restore it to the new computer. Which of the following must remain the same as the original server? [Check all correct answers]

❑ a. Site name

❑ b. Organization name

❑ c. Server name

❑ d. Drive partition information

Question 2

Your company upgrades one of your Exchange servers from version 4 to version 5.5. You enable POP3 support on the newly upgraded server. Your users complain that they cannot access their mailbox information using the POP3 protocol. What is the most probable cause for this?

○ a. The Exchange service account is set up incorrectly.

○ b. POP3 is disabled for the server.

○ c. The clients are using the wrong POP3 client.

○ d. Windows NT Challenge/Response authentication is disabled.

Question 3

Your users are complaining that their messages are not being delivered to remote locations. While troubleshooting your Exchange server, you notice a backed-up queue. What might be causing the backed-up queue? [Check all correct answers]

❑ a. A problem with the physical connection between the servers.

❑ b. A server or MTA configuration error.

❑ c. The Message Tracking Center was left open.

❑ d. An improperly configured connector.

Question 4

Your company's CEO accidentally deleted his mailbox contents. All the messages were stored on the server, not in personal folder files. The CEO's mailbox has a limit of 3MB set on it. The private message store is currently 4.2GB, and the Public Information Store is currently 3.3GB. How much disk space is required on your server to recover the lost messages?

○ a. 3MB

○ b. 4.2GB

○ c. 3.3GB

○ d. 7.5GB

Question 5

At a minimum, what is the proper version of NT Server, RAM requirement, and available hard-drive space for an Intel-based machine?

○ a. NT 3.51 SP 5, Pentium 60, 24MB RAM, 250MB available hard-drive space

○ b. NT 3.51 SP 5, Pentium 133, 32MB RAM, 500MB available hard-drive space

○ c. NT 4 SP 3, Pentium 60, 24MB RAM, 250MB available hard-drive space

○ d. NT 4 SP 3, Pentium 133, 32MB RAM, 500MB available hard-drive space

Question 6

What is the Internet Location Service used for?

○ a. Locating users for online meetings

○ b. Locating users for Microsoft Chat

○ c. Locating users for Microsoft NetShow

○ d. Locating a user's email address in the Exchange site

Question 7

What are the three types of directory synchronization (DirSync) objects that Microsoft Exchange uses? [Check all correct answers]

☐ a. Directory synchronization requestor post office

☐ b. Directory synchronization server post office

☐ c. Shadow post office

☐ d. Remote directory synchronization requestor post office

Question 8

You have a single Exchange server in your organization. Joe complains that he cannot access his inbox from home using his POP3 application, whereas other employees can. You verify that Joe is entering the correct configuration information into his POP3 application and that other users can access their mailboxes. Joe can access his mailbox at the office using Microsoft Outlook. What is the most likely problem?

○ a. POP3 is disabled for the site.

○ b. POP3 is disabled for the server.

○ c. POP3 is disabled for Joe's mailbox.

○ d. Joe is using a POP3 client that is not Microsoft Outlook.

Question 9

You have been given the task of installing and configuring an Exchange server for your organization. Most of your users will access the Exchange server locally, but there are several "road-warriors" who will access the server remotely through the Internet.

Required result:

Your remote users should have full email functionality from the Internet.

Optional desired results:

Your Exchange server should not be used to relay SMTP mail messages to the Internet.

Allow your remote users to access the internal Exchange server through the Internet while protecting your internal network from external attacks.

Proposed solution:

Install Microsoft Exchange Server version 5.5. Install the Internet Mail Service on the server. Place the Exchange server behind your company's firewall. Block all incoming SMTP traffic at the firewall. Which results does the proposed solution provide?

- ○ a. The proposed solution provides the required result and both optional desired results.

- ○ b. The proposed solution provides the required result and only one optional desired result.

- ○ c. The proposed solution provides only the required result.

- ○ d. The proposed solution does not provide the required result.

Question 10

You have two Exchange servers installed in your corporate head-quarters: NTExc1 and NTExc2. You also have two remote servers in three different locations: NTExc3, NTExc4, and NTExc5. NTExc1 has several public folders stored on it and replicated to the other servers. The public folder affinity is set to 50 for NTExc3 and 75 for NTExc4, and 95 for NTExc5. A user, whose mailbox resides on NTExc2, attempts to access one of these public folders. In what order will Exchange attempt to connect the user to the requested public folder?

○ a. NTExc1, NTExc2, NTExc3, NTExc4, NTExc5

○ b. NTExc5, NTExc4, NTExc3, NTExc2, NTExc1

○ c. NTExc2, NTExc1, NTExc3, NTExc4, NTExc5

○ d. NTExc2, NTExc5, NTExc4, NTExc3, NTExc1

Question 11

Your organization consists of only one Microsoft Exchange site. The number of users in your organization has grown beyond the capacity of your current site server.

Required result:

Install a new Exchange server to assist in distributing the system load.

Optional desired results:

Only one Exchange site can exist.

You would like the new server to join the existing site.

Proposed solution:

Install Exchange Server, and during installation, join it to an existing site. Provide the existing server name, and supply the Site Service Account password.

Which results does the proposed solution provide?

○ a. The proposed solution provides the required result and both optional desired results.

○ b. The proposed solution provides the required result and one optional desired result.

○ c. The proposed solution provides only the required result.

○ d. The proposed solution does not provide the required result.

Question 12

Your company has two Microsoft Exchange sites—one in London and one in New York. Both locations have dedicated connections to the Internet.

Required result:

Connect the two sites using the existing Internet connections.

Optional desired results:

Configure the sites so that there is a backup if the Internet connections get disconnected.

Make sure that the backup connection is only used in emergency situations.

Proposed solution:

Use the Internet Mail Service to connect the two sites.

Which results does the proposed solution provide?

- O a. The proposed solution provides the required result and both optional desired results.
- O b. The proposed solution provides the required result and one optional desired result.
- O c. The proposed solution provides only the required result.
- O d. The proposed solution does not provide the required result.

Question 13

A Dynamic RAS Connector connects two of your sites. How can you maintain a continuous dial-up connection?

- O a. Edit the Dial-Up Networking Phonebook entry for the connection.
- O b. It can only be done with an X.400 Connector.
- O c. Change the connector to IMS.
- O d. Create a schedule for the Dynamic RAS Connector.

Question 14

You want to connect your Exchange server to the Internet to allow users to access public and private information.

Required result:

Allow employees to send and receive messages using Microsoft Outlook Express.

Optional desired results:

Allow anonymous users access to specific public folders.

Allow Internet users to browse your address book.

Proposed solution:

Configure the POP3 protocol on Microsoft Exchange Server. Install and configure the Internet Mail Service. Configure and enable the LDAP protocol.

Which results does the proposed solution provide?

○ a. The proposed solution provides the required result and both optional desired results.

○ b. The proposed solution provides the required result and one optional desired result.

○ c. The proposed solution provides only the required result.

○ d. The proposed solution does not provide the required result.

Question 15

One of your sites needs to receive all attachments as MIME, whereas another site needs to receive all attachments as UUENCODE. What must you configure to accomplish this?

○ a. SMTP property page

○ b. Encoding property page

○ c. Site container

○ d. Internet Mail property page

Question 16

To control the transaction log file's size, you decide to enable circular logging. What events do you expect to occur on the server?

- ○ a. Fault-tolerance is disabled as circular logging is enabled.
- ○ b. After the checkpoint file is updated, the portion of the transaction log written to the database is discarded.
- ○ c. Checkpoints provide fault-tolerance.
- ○ d. After the checkpoint file is updated, the portion of the transaction log written to the database is moved to a server log.

Question 17

You have been given the task of installing and configuring an Exchange server for your organization. Most of your users will access the Exchange server locally, but there are several "road-warriors" that will access the server remotely through the Internet.

Required result:

Your remote users should have full email functionality from the Internet.

Optional desired results:

Your Exchange server should not be used to relay SMTP mail messages to the Internet.

Allow your remote users to access the internal Exchange server through the Internet while protecting your internal network from external attacks.

Proposed solution:

Install Microsoft Exchange Server version 5.5. Install the Internet Mail Service on the server. Place the Exchange Server behind your company's firewall. Allow ports 25 and 110 through the firewall.

Which results does the proposed solution provide?

- ○ a. The proposed solution provides the required result and both optional desired results.
- ○ b. The proposed solution provides the required result and only one optional desired result.
- ○ c. The proposed solution provides only the required result.
- ○ d. The proposed solution does not provide the required result.

Question 18

A user has deleted a message and would like to recover it. When would it be possible for the user to recover the deleted message?

- ○ a. Whenever the user wants; this is an automatic feature of Microsoft Exchange.
- ○ b. When they are part of the Backup Operators Windows NT group.
- ○ c. When the Administrator sets a Deleted Message Retention period.
- ○ d. Never. Once a message is deleted, it is lost forever.

Question 19

You have installed Microsoft Exchange on your server, which is a Pentium II dual processor machine. In order to improve the performance on the machine, you decide to add more memory to the server. Having successfully done so, what utility should you run from Microsoft Exchange Server to take advantage of the hardware upgrade?

- ○ a. Run the Microsoft Exchange Setup program.
- ○ b. Reinstall Microsoft Exchange Server.
- ○ c. Run the Microsoft Exchange Administrator program.
- ○ d. Run the Microsoft Exchange Performance Optimizer.

Question 20

You have just completed an Exchange installation. When is it desirable to run the Optimizer? [Check all correct answers]

- ❏ a. After installation of Exchange
- ❏ b. After a hardware change
- ❏ c. After a major software configuration change
- ❏ d. After the addition of many new users

Question 21

You have several connectors installed between two of your sites. You would like the Site Connector to always be used, unless it is unavailable. What must you do?

◯ a. Assign it a cost of 1 and the other connectors a cost of 100.

◯ b. Assign it a cost of 100 and the other connectors a cost of 1.

◯ c. Do not assign it a cost.

◯ d. Assign all the connectors a cost of 1.

Question 22

You are responsible for your company's MS Mail messaging system. Eventually, your goal is to migrate your messaging system to Microsoft Exchange Server. As a test, you would like to add an Exchange server to your network and integrate it with your MS Mail messaging system.

Required result:

Successfully transfer messages between the two messaging systems.

Optional desired results:

Synchronize the directory information between the two messaging systems.

Be able to share scheduling data between users of both messaging systems.

Proposed solution:

Add an Exchange server to your network, with the Microsoft Mail Connector installed. Configure the Microsoft Mail Connector correctly, and establish directory synchronization correctly. Send a message from the Microsoft Exchange client to an MS Mail recipient. Send a return message from the MS Mail Windows client to a Microsoft Exchange client.

Which results does the proposed solution provide?

○ a. The proposed solution provides the required result and both optional desired results.

○ b. The proposed solution provides the required result and only one optional desired result.

○ c. The proposed solution provides only the required result.

○ d. The proposed solution does not provide the required result.

Question 23

Your company has one Microsoft Exchange site, located in Austin. It is opening a new site in Dallas and needs to have mail services provided for that location. Both locations will be connected via a dedicated dual-channel ISDN connection providing 128K.

Required result:

Install Exchange Server at the new location as a new site.

Optional desired results:

Ensure that users at both sites will be able to view a comprehensive address book, consisting of users from both sites.

Make sure that all public folder information is replicated between the two sites.

Proposed solution:

Install Exchange Server at the new location. During installation, choose the Create A New Site option. Provide the existing organization name, and enter a new site name. After installation, use the Site Connector to connect to the Austin location.

Which results does the proposed solution provide?

○ a. The proposed solution provides the required result and both optional desired results.

○ b. The proposed solution provides the required result and one optional desired result.

○ c. The proposed solution provides only the required result.

○ d. The proposed solution does not provide the required result.

Question 24

To ease processor usage on a specific Exchange server when dealing with distribution lists, which of the following would you configure?

○ a. Home server

○ b. SQL server

○ c. Expansion server

○ d. Distribution server

Question 25

To connect to the Internet via a modem using the Internet Mail Service, which components must be installed? [Check all correct answers]

- ❑ a. RAS
- ❑ b. A valid RAS Phonebook entry
- ❑ c. NetBEUI
- ❑ d. TCP/IP

Question 26

You would like to receive a small number of newsgroups from your newsfeed provider. Which is the best way to configure your newsfeed?

- ○ a. Inbound push
- ○ b. Inbound push, outbound pull
- ○ c. Inbound pull, outbound push
- ○ d. Inbound pull

Question 27

Your company hosts several domains for its clients. Some of the clients complain that they cannot see any of the attachments that are sent to them. What is the most likely problem?

- ○ a. IMS does not route attachments.
- ○ b. The clients must upgrade their client software to handle your attachment type.
- ○ c. The clients need to change the attachment type for their domain in the IMS Properties pages.
- ○ d. The clients are using an Apple Macintosh and cannot read your attachments.

Question 28

You are the CIO of a multinational organization that uses Exchange Server for its email needs. The organization has offices in Chicago, London, and Taiwan. The Taiwan site needs to be restored from a backup. You have checked with the IT department within Taiwan, and they confirmed that they have a good backup of the directory and Information Store of the site from which to restore.

Required result:

Restore the Taiwan site from the backup.

Optional desired result:

Because the Taiwan site already existed, it should not be a new site for the other offices.

Proposed solution:

Advise the Taiwan site Exchange administrator to create a new site. You do not want the administrator to JOIN EXISTING SITE at the time of reinstalling the Exchange Server.

Which results does the proposed solution provide?

- ○ a. The proposed solution provides the required result and the optional desired result.
- ○ b. The proposed solution provides only the required result.
- ○ c. The proposed solution does not provide the required result.

Question 29

What must be installed on your Exchange server in order to share some newsgroups as public folders?

- ○ a. Install a newsreader client on the server and share its data.
- ○ b. Install and configure the Internet News Service.
- ○ c. Install newsreader client software on each user's desktop.
- ○ d. This cannot be done with Microsoft Exchange Server.

Question 30

You are responsible for your company's MS Mail messaging system. Eventually, your goal is to migrate your messaging system to Microsoft Exchange Server. As a test, you'd like to add an Exchange server to your network and integrate it with your MS Mail messaging system.

Required result:

Successfully transfer messages between the two messaging systems.

Optional desired results:

Have directory information synchronized between the two messaging systems.

Be able to share scheduling data between users of both messaging systems.

Proposed solution:

Add an Exchange server to your network, with the Microsoft Mail Connector installed. Configure the Microsoft Mail Connector correctly, and establish directory synchronization correctly. Send a message from the Microsoft Exchange client to an MS Mail recipient. Send a return message from the MS Mail Windows client to a Microsoft Exchange client. Install and configure the Microsoft Schedule+ Free/Busy Connector.

Which results does the proposed solution provide?

○ a. The proposed solution provides the required result and both optional desired results.

○ b. The proposed solution provides the required result and only one optional desired result.

○ c. The proposed solution provides only the required result.

○ d. The proposed solution does not provide the required result.

Question 31

Your company has two Microsoft Exchange sites—one in London and one in New York. Both locations have dedicated connections to the Internet.

Required result:

Connect the two sites using the existing Internet connections.

Optional desired results:

Configure the sites so that there is a backup if the Internet connections get disconnected.

Make sure that the backup connection is only used in emergency situations.

Proposed solution:

Use the Internet Mail Service to connect the two sites. Configure a Dynamic RAS Connector between the London and the New York sites. Assign both the IMS and the Dynamic RAS Connector a cost of 10.

Which results does the proposed solution provide?

- ○ a. The proposed solution provides the required result and both optional desired results.
- ○ b. The proposed solution provides the required result and one optional desired result.
- ○ c. The proposed solution provides only the required result.
- ○ d. The proposed solution does not provide the required result.

Question 32

You make a configuration change to the IMS. What should you do next?

- ○ a. Shut down and restart the Exchange Server computer.
- ○ b. Stop and restart the Internet Mail Service (IMS).
- ○ c. Stop and restart the SMTP service.
- ○ d. Pause and restart the Internet Mail Service.

Question 33

Your company would like to connect several of its branch offices together. It is your job as the senior system administrator to make sure that this is done correctly.

Required result:

Connect the offices together using the Internet.

Optional desired results:

Make sure that all connections to the Internet are protected.

Make sure that only mail messages are going to be delivered to/ from the Internet.

Proposed solution:

Use the Internet Mail Service to connect the remote sites. Install a firewall, and block all TCP ports.

Which results does the proposed solution provide?

- ○ a. The proposed solution provides the required result and both optional desired results.
- ○ b. The proposed solution provides the required result and one optional desired result.
- ○ c. The proposed solution provides only the required result.
- ○ d. The proposed solution does not provide the required result.

Question 34

You have a Site Connector installed. You would like to install a backup connector that will use a modem to connect to the remote site. What type of connector would you use?

- ○ a. Dynamic RAS Connector
- ○ b. Internet Mail Service (IMS)
- ○ c. Site Connector
- ○ d. X.400 Connector

Question 35

You would like to connect two of your sites together. They are on the same high-speed LAN. What type of connector would you use?

○ a. Dynamic RAS Connector

○ b. Internet Mail Service (IMS)

○ c. Site Connector

○ d. X.400 Connector

Question 36

What account must be available on all post offices that need to participate in sharing Microsoft Schedule+ data?

○ a. SchedAdmin

○ b. Domain administrator

○ c. AdminSch

○ d. All of the above

Question 37

Which of the following components are required to allow users to access your Exchange server through a Web browser? [Check all correct answers]

❏ a. Internet Information Server 3 or higher

❏ b. Outlook Web Access installed and configured on the Exchange server

❏ c. IMAP4 protocol

❏ d. POP3 protocol

Question 38

Which program would you use to create mailboxes for NetWare users?

○ a. NetWare Directory Synchronization

○ b. Gateway Services For NetWare

○ c. NetWare Extraction tool

○ d. Client Services For NetWare

Question 39

Which of the following statements is true about the X.400 Connector? [Check all correct answers]

❑ a. It is the most efficient connector.

❑ b. You can limit the message size transferred by it.

❑ c. You can control which users have access to it.

❑ d. You can configure the remote side of the connector automatically.

Question 40

What client component would you use to resolve a domain name to an IP address?

○ a. DNS

○ b. IMS

○ c. Microsoft Outlook

○ d. A resolver program

Question 41

Your server's GWART is corrupt. How would you recover it?

○ a. You can't. You must reinstall.

○ b. Copy the GWART0.MTA from another Exchange Server.

○ c. Copy the GWART1.MTA from another Exchange Server.

○ d. Copy the GWART1.MTA to GWART0.MTA on the server where the GWART is corrupt.

Question 42

You must establish a connection between the Microsoft Exchange Server computer in your company's main office and multiple Unix SMTP hosts in remote branches. What type of connector would you use?

○ a. Dynamic RAS Connector

○ b. Internet Mail Service (IMS)

○ c. Site Connector

○ d. X.400 Connector

Question 43

Your company has one Microsoft Exchange site, located in Austin, belonging to the AUSHQ Windows NT domain. It is preparing to open a second location in Austin, which will belong to the AUSMFG Windows NT domain. These locations will be connected via dedicated dual-channel ISDN providing 128K. You need to establish mail services at the new location.

Required result:

The two locations need to participate as separate sites within the organization.

Optional desired result:

Provide a means so that the site services account will be able to authenticate, allowing communications between the domains.

Proposed solution:

Establish a trust relationship between the Windows NT domains. Then, install Exchange Server at the new location, configuring it as a new site, within the same organization. Use the Site Connector to establish a connection between the sites.

Which results does the proposed solution provide?

○ a. The proposed solution provides the required result and the optional desired result.

○ b. The proposed solution provides only the required result.

○ c. The proposed solution does not provide the required result.

Question 44

You have a Site Connector installed. You would like to install a backup connector that will use a modem to connect to the remote site. Which connector would you use?

- ○ a. Dynamic RAS Connector
- ○ b. Internet Mail Service (IMS)
- ○ c. Site Connector
- ○ d. X.400 Connector

Question 45

In which file is the Microsoft Exchange Server directory database stored?

- ○ a. DIR.DB
- ○ b. DIR.STR
- ○ c. DIR.PUB
- ○ d. DIR.EDB

Question 46

Jane uses Microsoft Outlook to access her mailbox when she is in the office. When using a POP3 client from home, she cannot access a message in a folder named Private. What could be the problem?

- ○ a. Any folder named "Private" is not sent through POP3.
- ○ b. Jane can only access her mailbox using one product, either Outlook or a POP3 client.
- ○ c. The POP3 protocol can only read the user's inbox, not any subfolders within the inbox.
- ○ d. Jane must configure Outlook to share the "Private" folder with her POP3 client.

Question 47

> By default, how many recipient containers does the DirSync Requestor export?
>
> ○ a. One
>
> ○ b. All
>
> ○ c. Five
>
> ○ d. None

Question 48

> Your company would like to connect several of its branch offices together. It is your job as the senior system administrator to make sure that this is done correctly.
>
> *Required result:*
>
> Connect the offices together using the Internet.
>
> *Optional desired results:*
>
> Make sure that all connections to the Internet are protected.
>
> Make sure that only mail messages are going to be delivered to/from the Internet.
>
> *Proposed solution:*
>
> Use the Internet Mail Service to connect the remote sites.
>
> Which results does the proposed solution provide?
>
> ○ a. The proposed solution provides the required result and both optional desired results.
>
> ○ b. The proposed solution provides the required result and one optional desired result.
>
> ○ c. The proposed solution provides only the required result.
>
> ○ d. The proposed solution does not provide the required result.

Question 49

You want to connect your Exchange server to the Internet to allow users to access public and private information.

Required result:

Allow employees to send and receive messages using Microsoft Outlook Express.

Optional desired results:

Allow anonymous users access to specific public folders.

Allow Internet users to browse your address book.

Proposed solution:

Configure the POP3 protocol on Microsoft Exchange Server. Configure and enable the LDAP protocol.

Which results does the proposed solution provide?

○ a. The proposed solution provides the required result and both optional desired results.

○ b. The proposed solution provides the required result and one optional desired result.

○ c. The proposed solution provides only the required result.

○ d. The proposed solution does not provide the required result.

Question 50

Your Exchange server is functioning properly, but you determine that it needs more RAM and drive space. You purchase more RAM and another hard drive and plan to install them both on the server. You want Microsoft Exchange Server to fully utilize the additional resources. You also want to enable message tracking to resolve some MS Mail connectivity issues.

Required result:

Improve Exchange Server performance.

Optional desired results:

Take advantage of additional resources.

Establish message tracking on the MS Mail Connector.

Proposed solution:

Shut down the server and install the additional resources. Enable message tracking on the MS Mail Connector. Stop and restart the MS Mail Connector Interchange.

Which results does the proposed solution provide?

○ a. The proposed solution provides the required result and both optional desired results.

○ b. The proposed solution provides the required result and only one optional desired result.

○ c. The proposed solution provides only the required result.

○ d. The proposed solution does not provide the required result.

Question 51

You have three Microsoft Exchange sites in different parts of the city.

Required result:

Replicate all public folders to your remote site.

Optional desired results:

Allow users in your main site to sign and seal messages.

Allow users in your remote sites to sign and seal messages.

Proposed solution:

Configure public folder hierarchy and contents replication. Install Exchange Key Management (KM) Server on an Exchange server in your main site. Configure the Exchange servers in the remote sites with the KM Server in your main site.

Which results does the proposed solution provide?

○ a. The proposed solution provides the required result and both optional desired results.

○ b. The proposed solution provides the required result and one optional desired result.

○ c. The proposed solution provides only the required result.

○ d. The proposed solution does not provide the required result.

Answer Key

1. a, b, c	18. c	35. c
2. a	19. d	36. c
3. a, b, d	20. a, b, c, d	37. a, b
4. b	21. a	38. c
5. c	22. b	39. b, c
6. a	23. b	40. d
7. a, b, d	24. c	41. d
8. c	25. a, b, d	42. b
9. d	26. d	43. a
10. c	27. c	44. a
11. a	28. b	45. d
12. c	29. b	46. c
13. d	30. a	47. d
14. b	31. b	48. c
15. d	32. b	49. d
16. a	33. d	50. d
17. b	34. a	51. a

Question 1

The correct answers are a, b, and c. After completing a full backup of your Exchange server, shut down the old server, and install the new one with the same name. When reconfiguring the Exchange server, use the original site and organization name. You should also use the same Exchange service account as on the old Exchange server. The locations of the Exchange database files do not need to be in the same location after the restore. Therefore, answer d is incorrect.

Question 2

The correct answer to this question is a. The service account must be able to act as the operating system. This is not required in Exchange 4. If POP3 was disabled on the server, none of your users would be able to access the server. Therefore, answer b is incorrect. Basically, a POP3 client is a POP3 client, is a POP3 client. They may have extra bells and whistles, but they still use the POP3 protocol to receive messages. Therefore, answer c is incorrect. Windows NT Challenge/Response is not used with POP3. Therefore, answer d is incorrect.

Question 3

The correct answers to this question are a, b, and d. A problem with the physical connection between servers can lead to a backed-up message queue. A server or MTA configuration error, or an improperly configured connector, can also lead to this problem. The Message Tracking Center can be left open without affecting message delivery. Therefore, answer c is incorrect.

Question 4

The correct answer to this question is b. To restore a single mailbox from backup, you must restore the entire Private Information Store. Therefore, 4.2GB is required. Although the mailbox itself is a maximum of 3MB of information, you cannot recover a single mailbox using the Microsoft Exchange recovery tools. Therefore, answer a is incorrect. User mailboxes are stored in the private message store, not in the Public Information Store. Therefore, answer c is incorrect. Only the private message store needs to be recovered. The Public Information Store has no relevant data to the recovery of a mailbox. Therefore, answer d is incorrect.

Question 5

The correct answer to this question is c. At a minimum, Microsoft Exchange Server requires Windows NT Server 4 with Service Pack 3 or higher installed, a Pentium 60 with 24MB RAM, and 250MB of hard-drive space. Although this is not the ideal platform on which to install Exchange, it allows you to install and run Microsoft Exchange. Microsoft Exchange Server requires Windows NT Server 4 or higher. Therefore, answers a and b are incorrect. Although answer d is acceptable, it is not the minimum configuration required for Microsoft Exchange Server. Therefore, answer d is incorrect.

Question 6

The correct answer to this question is a. The Internet Location Service is used to schedule online meetings between users. None of the other answers are correct.

Question 7

The correct answers to this question are a, b, and d. A directory synchronization requestor post office submits directory changes to the directory synchronization server post office. Directory synchronization requestor post offices also request directory updates that other directory synchronization requestor post offices have submitted. Also, if an Exchange server is set up as a directory synchronization server post office, each MS Mail post office must be defined as a remote directory synchronization requestor. Answer c is incorrect.

Question 8

The correct answer to this question is c. If Joe cannot access his mailbox using POP3 and other users can, his mailbox access for POP3 must be disabled. Other users can access their mailboxes using POP3. Therefore, answers a, b, and d are incorrect.

Question 9

The correct answer to this question is d. Installing the Internet Mail Service on the Microsoft Exchange server provides internal users with full email functionality. Your external Internet users will not be able to communicate with the internal system. This is because the firewall blocks all incoming SMTP traffic, which does not allow your external users to send email. Blocking incoming SMTP traffic at the firewall satisfies the first optional criteria.

Question 10

The correct answer to this question is c. When the user logs on to NTExc2, the Information Store will attempt to access the public folder on the NTExc2 computer. If the public folder is not found or is unavailable, it then attempts to access it in other computers within the site. If no replicas are found within the site, the Information Store attempts to contact remote servers based on public folder affinity. The lower the affinity, the sooner the server is contacted. Therefore, NTExc3 with an affinity of 50 is contacted before NTExc4 with an affinity of 75, which is contacted before NTExc5 with an affinity of 95. Therefore, answers a, b, and d are incorrect.

Question 11

The correct answer to this question is a. Installing the new Exchange Server and joining the existing site will help to distribute the load between the servers.

Question 12

The correct answer to this question is c. Using the Internet Mail Service to connect the two sites solves only the required result. Should these Internet connections fail, the servers will not have a backup communication route. Therefore, the first optional result is not fulfilled. Because the first optional result is not met, there is no connection that can be used in emergency situations. Therefore, the second result is not fulfilled.

Question 13

The correct answer to this question is d. By creating a schedule for the Dynamic RAS Connector, you can select to maintain a continuous dial-up connection. The Dial-Up Networking Phonebook entry for the connection cannot control the times at which the connector is to be used. Therefore, answer a is incorrect. The Dynamic RAS Connector is one of the connectors that can be scheduled, and the X.400 Connector is another. Therefore, answer b is incorrect. The Internet Mail Service is one of the connectors that cannot be scheduled. It is either on or off. To give the Internet Mail Service this functionality, you must install the Dynamic RAS Connector along with the IMS. Therefore, answer c is incorrect.

Question 14

The correct answer to this question is b. The POP3 protocol is used to allow clients to receive email messages from your Exchange server. To send messages, the clients must communicate with the server using the SMTP protocol. This is accomplished by installing the Internet Mail Service. The second optional result is met by installing the LDAP protocol. This protocol allows anonymous Internet users to browse your address book. To allow users to access your public folders, you would have to install and configure the Outlook Web Access.

Question 15

The correct answer to this question is d. The Internet Mail property page is the only location where you can configure different sites to receive different types of attachments. Therefore, answers a, b, and c are incorrect.

Question 16

The correct answer to this question is a. As soon as circular logging is enabled, the Microsoft Exchange Server databases are no longer fault-tolerant. When you turn on circular logging, Microsoft Exchange overwrites the old log files as they fill up. This does not allow you to recover should the databases get corrupted. Answers b, c, and d are all untrue and therefore incorrect.

Question 17

The correct answer to this question is b. The first result is met when you allow both ports 25 (SMTP) and 110 (POP3) through the firewall. SMTP is used by the clients to send email messages, while POP3 is used by the client to receive email messages. Placing the Exchange server behind a firewall fulfills the second optional result and protects it from external attack originating from the Internet. The first optional result, however, is not met because anyone can use your Exchange server as a relay server.

Question 18

The correct answer to this question is c. A new feature in Microsoft Exchange 5.5 is the ability to specify an amount of time that the server waits before permanently deleting a message. This is not an automatic feature—it has to be configured manually. Therefore, answer a is incorrect. If a user is part of the Backup Operators group, then the user can restore from or back up to a tape system but cannot recover the individual message. Therefore, answer b is incorrect. By setting a Deleted Message Retention period, the administrator can allow users to recover their own deleted messages. Therefore, answer d is incorrect.

Question 19

The correct answer to this question is d. The Microsoft Exchange Performance Optimizer should be used whenever you change the hardware or software configuration of the Exchange server. The Microsoft Exchange Server Setup program gives you the option to either reinstall Microsoft Exchange Server or to uninstall it. Therefore, answer a is incorrect. Although reinstalling Microsoft Exchange Server automatically runs the Microsoft Exchange Performance Optimizer, it is not the best or easiest solution. Therefore, answer b is incorrect. The Microsoft Exchange Administrator program does not allow you to change the physical configuration of Microsoft Exchange Server, such as the location of the database files. Therefore, answer c is incorrect.

Question 20

The correct answers to this question are a, b, c, and d. The Microsoft Exchange Server Optimizer should be run after all of these situations.

Question 21

The correct answer to this question is a. By assigning this connector a cost of 1 and the others a cost of 100, you ensure that only this connector is used, unless it is unavailable. The lower the cost, the more desirable the connector is to Exchange Server. Assigning the Site Connector a cost of 100 causes Microsoft Exchange Server to use the other connectors first, unless they are unavailable. Therefore, answer b is incorrect. Not assigning the Site Connector a cost makes all the connectors seem equal to the Exchange Server. Therefore, answer c is incorrect. Assigning all the connectors a cost of 1 causes Microsoft Exchange Server to use all the connectors equally. Therefore, answer d is incorrect.

Question 22

The correct answer to this question is b. By installing Microsoft Exchange Server and configuring the Microsoft Mail Connector, you fulfill the required result. Sending messages back and forth between the Exchange and the Microsoft Mail environments is only used as a test. By configuring the Directory Synchronization option of the Microsoft Mail Connector, you allow the two systems to synchronize directory information, thereby fulfilling the first optional requirement. The only requirement that is not met is the ability to synchronize scheduling information between the two systems. For that, you need the Schedule+ Free/Busy Connector.

Question 23

The correct answer to this question is c. Installing an Exchange server at the new location with the same Organization name and a different site name will suffice the required result. A Directory Replication Connector must be installed to make a comprehensive address book viewable at each site. Public folder replication must be configured to replicate public folders. The Site Connector, though necessary for each of the optional desired results, only moves messages between two sites.

Question 24

The correct answer to this question is c. By configuring an expansion server, you offload the job of expanding a distribution list to another server. A home server is where a mailbox is located. Therefore, answer a is incorrect. A SQL Server is a database server and has nothing to do with distribution list expansion. Therefore, answer b is incorrect. There is no such thing as a distribution list server. Therefore, answer d is incorrect.

Question 25

The correct answers to this question are a, b, and d. RAS is the component that establishes the connection using the Phonebook entry over TCP/IP. Although NetBEUI is a valid RAS protocol, it is not required for connection to the Internet. Furthermore, it is not routable. Therefore, answer c is incorrect.

Question 26

The correct answer to this question is d. To receive only a small number of newsgroups, you must pull the specific newsgroups. An inbound push sends all the newsgroups to your server. Therefore, answers a and b are incorrect. An outbound push publishes newsgroups, rather than receiving them. Therefore, answer c is incorrect.

Question 27

The correct answer to this question is c. Microsoft Exchange Server can handle multiple types of attachments, including MIME and UUENCODE attachments. If some clients complain that they cannot see the attachments, it is most likely because Microsoft Exchange is sending them the wrong type. This can be changed within the IMS properties pages. The Internet Mail Service does, in fact, route email attachments. Therefore, answer a is incorrect.

Although the client can change their email client so that it handles the default Exchange Server attachment, it is not the best solution. Therefore, answer b is incorrect. One of the nice features of the protocols used by the Internet is that they are platform-independent. This means that any system running the TCP/IP protocol stack, Apple Macintosh included, can communicate with any other client. Therefore, answer d is incorrect.

Question 28

The correct answer to this question is b. By advising the Taiwan site Exchange administrator to create a new site and not to join the existing site, you do not fulfill the optional desired result. However, you do complete the required result to complete a restore of the site.

Question 29

The correct answer to this question is b. The Internet News Service has the ability to share newsgroup information in public folders. A newsreader cannot share its information—it can only read information from a News server. Therefore, answer a is incorrect. Installing a newsreader client on your user's desktops allows them to connect to an NNTP server to receive newsgroup information but stores newsgroups in private folders. Therefore, answer c is incorrect. Finally, because this can be done with Exchange Server, answer d is incorrect.

Question 30

The correct answer to this question is a. By installing Microsoft Exchange Server and configuring the Microsoft Mail Connector, you fulfill the required result. Sending messages back and forth between the Exchange and the Microsoft Mail environments is only used as a test. By configuring the Directory Synchronization option of the Microsoft Mail Connector, you allow the two systems to synchronize directory information, thereby fulfilling the first optional requirement. The second optional result is met by installing and configuring the Schedule+ Free/Busy Connector.

Question 31

The correct answer to this question is b. By installing the Internet Mail Service, you connect the two locations using the Internet as a medium. By installing and configuring a Dynamic RAS Connector, which uses regular phone lines as its medium, you effectively protect the connection from failure of the Internet connection. However, by assigning the same cost to both connectors, you ensure that Microsoft Exchange uses both connectors equally, thereby failing the second optional result.

Question 32

The correct answer to this question is b. Although all the solutions are valid, the best answer is to shut down and restart the IMS to ensure that the new configuration works correctly.

Question 33

The correct answer to this question is d. Configuring the Internet Mail Service effectively connects your two sites. Placing the Exchange server behind a firewall protects it from external attacks. However, blocking all the ports completely isolates your internal network from the outside world.

Question 34

The correct answer to this question is a. The Dynamic RAS Connector uses a modem to connect to a remote site. Although IMS can use the Dynamic RAS Connector, it cannot use a modem to connect. Therefore, answer b is incorrect. The Site Connector requires a high-speed connection and cannot use a modem. Therefore, answer c is incorrect. The X.400 Connector cannot directly use a modem to connect. Therefore, answer d is incorrect.

Question 35

The correct answer to this question is c. All of the connectors except for the Dynamic RAS Connector can be used over a high-speed LAN. The Site Connector, however, is the most efficient of the connectors. Therefore, it is the best solution.

Question 36

The correct answer to this question is c. MS Mail and Microsoft Exchange use the AdminSch account to share Microsoft Schedule+ data. Therefore, every MS Mail post office and Exchange server that needs to share Microsoft Schedule+ data must have access to an AdminSch account. Answers a, b, and d are incorrect.

Question 37

The correct answers to this question are a and b. Internet Information Server's Active Server Pages along with the Outlook Web Access extensions are required to allow your users to connect to the Exchange server through a Web browser. The IMAP4 and POP3 protocols are used to receive messages using an email client. Therefore, answers c and d are incorrect.

Question 38

The correct answer to this question is c. The NetWare Extraction tool can be used to migrate users from NetWare to Exchange. NetWare Directory Synchronization does not exist. Therefore, answer a is incorrect. Gateway Services For NetWare allows a Windows NT Server to act as a gateway to share information from a Novell NetWare server to a Microsoft network. Therefore, answer b is incorrect. Client Services For NetWare allows Windows NT Workstation to connect to a Novell NetWare server for services. Therefore, answer d is incorrect.

Question 39

The correct answers to this question are b and c. All the connectors except for the Site Connector can control both user access and maximum message size. The Site Connector is the most efficient connector. Therefore, answer a is incorrect. Only the Site Connector auto-configures the remote site. Therefore, answer d is incorrect.

Question 40

The correct answer to this question is d. The client portion of DNS is called the resolver. It passes any name resolution requests to the DNS server. DNS is the server component used for Internet name to IP address resolution. Therefore, answer a is incorrect. IMS is the Internet Mail Service. It is used to connect an Exchange server or site to the Internet using the SMTP protocol. Therefore, answer b is incorrect. Microsoft Outlook is the client portion of Microsoft Exchange Server. Therefore, answer c is incorrect.

Question 41

The correct answer to this question is d. The GWART1.MTA file is the previous version of the Gateway Address Routing table. Copying it over the corrupt file restores the older version. By copying the older version of the GWART, you can recover. Therefore, answer a is incorrect. The GWART on one Exchange server is different than on another. Therefore, answers b and c are incorrect.

Question 42

The correct answer to this question is b. The only connector that allows you to connect your Microsoft Exchange computer to a Unix SMTP host is the Internet Mail Service. It is the only service that uses the SMTP protocol. Therefore, answers a, c, and d are incorrect.

Question 43

The correct answer to this question is a. All of the results are met by the solution.

Question 44

The correct answer to this question is a. The Dynamic RAS Connector is designed to operate over a modem connection. The other connectors will work but are not designed for this type of connection. A Dynamic RAS Connector is the best answer. Therefore, answers b, c, and d are incorrect.

Question 45

The correct answer to this question is d. The Microsoft Exchange Server databases all have the .EDB extension. The directory database uses a file called DIR.EDB, the Public Information Store uses one called PUB.EDB, and the Private Information Store uses one called PRIV.EDB. The other files are invalid. Therefore, answers a, b, and c are incorrect.

Question 46

The correct answer to this question is c. The POP3 protocol only allows you to view messages stored in the top-most level. Because Jane is trying to access a folder that is below the top-level, the POP3 protocol does not allow this to take place. Therefore, answers a, b, and d are incorrect.

Question 47

The correct answer to this question is d. By default, the Microsoft Exchange directory synchronization requestor does not export any recipient containers. Using the Exchange Administrator, the recipient containers that should be exported to the MS Mail directory server can be specified. A trust level can be specified so that only certain recipients are exported. Answers a, b, and c are incorrect.

Question 48

The correct answer to this question is c. By using the Internet Mail Service, you successfully connect the remote sites through the Internet, but the optional results are not met. Your sites are not protected from attack, and messages are not controlled.

Question 49

The correct answer to this question is d. Configuring the POP3 protocol only gives users the ability to receive email messages, not to send them. For that functionality, you require the SMTP protocol, which is installed using the Internet Mail Service. You meet the second optional result by installing LDAP. LDAP allows anonymous users to browse your address book, but you did not configure any way for anonymous users to access your public folders.

Question 50

The correct answer to this question is d. Just because you restarted the server does not mean that your performance will improve. To take full advantage of the new hard drives and RAM, you must run the Microsoft Exchange Performance Optimizer.

Question 51

The correct answer to this question is a. All the results are met by the solution offered.

Glossary

Active Desktop—Microsoft's integration of Internet Explorer 4.0 with the Windows desktop that enables desktop components to connect directly to the Internet.

Active Server—A Web server or similar application that supports server-side scripting, also known as Active Server Pages.

Active Server Pages (ASP)—A Web programming technique that enriches commerce and business communications by improving script management. ASPs can execute with a transaction. Therefore, if the script fails, the transaction is aborted.

ActiveX—Represents a suite of technologies you can use to deliver business solutions over the Internet and intranets.

ActiveX controls—A stripped-down version of OLE controls with their size and speed optimized for use over the Internet.

ADMIN.EXE—The file used to start Exchange Administrator.

AdminSch account—The account used by MS Mail and Microsoft Exchange to share Microsoft Schedule+ data.

alias—A short name for a directory that is easy to use and remember.

Application Programming Interface (API)—A set of instructions that allows one program to invoke the functions of a second program.

assessment exam—Similar to the certification exam, this type of exam gives you the opportunity to answer questions at your own pace. This type of exam also uses the same tools as the certification exam.

Authorized Academic Training Program (AATP)—A program that authorizes accredited academic institutions of higher learning to offer Microsoft Certified Professional testing and training to their students. The institutions also are allowed to use the Microsoft Education course materials and Microsoft Certified Trainers.

Authorized Technical Education Center (ATEC)—The location where you can take a Microsoft Official Curriculum course taught by Microsoft Certified Trainers.

back-end program—With regards to the client/server architecture, a back-end program refers to the server software, which provides all the administrative tasks, storage, and distribution of data for the messaging system.

backfill—A process used by the Public Information Store to recover from lost replication messages, a public server being restored from a backup, or a public server that is being shut down and then restarted.

Backup Domain Controller (BDC)—A machine within a network that maintains a copy of the entire security accounts database. If the Primary Domain Controller (PDC) is busy or fails, the BDC takes control and logs on clients.

bandwidth—The range of frequencies that a communications medium can carry. For baseband networking media, the bandwidth also indicates the theoretical maximum amount of data that the medium can transfer. For broadband networking media, the bandwidth is measured by the variations that any single carrier frequency can carry.

beta exam—A trial exam that is given to participants at a Sylvan Prometric Testing Center before the development of the Microsoft Certified Professional certification exam is finalized. The final exam questions are selected based on the results of the beta exam. For example, if all beta exam participants get an answer correct or wrong, that question generally will not appear in the final version.

bottleneck—The component of a computer or network that's preventing at least one other component from operating at its maximum efficiency.

bridgehead server—A gateway for a site that receives mail from servers within the site and delivers those messages to either a messaging bridgehead server or a target server in the remote site.

cache—A temporary storage area that holds current information and is able to provide that information faster than other methods.

Challenge Handshake Authentication Protocol (CHAP)—An Internet term that describes an authentication method used to connect to your ISP.

change message—A message sent to Information Stores that stores replicated instances when a change to a public folder occurs.

change number—A number created using a globally (organization-wide) unique Information Store identifier and a server-specific change counter.

child object—An object that is located within a parent object. The permissions granted to a child object are inherited from its parent.

circular logging—A logging process in which you log the transactions and manage disk space by creating and using new log files and purging old log files.

configuration changes—Changes you make to Windows NT settings, Exchange Server Connector configurations, protocol addresses, path information, and so on.

configuration object—An object that contains configuration information about a specific site.

connections object—An object that contains all the connectors used to link Exchange sites with other Exchange sites, Microsoft Mail systems, or other foreign messaging systems.

connector cost—A numerical value (1 through 100) used to assign a cost to a specific connector.

connectors—A series of programs developed by Microsoft that act as translators between Exchange Server and foreign systems.

container object—In Exchange hierarchy, this is an object that encompasses other objects: either other container objects or noncontainer objects.

counter—An attribute of an Exchange Server object that you can track to measure an object's performance.

CSV files—A comma-separated file is produced when you use the Extract Windows NT Account List menu item from the Tools menu of the Exchange Administrator. This file can then be imported into Microsoft Exchange to batch create Exchange recipients.

custom recipient—A recipient in a foreign mail system whose address is in the Exchange Address Book.

cut score—On the Microsoft Certified Professional exam, the lowest score a person can receive and still pass.

database—A collection of information arranged and stored so that data can be accessed quickly and accurately.

decryption—The necessary flip side of encryption. Decryption is the process of unscrambling data.

defragmentation—A process that eliminates wasted space in a file.

deleted message retention—A new feature of Exchange 5.5 that allows messages deleted from mailboxes to be held for a specified amount of time before they are permanently deleted.

diagnostic logging—A process that helps pinpoint messaging problems. Using each component's Diagnostic Logging property page, you can specify the degree of diagnostic logging you want.

differential backup—A backup in which you back up only a subset of the Information Store and directory databases.

directory—The database that holds information about the organization's resources and users, such as servers, mailboxes, public folders, and distribution lists. The directory and its contents are replicated automatically to all servers within the same site.

directory database—The database that contains all the information about the objects in your Exchange server.

Directory Import—The menu item used by Exchange Administrator to create or modify recipients by reading the contents of a comma-separated text file. The Directory Import menu item displays a dialog box, from which the file name and appropriate options are specified.

directory information base (DIB)—The information or data contained within the directory information tree (DIT).

directory information tree (DIT)—The logical structure of the X.500 directory, containing objects and resources on the Internet.

directory replication (DR)—Updates the directories of all Microsoft Exchange Server computers within a site and between sites with the same information. Within a site, directory replication is automatic. Between sites, you can configure directory replication so only the desired information is replicated to other sites.

Directory Service (DS)—The service that manipulates the information contained within the directory database. This service processes requests from users and applications.

DirSync (directory synchronization)—The process of exchanging address information between a Microsoft Exchange organization and any other messaging system that uses the MS Mail directory synchronization protocol.

distinguished name (DN)—The digital equivalent of your formal name, address, city, state, and postal code or ZIP code.

distributed computer processing—A process in which the client sends a request to the server, and the server processes the request and returns the result to the client. Depending on the request made by the client, the server could also send data back to the client for processing. This would occur if the request made by the client required a local process (for example, moving email files from the server to a local directory on the client's computer system).

distribution lists—A logical grouping of recipients created to ease mass mailing of messages. All the members of the distribution list will receive any message sent to that list.

domain controller (DC)—The Windows NT Server computer that maintains the security database of all user accounts in a domain. Windows NT Server domains can have one Primary Domain Controller (PDC) and one or more Backup Domain Controllers (BDCs).

Domain Name System (DNS)—A distributed database that provides a hierarchical naming system for identifying systems on the Internet or intranets.

Dynamic RAS Connector—A connector that uses Microsoft's Remote Access Service (RAS) to provide message transport between sites that have no permanent connection.

encryption—The process of scrambling data (messages, streaming multimedia, data files, and so on) into a form that is unusable and unreadable by anyone except the intended recipient.

enterprise—The corporate organization.

ESEUTIL—An Exchange Server database utility that checks the consistency of the Information Store database and directory databases, defragments these databases, and repairs any inconsistencies in them.

Exam Preparation Guides—Guides that provide information specific to the material covered on Microsoft Certified Professional exams to help students prepare for these exams.

Exam Study Guide—Short for Microsoft Certified Professional Program Exam Study Guide, this guide contains information about the topics covered on more than one of the Microsoft Certified Professional exams.

Exchange Administrator—The program used by Microsoft Exchange administrators to manage the many aspects of Exchange, such as adding mailboxes, setting up address book views, establishing connections to other sites, establishing connections to the Internet, and setting up directory replication between sites.

Exchange form—A method of electronically posting and gathering information that might otherwise get lost in a sea of data.

Exchange Server performance chart—A chart that tells you the percentage of processor time utilized by each service.

EXPORT.EXE—The Lotus cc:Mail program used to export messages and directory entries from Lotus cc:Mail post offices.

Extract Account Lists—The Tools menu option used by Exchange Administrator to display a dialog box from which you can produce a comma-separated file (CSV) containing user information from a Windows NT domain user list.

firewall—A piece of equipment used to secure an Internet connection.

foreign systems—Any messaging system other than Microsoft's Exchange Server.

Frame Relay—A network service that uses variable-length packets in a packet-switching environment.

front-end program—In the client/server model, the software running on the client's computer is referred to as the *front-end program*. The front-end program is usually the client software (for example, Microsoft Outlook) that provides the interface for the data stored on the server.

Fully Qualified Domain Name (FQDN)—The full Domain Name System (DNS) path of an Internet host.

function call—A set of instructions within a program that allows it to access the functions of another program.

gateway—Any third-party (non-Microsoft) program that acts as a connector between the Exchange Server messaging system and a foreign system.

gateway address routing table (GWART)—The route table created by the System Attendant when it collects the set of addresses that can be reached through a connector.

Global Address List (GAL)—A global list in an address book that contains all the recipient addresses in an organization.

granularity—A computer activity or feature in terms of the size of the units it handles.

home server—The Exchange server where the mailbox is physically located.

Hypertext Markup Language (HTML)—The language used to create static Web pages.

Hypertext Transfer Protocol (HTTP)—The protocol used to communicate between a Web browser and a Web server (uses HTML).

IMPORT.EXE—The Lotus cc:Mail program used to import messages and directory entries into Lotus cc:Mail post offices.

inbound newsfeed—A newsfeed that allows you to pull messages from your provider's Network News Transfer Protocol (NNTP) host computer and to accept messages that your provider's host computer pushes to your Exchange server.

incremental backup—The same as differential backup, except the LOG files are purged within an incremental backup.

Index Server—A component of the Internet Information Server (IIS) that brings site content indexing and searching to IIS-hosted Web sites.

Information Store (IS)—Contains the messages in users' mailboxes and public folders. Its two main components are the Public Information Store and the Private Information Store.

Integrated Services Digital Network (ISDN)—A form of digital communication that has a bandwidth of 128Kbps.

Internet—The collection of TCP/IP-based networks around the world. Information on nearly every subject is available in some form somewhere on the Internet.

Internet Information Server (IIS)—Web server software by Microsoft; included and implemented with Windows NT Server.

Internet Locator Server—A server that allows Microsoft NetMeeting users to locate mailboxes to set up online meetings.

Internet Mail Service—Renamed from Exchange version 4, where it was known as the *Internet Mail Connector*. It allows you to connect your site to literally millions of other sites and users.

Internet Message Access Protocol version 4 (IMAP4)—The protocol that enables users with any IMAP4 client (that is compliant with RFC 2060) to access mail in their Microsoft Exchange Server mailboxes. It can also be used to read and post messages to public folders or to access other users' mailboxes that they have been granted access to.

Internet News Service—A method for your organization to connect to a Usenet host to exchange information with Usenet.

Internet Packet Exchange/Sequenced Packet Exchange (IPX/SPX)—Novell's NetWare protocol, reinvented by Microsoft and implemented in Windows NT under the name NWLink. It's fully compatible with Novell's version and, in many cases, is a better implementation than the original.

Internet Protocol (IP)—A network layer protocol that provides source and destination addressing and routing.

Internet Service Provider (ISP)—A service company that sells network access to the Internet. They purchase bandwidth in bulk and, in turn, resell it in smaller packages.

interoperability—The ability of one messaging system to coexist with other messaging systems.

intranet—An internal, private network that uses the same protocols and standards as the Internet.

IP address—Four sets of numbers, separated by decimal points, that represent the numeric address of a computer attached to a TCP/IP network, such as the Internet.

ISNTEG—An Exchange Server database utility that checks the consistency of the Information Store database at a database level.

job function expert—A person with extensive knowledge about a particular job function and the software products/technologies related to that job. Typically, a job function expert is currently performing the job, has recently performed the job, or is training people to do this job.

KM Server (Key Management Server)—A service used by Exchange Server to manage the different security keys.

Knowledge Base (KB)—An extensive database from Microsoft that contains a plethora of technical articles that provide information about products, answers to common technical support questions, and document errors.

Knowledge Consistency Checker (KCC)—The utility used by directory replication (DR) to perform the tasks of passing data. Also, it provides an easy way to add a server.

Lightweight Directory Access Protocol (LDAP)—An Internet protocol that allows access to directory information. Clients with access can use LDAP to browse, read, and search directory listings in the Exchange Server version 5.0 directory.

link monitors—An Exchange utility used to verify the efficient routing of test messages.

Load Simulator (LOADSIM.EXE)—An application used to identify the bottlenecks within an organization's Exchange mail system.

local area network (LAN)—A network that is confined to a single building or geographic area and comprised of servers, workstations, peripheral devices, a network operating system, and a communications link.

local procedure calls—A command, or set of instructions issued by a program, to be executed by the local processor.

Lotus cc:Mail—The "father" of Notes. This popular email system once competed with MS Mail.

Lotus Notes—The IBM/Lotus competitor to Exchange Server.

mailbox—A storage location on the Exchange Server computer that allows information to be sent, received, and stored. Each user who is to receive messages through Exchange must have a mailbox.

maintenance window—The period of time when you plan to execute the routine maintenance chores.

master encryption key—The key that maintains the security of the information contained within a file. The master encryption key is encrypted using passwords from each service that uses the KM Server database.

Message Queue Server—A component of the Windows NT Server 4.0 Option Pack that enables applications to communicate via a message queue system, even when remote systems are offline.

message tracking—Allows you to track messages to locate slow or stopped connections, find lost mail, and determine the delay on each segment of a route for link monitoring and performance tuning.

Message Transfer Agent (MTA)—The component responsible for routing messages to their destinations. The MTA provides addressing and routing information for sending messages.

Messaging Application Programming Interface (MAPI)—A series of Application Programming Interfaces (APIs) designed specifically for messaging.

Microsoft Certification Exam—A test created by Microsoft to verify a test-taker's mastery of a software product, technology, or computing topic.

Microsoft Certified Professional (MCP)—An individual who has taken and passed at least one certification exam.

Microsoft Certified Professional Certification Update—A newsletter for Microsoft Certified Professional candidates and Microsoft Certified Professionals.

Microsoft Certified Solution Developer (MCSD)—An individual who is qualified to create and develop solutions for businesses using the Microsoft development tools, technologies, and platforms.

Microsoft Certified Systems Engineer (MCSE)—An individual who is an expert on Windows NT and the Microsoft BackOffice integrated family of server software. This individual also can plan, implement, maintain, and support information systems associated with these products.

Microsoft Certified Systems Engineer + Internet (MCSE + I)—An individual with this certification has passed the nine necessary exams and is an expert not just on Microsoft operating systems, but also on Microsoft's Internet servers and TCP/IP.

Microsoft Certified Trainer (MCT)—An individual who is qualified by Microsoft to teach Microsoft Education courses at sites authorized by Microsoft.

Microsoft Developer Network (MSDN)—The official source for Software Development Kits (SDKs), Device Driver Kits (DDKs), operating systems, and programming information associated with creating applications for Microsoft Windows and Windows NT.

Microsoft Mail Connector—The connector that Exchange Server uses to communicate with MS Mail.

Microsoft official curriculum—Microsoft education courses that support the certification exam process and are created by the Microsoft product groups.

Microsoft Online Institute (MOLI)—An organization that offers training materials, online forums and user groups, and online classes.

Microsoft Roadmap to Education and Certification—An application, based on Microsoft Windows, that takes you through the process of deciding what your certification goals are and informs you of the best way to achieve them.

Microsoft Sales Fax Service—A service through which you can obtain exam preparation guides, fact sheets, and additional information about the Microsoft Certified Professional program.

Microsoft Schedule+—A messaging-enabled program that lets users access other users' schedules and reserve meeting times with those users.

Microsoft Solution Provider—An organization, not directly related to Microsoft, that provides integration, consulting, technical support, and other services related to Microsoft products.

Microsoft Technical Information Network (TechNet)—A service provided by Microsoft that provides helpful information via a monthly CD-ROM. TechNet is the primary source of technical information for people who support and/or educate end users, create automated solutions, or administer networks and/or databases.

MS Mail (Microsoft Mail)—The "father" of Exchange. MS Mail was Microsoft's first mail program. (Note: MS Mail isn't year 2000 compatible.)

MTACHECK—An Exchange Server database utility that checks the data the Message Transfer Agent (MTA) stores within the DAT files. This utility also automatically repairs errors, if any.

Multipurpose Internet Mail Extensions (MIME)—A standard that allows binary, audio, and video data to be attached to an email message and transmitted across TCP/IP networks.

multiple-rating item (MRI)—An item that gives you a task and a proposed solution. Every time the task is set, an alternate solution is given, and the candidate must choose the answer that gives the best results produced by one solution.

name resolution—The main function of the Domain Name System (DNS) that resolves Fully Qualified Domain Names (FQDNs) to IP addresses and IP addresses to FQDNs.

NetBEUI—A simple network layer transport protocol developed to support NetBIOS networks.

Network News Transfer Protocol (NNTP)—The protocol used to distribute, retrieve, inquire about, and post Network News articles.

network—A collection of server and client computers that communicate over a wire-based media for the purposes of sharing resources.

New Technology File System (NTFS)—A file system used in Windows NT that supports file-level security, fault tolerance, and file-level compression.

nondisclosure agreement (NDA)—A legal agreement signed both by Microsoft and by a vendor, rendering certain rights and limitations.

normal backup—A complete and full backup in Exchange that backs up everything, including transaction logs, the Information Store, and directory databases.

object—A messaging system resource, such as a server, mailbox, public folder, address book, and so on, that is listed in the Exchange directory.

Open Database Connectivity (ODBC)—A standard Application Programming Interface (API) used to construct platform/application-independent databases.

operating system (OS)—A software program that controls the operations on a computer system.

organization—The largest administrative unit in Microsoft Exchange Server, usually consisting of one or more sites. Organizations provide services for an entire group.

organization object—The top-most object in the Exchange hierarchy. It's a container object and all other objects are contained within it.

outbound newsfeed—A newsfeed that allows you to push (or send) messages posted by your users to a newsgroup public folder to your provider's host computer.

Outlook Web Access (OWA)—A component of Exchange that allows users to access data on your Exchange server using an Internet Web browser from a Macintosh, Unix, or Microsoft Windows computer.

parent object—An object that contains other objects. An object is a parent to all the objects within it.

parent-child relationship—The relationship that exists between the parent object and the child object. The relationship is dictated by permissions.

Performance Optimizer—An Exchange utility that analyzes and optimizes your hardware so it performs in the most efficient way.

permissions—A set of rules that controls objects, such as containers within the system. These rules dictate which users can access the objects and how those users can manipulate them.

personal address book (PAB)—A user's grouping of contact information, as opposed to a global or public list.

personal information manager (PIM)—A utility or an application that helps users organize various types of related information, such as email addresses, Web sites, phone numbers, fax numbers, and so on.

Post Office Protocol 3 (POP3)—A mail protocol that allows users to connect to the Exchange server to access their mailboxes remotely (from home or from anywhere on the Internet).

predecessor change list—A list of the Information Stores that have made a change and the last change number made by each Information Store. The predecessor change list is used to help identify public folder conflicts.

Primary Domain Controller (PDC)—A machine within a network that validates the username and password, thus authenticating the logons for clients. The first server within a Windows NT network must be a PDC.

Private Information Store—The component of the Information Stores that contains user mailboxes and messages.

proxy server—A software product that acts as a moderator or go-between for a client and a remote host. Most proxy servers also offer content caching and firewall capabilities.

PST file—The extension given to a personal folder file.

public folder—A repository for many different types of information, such as files and messages, that can be shared by a number of different users. Public folders make custom applications, such as customer tracking systems, possible.

public folders replication agent (PFRA)—When more than one instance of a public folder exists, the PFRA monitors all modifications, additions, and deletions to the public folder.

Public Information Store—The component of the Information Stores that contains public files, folders, and messages.

public/private key technology—The industry standard encryption technology used by Exchange Server that allows users to sign and seal their messages. Each mailbox is assigned a key pair; one key is publicly known, and only the user knows the other key.

pull feed—A newsfeed in which your provider's host computer initiates a newsfeed to your Exchange Server computer and then "pushes" the news article to your computer.

push feed—Best for a large newsfeed, but it does require you to interact with your newsfeed provider because the provider controls which newsgroups you receive.

recipient—An object in the directory that can receive messages and information. Exchange Server recipients are mailboxes, distribution lists, public folders, and custom recipients.

Redundant Array of Inexpensive Disks (RAID)—A standardized method for categorizing fault tolerance storage systems. Windows NT implements Level 0, Level 1, and Level 5 RAID through software, not hardware.

Registry—A database that stores all the configuration information for Windows NT.

Remote Access Service (RAS)—A secure method for dial-up networking. Think of RAS as a way to extend the network, using a very long and very slow network connection from the server to the client.

Remote DirSync Requestor—What MS Mail post offices are referred to when Exchange Server is set up to be the directory synchronization server.

remote procedure call (RPC)—A programming interface that allows software applications running on separate computers on different networks to use each other's services.

replicas—Copies or duplicates of public folders within the messaging system. The purpose of replicas is to prevent a single point of failure with regards to data access.

replication—A cloning process for information.

resolver—The client component of the Domain Name System (DNS).

Resource Kit—The additional documentation and software utilities distributed by Microsoft to provide information and instruction on the proper operation and modification of its software products.

scalable—Refers to an application's ability to be added to or expanded. Exchange Server is considered a scalable messaging system because it can grow to accommodate the largest of corporations without hindering functionality.

scripting—A type of programming language used to write custom code for Web pages.

sealing—The encryption of any message generated by either Microsoft Outlook or an Exchange client.

secret key—A security method that uses an algorithm (using a single key) to encrypt and decrypt messages. Both the sender and the recipient use a secret key. This is an efficient method of encrypting large amounts of data.

Secure Sockets Layer (SSL)—A protocol that creates secure communications using public key cryptography and bulk data encryption.

security—The protection of data by restricting access to only authorized users.

server monitors—An Exchange utility used to check the condition, including services and clocks, of one or more servers in a site.

server object—An object that represent a specific server in the server list.

server recipients object—A container for all Exchange recipient objects (for example, mailboxes) located on the server.

Service Pack—A patch or fix distributed by Microsoft after the final release of a product to repair errors, bugs, and security breaches.

signing—When a signature is added to any message generated by either Microsoft Outlook or an Exchange client.

Simple Mail Transfer Protocol (SMTP)—The mail protocol used to connect two hosts running the TCP/IP protocol.

Site Connector—A tool that connects sites within a local area network (LAN) or a wide area network (WAN).

site object—This object represents each site in your organization (a site is one or more Exchange servers that have been grouped together). The site object contains the configuration and recipients objects.

site—A server or series of servers that communicate with each other and use the same directory information.

status message—A message sent from one Information Store to another informing it of the current public folder hierarchy and contents status.

subnet—A portion or segment of a network.

subnet mask—A 32-bit address that indicates how many bits in an address are being used for the network ID.

System Attendant (SA)—A service that must be running for messaging processes to run. The System Attendant is a maintenance service that runs in the background.

target server—A server in a remote site that the local Message Transfer Agent (MTA) can use to send intersite messages.

time stamp—When messages arrive in a public folder, they are assigned a time stamp. When a message is modified, the public folders replication agent (PFRA) assigns a new time stamp using the greater of either the current system time or the old time stamp.

transaction log—A log that records all email transactions to permit Exchange Server to record messaging activity and to reconstruct recent messaging traffic in the event of a server crash.

Transaction Server—An Internet Information Server (IIS) component that allows distributed transaction applications to be developed for IIS.

Transmission Control Protocol/Internet Protocol (TCP/IP)—The most commonly used network protocol and the central protocol of the Internet.

trust level—A selection on the Advanced property page of a mailbox used to specify whether the mailbox is to be replicated to other servers during directory synchronization.

uninterruptible power supply (UPS)—A device that lets the server write all its data to disk. A UPS provides a safe and controlled shut down of the Exchange server and other servers.

Universal Resource Locator (URL)—The addressing scheme used to identify resources on the Internet.

Unix—An interactive time-sharing operating system developed in 1969 by a hacker to play games. This system developed into the most widely used industrial-strength computer operating system in the world, and it ultimately supported the birth of the Internet.

update sequence number (USN)—The unique number assigned to a replication when replication occurs.

VBScript—A Microsoft proprietary scripting language for HTML pages whose syntax resembles Visual Basic; used only in Microsoft Web products.

Visual Basic—A version of the BASIC programming language written by Microsoft for rapid programming of Windows applications by plugging together components in a visual designer environment.

wide area network (WAN)—A network that spans geographically distant segments. Often, a distance of two miles or more is used to define a WAN; however, Microsoft equates any Remote Access Service (RAS) connection as establishing a WAN.

Windows NT domain—A grouping of network servers and other computers that share common security and users account information. Users log on to the domain, not individual servers in the domain. Once logged on to the domain, the user has access to the network resources within the domain.

X.400—A set of standards related to the exchanging of electronic messages, such as voice mail, fax, telex, and email. X.400 is an internationally recognized message-handling system. A Message Transfer Agent is the server-based process in the message transfer system that's responsible for routing and delivering messages. It's the equivalent of a local postal sorting office.

X.500—Defines the standard protocols for a global directory service.

Index

G

Order Practice Tests From The
Authors Of The *Exam Cram* Series

. . . .

LANWrights offers diskette copies of practice tests for these MCSE exams:

70-058 Networking Essentials
70-064 Windows 95 (OSR2)
70-067 NT Server 4
70-073 NT Workstation 4
70-068 NT Server 4 In The Enterprise

70-059 TCP/IP for NT 4
70-081 Exchange Server 5.5
70-087 IIS 4
70-088 Proxy Server 2
70-098 Windows 98

Each diskette includes the following:

√ Two practice exams consisting of 50-70 questions, designed to help you prepare for the certification test. One test automates the test that appears in each *Exam Cram* book; the other is new material.

√ Feedback on answers, to help you prepare more thoroughly.

√ Access to the LANWrights Question Exchange, an online set of threaded discussion forums aimed at the topics for each of these books, where you can ask for help and get answers within 72 hours.

Note: These tests are written in HTML and use Java and JavaScript tools, so you must use Navigator 3.02 or Internet Explorer 3.02 or higher. (IE 4.01 is recommended.)

Fees for practice exam diskettes:

$ 25 for single diskette
$ 45 for any two
$ 65 for any three
$ 85 for any four
$100 for any five

$115 for any six
$130 for any seven
$145 for any eight
$160 for any nine
$175 for all ten

All amounts are US$

To order, please send a check or money order drawn on a U.S. bank. Please include complete delivery information with your order: Name, Company, Street Address, City, State, Postal Code, Country. Send all orders to LANWrights Exams, P.O. Box 26261, Austin, TX, USA 78755-0261. For orders from Mexico or Canada, please add US$5; for orders outside North America, please add US$10. For expedited delivery, online orders, or other information, please visit www.lanw.com/examcram/order.htm.

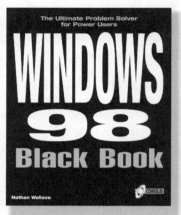

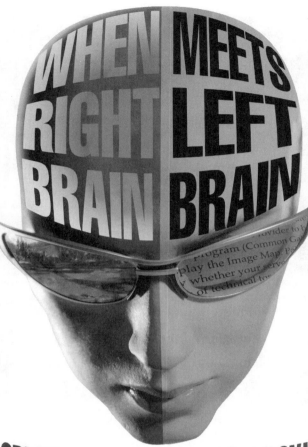

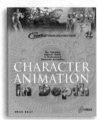

  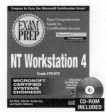